Praise for Mikhail Zygar and

WAR AND PUNISHMENT

"A superb account of all that led to Vladimir Putin's brutal and misbegotten invasion of Ukraine . . . Zygar's book provides an ardent, informed understanding of the present."

—The New Yorker

"This haunting history explores 350 years of 'Russocentric exceptionalism,' debunking the myths fueling Putin's imperialism. . . . A sorry tale of big brother chauvinism and oppression. [Zygar] seeks to demolish, myth by myth, the 'imperial mindset' that led to the current conflict. . . . The pattern of anti-Ukrainian persecution repeats from one era to the next, in Zygar's haunting telling. . . . A fine book."

—The Guardian

"[Zygar] feels he has taken up arms. . . . To change the future, the author believes we must understand the past. . . . [Thus] he writes entirely in the present tense as he journeys through the centuries."

—Stuart Miller, *Los Angeles Times*

"Sweeping and very accessible . . . compelling . . . important."

—Washington Post Live (podcast)

"Zygar approaches history like he's interviewing it—listening to what those involved had to say and expertly putting that in context. The result is a riveting unfolding of history as it was being lived."

—Foreign Policy

"Excellent . . . Cleverly weaves the story of independent Ukraine with an amusing look at the career as a comedian and actor of its president, Volodymyr Zelensky . . . Although a committed supporter of Ukrainian independence, Zygar is honest about Ukraine's record in the past three decades. While other recent works sympathetic to the Ukrainian cause elide over the epic corruption there, Zygar is clear that before Zelensky was elected Ukraine was near to being a failed state."

—*The Sunday Times* (UK)

"A brave, passionate book setting Russia's invasion and Ukraine's resistance into the broad sweep of history . . . authoritative . . . Zygar's knowledge is undeniable."

—*Kirkus Reviews*

"Zygar has invented a new genre. If Tolstoy's story is a wide river, Proust's is a slow river, Zygar's is a chase. Alas, under President Putin's rule, no one would dare to publish this terrific book in Russia. So it's easy to tell if the regime has changed—if Zygar is openly on sale in Moscow shops, then yes."

—Dmitry Muratov,
winner of the Nobel Peace Prize (2021)

"A sweeping, ambitious, and impassioned chronicle . . . makes for compelling reading with its searing portrayal of the 'long road to war.' It's a fiery, informed reckoning of past and present relations. . . . A bold prediction from a brave writer."

—*The Irish Times*

"Why is my country fascist—and what is my role in that? For Russia to ever change these are the questions Russians will need to ask. Zygar does it with a searing mix of history and self-reflection."

—Peter Pomerantsev, author of *This Is Not Propaganda: Adventures in the War Against Reality*

"Mikhail Zygar is a rare Russian journalist, objective, refusing to follow the herd, still holding the Putin era to account despite the obvious dangers. Knowing he could always follow many colleagues and activists into jail, hospital, or into the graveyard, Zygar persists nonetheless."

—Christiane Amanpour,
CNN chief international anchor

"A very cool book. I highly recommend everyone to read it."

—Ukrainian president Volodymyr Zelensky,
on Mikhail Zygar's *The Empire Must Die*

"Zygar demolishes Putin's myths about Ukraine with a fury born out of shame at what is being done in his country's name. It is just possible to dream that, one day, *War and Punishment* will be taught in Russian schools in place of the Kremlin's deadly lies."

—Oliver Bullough,
author of *Butler to the World*

"Passionate and perceptive, [Zygar is] one of Russia's best journalists."

—Anna Reid, author of *Borderland:
A Journey Through the History of Ukraine*

ALSO BY MIKHAIL ZYGAR

All the Kremlin's Men: Inside the Court of Vladimir Putin

The Empire Must Die: Russia's Revolutionary Collapse, 1900–1917

WAR AND PUNISHMENT

PUTIN, ZELENSKY, AND

THE PATH TO RUSSIA'S INVASION OF UKRAINE

―――――――

MIKHAIL ZYGAR

SCRIBNER

New York   London   Toronto   Sydney   New Delhi

Scribner
An Imprint of Simon & Schuster, LLC
1230 Avenue of the Americas
New York, NY 10020

First Scribner trade paperback edition April 2024

SCRIBNER and design are trademarks of Simon & Schuster, LLC.

Simon & Schuster: Celebrating 100 Years of Publishing in 2024

For information about special discounts for bulk purchases, please contact Simon & Schuster Special Sales at 1-866-506-1949 or business@simonandschuster.com.

The Simon & Schuster Speakers Bureau can bring authors to your live event. For more information, or to book an event, contact the Simon & Schuster Speakers Bureau at 1-866-248-3049 or visit our website at www.simonspeakers.com.

Interior design by Jaime Putorti

Manufactured in the United States of America

10 9 8 7 6 5 4 3 2 1

Library of Congress Control Number: 2023935453

ISBN 978-1-6680-1372-4
ISBN 978-1-6680-1373-1 (pbk)
ISBN 978-1-6680-1374-8 (ebook)

CONTENTS

PREFACE TO THE PAPERBACK EDITION

In February 2022, on launching his invasion of Ukraine, Putin had a very clear plan: he hoped to take Kyiv in three days.

Two years later, in the winter of 2024, he hatches another plot, which to him also seems fail-safe: wait for Donald Trump to return to the White House.

Time is on his side, Putin feels. He doesn't need to attack, but simply to wait for Western support for Ukraine to wane. And after the outbreak of war in the Middle East in October 2023, he is more confident than ever that this will happen sooner or later.

The problem is that Putin does not want negotiations or a peace treaty at all. Any talks for him are only a means to stall for time before resuming hostilities. He needs this war, for he unleashed it with the aim of perpetuating his power in Russia. And it will last as long as he lives.

For Putin, it is a war not for Ukraine, but for Russia. In this book I describe how he prepared for this war, how he exploited historical myths, how he brainwashed the Russian people, and how he falsified history.

The Russian Empire's war against Ukraine did not begin in 2022: it began three centuries earlier, but it cannot end while Putin is in power. And in this book I explain why.

I wrote this book to dispel the myths that led to the war in Ukraine. In it, I show how, over the course of centuries, historians and propagandists have created the myth of a Great Russia and how they have covered up the oppression of the peoples Russia conquered. Putin's propaganda has been brainwashing Russians for years, and now he is reaping the benefits.

Not only do millions of Russians believe in Putin's myths today, but a significant number of people in the West can be found ardently defending them. The mission of this book is to fight against Russian imperialism, against its fascism. *War and Punishment* is my contribution to the struggle for a Ukrainian victory and the struggle for freedom from an inhumane empire. Freedom for Ukrainians and Russians alike.

INTRODUCTION

This book is a confession. I am guilty for not reading the signs much earlier. I, too, am responsible for Russia's war against Ukraine. As are my contemporaries and our forebears. Regrettably, Russian culture is also to blame for making all these horrors possible.

Many Russian writers and historians are complicit in facilitating this war. It is their words and thoughts over the past 350 years that sowed the seeds of Russian fascism and allowed it to flourish, although many would be horrified today to see the fruits of their labor. We failed to spot just how deadly the very idea of Russia as a "great empire" was. (Of course, any "empire" is evil, but let different historians judge other empires.) We overlooked the fact that, for many centuries, "great Russian culture" belittled other countries and peoples, suppressed and destroyed them.

So that Russian culture may live on, we must act. We must start by looking inside ourselves and telling the truth about our past and our present.

Russian, Ukrainian, and indeed any history is made up of myths. Alas, our myths led us to the fascism of 2022. It is time to expose them.

This book is about myths and about people. People who lived one hundred, two hundred, three hundred years ago, and then turned into mythological figures. They died physically; then historians stripped away their human qualities: their weaknesses, their passions, their doubts, their true motives. They were subjected to the inexorable "logic of history," which serves the needs of those in power.

This book also tells about our contemporaries, such as Volodymyr Zelensky. He and many others appear real and knowable to us now, yet soon they, too, will become immortalized and heroized, and in a generation will seem like legendary characters. Moreover, one of the protagonists of this book, Putin, has already, in his lifetime, turned into an otherworldly, universal evil—and I try to trace how this happened.

I specifically wrote this book in modern language and the present tense, trying to convey and clarify historical terms, drawing present-day parallels, so that today's reader might grasp the spirit, not merely the letter.

I would like this book to be understandable to readers a century from now, to give them a glimpse into our thought processes. For this purpose, I have tried to depict all the characters as living people, not historical monuments, and to debunk the old myths without sparing historians, without pity for yesterday's idols, without being afraid to offend the feelings of fellow Russians.

This book will not undo the past and present, but it can change the future. Nationalist history is a disease that afflicts many peoples. The Russian people can stamp out the myths that have infected them; the Ukrainian people will deal with theirs on their own.

For many years, starting in 2004, I visited Ukraine as a journalist. During this time, I got to interview every Ukrainian president, and make the acquaintance of most politicians, big businessmen, well-known reporters, and even clergymen. I witnessed many events: from the talks between Presidents Leonid Kuchma and Vladimir Putin back in 2003 to the opening of the Babyn Yar memorial by President Volodymyr Zelensky in 2021, which commemorates the site where Nazis killed thousands of Jews.

Sometimes I spent lengthy periods in Kyiv and the surrounding region. For example, in Bucha, at the house of my friend Nadia, I wrote a significant portion of my book *All the Kremlin's Men*. Incidentally, Nadia no longer speaks to me: because I am Russian, she considers me an "imperialist."

Recent decades have seen me working as a political journalist in Russia, trying to uncover the hidden causes and motives behind events. I have followed the ever-changing Russian policy in respect to Ukraine. Often horrified by what I heard, I never concealed my thoughts as an opposition journalist and writer.

In 2010, I was one of the founders of the TV station Dozhd (Rain), the only independent news channel in Russia. In 2014, it was effectively shut down for its honest, detailed coverage of the Revolution of Dignity in Ukraine, when the Ukrainian government was overthrown by Ukrainians tired of corruption and abuse of power. A month before the occupation of Crimea, the Kremlin ordered all Russian cable and satellite networks to switch off TV Rain.

I remember well how on March 1, 2014, Russian senators authorized the president to "use the Russian armed forces outside the country"—that is, gave a green light to war in Ukraine. That day, as the station's editor in chief, I wrote a letter to my colleagues saying that from now on we should always write "in Ukraine"—even if it jars the ears of Russian grammarians—as a sign of respect and support for independent Ukraine. Before that for many years Russians have traditionally said *na Ukraine* ("on Ukraine") instead of *v Ukraine* ("in Ukraine"). Ukrainians usually considered it insulting, as the preposition "on" makes Ukraine sound like a territory, not a country. A similar distinction exists in English, where "Ukraine" has largely replaced "the Ukraine." But in March 2014 that became crystal clear for me: if it's important for Ukrainians, we must take heed.

On February 24, 2022, when Putin launched a full-scale invasion of Ukraine, I wrote an open letter that was signed by several Russian writers, filmmakers, and journalists. Later tens of thousands more Russian citizens put their signatures to it. Here it is:

> *The war launched by Russia against Ukraine is shameful.*
>
> *It is our shame, but, unfortunately, our children, as well as generations of still infant and unborn Russians, will also have to bear responsibility for it. We do not want our children to live in an aggressor country, to be ashamed that their army attacked a neighboring independent state. We call upon all citizens of Russia to say "no" to this war.*
>
> *We do not believe that an independent Ukraine poses a threat to*

Russia or any other state. We do not believe in Vladimir Putin's state-ments that the Ukrainian people are ruled by "Nazis" and must be "liberated."

We demand an end to this war.

Then I had to flee to Germany. During my first year of living in Berlin, I reviewed all the previous interviews I'd conducted over the past eighteen years of working in Ukraine and in Russia. And I kept talking to people, hundreds of people. And they recalled what had brought us to where we are now. From these conversations, old and new, this book was born.

But there are two parts. This book is not only about the present but also about the past—about the historical myths from which today's politics has grown and which it is founded upon. I carefully and impartially read the historical sources and tried to trace the origins and development of the brutal Russian Empire that gave rise to the current war. This book is by no means an attempt to write the history of Ukraine. Rather, it is a "detective story through the eyes of the criminal," a chronicle of how Russia has oppressed Ukraine for the past five centuries. How the empire tried to bring up the loyal elite, but in the end couldn't have suppressed Ukrainian society.

This book tells about the long road to war, and about the road to punishment that we have yet to travel.

Nadia, I am not an imperialist, and I am writing this book so that others will not be either.

PART I

SEVEN TALES OF COLONIAL

OPPRESSION IN UKRAINE

SWEDISH

EMPIRE

BALTIC
SEA

PRUSSIA

Königsberg

Vilnius

Moscow

LITHUANIA

TSARDOM

OF RUSSIA

POLISH-LITHUANIAN

Warsaw

COMMONWEALTH

POLAND

COSSACK

Kyiv

Pereyaslav

Hadiach

Lviv

HETMANATE

Chyhyryn

Zhovti Vody
×

ZAPORIZHIAN HOST

MOLDAVIA

CRIMEAN KHANATE

TRANSYLVANIA

SEA OF AZOV

Bahçesaray

OTTOMAN EMPIRE

BLACK SEA

COSSACK HETMANATE

IN 1654

Istanbul

200 miles

200 km

1

THE MYTH OF UNITY:

HOW BOHDAN KHMELNYTSKY SIGNED

A CONTRACT WITH MOSCOW

Inventing the Russian World

1670, Kyiv. A German monk is writing a history book. He is Innokenty Gizel; a native of Königsberg who grew up in a Protestant family but moved to Kyiv in his youth and embraced Orthodoxy.

Innokenty is not merely writing a book about history: he believes that it will help to champion Orthodoxy, his beloved Kyiv, and the entire Ukrainian territory. Who does he see as their main threat? Muslims, that is, the Ottoman Empire, as well as the West. As he is a German from East Prussia, Kyiv's sworn enemies in the seventeenth century are the Catholics, in particular those in Poland and the Jesuit order, which is very active in Eastern Europe at this time. Innokenty himself is not just a monk. He is the abbot of Kyiv's main monastery, that is, an important political figure. He incorporates into his book what the Kyivan monks wrote before him, but adds a very important conclusion of his own.

As is common for a medieval historian, Innokenty begins with the story of Noah, telling how his son Japheth was the progenitor of all Europeans. But then the narrative switches to Japheth's sixth son, Mosoch, from whom, according to legend, the Russian people are descended and the word *Moskva* (Moscow) is derived.

Innokenty Gizel has never been to Moscow, but his aim is to create the illusion that it and Kyiv share a common history.

A modern-day critic might say that the Prussian-born Innokenty invented what today is known as *russkiy mir* (the Russian world)—but that would not be entirely accurate. In essence, he invents a single nation, supposedly with a common history. And this Rus is inhabited by a single people, Gizel claims. Until the latter half of the seventeenth century, the Moscow rulers had a very muddled and mythologized idea of their history and ancestors. They consider themselves the descendants and successors of both the Roman emperors and the Kyivan princes. The Moscow rulers are sure their lineage extends from Emperor Augustus (63 BC–AD 14) himself. In Grand Prince Vladimir (Volodymyr) of Kyiv (c. 958–1015), they see the link that binds them to the Roman caesars. They also like to talk about Moscow's connection to Orthodox Constantinople, which the Turks captured around two hundred years earlier. In general, for Muscovites in the seventeenth century, Rome, Constantinople, and Kyiv are all distant, semi-mythical cities.

But Innokenty Gizel makes a connection and subordinates all historical logic to it. In his world view, Kyiv was once the capital of some abstract supranational Russia. Then it was Moscow.

For contemporaries of Innokenty Gizel, this revision of history is nothing short of revolutionary. In the seventeenth century, the Polish kings called themselves the rulers of Rus; after all, Kyiv and the surrounding lands had belonged to them for many centuries. Here, the term "Rus" refers to the part of the Polish-Lithuanian Commonwealth inhabited by Orthodox Christians. The Poles refuse on principle to refer to the more easterly "Moscow" tsars as *russkiye* (Russians), that is, "people of Rus." But Innokenty Gizel of Kyiv deliberately puts an anti-Polish spin on his version of history.

Moreover, he claims the existence of an all-embracing "pan-Russian Orthodox people," uniting all the East Slavs (the forebears of modern-day Russians, Ukrainians, and Belarusians) under one umbrella. Moscow, incidentally, thinks otherwise. The Muscovite Orthodox Church does not even consider the Christians of Kyiv to be coreligionists. If a resident of the city in the seventeenth century wants to move to Moscow, he must be rebaptized, as Muscovite priests consider Ukrainian Orthodoxy to be a different faith. But Innokenty pursues his own political goal: his book is not a historical study, rather a tool, or weapon, for diplomatic negotiations. Innokenty's target audience is Moscow-based diplomats—to exert moral pressure on them. He needs to induce the Muscovite tsar to enter into a military alliance with the Ukrainians and give them security guarantees in their war against Poland. He tinkers with history to achieve the desired end result: to prove that Kyiv and Moscow are directly related and hence the Muscovite tsar is duty bound to assist Kyiv.

Innokenty Gizel's tendentious tome is published under the title *Synopsis*. It quickly transcends immediate political interests and unexpectedly becomes a bestseller of the day. Naturally, *Synopsis* greatly appeals to Alexis Romanov, the Russian tsar at the time.

It is not long before a second, then third, edition of *Synopsis* is published. Translations into Latin and Greek soon follow. Finally, under the next Russian tsar, Alexis's son the future Peter the Great, *Synopsis* becomes in the 1700s the standard textbook on Russian history.

Over the coming centuries, *Synopsis* will form the blueprint for Russian scholars (Vasily Tatishchev, Nikolay Karamzin, Sergey Solovyov, Vasily Klyuchevsky, et al.) in penning their own versions of Russian history. After Gizel, the whole history of the Russian state will spring from the bygone Principality of Kyiv. In 1913, historian and future foreign minister in the short-lived Provisional Government of 1917 Pavel Milyukov, himself a student of the aforementioned Klyuchevsky, will write: "The spirit of *Synopsis* reigns supreme in our historiography of the 18th century; it defines the tastes and interests of readers, serves as a starting point for most researchers, and provokes arguments among the most serious of them. In brief, it forms the backdrop for the development of historical science in the last century."

The historical logic invented by Innokenty Gizel will please Moscow's rulers so much that it remains the official version of history until the twenty-first century. And so the Russian propagandists of that same century, it turns out, those who assert that Russians and Ukrainians are one people with a shared past, have simply bought into the ideology of a seventeenth-century propagandist.

Helen of the Steppe

It was all because of love. Her name is Elena (Helen). She is young and beautiful, just like her namesake in Greek mythology who sparked the Trojan War. She gets a job as a nanny in the family of a rich Ukrainian. The lady of the house, Hanna, is seriously ill and needs help with the children. The owner, Hanna's husband, takes a fancy to the young child-minder, and soon she becomes his mistress.

Also in love (or lust) with Elena is a wealthy Pole, who dreams of stealing her from his Ukrainian neighbor and marrying her. Even in the twenty-first century, such a story would end in tears; but the seventeenth century is a far crueler time.

The smitten Pole is named Daniel, and his Ukrainian rival Bohdan. In the spring of 1647, seizing a moment when Bohdan is away, Daniel and his servants attack his estate, set fire to it, kidnap Elena, and give Bohdan's ten-year-old son a vicious beating for good measure. The boy dies soon afterwards.

Thirsty for revenge, Bohdan goes to Warsaw, because Ukraine is a Polish province at that time. He turns, in the first instance, to the courts. But his offender, the Polish nobleman Daniel Czapliński, is a high-placed official, so the court awards Bohdan a derisory sum of compensation, 150 florins. He believes that his land (not to mention his son and mistress) is worth at least twenty times as much. So Bohdan goes in person to plead his case to the Polish king.

Legend has it that the king receives Bohdan in his palace, but secretly, late at night. They are the same age and rumored to be long acquainted, the king having previously entrusted Bohdan with various hush-hush assignments, such as securing Cossack help in the wars against the Ottoman Empire, which his own parliament, the Sejm, refused to finance. At their meeting, however, the king is the first to unburden his soul: he has no power, the nobles are out of control, he sighs. In response, Bohdan tells his harrowing tale. But the king does not wish to get involved, remarking rhetorically: "If you Cossacks [that is, free mercenary soldiers] are such brave warriors, if you have weapons, why don't you stand up for yourselves?" This off-the-cuff suggestion will change world history.

Bohdan returns to Ukraine and raises a revolt against the Polish overlords, an event known as the Khmelnytsky Uprising. Just a few months later, he exacts revenge on his nemesis Daniel Czapliński, seizing the latter's estate, reclaiming Elena, and marrying her. Daniel is forced to flee to Poland.

Now for some background about the world inhabited by Elena and Bohdan.

The Ways of the Seventeenth Century

In 1647, Bohdan is fifty-one years old. The land he lives in goes by many names, one of the most common of which is Ukraine. It is at around this time that the traveler Guillaume Levasseur de Beauplan's book *Description of Ukraine* is published in France. The author explains that Ukraine is ordinarily understood as being part of Poland, "located between Muscovy and Transylvania." Another, more common name for these lands is Rus or Malaya Rus (Little Rus)—a toponym of Greek origin. According to one version, supported by many Ukrainian historians today, "Little" simply referred to its being the historical core of the state. The lands to the north of it became known as "Great Rus," because they were larger. Over time, these names will turn into Malorossiya (Little Russia)—that is, Ukraine—and Velikorossiya (Great Russia), the lands around Moscow.

Bohdan lives in troubled times, even by the standards of the day. Europe is engulfed in the deadliest conflict in its history by percentage of population killed: almost all European states are sucked in, and 5–8 million people die as a result. Historians will call it the Thirty Years' War. It breaks out when Bohdan is twenty-two and lasts almost his entire adult life.

The main European superpower of the day is referred to simply as "the Empire"—because there is no other on the continent. Its full name is the Holy Roman Empire of the German Nation, a patchwork of duchies and principalities, most of which, when unified in the nineteenth century, will form modern Germany. The Empire has its capital at Vienna and is ruled by the Habsburg dynasty.

The war begins in 1618 as a conflict between the Empire and Bohemia in today's Czech Republic. This "world war" of the seventeenth century is ostensibly fought over religion: the Catholic Holy Roman Empire and its allies versus the breakaway Protestant principalities. But pretty soon everything gets mixed up and people start butchering each other regardless of religious affiliation.

In the seventeenth century, religion is the primary factor in self-identity. Like nearly all Ukrainians, Bohdan was born into an Orthodox family. At the age of fifteen, however, he was sent to study at a Jesuit school in Lviv, where he was naturally encouraged to adopt Catholicism—which he refused to do on principle.

Bohdan goes to war at the age of twenty-four along with his father, as part of the Polish army against Ottoman forces. The Turks are victorious; Bohdan's father is slain in battle, and he himself is taken prisoner and sold into Ottoman slavery (a common occurrence in the seventeenth century). But he is lucky: two years later his relatives buy back his freedom.

Having returned home from slavery, the irrepressible Bohdan is soon off to war again. War is the main occupation of many Ukrainian males in the seventeenth century. Most Ukrainians back then are Cossacks; as mercenaries, they earn their crust not only from farming or commerce, but mostly from fighting. In war-torn Europe, mercenaries are in great demand.

By this time, the French have entered the war against the Empire. Despite France being a Catholic country, First Minister of State Cardinal Richelieu (of *Three Musketeers* fame) eyes an opportunity for French expansion at Habsburg expense. Lutheran Sweden harbors similar imperialist ambitions; it, too, is at war with the Empire. When Richelieu dies, Cardinal Mazarin continues his predecessor's policy. It is Mazarin who in 1644 hires a detachment of Ukrainian mercenaries to capture the port of Dunkirk in France.

Legend has it that it is shortly after the Dunkirk mission that Bohdan returns home to find his estate devastated and his mistress kidnapped. At first he behaves like a loyal subject of the Polish king, Władysław IV, taking his complaint to the law courts, then to the monarch personally, as described earlier. But then, offended by the treatment shown to him, he gathers a Cossack army around him. He convenes a meeting of Cossacks from all over Ukraine and calls for an uprising. This idea proves very popular: Ukrainian peasants are tired of economic and religious oppression; everyone has many reasons to start a rebellion, it's not about Elena at all.

Bohdan needs an ally. The ideal ally to fight Poland would be the Tsardom of Russia to the north, he muses. But Moscow, its capital and center, is still too weak after decades of strife. There is nothing for it but to woo the southern neighbor, Crimea. At that moment, the peninsula is a large Muslim state—the Crimean Khanate, still ruled by the descendants of Genghis Khan.

Ambitionless Moscow

What is up with the Moscow-centered Tsardom of Russia (also known as Muscovy) in the seventeenth century? Why does Bohdan Khmelnytsky consider it weak and unable to help? The fact is that the country cannot move on from the reign of Ivan the Terrible, who sat on the throne for fifty years, the longest-serving ruler in Russian history (not even Putin will beat that . . . probably). Ivan significantly expanded the territory of the state, while inflicting so much inhuman repression on his people that after his death, in 1584, society remained crushed and demoralized for decades to come.

But Bohdan knows little about such internal politics. He was born ten years or so after the tsar's death and has never even heard of "Ivan the Terrible." Officially the tsar is Ivan IV, while the epithet "Terrible" will be coined by the historian Vasily Tatishchev only a century later.

Throughout his childhood, Bohdan heard much about Poland's wars with the Tsardom of Russia and its periodic attempts to place its own candidate on the Muscovite throne. When Bohdan is fifteen years old, in 1610, the Moscow elite (known as the boyars) depose the latest in a string of tsars and offer the crown to another fifteen-year-old: the heir to the Polish throne, that selfsame future king Władysław IV. He and Bohdan are not yet acquainted, of course.

The Moscow boyars have only one condition: the Polish prince must convert from Catholicism to Orthodoxy. Had the proposal been accepted, world history would have taken a different course. But Władysław's father, the current Polish king, Sigismund III, intervenes. He is categorically against his son's conversion. In any case, the king has a better idea. The Jesuit-raised Sigismund proposes himself as the new tsar of Russia, followed by the forced conversion of the Muscovite people to Catholicism. The boyars refuse; war breaks out; Polish troops occupy Moscow. Also fighting as allies of the Poles are the Cossacks.

For Bohdan, therefore, the Tsardom of Russia is not so much a threat as a dysfunctional land teeming with Orthodox Christians. When Bohdan turns seventeen, he learns that a Russian militia has recaptured Moscow and the Poles have retreated. And although young Władysław will continue to call himself Tsar of Muscovy, another young monarch from the new Romanov dynasty has been elected in Moscow. However, for a long time to come, the Muscovite rulers will assiduously abstain from campaigns of conquest. Even thirty-five years later, Bohdan and his Cossack army know they will never persuade the Muscovites to declare war on the Poles. So they turn to the Crimean Khanate.

Independent Ukraine

To launch a full-fledged uprising against Poland, Bohdan must follow democratic procedures: he needs the Cossacks to elect him as their hetman (that is, commander in chief). So he goes to the Zaporizhian Host. The Host is a defensive structure in southeastern Ukraine. It is essentially a fortress located at the end of the world protecting its inhabitants from raiders, in particular the troops of the Crimean Khan, who periodically attack Ukraine from the south, robbing the people and capturing slaves. For the people of the twenty-first century who watched *Game of Thrones* it would be fair to compare the Host to the Wall and the Night's Watch. Cossacks from the Host form a special part of Ukrainian society; they are the most daring and courageous, as reflected in the many folk legends about them. They are always ready to join in a revolt. The Host throws its full weight behind Bohdan, who is duly elected, and the Cossacks expel all Polish commanders. The Ukrainian uprising spreads rapidly.

Warsaw sends a huge army to suppress the Ukrainian revolt (the aforementioned Khmelnytsky Uprising), and even demands help from Muscovy (ironically, the Russian tsar agrees). In May 1648, the army of Bohdan Khmelnytsky wins its first major victory at the town of Zhovti Vody, very close to the site where, 120 years later, the Cossack city of Kryvyi Rih will spring up, and, 330 years later, future Ukrainian president Vova Zelensky will be born.

Just a few days later, in Warsaw, the Polish king, Władysław IV, dies from an attack of urolithiasis (kidney stones). Somewhat counterintuitively, Bohdan is taken aback by the news. Despite his rebellion, he still counted on maintaining relations with the Polish king. The plan was not to secede from Poland entirely, but to achieve greater rights and autonomy; now he has no idea who the next Polish king will be, or whom he will face at the negotiating table when the time comes.

The crown of the Polish-Lithuanian Commonwealth at that time is not passed on by inheritance; rather, the next monarch must be chosen by parliament (the Sejm), which consists of representatives of the nobility and clergy of Poland and Lithuania. Having pondered the question, Bohdan decides that, for him, the least bad option would be for the new

Muscovite tsar, Alexis Romanov, to occupy the Polish throne. The tsar is tempted, but hesitant about the suggestion. At the same time, Bohdan tries to negotiate with the younger brother of the late Polish king, Jan Casimir—he, too, is a strong candidate. Alexis is still of two minds; Jan Casimir is elected.

But the uprising continues: the rebel peasants start smashing up the homes of Poles and Jews living in the territory of Ukraine. About a third of all Jews in the Polish-Lithuanian Commonwealth live on Ukrainian soil. Many of them make a living by working for the Polish administration, in particular as tax collectors on behalf of the Polish nobility.

During the revolt, the Cossacks ransack Polish estates and kill their owners. In addition, there are mass anti-Jewish pogroms. The Jews are not the main target of the uprising; they are just in the wrong place at the wrong time. Bohdan does not personally like Jews. Since the revolt takes place under the banner of rights for Orthodox Christians, the Cossacks perceive the Jews likewise as enemies and massacre them along with the Poles. Anti-Semitism is widespread and deep-rooted in the seventeenth century. In Europe, trials of Jews accused of sacrificing Christian children are not uncommon. After the uprising, Bohdan will forever have a reputation as a virulent anti-Semite.

Within a few months, the Ukrainian lands have been cleared of almost all Polish nobles, officials, Catholic priests, and Jews. Estimates vary as to the number killed. In the seventeenth century, human life is of little value; any conflict claims many victims. At the same time, historians have a tendency to inflate the figures.

In December 1648, Bohdan's army triumphantly enters the ancient capital of Kyiv. He is solemnly greeted by senior clergy: the Metropolitan Archbishop (or simply Metropolitan) of Kyiv, the abbot of the Kyiv-Pechersk Monastery (now called Kyiv-Pechersk Lavra), Innokenty Gizel, and even Patriarch Paisios of Jerusalem, who happens to be passing through Kyiv on his way to Moscow. They congratulate Bohdan on his victory and even address him as *Knyaz*, a noble title that roughly translates as "Grand Duke" and suggests that he is a ruler. Hearing this, Bohdan experiences an inner revolution: never before has he thought that Ukraine could be a separate independent state, with him as its leader.

But, on seeing the patriarch, Bohdan first consults him on an entirely different matter: his beloved Elena was forced to convert to Catholicism and marry a Pole, who has now fled. Is it possible somehow for her to divorce her husband in his absence and allow her to get married anew, this time to Bohdan? The patriarch has no objection (and receives six horses and a thousand gold pieces for being so compliant). Bohdan and Elena exchange vows.

A New World Order

The Khmelnytsky Uprising coincides with another historical event: the end of the Thirty Years' War in Europe. In October 1648, peace talks are being finalized in the German city of Osnabrück. Historians call the treaty the Peace of Westphalia.

The document guarantees freedom of religion for the German Protestant principalities, and signifies defeat for the Empire. The Empire's decline is offset by the rise of two new European superpowers: France (which has claimed Alsace from the Empire) and Sweden (which has gained control over the Baltic Sea). "Russia" does not take part in the congress—this single-word designation for the country is still unknown in Europe, but the Swedish delegation mentions in the treaty that the "Grand Duke of Muscovy" was one of its allies, albeit nonbelligerent.

Bohdan Khmelnytsky, of course, hears that the war is over; he can barely remember a time without it. He seems to be trying out the rules of the Peace of Westphalia for himself: an attempt to secure freedom of religion, as did the German principalities, and autonomy, but under the Polish-Lithuanian Commonwealth.

From this moment on, Bohdan begins negotiations with the Polish king in an attempt to secure maximum autonomy for Ukraine and rights for the Orthodox clergy. Moreover, he wants a Ukrainian delegation to participate in the election of the new king, alongside the Polish and Lithuanian ones. During talks with the Polish delegation, Bohdan Khmelnytsky for the first time describes himself as the "sole ruler of Rus"—that is, he behaves toward the king like some Saxon or Bavarian duke toward the emperor. The Polish diplomats are not ready for such a sharp turn; the negotiations end in failure.

In addition to the Poles, Bohdan Khmelnytsky holds parallel negotiations with the Muscovite ruler about a possible military alliance against the Poles. Tsar Alexis refuses, saying that, of course, he is glad to accept the Cossacks under his patronage, but he will not oppose Poland. If, on the other hand, the Ukrainians join Moscow Tsardom through their own efforts, then so be it. The prospect of Ukrainian liberty is not exactly to Moscow's liking: from the tsar's point of view, Bohdan is an insurgent who rebelled against his monarch. The population of Ukraine is too "European": it consists of free Cossacks and peasants, plus a Western-educated elite and enlightened clergy who speak Latin, like all Catholic priests in Western Europe. In Moscow, strict centralization and bureaucracy rule. Cossack freedom, combined with a democratized nobility, looks too Western and alien to Moscow.

After the aborted negotiations with Poland, the war resumes and ends with another Cossack victory. In 1649, Bohdan and the Polish king, Jan Casimir, sign a treaty that effectively recognizes Ukraine as an autonomous region, a separate Cossack state. Under this agreement, Jews are barred from Ukraine and Chyhyryn, the hetman's hometown, becomes the capital.

Bohdan creates new state institutions, in effect applying the Polish and Turkish setups to Ukraine. The place of the elected king is taken by the hetman (Bohdan himself), that of the Polish nobility (the *szlachta*) by the Cossack chivalry, that of the Sejm by the General Rada. But all this is still in embryo.

The problem for the new state is that its inhabitants have abandoned agriculture en masse. The new Ukraine is a paramilitary state (its official name is the Zaporizhian Host); soldiers have a special status, which means everyone wants to be a Cossack. In times of war, this is beneficial, because large forces can be quickly mobilized. But in peacetime, the huge paramilitary population hinders development.

Bohdan Khmelnytsky is not the only European politician in 1649 who creates a new state for himself with a republican form of government. At exactly the same time, on the other side of the continent,

Oliver Cromwell replaces the headless monarch as ruler of England. This is just one of many parallels between Cromwell and Khmelnytsky: already in the seventeenth century, comparisons are drawn between them. They are almost the same age; they come to power at the same time; they die at roughly the same time; the states they create ultimately collapse; and their corpses are dug out of their graves and desecrated. But it is they who create a historical precedent that will forever resonate through the history of their respective lands: a successful uprising against the Crown in the name of freedom. It is unlikely that Cromwell knew about the existence of Bohdan Khmelnytsky; but in Ukraine they would surely have heard about the English Revolution and the execution of Charles I—a political and psychological milestone of epic proportions.

Eternal Love

The war continues: the Polish king, Jan Casimir, launches a new campaign against Ukraine. Bohdan and his army set out to meet him, while Elena and Bohdan's children remain in Chyhyryn. Then something terrible happens: Bohdan's eldest son from his first wife, Hanna, nineteen-year-old Timosh, attacks and kills his ex-nanny-now-stepmother, and hangs her naked body on the gate of his father's house.

Sources do not give an exact reason why. Timosh apparently considered Elena guilty of some awful crime: stealing money, committing adultery, spying for the Poles, secretly corresponding with her former husband, Daniel Czapliński—all these versions exist. According to some historians, Timosh laid out his suspicions to his father in a letter. Whether that was before or after the murder is not known.

Bohdan's reaction is not recorded, but in any case, he has other problems: he is again at war with the Poles. And the troops of his allies, the Crimean Tatars under the command of Khan İslâm Giray, retreat unexpectedly. Bohdan tries to stop them, whereupon the Tatars take him prisoner. In the absence of their hetman, the Cossacks continue to fight but suffer defeat. The Crimean Tatars release Bohdan only ten days later, when the battle is already lost. During this time, the troops of the Grand Duchy of Lithuania, advancing from the north through today's Chernobyl zone, have managed to capture Kyiv. Hetman Bohdan, freed from captivity, manages to cling to power, but the territory under his control is reduced to the Kyiv Voivodeship, the region around Kyiv.

His mind turns again to an alliance with Moscow, since his former Crimean allies proved so fickle and unreliable. Bohdan believes that Ukraine would be far better off if it were to separate from Catholic Poland and accept the patronage of Orthodox Muscovy.

After 1652, Moscow's attitude toward Ukraine begins to change. The former patriarch dies and the Russian Orthodox Church (ROC) is headed by Nikon, a man with vaulting ambitions. He sees himself as a kind of Russian Cardinal Richelieu (a cleric who controls a nation). It is Nikon who kick-starts the transformation of the Tsardom of Russia, the benighted Muscovy, into the mighty Russian Empire. Nikon explains to the tsar that with Cossack assistance he will be able to regain all the territories lost to the Poles.

Bohdan's position at this moment is rather precarious, having launched a failed military campaign in Moldavia, which, inter alia, claimed the life of Timosh.

On January 18, 1654, Bohdan and the Muscovite emissaries meet in the city of Pereyaslav, which lies exactly halfway between the old princely capital, Kyiv, and Bohdan's new capital, Chyhyryn. Bohdan, accompanied by Cossacks and Russians, goes to the city cathedral to swear allegiance to Tsar Alexis. But just at the crucial moment, a dispute arises. Bohdan demands that Alexis's representative, the boyar Vasily Buturlin, swear on behalf of the tsar to preserve all Cossack liberties. Buturlin refuses to do so but invites Bohdan to state his wishes in writing and send them to the tsar—but only after taking the oath. (For his firm negotiating stance, Buturlin will later receive a royal bonus: a fur coat, a gold cup, and 150 rubles.) The hetman agrees, the Cossacks take the oath to be "eternal subjects of His Majesty the Tsar of All Rus and His heirs." (Such text was common for the early modern period, when everyone swore "eternal love," "eternal loyalty," and "eternal friendship"—which never prevented bloodshed, because it always seemed that the other side broke the oath first.)

After the oath, Bohdan writes a detailed letter to Tsar Alexis, setting out the terms and conditions of Ukraine's accession to the Tsardom of Russia: the Ukrainians shall elect their own hetman, who is free to conduct his own foreign policy and can receive emissaries and ambassadors, having informed the tsar about this, but who vows to have no relations with the Polish king or the Ottoman sultan; Ukraine shall pay taxes to Moscow, but the tsar has no right to seize any Cossack lands; the entire political structure shall remain the same as under the Poles, and the Ukrainian nobility must retain all their former rights.

Tsar Alexis accepts all these demands—except for independent foreign policy. But the parties, of course, view the treaty differently. The Cossacks have signed various agreements with the Polish kings many times before. For them, this is just another diplomatic document, albeit with a new counterparty. According to Bohdan, the treaty can be broken should Moscow not fulfill its obligations. The hetman has already withdrawn his oath to the Polish king, believing him to have violated the terms by failing to protect the Orthodox faith.

But the Muscovite tsar has never before signed a treaty with any of his subjects. And so the document for him is primarily an oath of allegiance, and the fine print just for decoration.

Death and Deluge

On June 6–7, 1654, six months after Bohdan Khmelnytsky has sworn allegiance to Tsar Alexis in the cathedral of the city of Pereyaslav, two important ceremonies take place. In France, fifteen-year-old Louis XIV is crowned in the cathedral of Reims. And in Sweden, thirty-two-year-old Charles X Gustav is crowned in the cathedral of the city of Uppsala.

France and Sweden have been the most powerful countries in Europe since the end of the Thirty Years' War. The near-simultaneous coronation of the two monarchs is a symbolic coincidence. It is Louis and Charles Gustav who will soon carve out a new Europe.

Louis XIV has actually been the nominal king for a long time—from the age of four, after the death of his father, Louis XIII. His childhood was difficult. A noble uprising broke out in France against his mother, Anne of Austria, and her lover Cardinal Mazarin, forcing little Louis to flee from Paris. Yet in those days rebellions against royal power were par for the course: the German princes defeated their emperor in the Thirty Years' War; Oliver Cromwell overthrew and executed Charles I in England; Bohdan Khmelnytsky liberated his land from the Polish king. The civil war in France, known as the Fronde, lasted throughout Louis's childhood. It led, ultimately, to a dictatorship under the rebel leader, Louis de Bourbon, Prince of Condé. But when he lost popularity, power returned to Louis XIV. This time it was power on a scale that the medieval monarchs could not have imagined.

In 1652, the fifteen-year-old Louis writes a letter to the French parliament: "All power belongs to Us. We hold it according to God's will, so that no man, whatever his status, can claim it." Later Louis XIV will become famous for his phrase "*L'État, c'est moi*" ("The state is me"). Curiously, such childish maximalism will become the political mainstream for several centuries to come and many leaders, right up to the present day, will continue to believe wholeheartedly in their divine right to rule.

Charles X Gustav is older than Louis XIV. Having tasted victory, as he sees it, in the Thirty Years' War, he is full of imperial ambitions. In his view, the Baltic Sea should become a Swedish lake. The sooner, the better.

In 1654, the fashion for absolutism and imperialism has not yet reached Russia. But the army of the Muscovite tsar decides for the first time to attack the Polish-Lithuanian Commonwealth—in alliance with the Cossacks of Bohdan Khmelnytsky. The combined army occupies the territory of modern Belarus. It is here that the tsar and the hetman fall out, since both claim the acquired territories as their own. Meanwhile, the local nobility has acknowledged the rule of the Muscovite tsar, while the peasantry want to become subjects of the hetman in the hope of acquiring Cossack liberty. Belarusian peasants swell the ranks of the Cossacks in droves. And the first conflicts between the Ukrainian and Russian administrations break out.

Bursting with imperial ambition, the new Swedish king, Charles X Gustav, also attacks Poland and Lithuania. The united Commonwealth, which until recently was stable, finds itself fighting for its very survival. At this point, Moscow changes tack—Tsar Alexis seeks a truce with the Poles: it is better to have a weak Poland as a neighbor than a strong Sweden. Bohdan Khmelnytsky is against the move—he no longer wants peace with Poland. Bypassing Moscow, he begins negotiations with the Swedish king and enters into an anti-Polish alliance with him. And with that, despite being just one year old, the Treaty of Pereyaslav between Bohdan and the Muscovite tsar is forgotten.

In October 1656, in present-day Vilnius (then Vilna), negotiations begin between Russia and Poland. It turns into a real drama for the Ukrainian side. First, at the insistence of the Polish side, the Ukrainian emissaries are not allowed to attend the talks. Then the Poles play a trick on them, saying that the tsar has agreed to return the hard-won Ukrainian lands to the Poles. It is disinformation, but the Ukrainian emissaries take it at face value.

Bohdan and all Ukrainians are horrified—they are sure that Tsar Alexis has betrayed them. Bohdan, evidently, no longer considers himself a subject of the Muscovite tsar, bound by the Treaty of Pereyaslav. In alliance with Sweden and Transylvania, the Cossacks continue to wage war against Poland, and even capture Kraków. Soon Charles X Gustav of Sweden, Bohdan, and other allies are discussing how to carve up Poland.

In July 1657, Muscovite emissary Fyodor Buturlin pays a visit to Bohdan in Chyhyryn. By now seriously ill, Bohdan has already chosen a successor for himself: his sixteen-year-old son, Yuri. The talks are tough: Buturlin and Bohdan each accuse the other of violating the Treaty of Pereyaslav. Soon after the meeting with Buturlin, the hetman dies of a stroke. Bohdan's death breaks off the futile negotiations but also derails any further talks.

Ruin and Oblivion

The sixteen-year-old Yuri Khmelnytsky turns out to be a far less successful young ruler than his peer Louis XIV. Bohdan's right-hand man, the general clerk Ivan Vyhovsky, persuades the teenager to renounce the throne and go to study at Innokenty Gizel's academy. Vyhovsky himself becomes hetman. True, despite being an experienced politician, he lacks the charisma and common touch of Bohdan.

In September 1658, a year after Bohdan's death, Hetman Vyhovsky concludes an agreement with Poland, which managed, ultimately, to withstand the war against Sweden and its allies. Ukraine will join the Commonwealth as a third equal partner: alongside the Kingdom of Poland and the Grand Duchy of Lithuania, it will be known as the Grand Duchy of Rus. The Orthodox faith is granted equal rights with Catholicism, and Ukrainians receive as many seats in parliament as Poles and Lithuanians. The hetman will be elected without any interference from Poland and will mint Ukraine's own money in Ukraine. In the wars between the Commonwealth king and the Muscovite tsar, the Cossacks may remain neutral, but in the event of an attack by Moscow on Ukraine, the king is obliged to defend the latter. Lastly, the most symbolic clause of the agreement: "What happened under Khmelnytsky shall be consigned to eternal oblivion"—that is, the oath of allegiance of the Ukrainians to the Muscovite tsar is no longer relevant. Thus, legally, the unification of Ukraine with Russia has lasted less than four and a half years. (This will not prevent the Soviet leadership from marking the occasion three hundred years later.)

This so-called Treaty of Hadiach, much more detailed than that of Pereyaslav, is signed by the respective diplomats on September 16, 1658. Only in May the following year is the agreement discussed in the Polish Sejm—and a terrible thing happens. The Sejm throws out all the clauses that guarantee Ukraine's statehood, relating to both the Grand Duchy of Rus and the minting of coins. The treaty is ratified in a watered-down form, which means that Hetman Vyhovsky's ambitions are destined never to be realized, one of which is to bear the title "Grand Duke of Rus." It marks the collapse of his career—Bohdan's followers and anti-Polish opponents depose Vyhovsky and elect the now-eighteen-year-old Yuri Khmelnytsky as the new hetman.

Yet Bohdan's son cannot live up to his father. First he signs a new treaty with Moscow (the "eternal oblivion" is itself now forgotten), then again swears allegiance to the Polish king, then suffers a defeat at the hands of his own uncle's troops, renounces power, and retires to a monastery.

There begins a period that Ukrainian historians will describe, somewhat poetically, as the "Ruin"—the word encapsulates what remains of the Cossacks' dream of an independent state.

In 1667, Russia and Poland sign a truce and divide Ukraine between themselves. The area of West Ukraine to the right of the Dnieper River goes to Poland (also known as "right-bank Ukraine"), and the left to Russia ("left-bank Ukraine"). This is yet another body blow for the Cossacks, who see their land carved up without so much as a by-your-leave.

Enslaved People and Other Goods

Reconstructing a picture of the seventeenth-century European world is not easy today: the values and technologies are so wildly different. But the main disparity is that most of the countries we know today did not yet exist. And for many of those that did exist, it is a time of early and rapid colonial development.

While the annexation of Ukraine is raising all kinds of questions and doubts in Moscow, the expansion eastwards is progressing at breakneck speed. The area along the eastern border of Muscovy, in the Urals, is also home to Cossacks—the same free warriors as the inhabitants of Ukraine. Only they speak Russian and are in the service of the tsar. It is they who are leading the colonization of Siberia: the conquest of the indigenous peoples beyond the Ural Mountains.

It is in 1648 that the Cossack Semyon Dezhnev reaches America—via the strait between Chukotka and Alaska. In the decades that follow, Muscovite troops conquer eastern Siberia, fighting the local inhabitants, such as the Buryats, who live on the shores of Lake Baikal.

At the same time, the neighboring lands are being colonized by the Chinese, who seize the territory of modern Mongolia. The new Qing dynasty creates its own empire, one that will last until the early twentieth century and fall in the same decade as the Russian empire of the Romanovs. The mid-seventeenth century sees several clashes between the armies of the Muscovite tsar and the Chinese emperor, but in the end they come to an agreement: Mongolia shall belong to China, Buryatia to Muscovy.

There is a plenty of evidence pointing to the brutal treatment of the Buryats by the colonialists: the Cossacks rape women, kill children, and enslave the local population. This provokes frequent backlashes. Then, in 1661, in the former Buryat lands, Russian Cossacks found the city of Irkutsk.

Three hundred and sixty years later, it will be contract soldiers from Buryatia who will initially be accused of violence against residents in areas around Kyiv under Russian control, including Bucha, Irpin, and Hostomel. However, it would later be proved that Pskov paratroopers were responsible for the killing of civilians.

Back in the seventeenth century, trading slaves and massacring indigenous peoples are nothing out of the ordinary. The conquest of Siberia occurs simultaneously with the colonization of North America. In 1660, the English king introduces a state monopoly on the trade of "mahogany, ivory, Negroes, slaves, hides, wax and other goods" from African countries. The Royal African Company is created, one of the largest companies that will supply slaves to North America for almost a century.

The fate of modern-day New York City is also decided in those same years. In 1655, the Susquehannock tribe rises up against the Dutch settlers in the New Amsterdam area, killing several dozen of them. A decade later, in 1665, the British arrive and seize the land from their Dutch rivals. It changes ownership several times, during which time the indigenous population suffers at the hands of the British and the Dutch. Finally, in 1674, the Europeans agree that New York (formerly New Amsterdam) shall go to Britain and in exchange the Dutch shall receive the South American colony of Suriname.

Also in 1674, the monk Innokenty Gizel publishes his *Synopsis* in Kyiv. He wants to persuade the Muscovite rulers not to cede the Ukrainian Cossack lands to Poland or Turkey, but to protect them. The history of Russia in his book ends with the Treaty of Pereyaslav, the triumphant but brief reunification of Kyiv and Moscow. He never even mentions the name Bohdan. For twentieth-century Soviet leaders Khmelnytsky will become a folk hero, but for the seventeenth-century Tsar Alexis he is a dangerous rebel. Gizel is sure that his Moscow-based readership will not want to be reminded of him.

Stockholm

St. Petersburg

SWEDISH

EMPIRE

BALTIC
SEA

Moscow

PRUSSIA

Smolensk

Minsk

TSARDOM

OF RUSSIA

Warsaw

POLISH-LITHUANIAN

COMMONWEALTH

Hlukhiv

Baturyn

Dubno

Kyiv

Zhovkva

Lviv

HETMANATE

Poltava

× Perevolochna

ZAPORIZHIAN HOST

AUSTRIAN

MOLDAVIA

EMPIRE

Bendery   Ochakiv

CRIMEAN KHANATE

SEA OF AZOV

OTTOMAN EMPIRE

BLACK SEA

GREAT NORTHERN WAR IN 1707–1709

State borders in 1700

Partitioned Ukraine

Russian army in 1707–1709

Swedish army of Charles XII in 1707–1709

Flight of Mazepa

200 miles

200 km

2

THE MYTH OF BETRAYAL:
HOW IVAN MAZEPA BROKE
WITH PETER THE GREAT

Horsing Around

1817, Venice. Lord Byron, Europe's most celebrated and scandalous poet, is inspired by a scene he discovered while reading Voltaire: a naked young man is tied to a wild horse as punishment for having an affair with the wife of a wealthy count. An elaborate method of execution, Byron muses: the horse is set free, condemning the young man to near-certain death. Everything about the legend appeals to Byron.

In the protagonist he sees himself, of course. He has recently left England to escape the numerous scandals dogging him: his wife left him a year after their wedding, declaring him insane, the poet's alleged bisexuality is the talk of London society, and there are even rumors of a love affair with his own sister. Byron flees his native land, feeling as if strapped naked to a horse galloping into the unknown.

Byron's poem is titled *Mazeppa*, after its eponymous hero, Ivan Mazepa. (Byron adhered to Voltaire's spelling.) The work begins with a reference to the Battle of Poltava in 1709, when the army of the Swedish king, Charles XII, is defeated by the troops of the Muscovite tsar, Peter I (later "the Great"). Charles is accompanied by Mazepa, the ageing Ukrainian hetman. The Swedish king notes that Mazepa is more at home in the saddle than any other rider. In response, the hetman explains how this skill was acquired through suffering. He was twenty years old, a page of the Polish king, and the lover of the wife of a rich Polish count. One day, her elderly husband found them in bed together and devised an unusual punishment: to be tied naked to a wild steed let loose. But contrary to expectations, the young man not only survived but also went on to lead Ukraine.

Reaching the end of his tale, Mazepa sees that the young king has fallen fast asleep: the plight of a doomed man tied to a horse has clearly made little impression on him.

Byron's poem is published in 1819 to tremendous acclaim. More significantly, it inspires a galaxy of painters to continue the theme. For decades to come, artists depict the young Mazepa tied to a crazed stallion. For Europeans, he is a romantic hero, doomed to suffer because of the petty tyranny of a cuckolded old man.

Pushkin and His Horseman

Byron's work and lifestyle exert a huge impact on writers throughout Europe, including Russia, one of whom is Alexander Pushkin. Ten years younger than the English poet, he styles himself for a while as the "Russian Byron"—and readers, friends, and critics do likewise. Byron's most popular works are the long narrative, autobiographical poems *Childe Harold's Pilgrimage* and *Don Juan*, which inspire Pushkin to write his own novel in verse, *Eugene Onegin*, seen by many as the finest work in Russian literature. (Critics describe it as imitative.) Like Byron, Pushkin is eager to see the world, drawn to the romance of travel. But the Russian Empire's attitude to poets is very different from that of the British: Pushkin pens many politically charged poems, making no bones about his disdain for Emperor Alexander I, and is forbidden to leave the country as a result. Instead, he finds himself "internally exiled" to the Black Sea coast in the south: Crimea and Odesa (in present-day Ukraine), then Chisinau (in present-day Moldova).

In 1823, further burnishing his romantic image, Byron joins the Greek struggle for independence against Ottoman rule and dies of fever in Greece on his way to the front lines in April 1824. At that very moment, Pushkin's punishment is ramped up: his place of exile is changed to the remote village of Mikhailovskoye in northwest Russia.

December 1825 sees the death of Pushkin's nemesis, Emperor Alexander I, whereupon officers—all members of secret anti-government societies, remembered by history as the "Decembrists"—stage an uprising in St. Petersburg and Kyiv Province, which is suppressed. Pushkin has friends among the conspirators. Five of his comrades are sentenced to death, the rest to hard labor in Siberia. It is not long before Pushkin himself is summoned to the capital, where he, too, will be tried and condemned, he is sure. However, the new emperor, Nicholas I, on the contrary, allows Pushkin to return from exile. He does not release the poet from censorship but promises to personally read all his works and decide their fate.

A fan of the rebellious Byron, Pushkin knows that to keep the authorities happy he must produce patriotic poems in praise of the state. To square this circle, in 1828 he composes a poem that he initially calls *Mazepa*, after Byron. The plot is based on another myth from the life of the Ukrainian hetman: Mazepa, no longer young, but sixty-five years old, seduces his own goddaughter, the daughter of his friend Vasily Kochubey. At the same time, he betrays the Russian tsar, Peter I, and goes over to the side of the Swedish king, Charles XII. Kochubey writes to Peter, denouncing Mazepa, who in revenge kills his old friend and father of his beloved. The finale of the poem sees Mazepa and Charles XII defeated by the Russians at the Battle of Poltava. The poem is a paean to Peter the Great.

At the last moment, Pushkin renames the poem *Poltava*, lest anyone else accuse him of imitating Byron.

Pushkin's *Poltava* forms the example of a historical myth: that of Mazepa as a dastardly traitor. Describing his protagonist, Pushkin does not skimp on monstrous epithets: "wicked old man," "ravager," and "vile turncoat" are just a selection, while Kochubey, who betrays his friend, is "fearless" and "guiltless."

Incidentally, just a few years later Pushkin's attitude toward Peter the Great will change. In 1833, he composes the poem *The Bronze Horseman*, in which he portrays the Russian emperor (or rather his statue in St. Petersburg) as a monster who ruthlessly sacrifices the people at the altar of personal ambition. Unsurprisingly, this work falls foul of the censors, the honeymoon period between Pushkin and the authorities comes to an end, and the poet remains under suspicion for the rest of his days. He receives no recognition at all from the state, becoming a victim of persecution, rather like his erstwhile hero Byron.

The Real Mazepa

In reality, Ivan Mazepa was never tied to a bucking bronco—it is all the product of poetic license. Here is what actually happened: In 1662, the young Mazepa is serving as a page at the court of the Polish king Jan II Casimir. Only five years have passed since the death of Bohdan Khmelnytsky, but Ukraine is now split in half: the east is controlled by the Muscovite tsar, the west by the Polish king. Mazepa is highly educated: he graduated from the Kyiv-Mohyla Academy, the oldest and best institute in Ukraine, run by Innokenty Gizel, and studied in Holland, Italy, Germany, and France. But the Polish nobles at the court of Jan Casimir in Warsaw do not consider a Cossack as their equal, even an educated one. One day, the popular Polish writer Jan Pasek comes to see the king and meets Mazepa in the reception hall. Pasek, inebriated, takes a dislike to something about the young man's bearing, hurls a few insults, and hits him in the face. This Mazepa cannot tolerate. The two men reach for their sabers, but the servants pull them apart in time.

The king does not take sides and forces Pasek and Mazepa to publicly reconcile and embrace. But Pasek is unforgiving and unforgetting. Roughly three decades later, he will publish a semi-fictional memoir in which he invents the story about Mazepa's alleged punishment for adultery. After that, Pasek writes, the disgraced Mazepa left Poland forever and was never heard from again. This is a clear case of wishful thinking: Mazepa did indeed leave Poland soon after the quarrel with Pasek, but it had nothing to do with any punishment. And far from never being heard of again, he returns to lead his people. Nevertheless, the story sticks. So much so that in a hundred years Voltaire, and then Byron, will retell the legend of the young man strapped naked to a horse.

In fact, Mazepa leaves Warsaw with his clothes very much on. The king regularly uses him as a special envoy to deliver messages to the hetman of western Ukraine. Mazepa feels like a fish out of water in both lands: in Poland he is a Cossack, in Ukraine a Pole. So, after one such mission, he decides not to return to Warsaw but to establish himself in Ukraine. He duly marries a close relative of the new hetman. Thanks to Mazepa's fine education, he becomes a long-serving diplomat for special assignments, most often to Moscow.

In 1686, Mazepa is tasked with preventing a peace treaty between Muscovy and Poland but does not succeed: the two longtime foes sign the (not intentionally ironic) Treaty of Perpetual Peace, in which they officially carve up Ukraine between themselves. For Mazepa and all Ukrainians, it is an unbearable humiliation. Cossacks do not rebel; rather, they submit.

In May 1687, Moscow sends an army to Crimea under the command of Prince Vasily Golitsyn. The Ukrainian army joins the campaign, which ultimately ends in abject failure. Golitsyn somehow has to justify himself in the eyes of Moscow, and so shifts all the blame to Hetman Ivan Samoylovich, accusing him of sabotage.

Far from resisting, the Cossack leaders welcome the charge. In July 1687, they write a collective denunciation of Samoylovich, this time accusing him of treason. There are ten signatures on the document: the fourth belongs to Mazepa, the tenth to Kochubey. It is he, "General Secretary" Kochubey, who is the mastermind behind the conspiracy; his aim is to become the new hetman.

Golitsyn reads the denunciation, sends it to Moscow, and is instructed to arrest Samoylovich. Then, bribed by Mazepa, he helps the latter to be elected hetman. The fact of the bribe is confirmed by a surviving receipt, though some historians assert that it is not corruption.

Since Mazepa is a protégé of Moscow, he immediately accepts several humiliating conditions: for example, Ukraine can no longer elect a hetman unless approved by decree of the Muscovite tsar.

Mazepa's hetmanship begins terribly—he is totally dependent on Moscow and on Golitsyn personally and financially, and his fellow Cossacks are intensely hostile, because they did not expect Mazepa to exploit his Moscow connections to achieve the role of hetman, leapfrogging over everyone else. Most irksome of all is that the Zaporizhian Host, the Cossack heartland, does not accept him.

For his part, Mazepa is counting on Moscow's assistance to deal with the Host. But there is a problem: it turns out that his Muscovite patrons are obsessed by new, somewhat harebrained imperial ambitions.

An Inglorious Revolution

In 1687, there are two tsars on the Muscovite throne: Ivan and Peter, the young sons of the deceased Tsar Alexis. They have different mothers, so the two half brothers belong to two warring factions. In reality, however, their elder sibling Sophia (Ivan's sister, Peter's half sister) rules the country as regent. Golitsyn is her favorite courtier, and together they become intoxicated by a geopolitical fantasy: that Moscow is the Third Rome (that is, the capital of the third Roman Empire, after the fall of Rome proper and Constantinople). The idea is strange even then, since Europe already has a new Rome: Vienna, whose rulers reign over what is known as the Holy Roman Empire. But Sophia is very ambitious; she, too, wants an empire.

She is greatly inspired by contemporary politics: in 1688, the "Glorious Revolution" begins in England, culminating in the overthrow of the unpopular king, James II. The throne passes to his sister Mary and her husband, the talented military commander William of Orange. Sophia and Golitsyn fancy themselves in the role of Mary and William. But for this they require military victories. They become preoccupied with the idea of winning back the Christian lands in the Balkans from the Ottoman Empire, with Mazepa as an ally and adviser. He tries to dissuade them, but in vain.

Sophia's favorite, Golitsyn, returns to Moscow from the next campaign and invites Mazepa to go with him. The hetman does not understand why and is bemused by the red-carpet treatment laid out for him: he rides around the capital in a luxury carriage, and is received by Tsarevna Sophia herself, accompanied by one of the two young tsars, Ivan V, and the patriarch of the Russian Orthodox Church (ROC). Only then does Mazepa begin to guess that a military coup is being prepared in Moscow: the second tsar, the seventeen-year-old Peter, has left the city to raise an army and overthrow his half sister. Aware of the threat, Sophia and Golitsyn want to use Mazepa and the Cossacks as a loyal guard to protect their power and put down Peter's rebellion. Mazepa's troops are two or three weeks' journey away from Moscow, but he hesitates and does not give the order to advance on the city.

The crisis lasts throughout August 1689: Sophia attempts to negotiate with her half brother Peter. As a result, the patriarch, the head of the ROC, goes over to the side of the seventeen-year-old tsar, as does the army. At the end of August, even Golitsyn goes to visit Peter in the monastery to surrender. Peter does not receive him, sending him straight into exile.

In early September, it is Mazepa's turn to visit. Peter does not receive him immediately—the hetman has to wait until the tsar has finished torturing Sophia's close associates.

In Ukraine, meanwhile, preparations are under way for the election of a new hetman, since everyone is sure that Peter will punish Mazepa for his proximity to Sophia and Golitsyn. But, wholly unexpectedly, Peter is pleased to see him. The tsar, it seems, appreciates the hetman's refusal to deploy his troops in support of his former patrons. Had he decided otherwise, world history would have run a different course.

Sophia is confined to a nunnery. Thirty-two years old, she has successfully ruled the Russian state for seven years; contemporaries liken her to England's Elizabeth I. But, unfortunately for her, Sophia will go down in history as nothing more than the conniving elder sibling of Peter the Great.

The seventeen-year-old Peter and the fifty-year-old Mazepa unexpectedly find common ground. The tsar places his full trust in the hetman, revokes the most humiliating terms and conditions forced upon Mazepa after his election, and allows him to consolidate his power. Opponents of the hetman write denunciations to the tsar, accusing Mazepa of having links with Sophia. But Peter refuses to believe them and has their authors executed. For nearly two decades to come, Mazepa is one of the most influential figures in Peter's inner circle.

The First Emperor

Tsar Peter, in Russian history textbooks, is portrayed as a progressive ruler. He is the superstar of Russian history, albeit not free of controversy. The essential difference between Peter and all other Russian monarchs is that he does not fear Western influence but rather embraces it.

At the age of twenty-five, he travels incognito (under the pseudonym Peter Mikhailov) to Europe: Germany, Holland, England, and Austria. He is less interested in Europe's political structure and freedom of enterprise than in its technology, especially shipbuilding and weaponry. During the trip, he works at dockyards in Holland and England. In the latter, he also visits a foundry, the Houses of Parliament, the Greenwich Observatory, and Oxford University. He had an opportunity to meet Isaac Newton, then Master of the Royal Mint. However, the great scientist, knowing in advance about Peter's visit, simply did not show up at the Mint that day.

Returning to Russia, Peter undertakes a program of reforms, including some quite outlandish ones: for example, he introduces a beard tax. The tsar, influenced by clean-shaven Europe, seeks to wean his subjects off their traditional beard wearing, which he identifies with backwardness: "shave or pay" is the motto. It is in the spirit of the exotic taxation schemes of the age. The year before, for example, England had introduced a window tax, causing many people to brick them up, leading to a national health crisis.

Besides technology, the purpose of the trip is to find allies for a future war with Turkey. In 1700, Muscovite diplomats conclude a peace treaty with Turkey, allowing Peter to embark on another campaign—against

Sweden for access to the Baltic Sea. The Swedish king, Charles XII, like his predecessors, sees the Baltic as a "Swedish lake." But Peter has his own, far greater imperial ambitions.

The Ukrainian hetman, Ivan Mazepa, forms the bedrock of Peter's support, especially since the conclusion of a peace with Turkey has at last brought relative calm to the southern borders of Ukraine. Moreover, Mazepa gradually manages to extend his power to the areas of western Ukraine previously under Polish rule; that is, he almost restores Ukraine's borders to what they were under Bohdan.

In 1700, Mazepa receives the highest award of Russia, recently introduced by Peter: the Order of St. Andrew. Only much later will Peter confer this honor upon himself and his closest friend, Prince Alexander Menshikov.

All communication between Mazepa and Moscow effectively goes through Menshikov, but the two men do not see eye to eye. This is a serious problem for Mazepa. In 1703, Peter commissions Menshikov to build the future empire's new capital, St. Petersburg, on the site of uninhabited (and uninhabitable) swampland. In need of mass labor, Menshikov corrals the Zaporizhian Cossacks. Mazepa is furious but forced to obey.

As the military campaign against Sweden commences, Peter and Menshikov's plans for Mazepa and his troops change repeatedly. The hetman writes to Menshikov, who does not reply. In Mazepa's eyes, Moscow has nothing but contempt and disregard for Ukrainian blood (that said, Peter cares no more about the lives of his own soldiers).

Envoys from Sweden and its ally Poland pay visits to Mazepa, but he arrests them and informs Peter of all the details. Meanwhile, Ukrainian troops fighting against the Swedes under the command of the Russians complain bitterly about their mistreatment.

In the summer of 1706, Peter and Menshikov travel to Kyiv. Peter takes an immediate dislike to the city, ordering the fortress to be completely rebuilt. But even more insulting to Mazepa is that Peter appoints Menshikov commander of the united army, with Mazepa as his subordinate. It is clear to all that Menshikov sees Ukraine as his private fiefdom.

But in the eyes of Peter's entourage, there is nothing untoward: Mazepa is almost seventy years old, and his age is starting to count against him. Moreover, Prince Menshikov (a native of Moscow) expects to receive part of the Ukrainian lands as his own personal property, for which reason he acquits himself in a very businesslike manner.

But worse is to come for Mazepa, in April 1707. He arrives at a military council in Zhovkva, a city in western Ukraine, where he learns that Peter has decided to reform the state administration: all the Ukrainian territories are to be stripped of any autonomy and to become part of Russia on equal terms. This is presented to Mazepa as a necessary step to increase defense capability in the war with the Swedes. Peter additionally demands the return to Poland of the cities in western Ukraine under Mazepa's control; Peter has agreed to this condition with Poles fighting on his side.

Mazepa asks Peter to send a force of at least ten thousand troops to protect Ukraine from the Swedes. To which Peter replies: "Never mind 10,000, I can't even give you ten. Defend yourselves as best you can." Declining supper with the tsar and his entourage, Mazepa returns to his quarters and eats nothing all the next day.

In July 1707, having arrived in Kyiv, Mazepa receives detailed instructions from Peter on how to proceed in the event of an attack by Charles XII: retreat beyond the Dnieper River and employ scorched-earth tactics. That is, leave Kyiv—home to St. Sophia's Cathedral, the Kyiv-Mohyla Academy, and other places dear to Mazepa—to its fate.

The First *Zrada*

In late August 1707, Vasily Kochubey writes the first denunciation of Mazepa. This is the same Kochubey who twenty years earlier wrote a denunciation of the previous hetman, Ivan Samoylovich, in the hope of supplanting him. Now Kochubey has multiple axes to grind against his former rival Mazepa, who outmaneuvered him for the top job.

Back in 1704, the sixty-five-year-old Mazepa had an affair with his own goddaughter Motrya (or Matrena), the young child of Kochubey. It is this story that Pushkin will describe in *Poltava*. Almost everything in this tale is true, except that Pushkin will change the heroine's name to Maria. The love between Motrya and Mazepa is mutual, and the elderly hetman even asks his erstwhile friend Kochubey for her hand in marriage. But according to the rules of the Orthodox Church at the time, marrying one's goddaughter is tantamount to incest, so Motrya's parents are vehemently opposed. The love-stricken sixteen-year-old girl elopes with Mazepa, but after some time he sends her back to her parents. Motrya, however, cannot forgive them; she curses her parents and runs away again. But nor can Kochubey forgive Mazepa. Thus, in 1707, he writes a denunciation to Moscow, accusing Mazepa of treason and collusion with the Swedes. In Pushkin's poem *Poltava*, Mazepa avenges Kochubey's denunciation, but, in fact, it is Peter who orders the latter's execution, after Kochubey admits, under torture, that he unjustly slandered the hetman.

But Kochubey's accusations of betrayal really are true. Mazepa has indeed decided to go over to the side of Charles XII—but only if the Swedes and Poles go to war against Ukraine: "Unless absolutely necessary, I shall not renounce my allegiance to His Majesty the tsar," he says to his closest aide, Pylyp Orlyk. He explains to the latter in detail his motivation—that he is acting not for his own sake, but for that of his descendants, "for the common good of the motherland, poor Ukraine, and the people of Malorossiya."

For contemporary Ukrainian historians, the choice that Mazepa faces is a classic dilemma of that era: enlightenment or absolutism. On the one hand, there is autocracy, in the form of Peter the Great, who forges his empire at any cost; on the other, there is the enlightened West, intelligible to Mazepa, far more democratic than authoritarian Moscow. Whichever he chooses, there will be tough consequences. But, ultimately, he makes a conscious political and civilizational decision.

Meanwhile, Charles XII has been advancing with great success. The Swedish king has grand plans: to divide Russia into principalities, to enthrone Peter's son, Tsarevich Alexei, and to establish a political system along Polish lines, that is, an "aristocratic democracy" (in which nobles have voting rights). No one in Europe doubts that the campaign will be crowned with the same success as Sweden's previous military operations in Denmark, Saxony, and Poland. Mazepa is very much aware of such sentiments. Charles XII plans to pass through Minsk and Smolensk on his way to Moscow.

Peter orders Mazepa to send troops to defend Smolensk, but the Cossack commanders inform the hetman that they are ready to die on their native soil, but not in Russia under the leadership of Russian generals. Then, as if by providence, Charles XII, instead of advancing on Moscow, swings south to Ukraine. On hearing the news, Mazepa exclaims: "It's the devil leading him here!"

Mazepa is summoned to Peter's headquarters, but he wavers, complaining of poor health. Instead, he himself writes to Charles that he is thankful for the latter's arrival and to have been liberated from "the heavy yoke of Moscow." It appears, however, that the hetman has not yet made a final decision, since he does not share his plans with the army. Only on October 23, 1708, when a messenger arrives in Baturyn, northern Ukraine, bringing the rumor that Menshikov is approaching with a view to arresting Mazepa, does the hetman decide finally to join the Swedes and go with his army to Charles's headquarters.

Soon afterwards, on November 13, 1708, Peter declares Mazepa a traitor. Menshikov's troops sack Baturyn, slaughtering up to fifteen thousand people, among them many women and children. All houses and churches are burned on Peter's orders. The Baturyn massacre will later become an important symbol of Peter the Great's enslavement of Ukraine.

Mazepa is anathematized by the Orthodox Church. Peter himself stages the execution of Mazepa in absentia: the Order of St. Andrew is torn off an effigy of the hetman, which is then ceremoniously hanged, as are several real-life commanders captured in Baturyn. Then the Russian troops besiege the Host; Cossacks are executed, buildings razed to the ground.

Peter chooses a new hetman. Despite Peter's brutality, many Cossacks switch to the Russian side; only a handful remain loyal to Mazepa.

The Swedish troops, meanwhile, are battling the unusually harsh winter: many die from the cold even before they clash with Peter's army. Mazepa again vacillates, writing to the tsar and promising to give him Charles XII, but the Swedes intercept the message and place Mazepa under house arrest. In May 1709, Charles besieges the city of Poltava, three hundred miles east of Kyiv, but does not permit the out-of-favor Mazepa to join him on the battlefield, ostensibly because the old man is in poor health. The Swedish troops are defeated. Just three months later, the seventy-year-old Mazepa dies. His right-hand man, Pylyp Orlyk, proclaims himself the new hetman in exile, and even drafts the first Ukrainian constitution. Peter, after the end of what became known as the Great Northern War, declares himself emperor and gives his expanding state a new name: the Russian Empire.

Since Ukraine at that moment is a center of education in the Russian tsardom, Peter engages a Ukrainian scholar to develop his new imperial ideology. In 1716, he summons Feofan Prokopovich, rector of the Kyiv-Mohyla Academy, to St. Petersburg. He will become not only the metropolitan (archbishop) of the new capital, but also the architect of the new empire, and the "Russian Torquemada"—he will develop systems of torture under interrogation. In his numerous historical writings, he follows Gizel in asserting the existence of a "triune people": Russians, Ukrainians, Belarusians. And that the emperor, not the patriarch, should be the head of the church. Peter takes heed and abolishes the post of patriarch—for almost two hundred years. Finally, it is Feofan Prokopovich who, in his *History of Peter the Great* and other works, creates the historical myth of the vile traitor Mazepa, which Pushkin will later use.

Mazepa's defection to the Swedes and their defeat at Poltava is a defining moment in Ukrainian history. The theme of betrayal will echo down the centuries to the present day:

For Russian historians and propagandists, Mazepa has become a common noun, a symbol of treachery. Ukrainian historians will insist that Mazepa, despite his seesawing loyalty to Peter and Charles, never betrayed the interests of the Ukrainian people, which is the key point.

The disputes over Mazepa will resurface with renewed vigor in the 1990s. And in the twenty-first century, the Ukrainian word *zrada* (betrayal) is perhaps the most loaded in the country's political lexicon. After the Russian invasion of 2014, Kyiv will coin the concept of *zradophilia*—Ukrainian society's obsession with seeking out traitors to the national cause. And Ukrainian society today considers Kochubey, not Mazepa, to have been a real criminal.

St. Petersburg
Tsarskoye Selo

BALTIC
SEA

Moscow

PRUSSIA

Vilnius

R U S S I A N

E M P I R E

P O L I S H -

L I T H U A N I A N

Warsaw

C O M M O N W E A L T H

Baturyn

Lviv

Kyiv

Kharkiv

AUSTRIAN

N O V O R O S S I Y A

EMPIRE

Kryvyi Rih

Yekaterinoslav

Mariupol

MOLDAVIA

Kherson

CRIMEAN KHANATE

SEA
OF AZOV

O T T O M A N   E M P I R E

RUSSIAN EMPIRE, POLISH-LITHUANIAN
COMMONWEALTH AND NEIGHBORING COUNTRIES
AFTER THE ABOLITION OF COSSACK HETMANATE,
1775–1783

BLACK SEA

State borders in 1775

Territories annexed to the Russian Empire in 1783

Territories of Cossack Hetmanate (abolished in 1764)
and Zaporizhian Host (abolished in 1775)

200 miles

200 km

3

THE MYTH OF CRIMEA:
HOW CATHERINE THE GREAT TOOK
AWAY COSSACK FREEDOM

1831, St. Petersburg, the capital of the Russian Empire. The young writer Nikolay Gogol is busy creating a fantasy world. He is twenty-two years old and desperate for fame.

He moved to St. Petersburg from Ukraine a few years ago. While still at home, he wrote a poem, under the influence of German romanticism, titled *Hans Küchelgarten*. Now in the Russian capital, the first thing he does is seek an audience with his idol, the great wordsmith Alexander Pushkin. But Pushkin does not receive him: he has been carousing all night and is now fast asleep. Undeterred, Gogol publishes the poem at his own expense—and watches in horror as it gets trashed by every critic. In a fit of nervous anxiety, the young man buys up and burns the entire print run. Almost destitute, he takes a desk job in a government ministry. His romantic dreams of literary glory, it seems, are over.

But St. Petersburg in those days is home to many of Gogol's countrymen, fellow natives of Ukraine, and they begin to nurture the young talent. True, he notes with curiosity, almost all of his countrymen are ashamed of their roots and keen to become "Petersburgers"; Russian is the only language they use. And Gogol himself speaks and writes solely in Russian.

Gogol finally makes the acquaintance of Pushkin, who takes a liking to him, and strikes up friendships with other writers too. He quickly discovers he can make good use of his Ukrainian provenance. His ebullient tales from the southern climes of the empire are no less popular with the inhabitants of cold, dark Petersburg than Byron's exotically oriental (Greek, Turkish, Jewish) motifs were with Londoners.

Gogol creates phantasmagorical stories about the magical land of Ukraine. Inspired by the folk tales and rituals he learned in childhood, he populates his homeland with mystical creatures: wizards, witches, demons, supernatural beings. Gogol does not invent but rather codifies the myth that Ukrainians are not ordinary people, that theirs is a paranormal world of magic and mystery.

His first volume of Ukrainian tales Gogol publishes in 1831. That same year sees the release of Victor Hugo's *Notre-Dame de Paris* (*The Hunchback of Notre Dame*) and the start of Charles Darwin's five-year, round-the-world trip aboard HMS *Beagle*, during which he will frame his theory of evolution.

Petersburg society at this time is gripped by the uprising against the Russian Empire in Poland and western Ukraine. The Poles are inspired by the revolutionary events in France of 1830. After Russian troops invade Warsaw, Polish composer and pianist Fryderyk (Frédéric) Chopin, who is on tour in Paris, realizes that he will never see his homeland again.

European, and especially French, public opinion is wholly on the side of Poland, and the question of providing military assistance is even discussed in parliament. It is then that Pushkin composes his poem "To the Slanderers of Russia." He begins by saying that the suppression of the uprising in Poland is a "family quarrel" which strangers should keep out of: "These tribes have long been feuding." Then he addresses the French, declaring that they hate the Russians for having defeated Napoleon. And he promises that if the French want to send "their embittered sons" to Russia once more, they will die as surely as before. (Exactly the same idea will be trumpeted by Putin's militaristic propaganda in the early twenty-first century: "We can do it again," Russian jingoists will say, alluding to a potential replay of World War II.) True, unlike Putin's propagandists, Pushkin himself is a child of war. When Napoleon invaded Russia, Pushkin was thirteen years old, a student at a lyceum outside St. Petersburg. But the city where he was born and spent his childhood, Moscow, is captured and burned by French troops.

Pushkin's contemporaries are of two minds about the poem. Some applaud; others are full of shame and horror.

Gogol, on the other hand, does not react at all to the Polish uprising: he comes from near Poltava, the heart of eastern Ukraine, far from the hotbed of protest and where there is strong anti-Polish sentiment. The twenty-two-year-old writer is too caught up in his Ukraine-flavored fantasy world: that same year, 1831, he pens the story "The Night before Christmas"—his only work with real historical characters.

The tale is written in Russian, with a view to the Petersburg audience, but it is full of Ukrainianisms and folk sayings. And, like many of his later works, it is laugh-out-loud funny. It is perhaps one of the first examples of real comic literature in Russian: before Gogol, much had already been written in the language, of course, but nothing by a talented humorist.

Plotwise, the protagonist, the blacksmith Vakula, dreams of marrying his beloved Oksana, but she will accept him only if he brings her the tsarina's slippers. Vakula thinks of drowning himself, but then fortune magically intervenes: he manages to trick the devil into taking him to St. Petersburg, where he finds the Russian empress, Catherine the Great.

As envisaged by Gogol, at that very moment Catherine is receiving a delegation of Cossacks, headed by the tsarina's favorite, Prince Grigory Potemkin. Vakula manages to infiltrate their group and ask for the slippers. The rest of the Cossacks are shocked by Vakula's foolish scheme, but the empress is touched by his simplicity, and presents him her slippers. Vakula goes home to a fairy-tale ending: he and Oksana get married, and, on parting, he gives the devil a good spanking.

It is curious that the writer sets his magical Ukraine in the time of Catherine the Great. For him, this is the relatively recent past: he was born in 1809, just thirteen years after the death of the empress, and in childhood he surely heard many stories and legends about her. In Gogol's fairy tale, the Russian ruler acts as a kind sorceress who gives the lowly protagonist what he needs. But Catherine the Great's real-life role was very different: for Ukrainians; she was more like an evil genius. Gogol is well aware of this, knowing, as he surely does, the history of the Ukrainian Cossacks.

Cossack, Academician, Hetman

A century before Gogol wrote "The Night before Christmas," a story no less fanciful happens to a young Ukrainian named Alexei (or Oleksiy) Rozum. The son of a simple Cossack, he was born near the city of Cherni-hiv and ran away from home as a teenager to a neighboring village to sing in the church choir. In 1731, Alexei unexpectedly gets picked as a court chorister and is invited to St. Petersburg. There Elizabeth, the twenty-two-year-old daughter of Russian emperor Peter the Great, falls in love with the talented young singer.

Ten years later, Elizabeth stages a palace coup and seizes the throne. Alexei becomes the "night emperor"—in 1742 they secretly marry, where-upon he moves into the palace and sits next to the empress at all official events, taking the name Count Alexei Razumovsky. But their marriage is never officially announced.

Alexei loves Ukraine very much, and even takes the empress to his homeland, to his village, and introduces her to his mother. True, he is no statesman and does not show any particular concern for his coun-trymen. But he does what he can for his own family: for example, he sends his illiterate fifteen-year-old brother, Kirill, to study abroad and assigns him a tutor, the young scientist Grigory Teplov. For an illiterate Cossack son, Kirill receives an unheard-of education: he lives in Berlin, home to one of the greatest mathematicians of the eighteenth century, Leonhard Euler, who teaches him science. Two years later, the younger Razumovsky returns to St. Petersburg. When in 1746 he turns eighteen, Empress Elizabeth appoints him president of the Russian Academy of

Sciences. In reality, however, the academy is run by his thirty-year-old tutor and deputy, Teplov.

The young Kirill Razumovsky is certainly no intellectual, but he enjoys the favor of the phalanx of European scientific stars who are attracted to work at the Academy. His manner with them is courteous and straightforward, for he remembers well that not so long ago he was a cowherd. They treat him like a prince. Teplov, meanwhile, manages the Academy with an iron fist; the scientists, for the most part, despise him.

Scandals at the Academy are not long in coming. One of the most high-profile is connected with the first attempt to write the history of Russia. At this moment, the standard historical reference work is still the Prussian-born Innokenty Gizel's *Synopsis*. But in 1747 Teplov and Razumovsky appoint another German, Gerhard Miller, to the post of court historiographer.

In 1749, Miller delivers a report titled "On the Origin of the Name and People of Russia"—essentially one of the first scientific studies of the country's past. The author's central thesis is the Scandinavian origin of the Russian princes. Miller relies on the oldest Kyivan chronicle, *The Tale of Bygone Years* (also known as the *Russian Primary Chronicle*), which recounts that the chieftain Rurik, founder of the dynasty of Muscovite princes and tsars, was a Varangian, that is, a Viking. The notion that the Varangians were invited seems dubious to Miller; he believes they conquered the Russian lands.

In the twenty-first century this theory is generally accepted and almost indisputable, but in the eighteenth century it provokes a furore. As mentioned earlier, past tsars imagined themselves to be descendants of the Roman Emperor Augustus, no less. To many, Miller's report is highly offensive.

Miller is most vehemently opposed by the Russian-born academicians, although they represent a minority (most of the academicians come from Germany). Professor of Chemistry and the ardent fan of Synopsis Mikhail Lomonosov is especially outraged: he states that the Varangian theory is pure fiction and slander, that Miller is deliberately trying to smear Russia's past, play down her victories, and overstate her defeats.

Teplov backs Lomonosov and, on the advice of his assistant, the twenty-one-year-old president of the Academy, Razumovsky, demonstratively strips Miller of his professorial title. Now chemist Lomonosov is appointed to write his own version of the history of Russia. He firmly believes that the task of historiography is to underscore the greatness of the people and to conceal the dark pages of the past. It is thanks to his political instinct and back-office intrigues that Lomonosov will later be considered the founder of Russian science and of Moscow State University, which bears his name to this day.

The now-twenty-two-year-old Alexei Razumovsky finds a new post for his brother Kirill as hetman of Ukraine. Grigory Teplov is again by his side, ostensibly as the head of the chancellery in the Hetmanate, but in reality he holds the reins of government. Initially, he plans to write a history of Ukraine and collect documentary evidence, but nothing comes of it. His main claim to fame is being the first de facto ruler of Ukraine to be born outside its borders.

For sure, Hetman Razumovsky loves his homeland and its traditions and even rebuilds the old capital of Baturyn, which was destroyed by Peter the Great. But Razumovsky is a courtier at heart and spends little time in Ukraine. He writes to the empress, somewhat disingenuously, that the "damp Ukrainian climate" is harmful for him, unlike the "salubrious Petersburg climate."

The Princess and the Assassin

Just as the sixteen-year-old Kirill Razumovsky returns from Europe to Russia, his peer the German princess Sophie Augusta Frederica journeys to St. Petersburg. Empress Elizabeth has chosen her as the future wife of Peter, her nephew and heir to the throne. Peter, it must be said, is not much more Russian than his bride: he, too, was born in Germany, in Kiel. On the death of his father in 1739, the eleven-year-old Peter assumed the title of Duke of Holstein-Gottorp under his full name, Charles Peter Ulrich. He was still only fourteen years old when his maternal aunt Elizabeth seized the Russian throne, whereupon he was taken to St. Petersburg. Yet he remained German to the core: he had no desire to adopt Russian dress or master the Russian language.

The next seventeen years Frederica (who takes the name Catherine on converting to Orthodoxy) spends at the imperial court in St. Petersburg, where she fits in well and acquires many friends and acquaintances, one of whom is Kirill Razumovsky. Unlike Peter, she makes every effort to adapt to Russian ways: for example, on falling seriously ill, she sends for an Orthodox priest, which shocks even her mother.

It is at the age of twenty-seven that Catherine starts contemplating the idea of getting rid of her husband and ruling alone when the time comes. For the Russian Empire, this is par for the course: throughout the eighteenth century, women governed the country. Before Peter the Great his half sister Sophia had acted as regent, and after his death the crown passed to his widow, an ethnic Polish woman, then to his niece, then to his daughter. All these women came to power through palace coups, so Catherine is guided by long-standing tradition.

The time duly comes in 1762, when Empress Elizabeth passes away and Catherine's husband ascends the throne as Peter III. There is no love or affection between him and his wife: he openly lives with his mistress, while Catherine, in April 1762, gives birth to a child by her favorite, Grigory Orlov. So that the courtiers do not hear the cries of the woman in labor, a faithful servant sets fire to his own house nearby. The new emperor and his circle go to marvel at the bewitching sight of the fire, while the empress bears her offspring in the deserted palace.

Catherine is not loved in the Russian capital, but Peter III is hated even more passionately. Among his detractors is Grigory Teplov, who was once beaten by the young emperor in front of other courtiers and, on another occasion, arrested for twelve days over a trifling quibble.

Peter III lasts just six months on the throne. On July 9, 1762, the palace guards swear allegiance to the empress. Peter tries to resist but is forced to sign an act of abdication, authored by none other than Teplov. After that, the latter draws up a manifesto on the accession of Empress Catherine II to the throne.

But no sooner has this happened when the mood in the capital sours. The regular army is perplexed. How is it that the crown has been snatched from the grandson of Peter the Great and handed to some German woman?

Catherine and her lover, Grigory Orlov, are worried. He arranges a bodyguard for Peter III, the former emperor, and writes ambiguous letters to her, expressing fears of Peter's "accidental death." Catherine sends a doctor to her husband, but for some reason he takes with him autopsy instruments, not medicines.

On July 17, the brother of Catherine's favorite, Alexei Orlov, goes to see Peter III, accompanied by Grigory Teplov and several others. The former emperor is strangled. The doctor, having waited for the deed to be done, performs an autopsy and reports that the death was due to natural causes. Catherine, on learning of her husband's death, sobs a little too histrionically.

Teplov, who only yesterday was an aide to the hetman of Ukraine, soon becomes the empress's personal secretary and most important confidant. But then an unprecedented scandal befalls him. No fewer than nine serfs accuse him of sexual abuse. In the eighteenth century, the #MeToo movement has yet to gain momentum, and peasants are unlikely to have denounced Teplov on their own initiative. Most likely, it is Razumovsky's attempt to stop his former assistant's rise to power. And so begins "the trial of State Councilor Grigory Teplov, accused by serfs of buggery and sodomy" (as it is officially titled).

The final decision rests with Catherine: she punishes all the complainants. Teplov is untouchable. And the outcome of the case will have fateful consequences for Ukraine.

No More Hetman

Teplov, now bearing a grudge against Razumovsky, writes a long denunciation that basically states that Ukraine cannot be considered a separate country linked to Russia only by treaty. Teplov argues that it is native

Russian soil, it belongs to the Russian monarchy, and its governance should be no different from that anywhere else in the empire.

Razumovsky is unaware of Teplov's report, but he is sure that he enjoys the favor of the empress for his support during the coup. His long-term plan is to make the hetmanship a hereditary position and to pass it on to his children. Razumovsky draws up a petition to that effect, and asks the Cossack commanders to sign it. To Razumovsky's surprise, they refuse.

All the same, only mildly deterred, the hetman takes his petition to St. Petersburg. There, on the steps of the Winter Palace, Teplov welcomes him with open arms. Catherine's still-favorite Grigory Orlov, who witnesses the scene, comments on it in biblical terms: "Today a kiss, tomorrow betrayal."

Deeply vexed by Teplov's report, Catherine makes a drastic decision: to abolish the Hetmanate altogether. "These provinces, by the easiest means available, must become Russified and made to cease gazing like a wolf at the forest [wanting to run away]," writes Catherine in February 1764 in an instruction to senate officials. "When there is no hetman in Malorossiya [Ukraine], the names of past hetmans must be erased from memory. . . ."

In May 1764, Catherine summons Razumovsky and accuses him of all the violations documented by Teplov and interprets his desire to make the hetmanship hereditary as a conspiracy against imperial power. Teplov's accusations are fatal. Razumovsky realizes that voluntary resignation is the best outcome for him. He asks to be "relieved of such a difficult and dangerous position." Having survived, he is given a pension and an estate in Ukraine.

In November, Catherine issues a "manifesto on the liquidation of the Hetmanate": it is to be replaced by the "Collegium of Malorossiya"— a kind of Ministry of Ukrainian Affairs, to be headed by General Pyotr Rumyantsev, a distinguished military officer who is rumored at court to be the illegitimate son of Peter the Great. The empress, aware that to supporters of the late Peter III she is a usurper, fears a countercoup. It is in her best interests, she feels, to dispatch Rumyantsev from St. Petersburg to far-away Ukraine.

Rumyantsev has never lived in Ukraine and knows nothing about it. He adheres meticulously to the plan devised by Teplov: to scrap all of Ukraine's former liberties and to unify the local laws with those of Russia at large. The reforms proceed stepwise: first the Cossack stronghold in Kharkiv is destroyed, then the election of leaders at all levels is canceled throughout Ukraine. Most significantly of all, the majority of Ukraine's peasants lose their freedom as a result of the reform.

In Ukraine at that time, unlike in the rest of the Russian Empire, there was no serfdom, that is, slavery. In other parts of the country, the landowning nobles owned the peasants, who were known as "serfs" in the Russian tradition. Historians insist there is a technical difference between serfs and slaves: the former were indentured not only to the landowner but also to the land, which meant, in theory, they could only be sold together with that land. In practice, however, there was almost no difference: serfs could be bought and sold, or won and lost at cards, could be separated from their family, could be flogged and even beaten to death; and violence against serf women was commonplace, including rape. Another difference between serfdom and slavery (as practiced by other colonial empires) is that in Russia serfs and their owners were one people: they were of the same race, ethnicity, and religion.

Serfdom did not always exist in Russia: the process of enslaving the peasantry ended in the seventeenth century. But in Ukraine, Khmelnytsky's uprising set the peasants free. However, in 1767 a commission convened by Catherine concluded that free peasants in Ukraine posed a threat and recommended a policy of maximum unification of all territory under her control. Thus, Catherine extended the Russian system of serfdom (slavery in all but name) across Ukraine as well. But that was only the beginning of the new policy of the "enlightened" empress: in the following years, she will do her utmost to destroy Ukrainian independence and distinctness.

Interestingly, Catherine introduces serfdom in Ukraine at the height of her famous correspondence with Voltaire, the most illustrious philosopher of the era, whose name is synonymous with the European Enlightenment. Nevertheless, in her mind's eye the establishment of a barbaric political system does not run counter to her progressive views. On the contrary, the Enlightenment helps her to change the system of government, educate a new generation of officials, and develop a new political culture in Russia.

Another of Catherine's passions is imperial expansion. This makes her broadly akin to Britain's George III. He comes to power in 1760, just two years before Catherine, and under him British colonial power reaches its peak, with the consolidation of British rule in India. In 1764, just as Catherine II abolishes the Cossack Hetmanate in Ukraine, the British army scores a major victory over a combined Indian army at Buxar: in 1765, a humiliating treaty is concluded that enshrines India's total economic dependence on Britain.

Russian diplomacy under Catherine becomes aggressive and efficient. In 1764, her ambassador to Warsaw, Nikolay Repnin, secures the election of Catherine's former lover Stanisław Poniatowski as the new king of Poland. This once mighty European power is independent no more. But the 1770s are decisive not only for Russian history; they are a time of major transformation worldwide.

Two Wars of Independence

Human history has known periods of rapid change: technological and humanitarian breakthroughs have been accompanied by tectonic shifts in politics, economics, and culture; values considered unshakable only yesterday have been rocked to the core.

The 1650s, for example, can be considered such a time: the period of Cromwell, the French Cardinal Mazarin, and Bohdan Khmelnytsky. So can the early 1700s, the era of Louis XIV and Peter the Great. But an even more transformative decade is the 1770s, which sees the birth of the global political and geographical structure as we know it today, the start of the Industrial Revolution, and the laying of the foundations of the modern economy. James Watt invents the steam engine; Adam Smith writes *An Inquiry into the Nature and Causes of the Wealth of Nations*; Captain James Cook reaches the shores of Australia and New Zealand. Curiously, at the same time a new type of political confrontation emerges—the struggle not for one's homeland or monarch but also abstract values. It is the 1770s that give rise to both populism and the liberal idea.

By now, European states are ready to start redrawing the world map. This starts in 1772 with the First Partition of Poland, when Russia, Prussia, and Austria carve up their fatally weakened neighbor among themselves.

At the same time, a new conflict between Russia and Turkey flares up. This one will last a long time, and the main battlefield will be Crimea and the south of modern-day Ukraine. Russia will acquire new colonies there, the consequences of which are still keenly felt today.

Almost simultaneously, the world's two largest empires of the day are hit by uprisings.

In 1773, a protest breaks out that will go down in history as the Boston Tea Party: the descendants of British colonists in North America rise up against the British Crown, which develops into a war of independence. The leader of the rebels is George Washington, the future first president of the United States.

In the same year, 1773, the Yaik Cossacks—the descendants of the recent colonizers of Siberia—rebel against the Russian Empire. (The Yaik River is now called Ural—it's known as a border between Europe and Asia.) The scenario mimics the American one: new taxes and excessive regulation of previously autonomous areas provoke unrest. Catherine's government strips the Cossacks of their former liberties, and they protest. But the confrontation in the Urals, as in America, develops into a real civil war only with the appearance of a strong, charismatic leader. That man in Russia is a simple Cossack named Yemelyan Pugachev. To further stamp his authority, he claims to be Emperor Peter III, Catherine's husband, having supposedly survived the assassination attempt.

The rebel armies in America and the Urals are comparable in number: around forty thousand each. Pugachev's Cossacks are quickly joined by various colonized peoples living along the Volga and in western Siberia: Tatars, Bashkirs, Kazakhs, Kalmyks. France comes to the aid of the Americans fighting against George III. In 1778, she will declare war on England. The Cossacks, too, have an ally in the shape of Russia's main foreign-policy rival, Turkey. However, the war with the Ottomans is over by 1774, allowing Catherine to deploy more troops to the rebellious Urals.

Historians never draw parallels between the wars waged by George Washington and Yemelyan Pugachev. After all, one was successful, the other a failure. And the two rebel armies are very different in composition: the Americans are far more educated and better armed (that said, some nobles from St. Petersburg do side with Pugachev). But the main factor is that Britain's colonies are located overseas, while Russia's are simply an extension of the mother country. The Cossacks enjoy some early successes: they take several major population centers, including Kazan, then the fifth-largest city in Russia. But when Catherine goes on the offensive, the rebels are found wanting in morale, ideology, values, and a clear sense of what they are fighting for—all the things that drive the North Americans to victory. Part of Pugachev's army scatters, and he is eventually betrayed by his own.

How would world history have unfolded if Yemelyan Pugachev, similarly to George Washington, had separated the colonies beyond the Urals from the Russian Empire and created a "United States of Siberia"?

Two centuries later, in the 1990s, Russian writer Yuri Karyakin, after attending an official event at the Kremlin with the participation of the first president of Russia, Boris Yeltsin, will later liken what he saw to "a victorious Pugachev who succeeded in taking Moscow." Yeltsin can indeed be compared with Pugachev. Both spent many years in the Urals; their shared traits included a desire for freedom and a love of alcohol.

But that is all speculation. In reality, Yemelyan Pugachev was caught, convicted, and quartered in 1775 on Bolotnaya Square in Moscow— the site of the strongest protests yet seen against Vladimir Putin in the twenty-first century.

Crimea and Punishment

In the twenty-first century, the question of who owns the Crimean Peninsula is the subject of fierce political debate in Russia. Putin's propaganda emphasizes the special role of Catherine the Great in the development of Crimea and southern Ukraine, as if life had not existed there before her. However, few commentators know the history behind it, in particular that for a long time it was the territory of modern Russia that was subordinate to Crimea, not vice versa. The Crimean Khanate was essentially the last fragment of the once all-powerful empire of Genghis Khan, and was ruled by his descendants. And the Moscow tsars paid tribute to the Crimean leaders.

It all started like this: In the thirteenth century, Genghis Khan united the Mongol tribes and created a vast empire, which he divided among his sons. His grandson Batu undertook a campaign to the West, all the way to Eastern Europe, conquering major cities along the way, including Kyiv and Vladimir; the Mongols also took Moscow, which back then was more a provincial town than a big city. Batu got as far as Saxony in modern-day Germany, after which he headed back to the Volga region and founded a new capital there, Sarai, not far from the modern Russian city of Astrakhan. In the fourteenth century, Sarai was the second-largest city in Europe, behind only Paris.

The descendants of Genghis Khan called their state Ulus Jochi; in Russian chronicles, and later in Western historiography, it is known as the "Golden Horde." If we overlaid this state on a modern map of the world, it would cover the whole of southern Russia, southern Ukraine, northern Kazakhstan, and parts of Uzbekistan and Turkmenistan. For the next three centuries, it was the strongest state in Eastern Europe—a medieval superpower. It would be logical for Russian propagandists to hold this state up as the predecessor of the Putin empire. Territory-wise, it corresponded to large swathes of the former Soviet Union, so it fits the description of the great and lost empire that many in Russia pine for today.

In the fifteenth century, this enormous state disintegrated, and the Crimean Khanate was essentially its successor: the Crimean khans called their domain the Great Horde, with its capital at Bahçeseray, not far from modern-day Simferopol.

From the thirteenth century, the Russian principalities paid tribute to the Horde, which greatly contributed to the rise of Moscow: the Muscovite princes were appointed to collect taxes from their neighbors and take the money to Sarai. In Russian historiography, it is stated that Moscow "threw off the Mongol yoke" in 1480, with the collapse of the Great Horde. But in fact, Moscow continued to pay tribute to the Crimean Khanate until the seventeenth century—even during the time of Peter the Great. The Polish-Lithuanian Commonwealth also paid tribute to Crimea.

In the seventeenth century, Crimea fought several wars against the Ottoman Empire and eventually succumbed to it: the Crimean khan recognized himself as a vassal of the sultan in Constantinople. Crimea effectively becomes Turkish, and, in all subsequent wars against Russia, it sides with the Ottomans.

One of the important sources of income for the Crimean Khanate was the slave trade: Crimean troops regularly raided the neighboring territories, primarily in the south of Ukraine, kidnapped people, and sold them in the slave markets of Bahçeseray and Istanbul. Hence, as mentioned earlier, the main purpose of the Zaporizhian Host, a string of Cossack fortifications in southern Ukrainian lands, was to provide protection against such raids from Crimea.

But in 1768 Catherine the Great launches a war against Turkey and Crimea, and over the next few decades the map of the region is completely redrawn. The Russian army is led by Pyotr Rumyantsev. The Zaporizhian Cossacks take part in the campaign.

Rumyantsev seizes more territory and creates a defensive line, which essentially swallows up the Host—the border now runs south of it. In addition, Russian troops occupy several key fortresses in Crimea and the Khanate itself becomes a Russian protectorate.

Although almost all the Muscovite rulers waged war on Crimea, starting with Ivan the Terrible, Voltaire can be said to have inspired the Crimean campaign: since 1763, he keeps up a regular correspondence with Catherine and urges her to wage war against the Turks. The philosopher believes that the Ottoman Empire is a barbarian state that must be destroyed; Constantinople should then become the capital of Russia, and Catherine herself should learn Greek and reinstitute Plato's Academy. "Madame, by killing the Turks, Your Imperial Majesty shall prolong my days," Voltaire writes to the Russian empress in 1769.

Soon Voltaire acquires a like-minded pupil in the shape of Catherine's new favorite, Grigory Potemkin. Potemkin will play a key role in the further historical development of Russia: it is he who will convince Catherine that Russia must transform itself into a colonial empire and compete with Britain. For him, the implementation of Voltaire's so-called Greek project—to conquer Constantinople to make it Christian again—is a lifelong venture. And Catherine will even name one of her grandsons Constantine in the expectation that he will one day rule over Constantinople.

While still a junior officer, Potemkin took part in the coup that brought Catherine to power, and since then he has outmaneuvered Catherine's previous favorite Grigory Orlov. In April 1774, it is Potemkin whom the empress entrusts to manage the colonies south of the Host—an area then called the "Wild Fields" by the Poles. Today these are the Ukrainian regions of Kherson and Zaporizhzhia, which will be occupied by Russian troops in March 2022. The colonized territory Catherine calls Novorossiya (New Russia).

Catherine instructs Potemkin to build new fortresses and cities, something that twenty-first-century Putin propagandists will stress. The local inhabitants, Crimean Tatars and Cossacks alike, are treated the same as the indigenous peoples of North America were by the French and the British: their ancestral lands are confiscated.

The Cossacks try to protest lawfully, by taking documentary evidence to St. Petersburg confirming their rights to the territories. (It is this trip that Gogol describes in "The Night before Christmas.")

Catherine's expansion of the Russian state will have another important consequence. After the annexation of Poland, a large number of Jews become citizens of the empire. But Catherine decrees that they are forbidden to settle in the major cities. They are allocated a special zone where they can live, which becomes known as the "Pale of Settlement." Most of the Pale is located on the territory of modern Ukraine.

And it is under Catherine that Russia's colonization of Alaska begins, as the Siberian Cossacks continue their advance eastwards until they reach distant America.

No More Host

In June 1774, the Zaporizhian Cossacks arrive in St. Petersburg, seeking an audience with Catherine to request that they be allowed to keep their lands in the Zaporizhian Host. They bring with them a huge number of gifts for the capital's officials: horses, jewelry, expensive fabrics, sausages, lard, fish, wines, fruits. The top civil servants accept the gifts without promising to help. Most of all, the Cossacks are irritated by the behavior of their countrymen—natives of Ukraine in top positions in the capital, but wholly uninterested in the fate of the Host.

The Cossacks joke that "everyone is sitting in the dark"—Prince Potemkin, the empress's lover, holds the reins of power. (In Russian, the word *potemki* means "darkness.") The Ukrainians do not know that on June 19, just before their arrival, Catherine secretly married him.

In Gogol's tale, it is Potemkin who arranges the meeting of the Cossacks with the empress and instructs them what to say beforehand. But at the sight of the empress, the Cossacks are dumbstruck and their minds go blank. They eventually muster the courage to request her not to destroy the Host and turn them into regular soldiers. The real-life meeting, however, does not take place at all: Catherine refuses to receive the Cossacks. They are permitted only to dine with some nobles at her country residence, Tsarskoye Selo. The Cossacks return home with nothing.

It is then that the empress orders the court historiographer, Gerhard Miller, to study the Host. This is the same Miller who got it in the neck for his theory of the Varangian origin of the Russian tsars. He is already over seventy years old, bedridden, yet he does what is required of him and produces a character assassination of the Cossacks: they are lazy, prone to drunkenness and banditry; their "unbridled freedom" only brings trouble. Miller becomes the second (after Gizel) German historian to influence the future of Ukraine.

On May 4, 1775, Catherine makes the decision to liquidate the Host. Six weeks later, the Russian army surrounds the territory. Most of the Cossacks are away fighting the Turks, so there are only a few thousand people in the fortress. They are forced to surrender.

On August 14, the empress issues a manifesto stating that the Host must be destroyed and its name erased from history. She accuses the Cossacks of arrogance, robbery, insubordination, and violence against other citizens of Russia. The lands of the Host are distributed to senior officials, including Potemkin and the former hetman Razumovsky.

That same year, the city of Kryvyi Rih is founded on the former lands of the Host, where, in two hundred years' time, Volodymyr Zelensky will be born. A year later, in 1776, Prince Potemkin founds the city of Ekaterinoslav (Catherine's glory) nearby, which he earmarks as the capital of the new province. In the twentieth century, the city will be renamed Dnipropetrovsk, from where the clan that will rule the late Soviet Union (including General Secretary Leonid Brezhnev) will hail. In the twenty-first century, the city will be renamed once more, as Dnipro. Potemkin builds other cities too, including Kherson and Mariupol, which will be occupied by Russian troops in 2022.

In 1787, Catherine, accompanied by her vast retinue and also Holy Roman Emperor Joseph II, travels around Ukraine, then goes to the newly conquered Crimea. According to a popular, though unconfirmed, legend, Potemkin builds fake settlements along the route with beautiful external façades to showcase the idyllic the life of the local people. Catherine is impressed. Settlements did exist there, but not built by Potemkin, rather by Zaporizhian Cossacks long before his time. The term "Potemkin village" will later come to mean any attempt by zealous subordinates to please their superiors by means of deception. It is common worldwide, yet Russian bureaucracy turns it into an art form.

The most notorious example of a "Potemkin village" in recent Russian history will be seen in 2022: the Russian military assures President Putin that the Russian army is the second most powerful in the world, and Russian intelligence informs him that Ukrainians will greet Russian soldiers with flowers. Yet both Putin and Catherine find such toadying to their liking. They want—and even demand—evidence of the reality of their fantasies.

Potemkin will die in 1791 at the age of just fifty-two. He will be buried in Kherson, the city that he built as the future capital of Novorossiya (New Russia). In March 2022, Putin's troops will capture Kherson, and in October, shortly before retreating from the city, they will steal Potemkin's remains from his burial place in St. Catherine's Cathedral and take them to Russia.

RUSSIAN EMPIRE AND NEIGHBORING
COUNTRIES IN 1861

——	State borders
·········	Pale of Settlement
POLTAVA	Ukrainian provinces

200 miles
200 km

4

THE MYTH OF LANGUAGE:
HOW TARAS SHEVCHENKO
BATTLED SLAVERY

A Softly Spoken Word

1845. Christmas Eve. A thirty-one-year-old poet lies in bed at the home of his doctor in Pereyaslav. It is here in this city, in 1654, that Bohdan Khmelnytsky signed his infamous treaty with Muscovy. The poet is dying of pneumonia. He spent the whole of the previous day soaked to the skin in the freezing rain, and caught a cold. In the mid-nineteenth century, antibiotics have not yet been invented, so both the doctor and the patient himself know that there is no chance.

Saying farewell to life, the poet writes a short poem, which he calls "My Testament." He asks to be buried in his homeland, in Ukraine, on the banks of the Dnieper. At the same time, he vows to "rise from the grave when the waves of the Dnieper are stained with the blood of Ukraine's hated foes"—that is, the Russians. And only then will he be ready to pray; until that moment God for him does not exist. Next, the poet urges his compatriots to break their chains, shed the blood of their enemies, and, having won freedom, remember him with a "softly spoken word."

Laying down his pen, the poet drifts off to sleep. . . . But in the morning a miracle happens: he is feeling better. He soon recovers.

The poet's name is Taras Shevchenko. After composing "My Testament," he will live another fifteen years. But the poem will be one of the reasons for the tragic changes that will occur in his life. On the upside, it will later become the main work of Ukrainian literature, a national symbol of the struggle for freedom. It will be translated into 150 languages; more than sixty composers will set it to music. But Shevchenko himself will become an even greater symbol—for the sheer tragedy of his fate.

Throwing Off the Shackles

The eighteen-year-old Taras Shevchenko arrives in St. Petersburg in 1831, just as Gogol is writing "The Night before Christmas." Gogol is Taras's favorite writer, but he cannot even dream of meeting him. And all because Taras is a slave.

He was born into a family of serfs near Kyiv. His parents died when the boy was eleven years old, but he had a stroke of luck when the landowner, Pavel Engelhardt, decided to make him a "domestic Cossack"—that is, a personal servant, a footman, only dressed in traditional Ukrainian attire. Soon the landowner moves to St. Petersburg, where Taras asks to be allowed to train as an artist's apprentice. The landowner agrees, intending to use Shevchenko as his own private "home artist." He already knows about the young serf's ability to draw and often engages his services, for example, by asking him to draw portraits of his mistresses.

In the artist's workshop, Taras expands his social circle. In 1836, he makes the acquaintance of Ivan Soshenko, his countryman and a talented draftsman. Soshenko does not believe that such a capable artist should be enslaved, and decides to help Taras improve his lot in life. He even goes to see Engelhardt. But to no avail.

So Soshenko tells the most popular artists of the time about Taras, one of whom is Karl Bryullov, then the most famous painter in Russia.

In March 1837, Bryullov himself goes to Engelhardt, who is not fazed by the visit of such an eminent artist. He says that he will release the talented serf only for a large redemption payment.

On hearing this, the enraged Taras threatens to murder his owner. But Soshenko and Bryullov manage to calm him down.

Bryullov goes to see Vasily Zhukovsky, a very popular poet, a friend of the now-deceased Alexander Pushkin, and an influential courtier. He is employed as the personal tutor of the heir to the throne, the future Emperor Alexander II. Zhukovsky agrees to help. The "rescue plan" goes as follows: Bryullov paints a portrait of Zhukovsky, the painting is sold at auction, and the proceeds are used to buy Taras's freedom.

On May 4, 1838, Bryullov and Zhukovsky, respectively the most famous artist and the most famous poet in the Russian Empire, receive a "redemption certificate" from Engelhardt and hand it to the twenty-four-year-old Shevchenko. He races to Soshenko, jumps as high as the ceiling, and shouts: "Freedom! Freedom!"—and cries like a baby.

Immediately after his liberation, Taras enters the Imperial Academy of Arts in St. Petersburg. He is one of Bryullov's favorite students, and even lives at his house. Taras still cannot truly believe what has happened: literally overnight he has turned from a slave into a renowned artist in the capital, living in the home of a star painter's house, where he can admire the latter's canvases. Around the same time, Taras begins to write poetry in Ukrainian.

In the same year, on the other side of the world, a similar story unfolds. On September 3, 1838, an African-American slave by the name of Frederick Bailey arrives at the Baltimore train station. He is carrying false documents showing that he is a freeman, a sailor. Twenty-four hours later, having changed trains, Frederick pulls into New York, a city where slavery is already outlawed. A few days later, he is joined by the brains behind his escape, his fiancée, Anna Murray. They get married, and together take the surname Douglass. In the following years, Frederick Douglass will become America's most famous freed slave and the country's first Black writer and public figure.

Mutilating the Russian Language

At this exact time, the so-called Great Game begins, a mad rivalry between the empires to see who can conquer the most territory. Britain and Russia are the adversaries, Asia the venue. The British Empire is moving from south to north: already occupying the territories of present-day India, Pakistan, Bangladesh, Nepal, and Bhutan, it starts a war in Afghanistan. The Russian Empire is moving from north to south: having seized present-day Kazakhstan, Kyrgyzstan, Uzbekistan, Turkmenistan, and Tajikistan, it approaches the border with Iran. At the same time, Russia is conquering the Caucasus. Georgia became part of the empire back in the early nineteenth century, but for almost a century thereafter Russia waged war in the North Caucasus against the Chechens and Circassians.

Also in the early nineteenth century, Russia expanded its territory in Europe, annexing Finland, and in the Far East, taking the lands to the north of the Amur River from China.

At the head of this vast empire stands one man: Emperor Nicholas I. Russia is an absolute monarchy. Unlike Britain, there is no parliament here. And Taras Shevchenko, freed from serfdom only very recently, suddenly finds himself within touching distance of the pinnacle of power in Russia.

One day, the twenty-year-old heir to the throne, Grand Duke Alexander, pays a visit to Bryullov's home. The thirty-nine-year-old master artist, already tired of annoying royal visits, asks the twenty-four-year-old Shevchenko to inform the duke that he is not at home and show him his paintings. Taras takes Alexander on a long tour of the gallery, which the latter enjoys very much. This is the first meeting between the future Russian emperor and the future national poet of Ukraine.

Shevchenko intermingles more and more with his countrymen, as well as with Poles and Belarusians, whose territories have also been swallowed up by the Russian Empire. They read humorous poems to each other. A comic pastime at the turn of the nineteenth century is to translate Virgil's poem the *Aeneid* (about the legendary Trojan hero Aeneas) into different languages, turning it into a burlesque. First, there appear versions in French, German, and Russian; then, in 1798, Ivan Kotlyarevsky produces one in Ukrainian.

Kotlyarevsky is a very interesting figure. A professional military man from a Cossack family, during the war with Napoleon in 1812 he attempts to reintroduce a standing Cossack army, but to no avail. It is during military service that he creates his own mock-heroic version of the *Aeneid*, the first poetic work in the modern Ukrainian language, no less. Curiously enough, it all started with a parody. Future generations will accuse Kotlyarevsky of disrespecting and ridiculing the Ukrainians. But Shevchenko is a big fan.

In the 1820s, a similarly comic version of the poem appears in the Belarusian language, the text of which closely resembles the Ukrainian. This is how Shevchenko and friends entertain themselves. The most popular works of the day in the minority languages of the Russian Empire are, in fact, comic poems. Highbrow works are penned in Russian; "folk" literature is there to entertain.

This stereotype is soon smashed by Taras Shevchenko. In April 1840, he publishes the poem *Kobzar*—a lyrical work in Ukrainian. It provokes a scandal: it is not the done thing in St. Petersburg to write, still less print, works in Ukrainian. In general, the position of the Russian state is as follows: there is no Ukrainian language, only the Russian language, which has several dialects: Great Russian, Belarusian, and Little Russian (Ukrainian).

Meanwhile, Shevchenko's work provokes a wide variety of responses. The most famous literary critic in Russia back then, Vissarion Belinsky, offers faint praise for the poem, believing it will "bring great benefit to the simple reading public of southern Russia." But mostly the reviews are damning. "It is a pity to see Mr. Shevchenko mutilating thought and the Russian language in a khokhol-style imitation!" writes the literary magazine *Syn Otyechestva* (Son of the fatherland). "He has a soul, he has feeling, and his Russian poems could probably make a contribution to our proper Russian poetry."

But Shevchenko ignores the critics: in 1840, he publishes the poem *Haidamaky* about a bloody uprising in western Ukraine against the Poles. The author clearly sympathizes with the rebels, for which reason he runs into serious problems with the censors. He tries to show that the heroes of the poem were not fighting against Russia, but against Poland. But such a claim doesn't sound very convincing, since the uprising took place at the very beginning of the reign of Catherine II, shortly before the partitioning of Poland, when the Polish-Lithuanian Commonwealth was already under the near-complete control of Moscow, and the Russian army actively aided the Polish in quelling the rebellion.

Petersburg critics trash *Haidamaky*. Even Belinsky writes: "Works of this kind are published only for the delight and edification of the authors themselves: they have no other audience, it seems. If these gentlemen *kobzars* [bards] think their poems will benefit the lower class of their compatriots, they are very much mistaken: their poems, despite the abundance of the most coarse and vulgar words and expressions, lack the simplicity of fiction and storytelling, filled as they are with the conceits and mannerisms common to all bad poets—which are often not 'folk' at all, despite being supported by references to history, songs and legends, and are thus incomprehensible to the common people and have nothing that resonates with them."

Yet despite all the criticism, Shevchenko's star is rising: he is a welcome guest in the most fashionable salons of the capital; the Petersburg glitterati court his friendship. And he receives sackloads of mail from readers in Ukraine praising his works and complaining about the small print runs.

In 1843, the Academy of Arts allows the student Shevchenko to go to Ukraine. He has mixed feelings about the trip, however, and wonders if it's worth it: "I won't go to Little Russia. Except for wailing, I won't hear anything there," he writes shortly before the trip. But then he makes up his mind to go to his homeland for the first time as a freeman. There he meets his brother and sister, who are still serfs. By this time, Shevchenko is a celebrity in Ukraine and is warmly received in the richest houses. But everywhere he is struck by how inhumanely the serfs are treated. Often, having witnessed the host being rude to a servant, Shevchenko gets up and leaves without any explanation.

His popularity continues to grow: in 1844, the most influential Petersburg magazine, *Sovremennik*, likens Taras Shevchenko's fame and standing in Ukraine to Alexander Pushkin's in Russia.

At the very same time, Frederick Douglass is seeking recognition in the United States. In 1845, he publishes *Narrative of the Life of Frederick Douglass, an American Slave*, which becomes a bestseller. True, some readers of the day wonder if a Black former slave could possibly have created such a work of literature. After its success, Douglass travels to Europe—to Ireland, which is under the oppressive rule of Great Britain, just as Ukraine is of Russia. On the one hand, he is heartened that in Ireland there is no US-style racial segregation: he is allowed into hotels, restaurants, and churches. Nowhere is he made to feel like a second-class citizen. On the other hand, he is deeply struck by the grinding poverty of the people. His trip coincides with the start of the Great Famine: in the space of four years, poor potato harvests and total indifference on the part of the British authorities will take the lives of over a million people and drive more than 2 million into emigration. The famine is the great historical tragedy of the Irish people, which preordains the struggle against Great Britain for independence.

Taras Shevchenko, too, spends a lot of time on the road: he travels to historical sites in Ukraine associated with Bohdan Khmelnytsky. In 1845, he again goes to see his brother and sister and promises to earn enough money to buy their freedom. Then, just before Christmas, Shevchenko falls ill, bids farewell to life, and writes the poem "My Testament." He does not die, but nor can he now fulfill his promise to his siblings.

The United States of Ukraine

The year 1846 is a watershed in Shevchenko's life. The main happening takes place in April, when he settles in Kyiv, on Khreshchatyk street, and makes the acquaintance of one of his neighbors, the historian Nikolay Kostomarov, one of the most prominent authors in the field of both Ukrainian and Russian historiography. Shevchenko is thirty-two, Kostomarov twenty-nine. They immediately become close friends. Kostomarov teaches history at Kyiv University, where Shevchenko would very much like to work as an art teacher, but no one will hire him.

Kostomarov's life story is no less compelling than Shevchenko's. He, too, is a former serf, as well as illegitimate. His father, an elderly landowner, had an affair with his Ukrainian maidservant, sent her to Moscow to study, then married her. But their son was born before the wedding, so, according to the laws of the Russian Empire, he is an illegitimate serf owned by his own father. Kostomarov Sr. seemingly wanted to adopt the child but kept putting it off. When Nikolay was eleven years old, his father was killed by his own servants. It was partly his own fault, one could argue: the landowner loved to enlighten his serfs by telling them there was no God. One of them, a coachman, took these words at face value and concluded that, consequently, there would be no punishment in the afterlife for crimes committed on earth. So he stabbed and robbed his owner. Tortured by pangs of conscience, he later confessed to the deed.

Not only did Kostomarov Jr. receive nothing from his deceased father's estate, but he himself, as a serf, was "inherited" by relatives. He was lucky, however. They released him and gave him an excellent education. And in the course of his studies, he became fascinated by the history of Ukraine.

The now-adult Kostomarov views history quite differently from his colleagues: he is not satisfied that books talk about "statesmen while neglecting the lives of the masses." He is drawn to the idea of writing the history of the people as opposed to the history of the state, and thus finds himself at odds with "official historians."

Kostomarov studies the past "not just from dead chronicles, but from living people." He travels extensively in Ukraine, explores the era of Bohdan Khmelnytsky, and, in 1846, at the age of twenty-nine, becomes a professor of Russian history at Kyiv University.

Kostomarov is an underrated figure. Although born in southern Russia, he considers himself more of a Ukrainian. He learned Ukrainian through self-study and wrote many works in the language. But, ultimately, neither Russians nor Ukrainians truly accept him as their own.

However, Kostomarov is not only a historian but also a politician. He is convinced that the natural path of development for the East Slavic peoples must lead to a democratic federation. Autocracy, for him, is an alien concept, a legacy of the Mongol yoke. He sees the Cossacks as the embodiment of the free spirit. Kostomarov pins special hopes on the Ukrainian people, who, in his opinion, are particularly freedom loving. He dreams of creating a new Slavic state: a union of the republics (or states) of Ukraine, Russia, Poland, Serbia, the Czech Republic, and Bulgaria. In each republic, serfdom and class privileges should be abolished and freedom of conscience proclaimed.

He envisions Kyiv as the capital of this state, with supreme legislative power entrusted to a bicameral parliament (which Kostomarov, in the Polish tradition, calls the Sejm) and executive power invested in a president. In essence, he wants to copy the system of government of the United States of America.

The United States at this very moment is expanding its territory by incorporating new lands. In 1845, Congress accepts Florida as the twenty-seventh state and the Republic of Texas, recently seceded from Mexico, as the twenty-eighth.

Kostomarov first articulates his revolutionary thoughts to his close friends, among them Taras Shevchenko. Beginning in April 1846, he holds meetings to discuss their dreams for the future setup of their homeland. Twelve people take part in these amicable conversations. They call their circle the Brotherhood of Cyril and Methodius, in honor of Saints Cyril and Methodius, the creators of the Cyrillic alphabet.

The clandestine society is obviously inspired by the news that an uprising has broken out in the Polish city of Kraków. By this time, Poland has long lost its independence, its eastern part having been annexed by Russia, the northern part by Prussia, and the southern part by Austria. It is against Austrian rule that the Poles are rebelling. Russia sends troops to crush the uprising, and at the same time tightens the screws on dissent inside the country.

On December 25, 1846, members of the Brotherhood of Cyril and Methodius get together to celebrate Christmas. The conversation is even more feverish than usual: the topic is the future "federation of Slavic tribes" and the overthrow of monarchical rule in Russia. Their impassioned speeches are overheard by a neighbor, a student of Kyiv University by the name of Alexei Petrov. Showing interest, he asks to read what Kostomarov and his associates have written about their vision. Two months later, Petrov snitches on the society to the secret police.

At around the same time, a letter arrives in Kyiv from the Ministry of Education in St. Petersburg, offering Shevchenko a position as an art teacher at the university. Petrov's written denunciation goes in the opposite direction to the capital, where it falls into the hands of both the chief of the gendarmerie and the heir to the throne, Alexander. The young prince insists that the suspects be arrested without delay.

The hardest of them to find is Shevchenko, for he is journeying around Ukraine. He is detained only on April 5.

"Look at you, Taras, all dressed up in tails and white tie!" sneers the governor of Kyiv during the poet's first interrogation.

"I was on my way to Kostomarov's wedding. I was his best man," Shevchenko replies.

"Well, wherever the groom goes, so does the best man."

"What a wedding!" says Shevchenko, smiling. At this point, Kostomarov is already in a Petersburg jail.

On the way to the capital, Shevchenko laughs and jokes with the guards, so that from the outside no one would guess that he is under arrest.

In St. Petersburg, meanwhile, the interrogations are in full swing. Kostomarov claims there was no secret society, just a group of friends. But the secret police are keen to uncover a dangerous conspiracy, whether one existed or not.

Another detainee says that Kyiv University has been hit by a political epidemic: "Almost all students are obsessed with state reform and many have drafted their own constitution." And he admits that the secret society still exists and has two leaders: Kostomarov and Shevchenko. "The former belongs to the moderate party, the second to the immoderate; Shevchenko's number one rule is: 'Whoever is loyal to the sovereign is a scoundrel, whoever is a liberal is noble.'"

A Terrible Dream

During his detention, one of Shevchenko's fans offers the poet his help: to hide or even destroy his papers. But Shevchenko refuses. And so, during the subsequent search, his "My Testament" and an even more objectionable work—a poem called "Dream"—are discovered.

Shevchenko wrote it in 1845. The plot is very simple: The poet-protagonist dreams that he is flying over Ukraine. First he sees the suffering of his compatriots, then the anguish of shackled convicts, one of whom is Jesus Christ. The protagonist goes to St. Petersburg and meets there a fellow Ukrainian, who is a courtier. The latter inquires of the poet: "Don't you speak the local language?"

"I do," he answers, "but don't want to."

The Ukrainian grandee offers a tour of the palace in exchange for payment, but the poet becomes invisible and bodiless, and slips inside on his own. There he notices Tsar Nicholas I and his wife. The description of the tsarina is particularly unflattering: "lanky, all skin and bone, like a dried-up mushroom, shaking her head, hopping around like a heron." She and the tsar at first strut around "like puffed-up owls" and talk about the fatherland; then the tsarina sits down in an armchair and the tsar punches and kicks the courtiers. They, in turn, furiously strike those who are lower in rank. At the same time, all the victims are shouting: "Hurrah for the Father-Tsar!"

Shevchenko's poet-protagonist then flies out of the palace, circles over St. Petersburg, and spots the *Bronze Horseman*, the monument to Peter I, to whom Alexander Pushkin dedicated his anti-imperial poem of the same name. On the pedestal is carved: "To Peter the First from Catherine the Second."

Gazing at the monument, the protagonist reflects that it is these two individual rulers who are to blame for the tragedy of Ukraine: "It is the First who crucified our Ukraine, and the Second who gave the death-stroke to the prostrate widow. Executioners! Cannibals! They both ate their fill, looted to their hearts' content. And what did they take with them to the next world?" A miraculous bird then appears in the sky, which also curses the executioner Peter the Great.

Then the sun rises. Shevchenko views with disgust those courtiers who moved to the capital from Ukraine and forgot their native language. The tsar, nursing a hangover, crawls out of his lair in the form of a bear, and yells at the nobles so that they all sink into the ground, while he turns into a mournful bear cub. And then the author wakes up.

Most of the detainees in the "Brotherhood of Cyril and Methodius affair" try to shield Shevchenko: Kostomarov says he attended only a handful of meetings and had nothing to do with the political agenda. But it's clear to all that Shevchenko's poems are no less dangerous than the conspiracy of Kyiv professors.

The investigation lasts for six weeks. Shevchenko's punishment "for composing outrageous poems" is army service as a private. Nicholas I personally adds a note to the verdict: no writing or drawing allowed. Kostomarov is sentenced to a year in prison, followed by exile.

Does Petersburg society sympathize with the convicted conspirators? No. Critic Vissarion Belinsky, who once praised Shevchenko, assesses the situation in a letter to a friend: "This is what these brutish, brainless liberals get up to. Oh, these *khokhols*! These muttonheads playing at being liberal in the name of dumplings and pork-fat pies! How do they present their grievances to the government? What kind of government would allow them to preach secessionist propaganda in print?"

Belinsky retells the story of Shevchenko in his letter, claiming that the latter wrote two satirical poems ridiculing the tsar and tsarina. When Nikolay read the one about himself, he is reported to have laughed. But on his reading the one about his wife, his mood turned sour: "Let's suppose he has reason to hate me. But why her?" Belinsky admits that he himself has not read "Dream"; nor have any of his acquaintances. But he is sure that these verses are "not at all evil, only insipid and stupid," and "the lampooning of the empress is outrageously vile," because, he believes, no one should insult a woman. "I do not feel sorry for him. If I had been his judge, I would have done no less," concludes Belinsky.

Crimean Catastrophe

Meanwhile, liberal ideas are sweeping the world. Soon after the convictions of Shevchenko and Kostomarov, successive revolutions break out across Europe—these are the Revolutions of 1848 or, more poetically, the "Springtime of Nations." Everywhere people are demanding a constitution, freedom of speech, and universal suffrage (for men only).

The monarchy is once again overthrown in France. The Slavic Congress takes place in Prague, attended by delegations of Czechs, Slovaks, Poles, and Ukrainians, mainly from the Austrian Empire. Without realizing it, of course, they express ideas very close to those of the Brotherhood of Cyril and Methodius.

Western Ukraine (Galicia), which is part of the Austrian Empire, demands autonomy and the right to Ukrainian-language instruction in schools—the authorities make concessions.

Kostomarov and Shevchenko know little about what is going on. They are both serving time and have next to no access to news about world politics. But they do know that the repressions in Russia are continuing. Across the country, young people hungry for change are routinely arrested. In 1849, members of one of the capital's political circles are detained and sentenced to death, including the twenty-seven-year-old Fyodor Dostoevsky. At the last moment, when the condemned have already been brought to the place of execution, the sentence is commuted to hard labor.

Emperor Nicholas I seeks to nip any glimmer of revolution in the bud. He even sends an army to suppress an uprising in Hungary against the Austrian Empire, for which the tsar is labeled the "gendarme of Europe." That said, he also is taken by the idea of uniting the Slavic peoples. True, St. Petersburg has its own interpretation of Slavic independence:

liberation of the Slavs under the Ottoman Empire, followed by their subjugation by the Russian Empire itself.

In 1853, war breaks out between Russia and the Ottoman Empire. Britain and France, seeking to temper the imperial ambitions of Nicholas I, side with the Turks. The main battlefield is Crimea. In October 1854, there begins the siege of Sevastopol, the base of Russia's Black Sea Fleet.

In the twenty-first century, it is hard to imagine how this war was perceived in the middle of the nineteenth. It is only seventy years since the capture of Crimea by Potemkin. Prior to this, the Crimean Khanate was a vassal of the Ottoman Empire. That is, the Turks are fighting for the restoration of historical justice, although Crimea's demography has changed considerably in the past seven decades.

September 1854 sees that start of the siege of Sevastopol, the base of the Black Sea Fleet. When it becomes clear that the defenders cannot hold out, the Russian emperor conceives a plan to relieve them by attacking the enemy's base at Yevpatoria. But when this offensive fails in February 1855, it is no longer possible to keep Sevastopol. Unable to accept the news, Nicholas I commits suicide—a fact that Russian history textbooks almost never mention.

At the same time, in early 1855, the Petersburg magazine *Sovremennik* publishes reports from the front lines written by an officer named Leo Tolstoy. They will go down in history as the *Sevastopol Sketches*—about the senselessness of war and the illusory nature of patriotism.

The reports make Tolstoy's reputation as a war correspondent. Even the new emperor, Alexander II, after reading them, asks his generals to "save" the talented writer. Thus begins the literary fame of the future author of *War and Peace*.

The Crimean War, although lost by Russia, will sprout several myths in the country's history. The dead sailors will be glorified as heroes, and Sevastopol will be called a "city of Russian glory"—which will serve as one of the main propaganda justifications for Russia's occupation of Crimea in 2014.

End of Slavery

To mark the coronation of Alexander II, an amnesty is granted. Shevchenko, Kostomarov, and Dostoevsky write petitions asking for clemency; Dostoevsky goes so far as to compose a poem exalting the widow of Nicholas I—that same "dried-up mushroom" from Shevchenko's poem "Dream."

The new emperor is unforgiving and unforgetting: he releases Kostomarov and Dostoevsky but scratches Shevchenko's name from the list of pardons with the comment: "He insulted my mother."

Kostomarov is allowed to return from exile, and can publish again and even travel abroad. In St. Petersburg, meanwhile, a campaign gets under way in support of Shevchenko's release: the Academy of Arts petitions the emperor and collects money to help the exiled poet. Finally, in 1857, ten years after his conviction, Shevchenko is released.

The next few years he spends in St. Petersburg. His works are in print once more, and all reviews are overwhelmingly positive; he is recognized simultaneously as a living classic author and a literary star. He is even compared with Pushkin and Adam Mickiewicz. True, Shevchenko himself always stresses that he does not like Pushkin—because of his poem *Poltava*.

Shevchenko is reunited with Kostomarov in 1857, and the two remain bosom buddies for life. In 1859, despite his dubious past, Kostomarov is invited to head the history department of St. Petersburg University.

The new emperor sets himself the goal of reforming the entire country and overcoming Russia's clear backwardness in comparison to the West, which led to the humiliating defeat in the Crimean War. On February 19, 1861, Alexander II signs a manifesto on the abolition of serfdom. A week after this news, Taras Shevchenko dies.

Two months later, in April 1861, civil war breaks out in the United States, which will lead to the abolition of slavery.

Russia's defeat in the Crimean War is not only a blow to its imperial ambitions but also a disaster for the country's economy. One of the consequences of the Crimean War is Alexander II's decision to sell Russia's colony in Alaska to the United States: St. Petersburg realizes that it cannot maintain such a vast territory on another continent. For Alaska, the Russian Empire receives a little over $7 million.

However, the basic desire of the Russian Empire to expand does not go away: Russia establishes full control over the Caucasus and completes its conquest of Central Asia, taking the major historical centers of Tashkent, Samarkand, and Bukhara. At the same time, Russia annexes lands in the Far East: the island of Sakhalin from Japan and the present-day region of Primorye (an outlet to the Pacific Ocean) from China, where it establishes the city of Vladivostok. It is in the latter half of the nineteenth century that a powerful ideological current emerges in Russia, underpinning the imperial mission of the Russian people. One of the most infamous publicists of the day, Mikhail Katkov, argues in his writings: "Peoples unable to create a state must submit to the state-nation," that is, the Russian people.

But probably the most famous Russian imperialist of that time is Fyodor Dostoevsky. Having returned from exile and become one of the most popular writers and journalists in the country, he argues that Russia's historical mission is to protect the Slavs from the Turks. This means that all Slavic lands must be conquered, for their own good. Generally speaking, his mindset is surprisingly similar to the rhetoric of Russian propagandists in the twenty-first century, who call for the defense of Ukraine against "the Nazis."

In his novel *Demons*, Dostoevsky further articulates one of the most infamous postulates of Russian nationalism: the Russian people are "God-bearing folk." So says one of the characters in the novel, Ivan Shatov. Although Dostoevsky refers to him with a certain degree of irony, according to contemporaries, it is Shatov who voices the author's own thoughts.

Just like Voltaire wrote a century before, Dostoevsky dreams of conquering Turkey itself, of turning Constantinople into a Christian city and Hagia Sophia, the grand mosque of Istanbul, back into its original cathedral, a Greek Orthodox church. The Turks would not even have to be evicted, Dostoevsky argues: they would live peacefully under the rule of the Russian tsar. Lastly, in Dostoevsky's view, the people of Russia have a huge advantage over Europeans: the Russians "possess such spiritual unity which, of course, does not, and cannot, exist in Europe."

Strikingly similar imperial thoughts are propounded at the same time by British scholars and writers. Historian John Seeley writes a monumental work, *The Expansion of England*, in which he argues that Britain invaded India for her own good. And Rudyard Kipling will develop this idea in his 1899 poem-manifesto "The White Man's Burden":

> *Take up the White Man's burden—*
> *Send forth the best ye breed—*
> *Go bind your sons to exile*
> *To serve your captives' need*

A similar racist attitude toward ethnic groups supposedly "liberated" by Russia is common in the nineteenth century, and in the Soviet Union, and even in the twenty-first century.

But not all of Russia's popular writers of the nineteenth century are imperialists. There are those who mercilessly ridicule the idea of Russian exceptionalism. The most famous of them is the satirist Mikhail Saltykov-Shchedrin. He penned an entire collection of short stories, known in English as *The Tashkenters' Clique*, in which he rejected the propaganda that Russia is bringing civilization to the peoples around it. In his opinion, the Russian colonizers' main goal is to "stuff their faces."

An important symbol of this colonial period in the history of the Russian Empire is the monument to Bohdan Khmelnytsky, put up in 1888 in front of St. Sophia's Cathedral in central Kyiv to commemorate the nine hundredth anniversary of the Baptism of Rus. The monument was intended to symbolize the unity of the Russian, Belarusian, and Ukrainian peoples under the rule of Moscow.

The original design featured Bohdan on horseback atop a steep cliff, with the horse rearing up and knocking a Polish nobleman, a Jew, and a Jesuit off the cliff with its hooves. At the foot, a Russian, a Ukrainian, and a Belarusian listen to the singing of a blind *kobzar* (bard). But then, following the scandalous affront to Jews and Poles, the extra figures are excluded from the project. Only the equestrian statue of Bohdan remained. It stands in the center of Kyiv to this day.

No Such Language

Shevchenko's death ushers in hard times for Ukrainian literature. In 1863, a new revolt begins in Poland and western Ukraine. In response, the government decides to uproot all green shoots of independence, whereupon the Ministry of Interior scours all books published in Ukrainian for signs of liberal ideas.

Local officials zealously get down to business. For example, the military governor of Kyiv, Nikolay Annenkov, informs St. Petersburg that the publication of the New Testament in Ukrainian poses a great danger: "Having achieved the translation of the Holy Scripture into the Little Russian [Ukrainian] idiom, supporters of the Little Russian party will gain, so to speak, recognition of the independence of the Little Russian language, at which, of course, they will not stop, but, referring to the separateness of the language, will claim autonomy for Little Russia."

Other Kyiv officials embrace the trend and inform St. Petersburg that the Ukrainian language is a tool in the hands of the Poles, who want to push the province into separatism. At this point, Interior Minister Pyotr Valuyev officially prohibits the publication of any books in the Ukrainian language—except works of fiction. School textbooks, however, fall under the ban. In justifying the decision, Valuyev cites the alleged opinion of ordinary folk: "Most Little Russians themselves are fully aware that there has never been, nor can there be, a separate Little Russian language, and that their dialect, used by the common people, is the same Russian language, only corrupted by the Polish influence."

The chief opponent of the ban is Kostomarov. He writes a fiery article in defense of the Ukrainian language, which, ironically, does not get past the censors. In a few years, the situation will worsen. Alexander II will sign the so-called Ems Ukaz (Decree)—banning book printing in the Ukrainian language—to combat the "Ukrainophile propaganda," which is seen as synonymous with Ukrainian separatism.

Petrograd

BALTIC
SEA

Moscow

GERMANY

RUSSIAN

REPUBLIC

Warsaw

Brest-Litovsk

Zhytomyr

Kyiv

Kharkiv

Lviv

WEST UKRAINIAN
PEOPLE'S
REPUBLIC

UKRAINIAN

PEOPLE'S REPUBLIC

AUSTRIA-

HUNGARY

Rostov

Mykolaiv

Taganrog

ROMANIA

Kherson

Odesa

SEA
OF AZOV

CRIMEA

UKRAINIAN PEOPLE'S REPUBLIC

AND THE RUSSIAN CIVIL WAR, 1917–1919

BLACK SEA

	State borders in October 1917
	Ukrainian People's Republic in November 1917
	West Ukrainian People's Republic (1918–1919)
	Territory controlled by Ukrainian troops in October 1919
	Farthest advance of Denikin's army in October 1919
	French forces on the Black Sea coast of Ukraine

OTTOMAN

EMPIRE

200 miles

200 km

5

THE MYTH OF LENIN:
HOW INDEPENDENT UKRAINE EMERGED

Ukraine-Rus

1898. Lviv, Austria-Hungary. A thirty-two-year-old historian is writing a book. His name is Mykhailo Hrushevsky; he is from Poland, that is, a subject of the Russian Empire. He studied in Kyiv but works abroad, in the history faculty of Lviv University. Today both Kyiv and Lviv are part of Ukraine, but in the nineteenth century things are very different.

Hrushevsky's favorite author is Nikolay Kostomarov. Having read all his works, the young researcher decides to write a popular history book for the general reader. Immersed in historical sources, however, he realizes that his duty is to study the history of his homeland as thoroughly as possible, which means nothing less than a ten-volume work.

In 1898, the world is already a turbulent place: the European empires are not yet collapsing but are beginning to shake. In Geneva, an Italian anarchist assassinates Sisi (that is, Elizabeth, empress of Austria and queen of Hungary), whose portrait today adorns postcards and fridge magnets. In Minsk, the capital of today's Belarus, comrades of Vladimir Ulyanov (the future Lenin) set up the Russian Social Democratic Party (the future Communist Party that will rule Russia for seventy years).

France's Pierre and (Polish-born) Marie Curie discover radium, and America's Caleb Bradham starts selling Pepsi-Cola. Émile Zola rages against anti-Semitism in the Dreyfus affair in his famous letter "J'accuse! . . . ," for which he will do jail time. Anton Chekhov becomes a star after his play *The Seagull* is staged at the Moscow Art Theatre, although he is so afraid of failure that he skips the premiere.

The first volume of Mykhailo Hrushevsky's monumental magnum opus, titled *History of Ukraine-Rus'*, is published in Lviv in that same 1898. The author's central premise is that the history of Russia and the history of Ukraine have little in common; Ukrainians and Russians (Great Russians, as Hrushevsky calls them) are different peoples. By the end of the nineteenth century, the imperial historical narrative is the only one generally accepted in Russia. Thus, Hrushevsky is effectively swimming against all his predecessors who wrote about the Russian principalities and their history and believed, à la Innokenty Gizel, that Muscovy was a continuation of Kyivan Rus. Historians have framed all the events as the story of one people. Hrushevsky is the first author to contradict this view. In doing so, he argues that Kyivan Rus is the forerunner of Ukraine, not of Russia. The Moscow princes submitted to the Golden Horde, while the Ukrainian princes, in Galicia, remained independent from the so-called Tatar-Mongols.

Hrushevsky surrounds himself with like-minded people, including the poet Ivan Franko, with whom he forms a close bond. Together they dream of autonomy for Ukraine. In no way are they revolutionaries.

Hrushevsky's texts are banned in the Russian Empire until 1904, when the liberal interior minister, Prince Pyotr Svyatopolk-Mirsky, allows *History of Ukraine-Rus'*, published in Lviv, to be imported into Russia. And it is in 1904 that Hrushevsky writes his most provocative article: "The Traditional Scheme of 'Russian' History and the Problem of a Rational Organization of the History of the East Slavs." In it, he sets out his views on the Russian and Ukrainian historical narratives and comes to the conclusion that a revolution in Russia, which Russian civil society is forever discussing, is impossible without the liberation of Ukraine, which must become a democratic autonomy within a democratic and federal Russia.

Hrushevsky's books bring him fame not only in Ukraine. He travels freely between Kyiv and Lviv for many years, right up until 1914.

Home of the Revolution

In the early twentieth century, the most restless part of the Russian Empire is Ukraine. Due not to the Ukrainians, but to the Jews. As noted earlier, it is on Ukrainian soil that most of the Pale of Settlement is located, the area where Jews are permitted to live. The Jews, as the most disenfranchised people in Russia, are the first to pursue political self-organization. Ukrainian cities witness the emergence of the most powerful cells of the underground Jewish parties: the Bund and the Socialist-Revolutionaries. At the same time, anti-Semitism is on the rise. The trend is noticeable throughout Europe; in France, for example, the trial of the Jewish officer Alfred Dreyfus becomes the main political event of the decade. And in the Russian Empire, Jewish pogroms are becoming more frequent. They lead to the mass emigration of Jews from Russia; for instance, the five-year-old Golda Meir, the future prime minister of Israel, leaves Kyiv with her family in 1903. Others, on the contrary, set up militant self-defense units: for example, Ze'ev Jabotinsky (born Vladimir Zhabotinsky) of Odesa, one of the founders of the Zionist movement.

In 1913, the most famous trial in prerevolutionary Russia begins in Kyiv: Mendel Beilis, a Jew, is accused of the ritual murder of an Orthodox Christian boy. In terms of public reaction, it is comparable with the Dreyfus affair in France; the intelligentsia of the Russian Empire speak almost unanimously in defense of Beilis. And the case ends unexpectedly: the jury finds Beilis not guilty.

Nevertheless, the situation in the Ukrainian provinces remains explosive: the revolutionary parties are at their most popular here; inhabitants of the shtetls (Jewish villages) in the Pale of Settlement will become leaders of the future revolutions in Russia, one of the most famous of whom, from Kherson Province, is the leader of the failed 1905 revolution and a future organizer of the 1917 Bolshevik revolution, Leon Trotsky.

The "Jewish question" is the most problematic for the Russian state up until the outbreak of World War I, when it is superseded by the "Ukrainian question." The outbreak of the First World War is a terrible tragedy for the Ukrainian people. Ukrainians live on both sides of the front lines: one part in Russia, the other in Austria-Hungary. This is a huge problem, since they are now viewed with suspicion by both sides as a potential fifth column.

Shortly after the war begins, a highly typical article appears in the Russian-language magazine *Ukrainskaya Zhizn'* (Ukrainian life), authored by Symon Petliura, an insurance company employee. The text (titled "War and Ukrainians") says that Ukrainians stand side by side with Russia and nothing will change that. "Separatism with 'Mazepinism' or Austrophilia is a myth that exists only in the inflamed imagination of the most irreconcilable opponents of Ukrainianism," writes Petliura. The word used by Petliura is highly symbolic: like all his contemporaries, he calls Ukrainian nationalists Mazepinites. Soon, however, this concept will be forgotten, to be replaced by another—"Petliurites."

It is Austrian western Ukraine that becomes the site of the main battles in the first months of the war. When it starts, Hrushevsky is forced to flee to Kyiv—in Austria he is accused of being a "Muscovophile." On September 3, 1914, Russian troops capture Lviv. Austrian propaganda embraces the idea of merging its Ukrainian territory with all the Ukrainian lands, from Kharkiv to Odesa to Lviv, under the rule of the Austrian emperor. The Austrians, of course, interpret Hrushevsky's books in their own interests. Russian publicists are indignant.

In December 1914, Mykhailo Hrushevsky is arrested in Kyiv, accused of pro-Austrian sympathies, and sent into exile—first to Simbirsk and from there to Kazan. Petersburg academics mount a powerful campaign in Hrushevsky's defense, writing letters saying that life in the provinces will damage his health irreparably. So, in September 1916, the tsarist government allows the historian to move from Kazan to Moscow.

Democratic Russia

On March 15, 1917, Russian emperor Nicholas II abdicates from the throne: the war, his hapless government, his own personal shortcomings, and his unwillingness to reform the country have all brought about the collapse of the empire. The Provisional Government, made up of extremely liberal politicians, comes to power. It grants a general amnesty to opponents of the tsar and abolishes the death penalty. Moreover, they give the vote to everyone, including women. This is an incredibly progressive step at the time: in Germany, women will become fully enfranchised in 1918, in the United States in 1920, in Britain in 1928, in France in 1944—and in Switzerland in 1971. Such unprecedented liberalism is not surprising, as the first prime minister of the new Russian Republic is Georgy Lvov, a friend and disciple of the die-hard democrat and humanist Leo Tolstoy.

New local authorities are being set up in Kyiv too. March 17 sees the first session of the Central Rada, an assembly of representatives of labor collectives and public organizations. Mykhailo Hrushevsky is elected chairman in absentia: he is still in exile in Moscow. But he arrives shortly and sets out his stall as a political leader. According to the professor, this "great moment" must be used to demand national-territorial autonomy as part of the new Russian Democratic Federal Republic.

Also represented in the Rada are the "independists" (full name: the Ukrainian Party of Socialist-Independists), a faction advocating secession from Russia. But they are in the minority.

On May 11, members of the Central Rada write a letter to Petrograd (as the Russian capital was renamed on the outbreak of World War I), outlining their proposals. They do not ask for much: for Russia to recognize Ukraine's autonomy, to allow the creation of frontline Ukrainian units to raise morale, to introduce Ukrainian-language education in schools, and to establish the position of Special Commissar for Ukraine under the Provisional Government. There is pandemonium in the capital. The Provisional Government believes that the Central Rada has no right to speak on behalf of the entire Ukrainian people. And it decides not to decide, but rather to wait for the convocation of the long-hoped-for Constituent Assembly, a body that would set the new laws for a new Russian democratic republic.

The advocates of autonomy are somewhat taken aback. Their leader, Hrushevsky's deputy, Volodymyr Vynnychenko, tells his Rada colleagues in May 1917: "At this moment we must not break away from the Russian state, with which we are connected historically, economically and politically. We need only to eradicate the causes that divide us. Until now, their attitude toward us has been arrogant. They have viewed us as manure for fertilizer. To officials nourished by Ukrainian sweat and blood, the idea that a *khokhol* peasant could dare to lay claim to his rights seemed wild. But now we are to be reckoned with, because they have felt real force inside us."

To what extent Ukraine is to be reckoned with remains an open question. The Provisional Government bans the newly formed All-Ukrainian Military Congress from meeting, yet it goes ahead anyway in June. The Central Rada proclaims autonomy without waiting for a Constituent Assembly to be set up in Russia, and adopts the most important political declaration of the new Ukraine: the First Universal. It was authored by Vynnychenko:

"Without separating from the whole of Russia, without breaking with the Russian state, let the Ukrainian people have the right to govern their own lives on their own land," he reads out to applause from the hall.

The congress also establishes the first Ukrainian government (known as the General Secretariat) and imposes taxes to the benefit of Ukraine. Vynnychenko becomes prime minister, and Symon Petliura, that same insurance worker and journalist for *Ukrainskaya Zhizn'* magazine, becomes minister of war.

The question of secession from Russia is raised periodically, but the prime minister opposes it: "The path of insurrection is closed to us. We have strength in the villages, but that way lies anarchy," he explains, insisting that there is no need to hurry, that the Rada in any case will get what it wants.

In early July, a delegation from Petrograd arrives in Kyiv: four ministers from the Provisional Government, including Mikhail Tereshchenko, a major sugar refiner, himself originally from Kyiv, who has been appointed as Russia's foreign minister, and Minister of War Aleksandr Kerensky, currently the most popular man in Russia, idolized by millions. During the negotiations, they make concessions, recognizing the Ukrainian government and persuading it, in return, not to rush into declaring autonomy, but to wait for the Constituent Assembly. "We must set an example to all Russia of the unification of democratic forces," Vynnychenko tells the visitors from the Russian capital.

Instead, however, a scandal ensues. When the results of the talks with the Ukrainians become known in Petrograd, some members of the Provisional Government pointedly resign. They belong to the Constitutional Democratic (Kadet) Party, which, before the revolution, was seen as extremely liberal but, with the fall of the monarchy, has become highly conservative and imperialist. The party's leader, historian Pavel Milyukov, believes that Russia's goal in World War I should be to seize Constantinople (Istanbul), the Bosporus, and the Dardanelles—little wonder, then, that he brooks no compromise on the Ukrainian question. Milyukov and his fellow party members consider Ukraine to be "ancestral Russian land."

Relations between Kyiv and the Provisional Government in Russia remain strained but civil until late October and the Bolshevik coup in Petrograd. Prime Minister Kerensky flees the capital, and other ministers including the sugar baron Tereshchenko are arrested. Vladimir Lenin is declared head of the new government.

As with Petrograd, armed Bolshevik uprisings begin in other regions. In Moscow, for example, fighting erupts right inside the Kremlin, destroying part of the ancient fortress. In Kyiv, however, everything ends rather quickly. Ukraine is not short of Bolshevik supporters, but the Central Rada manages to suppress the revolt and arrest its leaders.

That said, a major outcome of the October Revolution of 1917 is that Kyiv no longer sees itself as part of Bolshevik Russia. It proves impossible to reach an agreement with Lenin and his comrades: they are striving for world revolution and the dictatorship of the proletariat, that is, Bolshevik rule everywhere. But Hrushevsky and Vynnychenko are considered leaders of a "bourgeois government." And that means Ukraine must become an independent state.

First Republic

In early November, the Central Rada announces the creation of the Ukrainian People's Republic, consisting of nine provinces, which roughly constitute today's internationally recognized territory of Ukraine, minus Crimea and part of western Ukraine. The latter remains part of Austria-Hungary. That is, when Vladimir Putin, declaring war in 2022, says that Ukraine was invented by Lenin and no such state existed beforehand it is a direct contradiction of the historical truth: an independent Ukrainian state was formed *in spite* of Lenin; he gave the Ukrainians nothing.

Defeat in Ukraine is, of course, a major problem for Lenin. Already in late November 1917, speaking at the First All-Russia Congress of the Navy, the new head of the Russian government explains his approach to this issue. As ever, Lenin's rhetoric is Machiavellian in the extreme: what he says and what he means are near polar opposites. As befits a Marxist, he begins his speech by paying lip service to the right of all nations to self-determination: "We shall say to the Ukrainians: as Ukrainians, you can organize your lives as you wish. But," Lenin suddenly develops his thought, "we shall extend a fraternal hand to the Ukrainian workers and say to them: together we shall fight the bourgeoisie, both yours and ours." This is essentially the same logic used by Putin when he promises to "save" the people of Ukraine from their own government.

But the Bolsheviks have other problems besides Ukraine: the ongoing war with Germany and the pro-tsarist generals who have raised an army in southern Russia. Since the Bolsheviks are called the Reds, they, in contrast, become known as the Whites. It is over these two issues that Lenin and Vynnychenko fall out for good. Ukraine wants Ukrainian army units to defend their own territory, and so encourages them to return home from Russia, where they have been serving during the hostilities. This, of course, undermines the defense capability of the Bolshevik state. In addition, Kyiv has no plans to interfere with the so-called White generals in their anti-Bolshevik plans. In December 1917, Lenin presents an ultimatum to Ukraine: withdraw all support for the White Army and not take away frontline Ukrainian soldiers, or else it's war. Vynnychenko and his war minister, Petliura, refuse.

Simultaneously, the Bolsheviks try once again to seize power in Ukraine: the All-Ukrainian Congress of Soviets is held in Kyiv—at similar gatherings of people's representatives in Russia, the Bolsheviks are generally in the majority. But in Kyiv, supporters of the Central Rada hold the upper hand. Then Lenin makes a trademark move that Putin will copy for the first time after the Orange Revolution in 2004: the Bolsheviks in Ukraine withdraw to the east of the country, to Kharkiv, already occupied by Soviet troops. There they hold their own congress and proclaim their own state: the Ukrainian People's Republic of Soviets, with its capital at Kharkiv. The former Chekist Mykola Skrypnyk, an entirely Lenin-loyal communist from near Bakhmut, will soon become head of this republic.

Prime Minister Vynnychenko blames the conflict with the Bolsheviks on the overly combatant War Minister Petliura, believing that his resignation, in January 1918, will help avoid another war. However, the opposite happens: that same month, Russian troops launch a full-scale offensive, and the new war minister is hopelessly out of his depth.

Lenin's troops in 1918 move along almost the exact same route as Putin's in 2022, but far more successfully: they take not only the industrial centers of Luhansk and Mariupol but also Dnipro and Odesa.

At the same time, Lenin establishes an irreversible dictatorship in Russia. On January 22, 1918, he disperses the Constituent Assembly, the body so eagerly awaited by the Provisional Government and which was supposed to create a new democratic state. But the sentry at the palace where the meeting is taking place disperses the delegates with the curt phrase: "The guard is tired." And the next day the members of the Constituent Assembly find that the building is locked. The Bolsheviks, having again prevented them from meeting, now start to actively clamp down on them.

Meanwhile, Bolshevik troops are approaching Kyiv. The Central Rada, headed by Hrushevsky, heads west toward Austria and Germany. The Reds take Kyiv and shoot those officers who remained in the city. On February 9, the commander of the Bolshevik army boasts in a letter to Lenin: "I set fire to Hrushevsky's big house, and for three days it blazed brightly. . . ."

The foreign minister of Soviet Russia, Leon Trotsky, meanwhile, is trying to make peace with Germany and Austria-Hungary. Earlier the Bolsheviks were not against Ukrainian representatives taking part in the negotiations, but now Trotsky says that the Ukrainian People's Republic is no more, which means that its representatives must be expelled. But Germans do the opposite by concluding, on February 9, a peace treaty with Ukraine. And already on February 19, on the basis of the signed agreements, a 230,000-strong German-Austrian force goes on the offensive. On March 2, they take Kyiv and reach all the way to the modern borders of Ukraine and beyond, occupying the Russian cities of Rostov and Taganrog.

The leadership of the Central Rada returns to Kyiv together with the German-Austrian military. But disillusionment with the Central Powers swiftly sets in. If at first Hrushevsky and the Central Rada viewed them as liberators from the Russian invaders, they soon come to see them as occupiers. The nascent conflict between the Central Rada and the German command is quickly resolved: the Rada is dissolved. According to legend, on the last day of its existence, April 29, 1918, the Central Rada elected Mykhailo Hrushevsky as president of Ukraine. But many historians consider this to be a romantic myth. In fact, Hrushevsky is the president of the Central Rada, that is, the speaker of parliament, and with expanded powers, which, however, he can no longer use.

The Germans change the form of government by appointing the loyal military leader Pavel Skoropadsky as hetman; in other words, democratic power is replaced by a dictatorship. He arrests just about all the former leaders of Ukraine, including Hrushevsky, Vynnychenko, and Petliura. However, Skoropadsky's power is wholly dependent on the strength of the German military, which collapses in November 1918 following a revolution: Kaiser Wilhelm abdicates and the new government capitulates, bringing World War I to an end. On November 11, 1918, an armistice between Germany and the Entente countries is signed in the Compiègne forest near Paris. Under the terms of the treaty, the Germans must surrender all occupied territories in Eastern Europe.

Hetman Skoropadsky tries to cling on to power: first he invites Vynnychenko to join the government, and when the latter refuses he begins to look for allies abroad, inviting all Russian anti-Bolshevik forces, to create a unified federal state.

But it's too late: Vynnychenko and Petliura raise an uprising, and on December 14 Skoropadsky relinquishes power and flees from Kyiv along with the departing German troops. The new Ukrainian government is called the Directorate (in coming up with the name, Vynnychenko was inspired by the French Revolution*). This time Hrushevsky is not offered a leadership role: Vynnychenko and Petliura accuse him of aiding the German occupation, while Hrushevsky believes they simply do not want to share power.

Partitioning the Former Russia

As a result of the First World War, four empires collapse almost at once, effectively shaping the political map of modern Europe.

The Russian Empire is the first to fall. The revolution occurs a year before the end of the war. Six months before the victory of the Entente in March 1918 the Bolsheviks sign the Treaty of Brest-Litovsk, forfeiting Russia's place among the future winners by surrendering to the future losers.

The others follow like dominoes. In October 1918, the Hungarian parliament severs the union with Austria and proclaims independence. In November, Austria acknowledges defeat, Poland and the newly formed Czechoslovakia secede, and the emperor abdicates. Galicia, the part of the empire inhabited by Ukrainians, is liberated and the West Ukrainian People's Republic is established there.

In November 1918, as mentioned, a revolution takes place in Germany; the Kaiser abdicates. And Bavaria even proclaims the Bavarian Soviet Republic, a short-lived unrecognized socialist state.

---

* Le Directoire was the governing five-member committee in the French First Republic from November 2, 1795, till November 9, 1799.

Lastly, in November 1918, the forces of Britain, France, Italy, and Greece occupy Constantinople. The last sultan of the Ottoman Empire abdicates in 1922.

Traditional historiography is firmly centered on Western Europe, for which reason the flare-ups in 1918 immediately after World War I outside of Western Europe are not considered wars at all. It is customary to view them as a series of disparate regional conflicts in Eastern Europe, the Middle East, and Asia, a time when the victorious countries of World War I carve up the losers' territory. In fact, they constitute another world war—for the assets of the fallen empires.

The British and French occupy the former colonies of Russia and Turkey: in the winter of 1918–19, the French seize control of Syria and Lebanon, while the British take control of Palestine, Iraq, and Jordan. Before that, in March 1918, British and French troops land in northern Russia near Murmansk and in August in Arkhangelsk. Then, in January 1919, a French-Greek force occupies the Black Sea coast of Ukraine (the cities of Odesa, Mykolaiv, and Kherson), and the British do likewise with the territories of the current states of Azerbaijan, Georgia, and Uzbekistan.

While this is going on, the newly independent Poland is making territorial claims against the West Ukrainian People's Republic with a view to regaining the lands that were once part of the Polish-Lithuanian Commonwealth. By November 1918, Polish troops have already taken Lviv; the government of the West Ukrainian People's Republic has fled east and announced its unification with the Ukrainian People's Republic.

In southern Russia, to add to the chaos, opponents of the Bolsheviks, mostly former tsarist officers, plot the overthrow of Lenin and the restoration of the empire.

General Anton Denikin, one of the last chiefs of the General Staff of the Russian army in World War I, becomes supreme commander of the White forces. Denikin's army plans to march on Moscow, while Lenin's army goes to meet it head on. Geography predetermines that the Reds and the Whites clash on Ukrainian territory. That is, at the beginning of 1919 Ukraine is not only surrounded by enemies but also being attacked from all sides simultaneously: by Poland, Czechoslovakia, and Romania from the west, by the Bolsheviks from the north, and by Denikin's army from the south. The two Russian armies are both extremely hostile to the independent Ukrainian state. Lenin believes the bourgeois government in Kyiv should be overthrown and power transferred to the Ukrainian Bolsheviks, while the Whites are fighting for the restoration of the "united and indivisible" Russian Empire. They don't even want to hear about an independent Ukraine, believing it to be ancestral Russian land, which is, after all, how the history books describe it. The West is placing its bets on the combined White army; in European eyes, it is Denikin who has the best chance of defeating the Bolsheviks.

This period of all-out war, everyone against everyone, is one of the bloodiest and most terrible in the history of both Ukraine and Russia. The future looks very bleak indeed.

As early as 1918 Vladimir Lenin, the head of the Soviet government, moves the capital to Moscow out of fear that Petrograd could be captured. And in March 1919 he writes a letter to US president Woodrow Wilson with a proposal to hold an international conference in Norway to seek ways to end the armed conflicts breaking out across the former Russian Empire. All twenty-three (!) wars going on in parallel must be stopped, and Lenin is prepared to recognize all states that exist de facto on the territory of the former Russia. Thus, the Bolsheviks are ready to make do with the strip of land from Petrograd to the Urals that they currently control. As a result, Ukraine will gain independence; the Russian Far East will become a protectorate of the Entente countries, northern, southern Russia, and Siberia will be made into separate states governed by the White generals.

Lenin proposes mutual recognition of all these states, a general amnesty, free movement of people throughout the former Russian Empire, and the joint payment of its debts. But the White House does not take Lenin's proposal seriously. Like other countries, the United States expects the imminent collapse of Bolshevik power.

Catastrophe in Kyiv

In 1918–19, Kyiv is full of people fleeing the Bolsheviks. One of them is the doctor and aspiring writer Mikhail Bulgakov, future author of the novel *The Master and Margarita*. Various attempts are made to mobilize him: first he is drafted into the army of Symon Petliura but manages to escape; then the Red Army tries to enlist him, but he evades it.

The Bulgakovs have a dacha (country house) near Kyiv, in the village of Bucha. In 1918, their house burns down—his wife is sure it was done by the "Petliurites." The name Bucha will resound around the world in 2022, when this now city near Kyiv is occupied by Russian soldiers who massacre over a thousand local residents.

In February 1919, the Red Army occupies Kyiv. Vynnychenko, deprived of all support, emigrates. The Directorate is headed by Petliura, who is preparing a new offensive with a united Ukrainian army comprising units from Galicia, former subjects of Austria-Hungary, and Cossacks from eastern Ukraine, born in the Russian Empire. They all have their own perspective on the situation. The Galicians are fairly tolerant of the idea of broad autonomy within Russia—they did not experience life in the Russian Empire, so such a prospect to them seems like deliverance. The Cossacks, however, are categorically opposed to both the Reds and the Whites, and are fully committed to independence. The Galicians lived about four hundred years under Polish rule, so the leadership of the West Ukrainian People's Republic is as historically traumatized by Poland as the leadership of the Ukrainian People's Republic is by Russia. Military units from Galicia will help the former to unite with White Russia against Poland, while Petliura wants to join with Poland against any form of Russian power.

In August, Ukrainian troops approach Kyiv from the west, and the White Army does likewise from the east. On August 31, 1919, the Ukrainians enter the city, and a celebratory parade is scheduled for 4:00 p.m. on the main square, in those days called Dumskaya, the future Maidan Nezalezhnosti (Independence Square). Intelligence reports predicted the Whites would not reach the city until September 3, but in fact they enter Kyiv from the east on the same day as the Ukrainians. Around noon, Ukrainian units are stationed on Dumskaya Square near the Kyiv City Duma, hoisting the Ukrainian yellow-and-blue flag on the balcony. At about 2:00 p.m., the Whites also arrive on Dumskaya Square. A representative of the White Army asks the Ukrainian commander if they can raise their flag, the red, white, and blue tricolor, the former flag of the Russian Empire, next to the Ukrainian one and take part in a joint parade. The general from Galicia answers in the affirmative to both questions.

Later, however, Zaporizhian Cossack units move into the square. Seeing the Russian tricolor over the Duma, the Cossack leader orders it to be torn down. A Ukrainian soldier climbs up onto the balcony and hurls the Russian flag down under the horses' hooves. Gunfire erupts.

The Galician Ukrainians are mostly villagers unaccustomed to the big city. Panic breaks out in their ranks. The White Guards disarm the Ukrainians and take them prisoner en masse. The commander of the Whites, General Nikolai Bredov, then proclaims: "Kyiv, the mother of Russian cities, has never been, and never will be, Ukrainian. There can be no negotiations with the Ukrainian army. If they come, they will be arrested and shot as traitors and bandits." Symon Petliura will later describe the events of August 31 as the "Kyiv catastrophe."

Denikin's army begins to mobilize, and Bulgakov is drafted for a third time, which this time he cannot avoid. These events will later form the basis of his breakthrough novel, *The White Guard*.

Having captured Kyiv, Denikin's White Army continues its advance on Moscow. There, in the capital, the panic-stricken Bolsheviks are preparing to go into hiding. Unexpectedly, however, in the region of present-day Donbas, Ukrainian anarchists—detachments under Field Commander Nestor Makhno—strike at the rear of Denikin's troops. The anarchists support neither the Reds nor the Whites.

Petliura also declares a new war on Denikin, and even calls on the European powers for support: "General Denikin, basing his actions on the reactionary laws of the old times, is ruthlessly destroying Ukrainian culture, depriving us of the right and opportunity to study in Ukrainian schools. He has prohibited the use of the Ukrainian language in church, closed our cultural institutions and banned Ukrainian books." But the European allies prefer to support the Whites, because they have a better chance of defeating the Bolsheviks.

The final collapse of the Ukrainian army occurs in November 1919: the western Ukrainian part of the army goes over to Denikin's side. The Galicians consider Petliura's negotiations with Poland and his readiness to cede part of their land as a betrayal.

October 1919 marks a turning point in the war. The Red Army successfully halts Denikin on the approach to Moscow. The Bolsheviks go on the offensive, taking Kyiv and most of Ukraine. By April 1920, only Crimea remains under the control of the White Army. Denikin resigns and goes into exile. Sixty years later, the Soviet writer Vasily Aksyonov will write his dystopian novel *The Island of Crimea* about an alternative history in which the White Army managed to keep hold of Crimea— a kind of Russian Taiwan, an anti-Soviet enclave right next to the Soviet Union. In reality, however, by November 1920 the remnants of the White Army have been evacuated from Crimea aboard British and French warships.

In May 1920, the Polish army, in alliance with Petliura, invades and captures Kyiv. But the Bolsheviks retake it just a few months later, in November. Every transfer of Kyiv and other cities from one army to another is always accompanied by killings, violence, and destruction. In 1921, famine is added to this list of horrors: Ukraine's agriculture is wrecked, and the reduced harvest that could be gathered is requisitioned by the Bolsheviks.

In December 1922, Ukraine becomes part of the Soviet Union. The task of state building is assigned to the minister for nationalities of the Bolshevik government, Joseph Stalin. Officially, he will become head of the country two years later, in 1924.

In the 1920s, Moscow pursues a policy of "indigenization" (*"korenizatsia"*) in the national republics. In Ukraine this leads to a spread of the Ukrainian language, the establishment of Ukrainian schools, and the appointment of Ukrainians to ruling positions. The main promoter of indigenization in Ukraine is Bolshevik Mykola Skrypnyk, former head of the Ukrainian People's Republic of Soviets with its capital in Kharkov. He carries out reforms of the spelling of the Ukrainian language and opens Ukrainian-language schools throughout the republic. There is a remarkable cultural boom in Ukraine.

Also in 1924, Mykhailo Hrushevsky writes a letter from exile in Vienna to the Soviet government, in which he denounces his former "counterrevolutionary activities" and requests permission to return to Ukraine. He receives a positive response and relocates to Kyiv, where he devotes himself to academia at Kyiv State University as a professor of history. In 1929, Hrushevsky is elected a member of the Academy of Sciences of the Soviet Union.

BALTIC
SEA

ESTONIA

LATVIA

LITHUANIA

EAST
PRUSSIA
(GERMANY)

Moscow

R U S S I A N

S F S R

BELORUSSIAN
SSR

U . S . S . R .

Warsaw

P O L A N D

Kyiv

Myrhorod

Kharkiv

Lviv

Poltava

CZECHO-
SLOVAKIA

U K R A I N I A N   S S R

Dnipropetrovsk

K U B A N

R O M A N I A

SEA
OF AZOV

CRIMEA

Simferopol

BLACK SEA

UKRAINIAN SOVIET SOCIALIST REPUBLIC
AND THE HOLODOMOR, 1932–1934

————— State borders in 1932

░░░░░ Areas most affected by the Holodomor

⊙ Transfer of the capital from Kharkiv
to Kyiv in 1934

T U R K E Y

200 miles
200 km

6

THE MYTH OF PROSPERITY:
HOW STALIN ENGINEERED
THE HOLODOMOR

Leninist Rus

In 1935, the fifty-three-year-old Soviet academic Boris Grekov writes a historical treatise. He is very afraid. His memories of prison are still fresh. Although he served only a month, it has aged him prematurely. Grekov was accused of having allegedly fought against the Red Army in 1920 as a soldier in a White Army. He did no such thing, of course. Grekov was a history professor at the University of Simferopol (present-day Tavrida National University) when Crimea was controlled by the Whites. In the 1930s, that was enough to end up on the "enemies of the people" list.

Grekov is by no means the only historian to suffer political repression in the 1930s. The so-called academic case in the Soviet Union has been ongoing since 1929, in which ideologically suspect historians are put on trial charged with setting up the secret organization "The All-People's Union for the Revival of a Free Russia" with the intention of overthrowing the Soviet government. The organization was entirely concocted by the investigators, but some victims, under torture, confess that it exists.

The campaign against "wrecker" historians spreads nationwide. In

Ukraine, it goes hand in hand with the search for nationalists. In 1931, the sixty-five-year-old Mykhailo Hrushevsky, a former chairman of the Ukrainian Central Rada and now just a member of the Soviet Academy of Sciences, realizes that he will soon fall victim to the witch-hunt. Public hearings have already been organized, at which he is branded as a petit bourgeois scholar, a counterrevolutionary who distorts Soviet historical science. In March 1931, he is removed from his teaching post, bids farewell to his students, and leaves Kyiv for Moscow. He has been summoned to an interrogation by the OGPU, the secret police later to be renamed the NKVD and then the KGB. He is immediately charged with creating a secret Ukrainian nationalist organization. True, a few days later the charge is dropped—it seems that Lazar Kaganovich, Joseph Stalin's right-hand man and the former head of Soviet Ukraine recently transferred to Moscow, has interceded on the historian's behalf. But Hrushevsky continues to face regular interrogations by the OGPU.

The "academic case" is eventually put on ice. Despite the gravity of the accusations and the sordid details of the historians' alleged underground activities, most are exiled at worst. True, some of them die there. Hrushevsky, who is arrested for just a few days, and Grekov, who spent a month in prison, are among the lucky ones.

All the same, Hrushevsky is not permitted to return to Kyiv. He resides in Moscow and once a year receives a ticket to a sanatorium in Kislovodsk in southern Russia. It is there, in October 1934, that he falls seriously ill. Dying, he says to his wife, "When I'm gone, don't stay with the Bolsheviks. Go to Galicia [western Ukraine]."

Grekov, of course, knows about the death of his fellow historians in exile on false charges, and about Hrushevsky's untimely end. Against this backdrop, fearing for his life, he works on a new version of the history of Russia and Ukraine within a Marxist framework. Grekov is instructed to create a new canon: history through the prism of the teachings of Marx and Lenin. The Soviet Union is an ideological state in which everything must comply with the precepts of Marxism.

Does Grekov know about what is happening in Ukraine at that time? He himself comes from the region, having been born in Myrhorod, a city in the Poltava region, made famous by Nikolay Gogol's eponymous collection of short stories. In the early 1930s, the population of Ukraine suffers mass starvation, but not a single Soviet newspaper even mentions it. Officials from Moscow, arriving, for example, in Kharkiv or Kyiv, leave the station and calmly walk to their government cars, ignoring the corpses littering the roadside. After all, real communists are able to filter out such nuisances through their rose-tinted glasses.

Most likely, Grekov knows what is happening: rumors are swirling all over the country about starving peasants and whole villages dying out. In 1936, Grekov pens a book titled *Feudal Relations in the Kyivan State*. He attempts to show that in the ninth through twelfth centuries there existed a "Kyivan Rus"—not Ukraine at all, but the common cradle of the Russian, Ukrainian, and Belarusian peoples. For Grekov, the Principality of Kyiv is a protoempire that gave birth to the "empire of the descendants of Rurik," that is, the future Russian Empire. It is an eastern version of the Carolingian Empire under Charlemagne. But the most important thing is to introduce Marxist terminology.

The Great Break

October 24–29, 1929, are among the darkest days in world history, literally. On October 24, known as Black Thursday, the New York Stock Exchange crashes. It is followed by Black Friday, then Black Monday and Black Tuesday. The Great Depression hits the United States; millions of people lose their jobs.

In the Soviet Union, Stalin declares 1929 to be the year of the "Great Break": he sets about implementing his plan to industrialize the country. Taking advantage of the crisis and unemployment in the United States, he attracts tens of thousands of Western engineers to work in the Soviet Union and strikes deals with dozens of foreign companies to bring in new technologies and build new factories. In 1930, Ford and Austin set up automotive plants in Moscow and Nizhniy Novgorod, International Harvester establishes a tractor factory in Stalingrad (now Volgograd), Cooper Engineering, together with General Electric and Siemens, work on the largest hydroelectric power plant in Ukraine, DniproHES, built exactly where the Zaporizhian Host used to be.

US technology and the highly skilled workforce need to be paid for. And that is where part two of Stalin's plan comes in: sell grain on the world market and spend the money on industrialization.

The method invented by Stalin to take away the grain from the peasants is called "collectivization." Farmers throughout the country are obliged to join *kolkhozi*, or collective peasant farms, where no one owns property, everything is in common, or belongs to the state. Some in the Soviet leadership, such as economist Nikolay Bukharin, are against collectivization. But he and his supporters are expelled from the Politburo. Collectivization proceeds slowly in the face of resistance from the peasants, who see it as a return of serfdom, which was abolished by Alexander II just seventy years earlier.

In 1929, the governing body of the Soviet Communist Party adopts a "grain requisition plan" according to which grain grown by the peasants must be handed over to the state and anyone who resists faces punishment, up to and including execution. These prosperous peasants were known as "kulaks" (literally "fists"). In November 1929, Stalin announces at a party meeting that the grain requisition policy is not an emergency government measure, but simply a demand from the impoverished, who want to see an end to exploitation in the countryside. According to Stalin, the peasants are demanding faster collectivization and are eager to join the *kolkhozi*.

By the end of the year, almost 100,000 peasants across the country who resisted the grain requisitioning have been arrested. In January 1930, the Politburo votes to make the repression systemic: from February to May, it is decided to send 60,000 kulaks to forced-labor camps and evict 150,000 to remote areas.

The deportation of kulaks in Ukraine meets with huge resistance: peasant unrest breaks out in February 1930; more than a million people take part in the protests.

In response, on March 2, 1930, Stalin publishes an article in the newspaper *Pravda* titled "Dizzy with Success." In it, he claims the collectivization has been carried out with excessive zeal, leading to "excesses," and that only enemies of the party need to be purged. But the "dekulakization" continues unabated. A month later, the deputy head of the Ukrainian secret police, Karl Karlson, reports to Commissar Genrikh Yagoda in Moscow that 32,436 men, 28,480 women, and 32,054 children have been deported on schedule. And that is just the beginning.

The repression of the peasantry and the confiscation of grain from the population turn the Soviet Union into one of the largest exporters of grain on the world market. "Force the export of as much grain as possible. Otherwise, we risk being left without our new metallurgical and machine-building plants," Stalin writes to another of his henchmen, the head of the Soviet government, Vyacheslav Molotov.

Wreckers, Simulators, Agents of Poland

The construction of factories continues apace, as more and more foreign specialists arrive in the Soviet Union. But from 1929 to 1931, world wheat prices fall sharply, twice.

Stalin understands there is not enough money, and much more grain must be sold. The harvest of 1930 is very large, but all the successful farms have been destroyed and all the grain taken away. As a result, output in 1931 takes a nosedive. This means that even more must be seized, Stalin is convinced.

In the spring of 1932, the head of Soviet Ukraine, Stanislav Kosior, writes a report to Moscow that first mentions the famine. He says there are "isolated cases and even villages that are starving," but this is "a consequence of local ineptitude and excesses, especially in relation to the kolkhozes." Kosior is lying. On his desk is a letter from the head of the republican parliament, who asks that grain requisitions in Ukraine be suspended because of the nascent famine.

Lazar Kaganovich passes on the Ukrainian leaders' tentative complaints to Stalin, but the latter rejects them out of hand, calling Kosior and other Ukrainian communists "rotten opportunists." Stalin concludes, "Ukraine has received more than enough already."

In August 1932, Stalin goes on vacation to Sochi, thereby starting the tradition, continued by other Soviet leaders, of holidaying on the Black Sea. Later, Sochi will become the favorite summer residence of Putin, who even selects the city to host the 2014 Winter Olympics.

While resting, Stalin receives a report that hungry peasants are increasingly taking possession of collective farm property. He writes a letter to Moscow proposing a new, draconian measure: the so-called "law of three spikelets," which enters into force on August 4, 1932. The entire crop is now considered state property; it is sacred, and any attempt to steal it carries a sentence ranging from ten years' imprisonment to execution, plus confiscation of personal property. This means that farmers cannot make use of their own harvest, not even three spikelets—that would be regarded as theft from the state. Stalin assigns the task of implementing the law to Lazar Kaganovich, a recent former general secretary of the Communist Party of Ukraine, now the curator of the entire agrarian policy of the Soviet Union. By the end of the year, 4,500 people will be shot, and more than 100,000 sent to the Gulag.

Stalin is still vacationing in Sochi when he receives a sweeping denunciation of the leadership of the Ukrainian Communist Party. It contains a list of criticisms and protests made by Ukrainian communists about the grain requisition plan. Stalin is furious: collectivization is his brainchild, and he perceives any opposition to it as a personal insult. The head of the Soviet state has never trusted the Ukrainians anyway: he remembers the recent civil war and all subsequent peasant revolts, and believes that Ukrainians make unreliable communists. After reading the denunciation, his imagination paints the following picture: a conspiracy is being hatched in Ukraine to disrupt collectivization, split the republic from the Soviet Union, and annex it to Poland.

"The chief thing now is Ukraine. Things in Ukraine are terrible. It's terrible in the party. . . . If we do not make an effort now to improve the situation in Ukraine, we may lose Ukraine," he writes to Kaganovich. Remarkably, eighty years later, this exact same sentiment will be expressed by Putin: "We need to deal with Ukraine or we'll lose it."

In October 1932, Stalin, aware that the harvest is declining and there is nothing to sell, takes emergency measures: he sends two of his most trusted people to the Soviet Union's two main grain-growing regions to confiscate grain in the required volumes. Prime Minister Vyacheslav Molotov travels to Ukraine, and Deputy Prime Minister Lazar Kaganovich to the Kuban region. These lands, the most fertile in southern Russia, directly border Ukraine, and a large part of the population there is Ukrainian-speaking. Both of Stalin's envoys are sure that "wreckers" are to blame for all the problems and must be punished.

Arriving in Kharkiv, then the capital of Soviet Ukraine, Molotov analyzes the situation, admits that the grain requisition plan set for the republic is unfulfillable, and agrees to reduce it by 20 percent. At the same time, he establishes circuit courts that move around the villages and hand down on-the-spot sentences to those found guilty of impeding the grain requisitions. All supplies are confiscated from the Ukrainian peasantry, and not only grain, but also cows, chickens, and potatoes—the "fine" for not fulfilling the plan.

So-called "black boards" are drawn up: lists of settlements that have failed to fulfill the plan. They are banned from all trade. The Dnipropetrovsk region's performance is particularly poor, for which Molotov decides to punish it: he prohibits the sale of essential items there, including salt, matches, and kerosene. One of the leaders of Soviet Ukraine, Second Secretary Mendel Khatayevich, tries to reason with Molotov, even writing to Stalin to explain why the plan is unrealistic. Stalin reads Khatayevich's report and writes a one-word comment on it: "Interesting." Molotov, meanwhile, considers Khatayevich to be deluded and too persistent; he demotes him. Khatayevich ceases to argue.

On November 9, 1932, Stalin's wife, Nadezhda Alliluyeva, commits suicide in the Kremlin. She shoots herself in the heart, but Molotov and Kaganovich force the doctor to report the cause of death as "post-appendicitis complications." This tragedy raises Stalin's paranoia to a new level: there are traitors in the woodwork; even his own wife betrayed him by committing suicide.

Stalin's wrath falls on Ukraine, which he suspects most of all of disloyalty. The Kremlin orders a campaign of repression against the Ukrainian political and cultural elite. Politburo members Lazar Kaganovich and Pavel Postyshev arrive in Ukraine to oversee the purges. In December 1932, almost two thousand Ukrainian collective farm leaders are sent to prison. The special services uncover a "Polish-Petliura underground" in Ukraine, allegedly orchestrated by Symon Petliura, White Army officers, as well as the Polish and Romanian intelligence services. (The fact that Petliura was assassinated in Paris five years earlier is of no concern to the Chekists.) This underground movement, it is said, is the dark force responsible for sabotaging the harvest, concealing grain, and exterminating livestock and poultry.

In December 1932, the Politburo issues two decrees on the curtailment of Ukrainization, which has been labeled as the cause of all the problems in the republic. The campaign against Ukrainian cultural figures, whom Stalin accuses of nationalism and betrayal, begins with the persecution of Hrushevsky. The next victim is Mykola Skrypnyk, former head of the republic and ideologist of Ukrainization, and by this time Ukraine's education minister. Stalin's personal emissary Postyshev accuses the Old Bolshevik of "flooding the Party with Petliura pigs." Skrypnyk is removed from office. Ukrainian-language schools are closed down; books in Ukrainian are banned.

With the coming of winter, famine breaks out not only in Ukraine but in other agricultural lands of the Soviet Union too: in the Volga region, the North Caucasus, in the Urals, and Siberia. The Kremlin is fully aware of this, of course. In January 1933, Stalin prevents peasants from leaving the Ukrainian republic in search of food. Those who try are branded as "agents of Poland" seeking to penetrate the central regions of Russia to stir up rebellion on the collective farms. Of the 219,500 starving people detained, 186,600 are returned home; the rest are sent to the Gulag. Stanislav Kosior continues to head Ukraine. He does not complain to Moscow about the humanitarian catastrophe or ask for assistance, thereby avoiding punishment, because officially there are no problems. He orders that the famine be "localized" and that checks be carried out to determine if the starving are "simulating" hunger. Throughout the winter, local leaders turn to the republic's central authorities for help, for people all over Ukraine are dying of hunger. In response, Khatayevich writes to his superiors that he is not at all perturbed by the reports of starvation, since, in his opinion, the peasants themselves are to blame: they "stole bread for themselves," so those now dying are the ones "who stole the least or had their ill-gotten gains taken away."

Since February 16, 1933, the Ukrainian authorities have forbidden that starvation be recorded as a cause of death, in order to hide the scale of the disaster. Only in March does Kosior admit in a report to Moscow that there is mass famine in Ukraine, but he gives assurances that the numbers are limited to the tens of thousands, mainly in the Dnipropetrovsk and Kyiv regions. In fact, millions of Ukrainians are already swollen from hunger, eating plant roots or even resorting to cannibalism.

Stalin is fully informed of what is happening, but maintains the line that the dying have only themselves to blame: they are nationalists, kulaks, and enemies of collectivization, and therefore deserve no sympathy.

Meanwhile, all public mention of the famine in the Soviet Union is strictly forbidden, so not a single Soviet newspaper reports it. Western media also prefer to sidestep the subject. The *New York Times* even writes that the rumors of famine in the Soviet Union are not credible.

The death rate in rural Ukraine in 1933 exceeds the birthrate by four times. This year alone, about 2.9 million people die of hunger, and the total number of victims of the Holodomor (or the Great Famine) is 3.9 million, more than 12 percent of Ukraine's population. Already in 1933, the Kremlin authorizes the mass resettlement of peasants from Russia and Belarus to the deserted Ukrainian villages.

At the same time, the purges against the intelligentsia continue. Dozens of prominent Ukrainian writers and poets are arrested—an event that will go down in history as the "Executed Renaissance."

One of the brightest literary suns, Mykola Khvylovy, in the 1920s urges his contemporaries to look not to Russian but to European culture. Resisting Ukraine's transformation into a colony, he coins the slogan: "Get away from Moscow!" But in 1933, Khvylovy watches as his friends are arrested one by one. On May 13, he invites some guests round to his place and, having retreated to an adjoining room, writes a suicide note: "This is the execution of an entire Generation. . . . For what? For the fact that we were the most sincere communists? I don't understand anything. . . . It hurts terribly. Long live communism. Long live the socialist construction. Long live the Communist Party." And, with that, he kills himself.

On July 7, the former head of the republic and ideologist of Ukrainization, Mykola Skrypnyk, attends a meeting of the Ukrainian Politburo, where he is branded a "nationalist" and a "saboteur." He is ordered to sign a letter admitting his mistakes. He refuses, walks out of the room—and shoots himself in his office.

Throughout the coming year, the Soviet secret services will invent an underground organization called the "All-Ukrainian Central Bloc" and arrest practically all of Ukraine's leading cultural figures for belonging to it.

The Stalin Prize

In 1934, the capital of Ukraine is moved from Kharkiv to Kyiv. The famine finally comes to an end, and the leaders of the republic receive awards. Kosior, for example, is awarded the Order of Lenin in 1935 "for outstanding achievements in agriculture." Also in 1935, the Second Secretary of Ukraine, Postyshev, for the first time in the Soviet Union, organizes a New Year's celebration for Ukrainian children.

All the instigators of the Holodomor will soon be promoted. Kosior will move to Moscow in January 1938 and become deputy prime minister of the USSR. His replacement is Nikita Khrushchev, a forty-four-year-old official who grew up in Donetsk but does not speak Ukrainian, for which reason many local communists oppose his appointment.

The year 1937 sees the start of Stalin's Great Terror: approximately 1.5 million Soviet citizens are arrested and 700,000 are shot. The first victims are military commanders, the Red Army leaders who conquered Ukraine in 1918–20. The next to be purged are top party officials, including the recent architects of the Holodomor. Khatayevich is the first to be arrested, accused of being a member of a terrorist group. He is shot in October 1937.

More than a hundred representatives of the Ukrainian "Executed Renaissance" will be sentenced to death on November 3, 1937. They will be murdered and buried in a mass grave in a forest in northern Russia.

In 1938, Pavel Postyshev confesses to having been a Japanese spy. Shortly afterwards, Kosior is accused of belonging to the "Polish Military Organization." Both will be shot in 1939.

That same year, 1939, Boris Grekov republishes his already classic book on ancient Russian history under the title *Kyivan Rus*, and later receives the Stalin Prize for it. Each subsequent edition of Grekov's book differs slightly from the previous, mainly in its rising criticism of Hrushevsky. First, Grekov writes that Hrushevsky tried to artificially restrict *Kyivan Rus* solely to the history of Ukraine. In the next version, Grekov denounces Hrushevsky's concept as unscientific. The latest edition of Grekov's work reads like a court verdict: "Tendentiously recognizing the Old Russian state as a 'Ukrainian' state, Hrushevsky deprived himself of the opportunity to understand the history of that state correctly, according to the sources."

Also in 1939, the Soviet Union and the Third Reich sign a nonaggression pact, including secret protocols on the partition of Poland. On September 1 German troops enter Poland from the west, and on September 17 Soviet troops enter from the east. The territory of western Ukraine (Galicia), which since the 1920s has belonged to Poland, is occupied by the Soviet Union and incorporated into Soviet Ukraine.

The topic of the Holodomor does not get a mention in the press or in the history books until the 1980s. However, since the 1970s it has been extensively researched in the West. In post-Soviet Ukraine, the Holodomor becomes an essential part of the historical discourse: during Viktor Yushchenko's presidency, the memory of this tragedy is even declared to be a key component of national identity.

BALTIC
SEA

ESTONIA

LATVIA

LITHUANIA

GERMAN
REICH

• Leningrad

• Moscow

U   S   S   R

• Minsk

• Kursk

Warsaw •

P O L A N D

V O L H Y N I A

Brody •

Lviv •

• Kyiv

Kharkiv •

Vinnytsia •

U K R A I N I A N   S S R

HUNGARY

R O M A N I A

SEA
OF AZOV

CRIMEA

• Yalta

BLACK SEA

TURKEY

**UKRAINIAN SOVIET SOCIALIST REPUBLIC
DURING WORLD WAR II**

Borders before September 1, 1939

Partition of Poland by September 29, 1939

Ukrainian SSR after November 1939

Reichskommissariat Ukraine (1941–1944)

Farthest German advance, 1942

200 miles

200 km

7

THE MYTH OF BANDERA:
HOW UKRAINIANS FOUGHT
IN WORLD WAR II

Soviet James Bond

Moscow, 1975. A forty-three-year-old author is writing a detective novel. His name is Yulian Semyonov, and he is perhaps the most published writer in the entire Soviet Union. John Le Carré, Graham Greene, Ian Fleming, et al. are not published in the country, nor are the James Bond movies shown: they are all replaced by Semyonov and his beloved character: the superspy Maxim Isayev, aka Stierlitz.

Yulian Semenov was born into a Soviet elite family; his father worked as an editor for the country's most important newspaper, *Izvestia*, and retained his post even when its editor in chief, Nikolay Bukharin, was shot as an enemy of the people. Yulian was ten years old when Nazi Germany attacked the Soviet Union. Together with the entire Soviet elite, his family was evacuated to the Volga region. At the age of thirteen, in May 1945, thanks to his father's connections, he visited Berlin, recently taken by Soviet troops. In 1952, however, his father was imprisoned—but only for two years. After Stalin's death, the purges ended and political prisoners were amnestied.

During the political thaw that follows, the young journalist Semyonov reads Hemingway and dreams of emulating his fame. He also works as a war correspondent, traveling to Afghanistan, Cuba, Vietnam, Paraguay, and Chile. And he then starts writing political detective fiction.

Semyonov is a patriot who spends most of his time abroad, for which reason he idealizes his homeland. He collaborates with the KGB—in the sense that he acts as an "agent of influence." His articles and books are enormously popular with the Soviet secret services, especially the omnipotent head of the KGB, Yuri Andropov. Andropov himself suggests plot lines for Semyonov's new novels. And Andropov doesn't say no when the author asks to see the KGB archives. Semyonov greatly appreciates this level of access, denied to other writers. "Who controls the past won't lose their head in the present or go astray in the future," he is fond of saying. Semyonov romanticizes the life of KGB officers to an improbable degree: in his world, they are at once brave knights and cold-blooded intellectuals, always ready to make the ultimate sacrifice for the Motherland.

In 1969, he writes his most famous novel, *Seventeen Moments of Spring*. Part of a larger cycle, it tells of Soviet intelligence officer Maxim Isayev, who is embedded in the Third Reich leadership, where he is known as SS Standartenführer Max Otto von Stierlitz. In the spring of 1945, shortly before the end of the war, Stierlitz is informed by Moscow that the Nazis are in secret talks with the Americans, namely with Allen Dulles, the future director of the CIA, on a separate peace. Stierlitz is tasked with disrupting the negotiations, which he duly does.

The Cold War is in full swing, so Semyonov's tale about the Soviet Union's current enemies, the Americans, allegedly plotting with its recent foes, the Germans, is not at all surprising.

In 1973, the book is made into a TV series, which becomes a smash hit in the Soviet Union. During each episode, the streets are utterly empty, for everyone is glued to the TV screen, watching the exploits of the Soviet James Bond. Women are in love with him; boys and men want to be him.

One of Stierlitz's many fans is Vova, a student in Leningrad. After watching *Seventeen Moments of Spring* and devouring all of Semyonov's Stierlitz novels, he decides that he, too, will become a secret agent. After university he jumps at the opportunity to join the KGB. Vova is short for Vladimir. His surname is Putin.

Semyonov's plots are completely fictional. Although real people appear in all his novels, the foreground belongs to Stierlitz and his adventures. However, many readers will remember historical events as told by Semyonov, and this will shape their future actions.

Putin is twenty-five years old and already working at the Leningrad KGB Directorate when his favorite writer's new novel, *The Third Card*, is released. The action takes place in 1941. Stierlitz is fighting Ukrainian nationalists who are collaborating with Hitler. From this novel, Putin learns the name of Stepan Bandera.

Between Two Empires

On October 21, 1933, the nineteen-year-old Ukrainian Mykola Lemyk shows up on the doorstep of the Soviet consulate in Lviv, then part of Poland. He walks up to the desk of Secretary Andrey Maylov and shoots twice, hitting him in the heart and the head. Lemyk does not try to flee the scene of the crime. On the contrary, his objective is to be arrested by the Polish police.

In court, he will claim that the attack was carried out by the Organization of Ukrainian Nationalists (OUN) and masterminded by Stepan Bandera, its leader in western Ukraine. The purpose was to draw international attention to the Holodomor in Ukraine.

A year later, Bandera orchestrates the assassination of Poland's interior minister, who ordered a crackdown on Ukrainians in Lviv. In 1935, Bandera is arrested. At his trial, he gives a consummate performance, clearly outlining the goals of the OUN: to restore the Ukrainian state and not rely on anyone: "We know from history that when it comes to Ukraine, there has always been agreement between Poland and Moscow." Bandera is sentenced to death, but this is later commuted to life imprisonment.

On August 23, 1939, German foreign minister Joachim von Ribbentrop arrives in Moscow. As mentioned earlier, the Soviet Union and the

Third Reich sign a nonaggression pact, which includes secret protocols on the partition of Poland and the Baltic region.

On September 1, 1939, Germany invades Poland, and World War II begins. The Soviet Union does not enter the war immediately. Only on September 17 does the Soviet government send a note to Warsaw stating that, since the Polish state has collapsed, Moscow will be taking the Ukrainians and Belarusians in eastern Poland under its "protection"; in other words, the Soviet Union plans to invade and occupy the territory.

With the arrival of Soviet troops, Bandera's prison guards flee. He and the other prisoners are free, and he returns to Lviv. There the Soviet Union is already laying down its own rules, nationalizing land and enterprises.

The repression of Ukrainian nationalists gets under way. One of them is the father of the OUN leader, Andriy Bandera, a priest. He is arrested and sent to Kyiv. His son Stepan manages to escape from the Soviet-occupied territories to the German-occupied Kraków.

There he soon falls out with the pro-German head of the OUN, Andriy Melnyk, who is hoping for assistance from the Third Reich. Bandera clashes with him, arguing that the organization should be totally independent. The movement splits in two: The young nationalists who took part in the terror attacks in Galicia and Poland follow Bandera. The OUN is divided into "Melnykites" and "Banderites."

Nevertheless, Bandera himself does not refuse to work with the Germans. His wing of the OUN enters into an agreement with German military intelligence to create two Banderite sabotage battalions, one called Nachtigall (German for "nightingale"), commanded by Roman Shukhevych, and the other Roland, led by the Austrian-born Richard Yary. Bandera expects these battalions to become the backbone of the Ukrainian army.

On June 22, 1941, the German invasion of the Soviet Union finds Bandera in Kraków. The Gestapo bars him from returning to Lviv in the Soviet-occupied territories. At the same time, OUN units rise up against Soviet power in western Ukraine, capturing several dozen settlements even before the German military arrives. When the Germans do get there, the OUN units are reorganized into a people's militia, and villagers help it to track down Red Army soldiers, NKVD officers, and Jews.

The Soviets evacuate industrial plants and factories from Ukraine to the Urals, Siberia, and Central Asia, as well as around 3.5 million people. They take out what food they can, or destroy it.

On June 29, the OUN battalions take part in the capture of Lviv. Before the Red Army retreats, Moscow orders the execution of about two thousand prisoners, mostly political. When the Nachtigall and Roland battalions take the city, word spreads that the Jews helped to execute these prisoners. A Jewish pogrom breaks out in Lviv.

The next day, also in Lviv, Stepan Bandera's deputy, Yaroslav Stetsko, proclaims a Ukrainian state. The founding act declares that this is part of a future independent Ukraine with its capital at Kyiv, that the state "will closely cooperate with the National Socialist Greater Germanic Reich, which, under the leadership of Führer Adolf Hitler, is establishing a new order in Europe and the world, and helping the Ukrainian People to free themselves from Moscow's occupation."

That same Moscow is, by now, in a state of utter panic. The Germans have just taken Minsk, the capital of Belarus, and look unstoppable. On June 29, at a meeting in the Kremlin, Stalin says, "Lenin left us a great legacy, and we, his heirs, screwed it all up." The Soviet leader leaves for his dacha outside Moscow. When he fails to show up at the Kremlin the following morning, members of the Politburo, worried, go to see him.

In the words of one of them, they find Stalin huddled in a chair, terrified, expecting to be arrested. But they assure him they have come to persuade him to continue as leader. By July 3, Stalin finally recovers his senses and makes his first radio address of the war to the Soviet people.

Back in Kraków on that same day, Bandera is summoned for questioning. The German command is shocked by the Ukrainian nationalists' declaration. Bandera claims it was done on his orders, adding that the OUN has been fighting the Bolsheviks for more than a decade. He refuses to revoke the proclamation of the Ukrainian state. On July 5, he is detained by the Gestapo and sent to Berlin.

On July 10 in Kyiv, the NKVD shoots Stepan's father, Andriy Bandera.

The German command continues to pressure Stepan to revoke the proclamation. He refuses, and so, in September, the OUN is banned.

Bandera and his associates are sent to prison, and then, in January 1942, to Sachsenhausen, a kind of "elite" concentration camp for political prisoners. Stepan's brothers are dispatched to Auschwitz, where they perish soon afterwards.

It is these first weeks of the war that are described in Yulian Semyonov's novel *The Third Card*, only this time the central character is Stierlitz, Vova Putin's hero. In this fictional tale, Stepan Bandera is a sadist and a criminal, a paid agent of his Nazi puppet masters in the Abwehr, the military intelligence service of the Third Reich. "He is a pawn, an artificial creation, who utters words learned by rote, instilled in him by his handlers," the spy Stierlitz reports to Moscow. "Bandera is a man stripped of his past—it is criminal, lawless, bloody. He seems intent on fighting for his 'piece of the pie' with particular ferocity; as for demagogic slogans, they are apparently formulated here in Berlin by his immediate supervisors, whom he obeys unconditionally." The Soviet command orders its embedded secret agent to use Bandera to sow discord within the German elite. And it is Stierlitz who nudges the Ukrainians into proclaiming their own state. Hitler is livid, the Nazi leaders start feuding among themselves, and Stierlitz, having outsmarted them all, rubs his hands.

The style of *The Third Card*, written in 1975, is surprisingly similar to the propaganda of Russian television in 2022. The author proves step by step that Ukrainian nationalism was invented in the Austrian Empire: the insidious Habsburgs purposely supported Ukrainian culture in Lviv to spite Russia. All Ukrainian independence fighters are in the pocket of the Nazis, while all honest Ukrainians are ready to give their lives for the Soviet Union.

Against Everyone

In August 1941, the German command disbands the Nachtigall and Roland battalions. And Ukraine is carved in two: Galicia becomes part of the Nazi-controlled Polish General Government; the rest of the territory is named the Reichskommissariat Ukraine.

In late September, German troops approach Kyiv and surround the Red Army's Southwestern Front, tasked with defending the city. More than six hundred thousand people are forced into the "Kyiv cauldron"; some die, and some are taken as prisoners of war.

Retreating from the Ukrainian capital, the Soviets destroy bridges and mine buildings in the city center. On September 24, downtown Kyiv is rocked by explosions; the main street, Khreshchatyk, is engulfed in flames. To contain the fire, the Germans knock down buildings in neighboring streets. One side of Khreshchatyk is totally destroyed.

The sabotage is blamed on the Jewish population. On September 29, 1941, German soldiers and Ukrainian police round up the city's Jews and take them to Babyn Yar, a ravine. Over the next two days, they shoot forty-three thousand people. It is the first massacre of Jews during World War II.

In October, the Germans establish local authorities in Kyiv, betting on the Melnykites, Bandera's rivals in the OUN. They set up a National Rada, which is seen as a step too far, and by November it has been banned. Ukrainian nationalists are repressed; several are executed. At the end of 1941, Germany occupies the entire territory of Ukraine. About 3 million people are sent to forced-labor camps in Germany. In central Ukraine, not far from Vinnytsia, a bunker is built for Hitler, from where he will direct various operations in 1942–43.

In October 1942, at the height of the Battle of Stalingrad, the Banderite faction of the OUN holds an underground congress in Lviv. It discusses the situation on the front lines and concludes that a German victory, which six months ago seemed inevitable, is now in the balance. The OUN decides to create its own army and resume the struggle for an independent Ukraine. This becomes known as the Ukrainian Insurgent Army (abbreviated as UPA, after its Ukrainian name, Ukrayinska povstanska armiia).

Also fighting the Germans are partisan units on the side of the Red Army, one of which is commanded by Sydir Kovpak. Although the communist Kovpak is fighting the Germans, he is wanted by the NKVD for insubordination. Officers come to arrest him, but he takes refuge in the forest, from where he continues to fight for the Soviet cause.

After the Battle of Stalingrad, which lasted from July 1942 to February 1943, the Red Army goes on the counteroffensive. At the same time, over in western Ukraine, the Ukrainian nationalists decide to intensify their own war. Some Ukrainians, meanwhile, agree to fight for the Third

Reich against the Soviets. In the spring of 1943, the Germans create the Fourteenth SS Volunteer-Division Galicia, consisting entirely of Ukrainians.

In April 1943, the OUN acquires a new leader, Roman Shukhevych. He holds a congress of the OUN, at which participants declare their struggle to be against empires, against the exploitation of one nation by another. They are equally opposed to communism and Nazism.

On top of all this, the UPA, created by the OUN, takes the fight to the Poles as well, who form an ethnic minority in Volhynia, part of western Ukraine.

The calculation is this: to ensure this territory stays out of Polish hands after the war, the Polish population must be eliminated. In July 1943, the UPA slaughters Poles en masse, which will go down in history as the "Volyn Massacre." Ukrainian historians, however, insist these events should be perceived as part of the hostilities: Poles killed Ukrainians just as Ukrainians killed Poles. And the UPA murders Ukrainians from other factions too, be they Melnykite nationalists or Kovpak partisans.

After the titanic Battle of Kursk, which lasts from July 5 to August 23, 1943, the Soviets gradually push the Germans out of Ukraine, taking Kyiv in November 1943.

In April 1944, the commander of the First Ukrainian Front of the Soviet Army, General Nikolay Vatutin, is ambushed by the UPA. Badly wounded, he dies soon after. He is buried in central Kyiv's Mariinskyi Park. The NKVD unrolls a major operation to destroy those responsible for the general's death.

In May 1944, Crimea is liberated from German occupation, whereupon 165,000 Crimean Tatars and 35,000 people of other ethnicity are immediately deported from the peninsula, accused by Stalin of "collaborationism."

Then, in July 1944, the Red Army takes Lviv. But that does not put an end to the fighting in Ukraine: the UPA still needs to be dealt with. In August–September, around 11,000 Ukrainian nationalists are killed and the same number taken prisoner.

In July 1944, near the city of Brody in western Ukraine, Soviet troops encircle eight German divisions, including 10,000 soldiers of the SS Galicia unit. About 3,000 of the "Galicians" manage to escape captivity and join the UPA.

In September 1944, the German authorities change tack and decide to unite all forces that are anti-Soviet. Bandera is transported from the Sachsenhausen concentration camp to Berlin. There he is invited to collaborate with Russian general Andrey Vlasov, who has defected to the Nazis. But he declines. According to the report of the interrogating SS officer, Bandera "hates both Great Russians and Germans in equal measure."

In February 1945, the words "Bandera" and "Banderite" appear for the first time in *Pravda*, the main newspaper of the Soviet Union, in an open letter from the Congress of Teachers in western Ukraine to Stalin. The authors of the text curse "the Ukrainian-German nationalists, the Judases, the not-yet-killed Banderites and 'OUNites.'"

That same month, Stalin, Roosevelt, and Churchill meet in Crimea to discuss the post-war world order, where they agree to create the United Nations. On Stalin's initiative, the Soviet Union is given three seats in the organization, representing the Russian, Ukrainian, and Belarusian republics, which suffered the brunt of the war. The Yalta Conference forms the basis of the entire system of the post-war world order, later becoming Putin's idée fixe. Throughout his rule, he will dream of holding a new Yalta, one that would confirm his standing as a respected global player. This will never happen, which spurs his military adventures.

In February 1945, Bandera relocates from Berlin to Austria under forged documents, while in western Ukraine the commander of the UPA meets with representatives of the Soviet KGB in an attempt to negotiate a truce. The talks are unsuccessful.

When the war in Europe finally ends in May 1945, UPA commander Roman Shukhevych calls on the Ukrainians to continue the armed struggle against the Soviet Union. For their part, on May 9, 1945, Victory Day for the Soviet Union, the Soviet authorities call on the UPA fighters to lay down their arms and turn themselves in by July 20. As a result, ten thousand of them surrender during 1945.

Regular clashes with the UPA continue in western Ukraine throughout 1946, before waning and finally ending only in 1949. All this time, the key method deployed by the Soviet authorities against Ukrainian nationalism is deportation of all potential supporters to Siberia. In February 1946, at a session of the UN General Assembly in London, the Soviet

Union demands the extradition of all suspected Ukrainian nationalists hiding in Europe. The West refuses, so the KGB launches a worldwide hunt for all OUN leaders.

In 1947, Bandera is again elected leader of the OUN and reaffirms his former principle of relying only on one's own forces, not on other countries. The attempts on Bandera's life by Soviet agents begin in 1948.

Only in September 1949 does UPA commander Roman Shukhevych give the order to disband the organization's last combat units and head-quarters: the fighters are instructed to move to the West or go underground. On March 5, 1950, Shukhevych is killed in the Lviv region during an attempted arrest.

Stepan Bandera survives until March 15, 1959, when he is assassinated by an NKVD agent in Munich.

Bandera will become a household name in the Soviet Union. Supporters of Ukrainian independence were known before World War I as "Mazeparites" (after Ivan Mazepa) and between the world wars as "Petliurites" (after Symon Petliura). As of 1945, Ukrainian nationalists in the Soviet Union are called Banderites. This psychological ploy is to disassociate Ukraine from Bandera. Banderites support Bandera, not Ukraine, as the propagandists would say. From the late 1940s, Banderites are regularly mentioned in Soviet newspapers in the same breath as the Nazis. They rarely mention Bandera himself, however. Neither does the Soviet press ever mention the Molotov-Ribbentrop Pact. Or that Bandera was, in fact, an ally of the Nazis at the very same time as Stalin. But to fans of Yulian Semyonov, such as Vova Putin, everything is crystal clear.

Seventeen Moments of Spring and its hero Stierlitz will become immortalized in the Soviet Union. Even after the country's collapse, they remain phenomenally popular. In 1998, when Boris Yeltsin is still president of Russia, the influential weekly magazine *Kommersant-Vlast* polls the Russian public to find out which movie character they would most like to see as president. Stierlitz wins by a country mile. At that moment, the name of Vladimir Putin is still unknown.

PART II

SEVEN TALES OF PRESENT-DAY
OPPRESSION IN UKRAINE

ESTONIAN
SSR

BALTIC
SEA

LATVIAN SSR

LITHUANIAN
SSR

RUSSIAN SFSR

Moscow

R U S S I A N

S F S R

BELORUSSIAN SSR

POLAND

U   S   S   R

Chernobyl

Kyiv

Kharkiv

Lviv

U K R A I N I A N   S S R

Dnipropetrovsk

Donetsk

Kryvyi Rih

Zaporizhzhia

MOLDAVIAN
SSR

Odesa

ROMANIA

SEA
OF AZOV

BLACK SEA

BULGARIA

UKRAINE IN THE LATE
SOVIET PERIOD

TURKEY

200 miles
200 km

8

UNITY AGAIN:
HOW SOVIET UKRAINE
SEARCHED FOR ITSELF

Bohdan Khmelnytsky Park

On January 25, 1978, in the Ukrainian city of Kryvyi Rih in the Dnipro-petrovsk (today Dnipro) region, the protagonist of this book, Volodymyr Zelensky, is born into a typical Soviet family. Mom, dad, and friends will all call him by the abbreviated name Vova. Like the other Vladimirs, including Vladimir Lenin and Vladimir Putin, he was named after Vladimir (Volodymyr) the Great, the baptizer of Rus and the central figure in Synopsis.

Vova and his parents do not speak Ukrainian. They are Jews, not ethnic Ukrainians, and in any case Dnipropetrovsk is a Russian-speaking region. In the 1970s, Russian is far and away the dominant language.

Ukraine at this moment is part of the Soviet Union. Volodymyr Shcherbytsky, little Vova's namesake and countryman, is in charge of the Ukrainian Soviet Socialist Republic (SSR); he, too, was born in the Dni-propetrovsk region.

Shcherbytsky speaks Surzhik, a mixture of Russian and Ukrainian. But his working language is Russian, in which he was educated and made a career. If Shcherbytsky needs to say anything in Ukrainian, he reads a speech from a sheet of paper. The texts are prepared for him by one of his deputies, Leonid Kravchuk. Kravchuk recalls how one day Shcherbytsky returned from an official event in a sour mood: "If you ever try to get me to speak in Ukrainian again, it will be our last conversation." Shcherbytsky has a solid reputation for his pro-Russia stance and opposition to "Ukrainian nationalism." For example, Ukrainian language teachers in schools are paid 15 percent less than their Russian counterparts.

Volodymyr Shcherbytsky is not just First Secretary of the Ukrainian Communist Party; he is also a close friend of then Soviet leader Leonid Brezhnev. Inside the Soviet political elite, many have Ukrainian roots. Some even say that the Soviet Union is run by the "Ukrainian clan"—not all of whom speak Ukrainian.

Former Soviet leader Nikita Khrushchev also had Ukrainian ties, having grown up and studied in Donetsk. For more than ten years, from 1938 to 1949, he led Ukraine as First Secretary of the Ukrainian Communist Party and chairman of the Council of Ministers of the Soviet Union. It was Khrushchev, as head of Ukraine, who helped Brezhnev up the career ladder, appointing him in the post-war years as First Secretary in Zaporizhzhia, then in Dnipropetrovsk, both in southeastern Ukraine. When Brezhnev took the reins of the Soviet Union in 1964, his "Dnipropetrovsk clan" became the most powerful group in the Kremlin. The Soviet Union was run by the Politburo, a sort of board of directors of the Communist Party. A third of the members of Brezhnev's Politburo hailed from Ukraine, and Shcherbytsky was among the most influential. Many in the Politburo believed that Brezhnev was grooming Shcherbytsky as his successor.

There are many strange historical myths in the Soviet Union, some of which are dressed up as national celebrations. In 1979, for instance, when Vova Zelensky turns one year old, Shcherbytsky organizes a massive celebration to mark the 325th anniversary of the reunion with Russia. When he was a child, Vova's parents often took him to Bohdan Khmelnytsky Park, one of the main sights in Kryvyi Rih.

Ukraine's "reunification" with Russia is one of the ideological pillars of Soviet history. The official myth goes as follows: in 1654, the then leader of Ukraine, Bohdan Khmelnytsky, placed his land under Russian control by concluding the Treaty of Pereyaslav, which allied the Cossack Hetmanate with the Tsardom of Russia. In Soviet times, this event was propagandized. In 1943, for example, in the midst of the Second World War, the Soviet army introduced the Order of Bohdan Khmelnytsky, awarded to soldiers and commanders who distinguished themselves during the liberation of Ukraine. And in 1954, the three hundredth anniversary of the "reunification" was celebrated with pomp, culminating in Nikita Khrushchev transferring Crimea from Russia to Ukraine as a gesture of goodwill. It was on this occasion, too, that Bohdan Khmelnytsky Park opened in Kryvyi Rih.

In 1982, the four-year-old Vova and his parents move to Mongolia, where his father becomes head of IT at the new metallurgical plant.

By this time, the Soviet Union is already struggling to maintain its colossal empire, not helped by the war in Afghanistan, which began in 1980. The Soviet standard of living is very low, especially in comparison with Europe and the United States. Almost all goods made in the Soviet Union—cars, machinery, clothes, food, cigarettes, et cetera—are of extremely poor quality. The country is even forced to import grain. Yet Soviet citizens do not feel that the empire is at a breaking point.

"Do We Really Deserve Pariah Status?"

On September 29, 1979, a trial gets under way in Kyiv. It is held behind closed doors; even the family of the defendant is not allowed into the courtroom. No wonder, for the case is political.

The accused, the Ukrainian poet and dissident Vasyl Stus, born in Donetsk oblast, is charged with distributing "hostile literature denigrating the Soviet state and social system." It is not the first trial of Stus. Back in 1972, he was sentenced to five years in a prison camp for anti-Soviet propaganda. That was the first year of Volodymyr Shcherbytsky's rule in Ukraine, which also marked the apogee of the persecution of the Ukrainian intelligentsia. The repressive campaign in Ukraine laid the groundwork for a nationwide sweep. Also in 1972, the Leningrad poet Joseph

Brodsky was expelled from the Soviet Union and stripped of his citizenship. And in 1974, the writer Alexander Solzhenitsyn, Nobel laureate in literature, author of *The Gulag Archipelago* and documenter in chief of the Stalinist camps, was sent into exile.

While in prison, Stus writes an open letter in which he demands to be stripped of Soviet citizenship: "Soviet citizenship for me is impossible. To be a Soviet citizen means to be a slave," he says. "I have fought for democratization, and this is condemned as an attempt to defame the Soviet order; my love for my native people, my concern about the crisis of Ukrainian culture, was interpreted as nationalism." But the authorities do not react: unlike with Solzhenitsyn or Brodsky, they ignore Stus.

The Soviet Union has two faces: one official, one underground. There is the Communist Party, propaganda, mass holidays celebrated by citizens who pretend to believe in communism and a brighter future, while in reality they chase after scarce items of food or imported clothes and dream of living "like in the West." And there are the "internal exiles"—those who try not to pay attention to the communist ideology or to have anything to do with the state. The most radical among them are the dissidents who, like the early Christian martyrs, are ready to be burned at the stake rather than betray their values, knowing that their struggle is doomed. Vasyl Stus is one of them.

Russian dissidents fight for human rights in general, while Ukrainian ones also stand up for the right to speak their native language. As a consequence, Russian dissidents are usually accused of "selling out to the West," while their Ukrainian counterparts get branded as "bourgeois nationalists" and "Banderites"—such are the clichés of the Soviet KGB.

From prison, Stus writes a letter to the most famous Soviet dissident of all, the physicist and human rights advocate Andrey Sakharov. Stus complains at length about the treatment he has faced from both the KGB and Moscow dissidents, who have little sympathy for the national struggle of Ukrainians: "Do we really deserve pariah status?" asks Stus.

After his first stint behind bars, the poet is released for eight months. Then, in May 1980, he is rearrested: all active dissidents nationwide are imprisoned ahead of the Olympic Games in Moscow.

Before his second trial, the poet refuses a state-appointed lawyer: "Official lawyers in the USSR act like a second prosecutor. I do not need a second prosecutor," he declares in writing. Nevertheless, a young public defender named Viktor Medvedchuk attends the proceedings as Stus's counsel.

At the very first hearing, the defendant demands that the entire court be disqualified, stating that a fair trial in the Soviet Union is impossible by definition. He pleads not guilty and insists that the Soviet and foreign press be present, as well as a foreign lawyer provided by PEN International, a worldwide association of writers that fights for freedom of expression. The prosecutor asks to reject the motion. Medvedchuk agrees with the prosecutor: "I defer to the discretion of the court"—a phrase the lawyer will repeat many times during the trial.

During the proceedings, Medvedchuk cross-examines hardly any witnesses. In his brief concluding statement, he declares that he "considers the classification of [Stus's] actions to be correct."

Stus intends to use his own last plea to demand that the KGB be put on trial as a "terrorist organization." But this opportunity is denied, and the sentence is passed in his absence: ten years in prison and five in exile.

Ten days later, Sakharov, who is in exile in the city of Gorky (now Nizhny Novgorod), writes an open letter in defense of Stus: "The year 1980 was marked in our country by many unjust prosecutions and hounding of human rights activists. But even against this tragic backdrop, the sentence against Ukrainian poet Vasyl Stus stands out for its inhumanity. A human life is completely shattered as retribution for basic decency, for nonconformity, for loyalty to one's convictions, one's self. The verdict against Stus brings shame upon the repressive Soviet system."

Having led the Soviet Union for eighteen years, Brezhnev gives up the ghost in 1982. Over the next three years, a string of elderly successors are buried one after the other. In 1985, everyone expects the Politburo to elect a new, this time younger leader. One of the favorites for the post is the head of Ukraine and persecutor of dissidents Volodymyr Shcherbytsky. In March 1985, he flies to the United States, where he is received at the White House by President Ronald Reagan. This is the first meeting in a long time between an American leader and a top Soviet official: relations between the countries are at rock bottom.

Shcherbytsky behaves like the future lord of the Kremlin. After meetings in New York, he goes to San Francisco, where he receives an urgent message: General Secretary Konstantin Chernenko has died in Moscow; the Politburo is in the process of choosing a successor. Stuck on the other side of the world, Shcherbytsky rushes home, but he is too late. While he is airborne, his main rival, Mikhail Gorbachev, is elected. The party elite decides that the young, inexperienced Gorbachev is a good compromise candidate; he will be easy to manage, unlike the seasoned Shcherbytsky.

In early 1985, the German writer Heinrich Böll nominates Vasyl Stus for the Nobel Prize in Literature, and a campaign in support of Stus begins in the West. But in August 1985, the poet is placed in solitary confinement, where he goes on a hunger strike. On September 4, 1985, Vasyl Stus passes away.

The Nobel Prize is not awarded posthumously. But two years later it is presented to another enemy of the Soviet state, US citizen Joseph Brodsky.

In the same facility where Stus died, there is another Ukrainian dissident, Stepan Khmara. He recalls that in 1986, after the election of Gorbachev, the prison regime becomes markedly stricter. Apparently, the local authorities feel a sense of impunity: Moscow has other things to worry about. The change is so sharp that in June inmates go on strike, refusing to do the manual tasks assigned to them. "Of course, they threw us all into the isolation facility. There weren't enough cells for everyone; some were sent to other units. We didn't receive any letters from home for six months. And our letters didn't get sent. There were no visits either," says Khmara.

This continues until October 1986, when Gorbachev meets with Reagan in Reykjavik, the capital of Iceland. The American president unexpectedly raises the topic of human rights and demands the release of Soviet political prisoners. Gorbachev, taken aback, replies that there aren't any in the Soviet Union. Then Reagan hands him a list that Sakharov managed to have smuggled abroad.

In November, Sakharov is allowed to return from internal exile in Gorky to Moscow. That is followed on February 15, 1987, by the release of Khmara and the remaining dissidents. Vasyl Stus missed out by just eighteen months.

Environmentally Unfriendly

In 1985, Vova Zelensky and his mother return home to Kryvyi Rih: life near the metallurgical plant in the harsh Mongolian climate is very hard; the child often falls sick. Dad stays behind in Mongolia to work. Back in Ukraine, however, life is no day at the beach either. Kryvyi Rih is home to the Krivorozhstal factory, the largest steelworks in the country.

April 26, 1986, is a dark day in history: reactor No. 4 at the Chernobyl nuclear power plant near Kyiv explodes. Soviet media report next to nothing, issuing only short official bulletins that everything is under control. Meanwhile, Western media talk of thousands of fatalities, which only infuriates the Soviet Politburo (according to the official version, only two people were killed in the explosion itself and twenty-eight more within three months). The Kremlin believes this is a premediated campaign by Western intelligence agencies to discredit the Soviet Union. So, as usual, it denies everything.

A public parade is scheduled for May 1 in Kyiv—one of the main Soviet holidays, the day of workers' solidarity. Thousands of people are due to proceed along the city's central thoroughfare, Khreshchatyk street, where Ukraine's leaders will acknowledge them from the podium. On the eve of May 1, these same leaders are nervously discussing what to do. Should they evacuate the population to save them from the fallout, or is it not worth upsetting Moscow?

Shcherbytsky is a typical Brezhnevite leader: he is used to anticipating the directives of his superiors and acting accordingly. So he issues a two-part instruction: go ahead with the parade, but with half the number of participants. At the same time, he orders the heads of Kyiv and Ukraine to attend the festivities with their families, including children and grandchildren. (They are already in a state of panic, desperate to get their loved ones out of Kyiv.)

A rumor surfaced decades later that Shcherbytsky had, in fact, fought tooth and nail to get the event canceled, but Gorbachev had allegedly told him, "I'll see you rot if you don't hold it!" and threatened him with expulsion from the party. But this version of events is not entirely convincing: in the days before the parade, Shcherbytsky effectively behaves like a cheerleader. "No one in Kyiv asked Moscow whether it was possible to cancel the May Day procession," claims then Soviet prime minister Nikolay Ryzhkov.

Shcherbytsky is a shrewd Soviet leader, having learned over decades in the vipers' nest that he will indeed "rot" if he disappoints Moscow. Therefore, this rumor of him taking a stand is likely a figment of his imagination. Although Gorbachev knew, of course, about the forthcoming parade on Khreshchatyk street, it is hard to imagine that he would threaten reprisals against the party old-timer Shcherbytsky.

Despite the radiation and the obvious health threat to the public, the parade in Kyiv goes ahead—this shocks Ukrainian society even more than the actual explosion. The leadership's lies are the last straw: millions of Ukrainians realize that officialdom at all levels doesn't care a jot about them.

Gorbachev, too, is shocked by Chernobyl and the cover-up that kept even him in the dark. Tellingly, Vitaly Korotich, one of the few Ukrainian journalists who dared to tell the truth about Chernobyl, is promoted at Gorbachev's behest and appointed editor in chief in Moscow of the country's most popular weekly magazine, *Ogonyok* (Little flame).

The party elite is mistaken about Gorbachev: he is not soft and pliable at all, but ambitious and focused on change. He gradually dismisses the entire old guard that brought him to power. Shcherbytsky is the last veteran to be pensioned off by Gorbachev, in September 1989, six weeks before the fall of the Berlin Wall.

Just four months later, Shcherbytsky dies suddenly. The official cause of death is pneumonia, but soon the rumor spreads that he committed suicide, knowing that the new-look Ukrainian parliament planned to launch its own inquiry into what happened at Chernobyl. This is not confirmed by any of the then members of parliament, and no independent investigation commission had been set up at the time of Shcherbytsky's death.

Chernobyl marks a turning point for Ukrainian civil society. It spurs the creation of mass environmental movements, which gradually morph into political ones. Even thirty years from now, the area around Chernobyl will look like a piece of the Soviet Union frozen in time. In 2021, I will get there and be able to study the site, isolated from the rest of the world, in detail. And already in February 2022 there will be Russian troops advancing toward Kyiv through the Chernobyl zone.

Accidental Perestroika

In the summer of 1989, miners' strikes break out across the Soviet Union. The protest movement has many centers, but the most active are the regions of Vorkuta and Kuzbass in Russia, Donbas in Ukraine, and Karaganda in Kazakhstan. Everywhere the strikers voice economic, as well as some political, demands. The miners of Donbas, for example, want Shcherbitsky's resignation and then separation from the Soviet Union. Gorbachev is happy to meet the miners halfway, because he too wants to get rid of the leaders of the older generation. He duly pensions off the head of Ukraine.

In September 1989, a few days before Shcherbytsky's removal from office, the first Ukrainian movement for independence, Narodnyi Rukh (People's Movement), is created in Kyiv. Its founders are Ukraine's most famous writers, among them several dissidents recently released from prison. True, they are still wary of stating their goals too loudly, for which reason the full name of the organization is Narodnyi Rukh Ukrainy za Perebudovu (People's Movement of Ukraine for Restructuring). To avoid being banned immediately, they pretend to be supporters of Gorbachev.

November 1989 sees the first major protest demonstration in Kyiv: the authorities allow Narodnyi Rukh activists to rebury the body of Vasyl Stus and two other dissidents who died in the Soviet camps. The three coffins are carried around the city, followed by thousands of people with the still banned yellow-and-blue flag of Ukraine. Arriving at the building of the KGB of Ukraine, they start chanting: "Shame! Shame!" Then the coffins are carried to Baikove Cemetery, where the nation's most distinguished lie undisturbed.

Having dismissed Shcherbytsky, Gorbachev appoints in his place Volodymyr Ivashko, former First Secretary of the Dnipropetrovsk region. Like Gorbachev, he is a man of the new generation, understands that Moscow welcomes democratization at the local level, and does not hinder the process. As early as 1990, elections to local parliaments are held in all the republics of the Soviet Union. All across Ukraine, opposition candidates claim victory; many of them are members of Rukh. And in the western regions, not a single communist wins a seat.

The elections in Lviv, for example, are won by Ihor (in Russian, Igor) Yukhnovsky, a physicist and member of the Soviet Academy of Sciences, who, back in 1988, stated at a press conference that the Soviet Union would soon collapse: he is said to have studied all of Lenin's calculations from a scientific point of view and found them to be incorrect and the Soviet Union to be unworkable. It provoked a minor scandal, but Yukhnovsky was not punished—times had changed.

According to the election results, the Communist Party still retains an absolute majority in the parliament of Soviet Ukraine. Ivashko is elected chairman. But he makes an unexpected move by inviting Yukhnovsky to head the parliamentary opposition, saying that he is ready to give the opposition control over a third of the committees in the new Supreme Soviet (or Verkhovna Rada in Ukrainian).

In the summer of 1990, Gorbachev holds the 28th (and last) Congress of the Communist Party of the Soviet Union in Moscow. He understands that his reforms have provoked a great deal of criticism, primarily among communists. To strengthen his own position, Gorbachev decides to introduce the post of Deputy General Secretary, whose job will be to lead the party, while Gorbachev leads the country.

He offers the post to Ivashko, since he needs the leader of the "Ukrainian clan" on his side. Such promotions are rarely declined in the Soviet Union, but Ivashko has no opportunity even to consider it.

While Ivashko is at the Communist Party Congress in Moscow, a huge scandal flares up in Kyiv. The oppositionists in parliament, having learned that the chairman and a group of communists have gone to Moscow to attend the congress without informing anyone, are seething—the delegates should have requested leave from their fellow parliamentarians, they believe. The opposition demands that they be ordered back to Kyiv.

The situation is so febrile that the communist majority votes in favor of this proposal. As a result, most of the Rada members taking part in the congress decide to return.

Meanwhile, Ivashko, knowing about his upcoming election as deputy general secretary, himself resigns from the post of chairman of the Rada. At the same time, he summons two of his subordinates and assigns them various positions in the party: one of them, Second Secretary Stanislav Hurenko, is to become the party's new First Secretary; the other, Secretary for Ideology Leonid Kravchuk, will head the Rada.

According to Kravchuk, he and Hurenko try to dissuade their boss from going to Moscow. But Ivashko is firm: "I have already given my consent to Mikhail Sergeyevich [Gorbachev]. The parliamentarians can only criticize and name-call," Kravchuk recalls Ivashko's words.

Ivashko has no inkling that the times are changing, that the parliament is becoming a key body of power, and that no one needs the Communist Party anymore—and not only in Ukraine but in all the other Soviet republics too. He believes that as deputy general secretary he will be the second most important person in the country. Little does he know that the Communist Party of the Soviet Union has only one year left to live. As such, the party functionary Leonid Kravchuk, until yesterday completely unknown, becomes the de facto leader of Ukraine.

I met with Ihor Yukhnovsky in Lviv in the summer of 2021. Even thirty years later, he regretted that his then opponent Ivashko had not become the first president of Ukraine. He, says Yukhnovsky, was a more competent leader.

Kravchuk is a little different from any other party leader in Ukraine. Until the age of five, he was a citizen of Poland. When in 1939 Joseph

Stalin and Adolf Hitler signed a nonaggression pact and carved up Poland, the lion's share went to Germany, while the eastern lands went to the Soviet Union. Thus, Wołyń Voivodeship, the region where the five-year-old Leonid Kravchuk lived, became part of the Ukrainian SSR.

It does not take long for Kravchuk to pursue his own policy without regard to Moscow. He takes his cue from the mood on the street.

On the one hand, he is duty bound to fight against anti-Soviet and "bourgeois nationalists"—he even takes part in public debates with Rukh activists. On the other, he has no desire to quarrel with the "Rukhovites," who are gaining popularity. At one event, for instance, he is invited to pin a badge with the trident, then the symbol of Ukrainian nationalists, on his jacket lapel. He takes it and pins it next to the red flag badge he wears as a member of the Supreme Soviet of the Ukrainian SSR. He then goes to his chair, sits down, takes off his jacket, and hangs it on the back. That's it. Not a single compromising photo will appear; no need to justify himself to his superiors.

Many years later, Kravchuk will joke about himself that he never takes an umbrella with him, because he knows how to run between the raindrops.

The Russian Union

Many Soviet human rights activists, such as Andrey Sakharov, have tremendous sympathy for Ukrainian dissidents—they uphold the same values and fight the same enemies. However, as noted by Stus, Russian dissidents at times appear prejudiced. Among the protest movement in the Soviet Union, there is a separate imperial-religious current. Its spiritual leader is the writer and Nobel laureate Alexander Solzhenitsyn, who was stripped of his Soviet citizenship and forced to emigrate.

As the first to write about the Gulag, Solzhenitsyn became a literary star. His exposés of slave labor in the Stalinist camps brought him first fame in the Soviet Union, then trouble. However, after moving to the West, where he settled in the US state of Vermont, Solzhenitsyn became a fierce critic of the West for supposedly being soulless and anti-Russian. Back then, most other Soviet liberals viewed Solzhenitsyn as some kind of imperialist apostate.

In August 1990, Solzhenitsyn writes a long essay (titled "Rebuilding Russia" in English) addressed to the protest-hit Soviet Union. The text is a sensation; everyone is talking about it. The first premise of the article is that the Soviet Union will collapse anyway, so why resist it?

"We have no strength for the Empire!—and no need, let's be rid of it!" writes Solzhenitsyn. "Now we face a hard choice: between the Empire . . . and the spiritual and bodily salvation of our own people." He goes on to describe in detail what he means by "our own people": Russia, Ukraine, Belarus, and Kazakhstan. These four Soviet republics form a single whole and must be preserved under the name Rus or the Russian Union. All the other eleven republics of the Soviet Union can be jettisoned.

Solzhenitsyn's reflections that Russians and Ukrainians are one and the same still resonate today:

> *I myself am almost half-Ukrainian, and in my early years I grew up to the sound of Ukrainian speech. . . . It is a recently concocted false-hood that ever since the 9th century there has been a separate people with its own separate non-Russian language. We are all descended from precious Kiev,* "whence the Russian land came to be," according to the annals of Nestor, whence the light of Christianity shone upon us. The same princes ruled over us. [. . .] The people of Kievan Rus also created the Muscovite state. In Lithuania and Poland, Belarusians and Little Russians [Ukrainians] recognized themselves as Russians and fought against Polonization and Catholicism. The return of these lands to Russia was understood by everyone back then as Reunification.*
>
> *Today, to sever Ukraine means cutting through millions of families*

---

*   Kyiv is the correct Ukrainian spelling; Kiev is the Russian version. Nestor the Chronicler was the reputed author of the *Russian Primary Chronicle*, the oldest preserved East Slavic historical document.

and people: what a mix of population; entire regions with a Russian majority; so many people who struggle to choose their nationality from two; so many of mixed origin; so many mixed marriages. Yet no one has ever considered them "mixed." Among the general population, there is not a hint of intolerance between Ukrainians and Russians. Brothers! No need for this cruel division! It is the obscuration of the communist years. We have endured the Soviet era together, we fell into this pit together, and together we shall climb out.

Of course, if the Ukrainian people genuinely wish to secede, no one will dare to hold them by force. But this vastness is diverse, and only the local population can decide the fate of its locality, its region.

The text makes a strong impression on one Boris Yeltsin, then head of the Supreme Soviet of the Russian Federation and the most powerful opposition politician in the Soviet Union, Mikhail Gorbachev's most dangerous opponent. According to the memoirs of Galina Starovoytova, Yeltsin's adviser on national issues, her boss is gripped by the thought of bringing Solzhenitsyn's idea to life. So Yeltsin begins to test the water in conversations with the leaders of Ukraine, Belarus, and Kazakhstan—is the appetite there to create a new union of four republics? They are dumbfounded. In 1990, no one is yet ready to leave the Soviet Union, with or without Yeltsin.

First Elections

In the summer of 1990, another revolutionary event takes place in the Soviet Union: the death of the head of the Russian Orthodox Church (ROC), Patriarch Pimen. A successor must now be elected.

For a long time, religion in the Soviet Union was officially banned, replaced by Soviet ideology, which held that God does not exist. Universities taught "scientific atheism." In the 1920s and '30s, priests were executed en masse. In subsequent years, they were gradually allowed to conduct services, but only under the strict supervision of the KGB. Almost all of the top hierarchs of the Church collaborated with the authorities in one way or another, and some were even permanent agents. And it was usual practice for the patriarch to be chosen by the head of the Soviet secret service. Another force that seeks to control the Church is the Communist Party. In the Soviet Union, oddly enough, the party apparatus and the KGB cooperate and constantly fight for influence both at the same time.

But now times have changed. Soviet leader Mikhail Gorbachev talks of democracy and wants the new head of the Church to be elected according to proper procedure, that is, by a vote in the Local Council, a large congress of Orthodox clergy from around the world. The KGB is horrified at the prospect of losing influence over such a powerful organization as the ROC. So it starts playing its own game.

This effort, it should be noted, is not initiated by the KGB leadership. The shadowy organization itself is in crisis at this moment; its chairman, Vladimir Kryuchkov, is aghast to think it might surrender control over the situation in the country. He and other KGB heads, therefore, have no time for Church matters. It is mid-ranking officials who organize the election of the patriarch—at their own peril and according to their own ideas about what's best for the empire and their organization.

Immediately after Pimen's death, the Holy Synod (a kind of Church Politburo) convenes. Most of its members are KGB agents, so it is under state control.

The Synod's choice as the locum tenens, or placeholder, on the patriarchal throne is Metropolitan Archbishop (or just Metropolitan) Filaret Denysenko, who is hand in glove with both the authorities and the party. He is a Kremlin favorite. Now it is up to the Local Council to seal the deal.

The process is very similar to approving the appointment of the General Secretary of the Soviet Union. When a leader dies, the Politburo sets up a funeral commission and elects its head, who is also a kind of placeholder on the throne, after which the party's Central Committee obediently confirms the chosen one as General Secretary. The KGB initially assumes that Filaret is home and dry. But it soon realizes that the huge Local Council is unwieldy. The party elite and the KGB leadership are self-absorbed. Aware of this, the Church hierarchs understand that, for the first time in their lives, they can vote as they please. Besides, among the Synod members are several foreigners, whom the KGB can manipulate even less.

On June 7, 1990, opening the Local Council, Metropolitan Filaret delivers a speech about the importance of maintaining the unity of the Church. To avoid an unnecessary split, he proposes not to elect a new patriarch by secret ballot, but to cast lots, as happened in 1917 after the February Revolution. He hopes that the KGB will help arrange the lot so that he is the winner. However, the clergy are opposed, and insist on a vote. There are three in the running. Alongside the placeholder, Metropolitan Filaret Denysenko of Kyiv, there is another Ukrainian, Metropolitan Volodymyr Sabodan of Rostov, and Metropolitan Alexy Ridiger of Leningrad. The latter is the most non-Soviet candidate, born in Estonia even before his country was annexed to the Soviet Union following the pact between Stalin and Hitler in 1939. He is a living symbol of the Church's desire to break free of the KGB and the party. The government-backed candidate, Filaret, is eliminated in the first round, Alexy wins in the second.

This represents a crucial moment in the history of the ROC—it gains independence from the KGB, albeit short-lived.

The First Maidan

On October 2, 1990, around a hundred students, mostly from Kyiv and Lviv universities, assemble on the main square in central Kyiv, which does not yet bear the name *Maidan* Nezalezhnosti (Independence Square) but is called October Revolution Square. They sit right there on the granite slabs. The student leader from Kyiv, Oles Doniy, expects all the protesters to be arrested straightaway, after which, according to the plan, another group will gather on the second day, and another on the third, and so on, until Kyiv's detention facilities are overflowing and other students have joined in—then together they will stage a nationwide protest.

Around the square are many more police officers and police buses than students. The protesters come armed with tents, which they plan to set up right on the square, but the police tell them: "Just you try. As soon as the first tent goes up, we'll take you away." All the same, the police are waiting for something: they could round up the students immediately, but they don't.

The fact is that at the very same time a meeting is under way of the City Council, the newly elected parliament in Kyiv, in which democratic forces have a majority of exactly one seat. And the City Council suddenly declares that protests on the three main squares of Kyiv, including October Revolution Square, are allowed without prior approval. So, by the evening, the student rally is perfectly legal. Then, at 8:00 p.m. on the dot, in literally two minutes, the students set up camp and announce a hunger strike.

The action is the brainchild of Doniy, then a fifth-year student in the history department of Kyiv University. He says that he grew up in an exclusively Russian-speaking family and could not speak Ukrainian: "My self-identification as a Ukrainian and willingness to fight for independence did not come from political nationalism, but from the family cult of justice." As early as ninth grade in school, he made the decision to dedicate himself to the struggle for the marginalized Ukrainian language and to go to college specifically to seek out the "Ukrainian underground." He warns his mother not to be surprised if at some point their apartment is searched.

For a long time at Kyiv University he sees no trace of any underground movement—the teaching is conducted solely in Russian, and no one seems bothered about the lack of Ukrainian. Then Doniy begins to express his position publicly.

The university newspaper immediately brands him a disruptor and an enemy of the Soviet system—and soon he is a local celebrity. One after another, a string of fellow students come out of hiding and declare for Ukrainian independence. The administration tries to expel Doniy, but the professors resist: no one wants to give him low grades, and without that there are no grounds for expulsion.

Doniy soon learns that a strong student organization already exists in Lviv and arranges a joint protest with it. They agree on a date but do not discuss tactics or location so that the KGB does not get wind of it.

The Lviv students put forward two conditions: Ukrainians must not serve in the army outside of Ukraine, and the government must resign. Doniy and the Kyiv students have other slogans: reelections to the

Supreme Soviet and the nationalization of Communist Party property. Only their third demand is obliquely connected to independence: to reject the new union treaty being prepared by Soviet president Mikhail Gorbachev.

"We understood that the idea of independence back then was unpopular, so we had to count on gradual enlightenment," says Doniy. "Our whole liberation movement of the late eighties and early nineties was not xenophobic, which is very important. It was not driven by hatred; otherwise it would not have achieved success."

On the third day of the hunger strike, the chairman of the Supreme Soviet, Leonid Kravchuk, comes to the square to negotiate. "Kravchuk copied Gorbachev. Gorbachev went to the people, so Kravchuk came to the square," says Doniy.

The hunger strike drags on. A week later, many students in the square are starting to lose heart. So Doniy decides on a more proactive course: on October 12, on the tenth day of the protest, the students block the traffic on Kyiv's central thoroughfare. "It took only ten people and five folding beds to block Khreshchatyk," says Doniy. "Drivers can hit people, but they will always avoid a metal barrier for fear of scratching their beloved bumper. It's very easy to set up a few folding beds and close off the street in two minutes."

From that moment on, the whole of Kyiv is talking about them. Other school and college students join the action. On October 15, the students surround the parliament, and in the evening that same day they seize the building of Kyiv University and raise the blue-and-yellow flag (then still associated with the "bourgeois nationalists") above it for the first time. In the evening, Doniy and the other leaders of the student protest are invited to appear on television.

On the same day, news breaks that Mikhail Gorbachev has been awarded the Nobel Peace Prize. Tellingly, there has been no pressure from Moscow on the Kyiv authorities for a long time—Kravchuk claims that during the entire student protest he never once discussed it with Moscow.

Finally, on October 17, the Supreme Soviet of Ukraine considers the students' demands. According to Doniy, they agree to the least important ones: the resignation of the government; the limited conscription of Ukrainians into the army; and the creation of a commission on the nationalization of Communist Party property.

The main demand for new parliamentary elections to excise the old communist elite from politics the Supreme Soviet waters down.

Any feeling of triumph among the students, however, does not last long. On November 7,* they try to prevent the annual October Revolution military parade from taking place in Kyiv. But this time the police are under orders to stop the picket immediately. The activists are dragged away and interrogated, and on January 2, 1991, Doniy is arrested and sent to Lukyanivska, a notorious prison in Kyiv. The fleeting sense of euphoria is again replaced by one of powerlessness.

I met with Oles Doniy in Kyiv in the summer of 2021. Unlike many of his fellow protesters of 1990, he had not carved out a brilliant political career. "Ukraine lost in 1990," says Oles Doniy. "If reelections had taken place, there would have been a change of elite: communist to democratic. Instead, the monster remained in power, which prevented reform in Ukraine for decades."

The Greatest Showman

In 1990, the twelve-year-old Vova Zelensky is fixated on a group of Ukrainian students. But not Doniy and friends. Rather, participants in *KVN—Klub Vesyolykh i Nakhodchivykh* (literally "Club of the Merry and Resourceful")—a student comedy sketch show and the most watched program in the Soviet Union. *KVN* features teams of students competing against each other for the comedy crown; the best performers become instant celebrities.

The show's format was created back in 1961, and its then-unknown host was the fresh-faced Alexander Maslyakov, who became (and re-

---

* The October Revolution of 1917 took place on October 25 according to the Julian calendar. When the Bolsheviks introduced the Gregorian calendar, the date became November 7.

mains) an iconic figure. In 1972, the KGB and state censors banned the program as anti-Soviet: it was the "Brezhnev stagnation" period in the Soviet Union, and the jokes were too near the knuckle.

But the 1980s and perestroika saw *KVN* back on the small screen. The host was the same, now-matured Alexander Maslyakov. *KVN* quickly became a phenomenon, the focal point of Soviet student life. There was no other entertainment show (and very few TV channels) in the Soviet Union, so *KVN*ers were hundreds of times more famous than any of today's "stars" from *Pop Idol* and the like.

KVN contestants did not just tell jokes but staged mini-performances, like *Saturday Night Live* sketches or very short Broadway musicals. The teams created sketches on a given topic; a jury evaluated them and chose the winner. One season lasted a whole year, and the champion would be announced just before New Year.

Participants in the show were just as recognizable in the Soviet Union as, say, the top college basketball players in the United States. But college sport in the Soviet Union was not of national interest. On the other hand, every institute had a *KVN* team hungry for nationwide fame. For artistic young people, it was the fastest route to stardom.

At School No. 95 in Kryvyi Rih, Vova Zelensky takes part in a school version of *KVN*. He watches every episode of the TV show and idolizes the participants.

The show's popularity is so great that it even features advertising—still a rare phenomenon on Soviet television. Money is starting to revolutionize the industry. In 1990, host Alexander Maslyakov privatizes the *KVN* brand and creates a company called AMiK (Alexander Maslyakov and Company).

The 1990 season is particularly strong in terms of Ukrainian talent: there are four teams from Russia and four from Ukraine. Three of the Ukrainian teams make it to the final round: Donetsk, Odesa, and Dnipropetrovsk. Twelve-year-old Vova is a fan of the Dnipropetrovsk team, since his hometown of Kryvyi Rih is located in the Dnipropetrovsk region.

A sketch by the Dnipropetrovsk team becomes the most memorable of the season. They sing a song by the Soviet group Pesnyary called

"Belovezhskaya Pushcha"—the name of a national park in Belarus. But instead of that two-word chorus, they sing one of Lenin's aphorisms: *Luchshe mensche da luchshe* (literally "Better less, but better," that is, quality is more important than quantity). However, the subtext is clear: the Soviet empire is too big; less would be better.

The full prophetic significance of the sketch will manifest itself a year later, in December 1991, when the leaders of Russia, Ukraine, and Belarus sign an agreement (the Belovezh Accords) to terminate the Soviet Union in that selfsame Belovezhskaya Pushcha.

BALTIC
SEA

ESTONIA

LATVIA

LITHUANIA

RUSSIA

Moscow

POLAND

Minsk

BELARUS

RUSSIA

× Belovezhskaya
Pushcha

Kyiv

Kharkiv

Lviv

U K R A I N E

Dnipropetrovsk

Donetsk

MOLDOVA

Kryvyi Rih

Zaporizhzhia

Odesa

ROMANIA

SEA
OF AZOV

CRIMEA

Sevastopol

BULGARIA

BLACK SEA

INDEPENDENT UKRAINE
IN 1991

TURKEY

200 miles

200 km

9

BETRAYAL AGAIN:
HOW LEONID KRAVCHUK DESTROYED
THE SOVIET UNION

Chicken Kyiv

Winter 1991. Ukraine is still part of the Soviet Union. The leaders of the Soviet republics are pushing for more independence, emboldened by the mood of protest throughout the union. The two most vocal are the respective heads of the Russian and Ukrainian parliaments, Boris Yeltsin and Leonid Kravchuk. Until recently, both were party leaders and steadfast supporters of the General Secretary of the Communist Party, Mikhail Gorbachev. But that time has passed.

Gorbachev, trying to keep the regional elites in check, consults his right-hand man, lawyer Anatoly Lukyanov, who is the chairman of the Supreme Soviet (the country's top legislative body). He proposes to hold a referendum throughout the Soviet Union to determine the future of the state. In doing so, the experienced (that is, wily) Soviet lawyer Lukyanov words the referendum question in such a way that the Soviet public cannot answer in the negative. "Do you want to be rich and healthy, or poor and sick?" is how Soviet journalists poke fun at this nationwide expression of will. The question put to the vote on

March 17, 1991, reads, in classic Soviet bureaucratese, as follows: "Do you consider necessary the preservation of the Union of Soviet Socialist Republics as a renewed federation of equal sovereign republics in which the rights and freedom of an individual of any ethnicity will be fully guaranteed?"

In the six Soviet republics where supporters of independence are already in power, the referendum is boycotted. But in Ukraine, it goes ahead. Seventy percent of voters say yes.

However, Ukraine's political elite is already preparing for a new life independent of Moscow: in April 1991, a group of artists is summoned to the Ukrainian Supreme Soviet to discuss designs for Ukraine's new currency; the Soviet ruble is to be replaced with the hryvnia. They discuss which historical figures to depict on the banknotes. The first candidate is, naturally, Bohdan Khmelnytsky. The second is the great Ukrainian poet Taras Shevchenko. The next name to be floated is Ivan Mazepa, to which Leonid Kravchuk (according to artist Vasyl Lopata, who was present) immediately replies: "It's still early; let's not tease the geese."

Meanwhile, in Moscow, Mikhail Gorbachev is fighting to preserve the Soviet empire. In line with the referendum result, he must come up with a new version of the Soviet Union and draft a new union treaty. With this in mind, Gorbachev gathers together at his Novo-Ogaryovo residence near Moscow the heads of the nine union republics that held the referendum and tries to thrash out how the new state will be structured. This proves far harder than holding the referendum in the first place: Gorbachev has only one ally (President Nursultan Nazarbayev of Kazakhstan) and two powerful opponents (Boris Yeltsin and Leonid Kravchuk). The others are biding their time.

The first meeting happens on May 24. Nazarbayev makes a fiery speech in support of the Soviet Union: "They think we're mad: the United States of America has three hundred and fifty nationalities and ethnicities, but there's not a murmur of protest, all live in one state. The whole of Europe [. . .] is scrapping borders, promoting the movement of capital, establishing a single currency for the whole continent. . . .

And we, with seventy-five percent integration, are moving away from what everyone else in the world is heading for. Does anyone think we're smart people?"

Nazarbayev's speech convinces almost everyone, and Gorbachev happily declares that the results of the meeting can be announced to the press: the heads of the republics have agreed to strive for unity. But Kravchuk objects. He insists that the Ukrainian Supreme Soviet did not give him the authority to negotiate: "Better not to print that we agreed. Once the press writes that, there's no getting away from it."

In July 1991, Gorbachev and his aides come up with a plan for the gradual transformation of the USSR into the USS: the Union of Sovereign States. Russia, Kazakhstan, and Uzbekistan are set to sign the founding document (the New Union Treaty) on August 20, 1991, with the other republics following suit later. The last will be Ukraine, scheduled for October 22 or thereabouts.

Even US president George H. W. Bush believes that the Soviet Union must be preserved. He visits Moscow on July 30, followed by Kyiv on August 1, where he urges Ukraine's political elite to support Gorbachev. In his view, the collapse of the Soviet Union could result in the spread of nuclear weapons around the world. Besides, Bush is accustomed to dealing with Gorbachev.

There in Kyiv, addressing parliament in what is still the Ukrainian Soviet Socialist Republic, Bush delivers a warning: Americans will not recognize Ukraine's secession from the Soviet Union.

> *We will maintain the strongest possible relationship with the Soviet Government of President Gorbachev. But we also appreciate the new realities of life in the USSR. And therefore, as a federation ourselves, we want good relations—improved relations—with the Republics. So, let me build upon my comments in Moscow by describing in more detail what Americans mean when we talk about freedom, democracy, and economic liberty.*
>
> *No terms have been abused more regularly, nor more cynically, than these. Throughout this century despots have masqueraded as*

democrats; jailers have posed as liberators. We can restore faith to gov-
ernment only by restoring meaning to these concepts.

Yet freedom is not the same as independence. Americans will not
support those who seek independence in order to replace a far-off tyr-
anny with a local despotism. They will not aid those who promote a
suicidal nationalism based upon ethnic hatred.

The speech provokes outrage: it is slammed by all Ukrainian supporters of independence, and the *New York Times* dubs it the "Chicken Kiev
speech." No one knows that just three weeks later everything will change:
on August 19, there will be an attempted coup in Moscow; President
Gorbachev will be placed under house arrest in his dacha in Crimea.

Closing Time

At 6:00 a.m. on August 19, 1991, the chairman of the Ukrainian Supreme Soviet, Leonid Kravchuk, is woken by his grandson saying that
the loudest phone in Granddad's office is ringing, which the family calls
the thistle—a large contraption for secure state-level communications.
Kravchuk picks up the receiver. At the other end is First Secretary of the
Ukrainian Communist Party Stanislav Hurenko, who tells Kravchuk to
turn on the radio. There, in a deathlike voice, the newsreader announces
the introduction of a state of emergency in the Soviet Union. President
Mikhail Gorbachev is "unwell" and all power in the country has passed to
a group of eight men: the State Committee for the State of Emergency
(the State Emergency Committee [SEC] for short).

Hurenko conveys another piece of news over the phone: "Listen, the
representative of the SEC, General Varennikov, commander in chief of
Soviet Ground Forces, wants to meet with you. I think we should talk
to him at my place." Kravchuk understands that Hurenko wants him
to think that the old order has returned, that everything is again in the
hands of the Communist Party.

He stands his ground: "Stanislav Ivanovych [Hurenko], as long as I chair the Supreme Soviet, I shall meet with Varennikov in *my* office. If you want, you can come too."

Kravchuk is on his way to work when he receives a phone call from Russian president Boris Yeltsin, who asks him to contact Gorbachev. The latter is at his dacha in Crimea and can't be reached by phone from Moscow, but maybe no one will dare not to put the leader of Ukraine through. Kravchuk dials the number, and a brusque female voice informs him that Mikhail Sergeyevich [Gorbachev] is not feeling well and cannot come to the phone.

Varennikov arrives at Kravchuk's office and demands that a state of emergency be declared in Ukraine. In response, Kravchuk asks the general to show him a written order from Moscow: "Even Lenin, when he sent his representatives on missions, gave them a written power of attorney to handle matters."

"Written order?" Varennikov exclaims. "Haven't you been listening to the radio?" Kravchuk does not yield, insisting that he must have a written order to show to parliament and will not raise the matter of introducing a state of emergency on the basis of a radio report.

Kravchuk feels the attempt to exert moral pressure on him but decides that no one will punish him for excessive bureaucratism. Indeed, in Moscow, Russian president Boris Yeltsin's behavior is far more defiant: he declares what is happening to be a coup and demands that the orders of the SEC be ignored. Compared to Yeltsin's open rebellion, Kravchuk's wait-and-see approach poses no threat to the hard-liners. After the meeting, Varennikov flies to Lviv to assess the situation. The SEC is expecting civil unrest. For it is there, in western Ukraine, that the supporters of independence are most active. But all is quiet in the city.

That evening, Kravchuk makes a very cautious televised address, in which he calls upon Ukrainians to remain calm and carry on; unlike in Moscow, there are no mass protests against the coup in Kyiv.

The SEC lasts only three days. Several thousand supporters of Yeltsin gather outside the building of the Supreme Soviet of Russia in Moscow. The army does not dare to open fire on them; on the contrary, it withdraws from the city. By August 21, Yeltsin has already ordered the arrest of all members of the SEC.

The leaders of the union republics who supported the SEC suddenly find themselves in a tight spot. One of them, Mikalay Dzyemyantsyey, chairman of the Belarusian Supreme Soviet, takes preemptive action by announcing his resignation on August 22.

Two days later, the Ukrainian Supreme Soviet sits for the first time following the failed coup. On the square in front of the parliament building, supporters of independence hold an hours-long, thousands-strong rally. The communists are demoralized.

Parliamentarian Levko Lukyanenko, Ukraine's oldest dissident, who back in the 1960s fought for Ukrainian secession from the Soviet Union and was sentenced to death for his troubles (later commuted to fifteen years in a prison camp), on the morning of August 23, 1991, takes a ruled exercise book and writes a one-page text. This he calls the "Universal on the Declaration of Independence"—by analogy with the series of "universals" (legal acts) issued by the Central Rada of Ukraine in 1917–18, the fourth and last of which, authored by the preeminent historian Mykhailo Hrushevsky, declared independence from the collapsing Russian Empire. But Lukyanenko's allies persuade him to drop the word "universal"; they feel the historical parallel would spook the communists unnecessarily, and suggest the more neutral word "act."

Kravchuk, chairman of the parliament, is afraid to put the document to a vote; he proposes postponing it for several days. Then, according to popular rumor, an activist of Narodnyi Rukh (People's Movement) by the name of Dmytro Pavlychko approaches him and threatens to strangle him if he does not announce a vote. Kravchuk yields, and the Declaration of Independence Act is adopted unanimously.

A week later, the Presidium of the Ukrainian Supreme Soviet, given the Communist Party of Ukraine's support for the August coup, decides to ban the organization. Kravchuk's former party comrades immediately demand an audience with him, claiming that only the Supreme Court can ban the Communist Party. "You want to be tried as well as banned?" Kravchuk asks. They retreat.

A situational alliance suddenly breaks out between the communists and the fighters for Ukrainian independence. Yesterday's communists, headed by ideology secretary Kravchuk, essentially abandon Marxism and adopt the ideas of the Ukrainian nationalists. They, in turn, delighted that their ideology has won and lacking experience in public administration, are ready to retain the most important posts for the communists.

Soon afterwards, the artist Vasyl Lopata receives a call from the National Bank of Ukraine, saying that, in light of the new situation, Ivan Mazepa can be depicted on the new currency after all: he appears on the new ten-hryvnia bill.

My Motherland, Drunk or Sober

In late September 1991, Leonid Kravchuk flies to America for the first time as the head of an independent, though not yet recognized as such, Ukraine. He knows that President George H. W. Bush is wary about the idea of a Soviet breakup and would prefer to keep a centralized state in place, with Gorbachev at the head. Kravchuk needs to convince him somehow that it is time to establish relations with Kyiv directly. During the meeting, the head of the Ukrainian parliament keeps his cards close to his chest. He does not ask for recognition of independence, noting that he will raise the issue only after a referendum scheduled in his country for December 1. But he does ask for economic aid, since nothing that Washington sends to the center in Moscow ever reaches Ukraine. He also states that Ukraine does not need food supplies but rather financial support and new technologies to make the country's industry competitive. Bush hesitates. His instinct still tells him to deal with Moscow. So Kravchuk plays his ace, declaring that Kyiv will give up its nuclear status: let Russia be the custodian of all Soviet atomic weapons. Bush likes what he hears.

After the August coup, the Soviet Union is rapidly disintegrating: even the Soviet government is no longer functioning, its powers having been transferred to the republics. Naturally, the chaotic goings-on are lampooned mercilessly on the university sketch show *KVN*. In the autumn of 1991, the first semifinal sees teams from Lviv, galvanized by Ukrainian independence, and Yekaterinburg (recently renamed from Sverdlovsk), the birthplace of Russian president Boris Yeltsin, go head-to-head. Yeltsin is a big fan of *KVN*, and especially of his hometown team—a year earlier he was even spotted in the audience.

Both teams joke about the ineptitude of the coup plotters and the collapsing Soviet Union, but it is a song by the Yekaterinburg team that provokes outrage. The lyrics, set to the music of the Soviet national anthem, alternate line by line between the words of the original composition and a slightly modified version of a work by Russian poet Nikolay Nekrasov, memorized by all Soviet schoolchildren. The result in Russian is an absurdist masterpiece. For a flavor, here are the first two verses in English:

> *Once in the freezing wintertime,*
> *The mighty Rus was forever united.*
> *I see, climbing slowly up the hill,*
> *The great and powerful Soviet Union.*
> *Through the thunderstorm shone the sun of freedom,*
> *And here's a little peasant leading us by the bridle.*
> *He set the people on the righteous path,*
> *Wearing large mittens, himself knee-high to a grasshopper.*

In each verse, two rhyming lines are from Nekrasov's plain-talking poem about a peasant on his way to chop wood, while the two others eulogize Lenin and the Soviet Union in increasingly grandiloquent style.

The audience is spellbound and shocked in equal measure. Never before has the revered national anthem, penned in 1943 at the height of the Great Patriotic War, been used for comic effect. Even in 1991, when censorship is dead and anything goes, the judges—all popular actors, movie directors, and journalists proud of how wonderfully liberal and democratic they are—are taken aback by such chutzpah. Nearly all of them give the Yekaterinburg team two out of five. Anatoly Lysenko, general director of Russian television, appointed by Yeltsin, takes the floor: "The Americans have a very important principle: 'My country, right or wrong.'" The team from Yekaterinburg loses; the far less provocative Ukrainians from Lviv go through to the final.

The phrase "My country, right or wrong" was first uttered by the US naval commander Stephen Decatur in 1816 and was originally a toast. Then the slogan became a symbol of English jingoism. It was ridiculed by the writer G. K. Chesterton, who said that "My country, right or wrong" is equivalent to "My mother, drunk or sober." Amazingly, in 2022 Russian propagandists will cite these words in defense of the war against Ukraine.

Independence on a Silver Platter

On December 1, Ukraine holds a double vote: presidential elections and another referendum on independence.

This is the second such referendum in 1991, but after the failed coup the landscape has changed. Now Leonid Kravchuk comes up with his own (somewhat shorter) wording of the question: "Do you confirm the Declaration of Independence Act of Ukraine?" There is no explanation on the ballot paper of what is at stake, no mention of secession from the Soviet Union, since, according to Kravchuk, such a proposal would have garnered significantly fewer votes. But the very idea of independence is overwhelmingly popular. Ninety percent vote in favor.

In the presidential election, the recent communist (now-anti-communist) Kravchuk gains 61.6 percent in the first round, defeating the dissidents: Rukh leader Vyacheslav Chornovil and Levko Lukyanenko. Following the referendum, Ukraine is recognized globally as an independent country by many, including Poland and Canada. Nevertheless, the Soviet Union still exists de jure—no one knows what to do with the lifeless carcass.

Kravchuk flies to Minsk at the invitation of the new chairman of the Belarusian Supreme Soviet, Stanislav Shushkevich. At the exact same time, Yeltsin arrives in Belarus on a state visit. All three leaders had agreed in early autumn to meet and discuss the situation at the first opportunity, without Soviet president Gorbachev. While the Russian delegation is negotiating with Belarusian prime minister Vyacheslav Kebich on oil and gas supplies, Shushkevich invites Kravchuk to Belovezhskaya Pushcha National Park: "Leonid Makarovich, let's go hunting while Yeltsin is busy."

In the middle of the forest, they spot a wild boar. Shushkevich says to Kravchuk, "Leonid Makarovich, shoot!" Kravchuk takes aim, but Shushkevich grabs him by the arm: "No, not here, let's get closer." They approach, but the boar is startled and runs off. Kravchuk is crestfallen: he's lost a certain kill. *A hunter should never listen to anyone. Never!* he muses to himself.

Things get serious the following morning when six people gather round the negotiating table: two from each country. Yeltsin asks Kravchuk if he will agree to sign the New Union Treaty, an agreement on reforming the Soviet Union, which Gorbachev repeatedly redrafted and which now, after the coup, proposes the creation of a confederation. Yeltsin tests the water: "Will you sign the Union Treaty if it takes into account Ukraine's and your own proposals?"

"Boris Nikolayevich, I can't," Kravchuk replies. "The Ukrainian people have voted for independence in a referendum. If I answer yes to this question, it will be a betrayal of my people. I will then have to fly back to Kyiv and say: you elected me, but I let you down. . . ."

Kravchuk ends with a question of his own: "If it were like that in Russia, who would you listen to, Gorbachev or your own people?"

"My own people, of course," Yeltsin replies glumly. "But without Ukraine, there can be no Soviet Union. We need to think about drawing up another document."

Until that moment, the host of the meeting, Stanislav Shushkevich, never imagined he would have to sign anything. He thought the proceedings would consist solely of talking, hunting, and steaming in the *banya*. He instructs his subordinates to get hold of a typewriter. After a great deal of effort, an old one is finally found in a neighboring village.

While the search is going on, Gennady Burbulis, Russia's secretary of state and de facto head of government, proposes the following wording for the document: "The Soviet Union as a geopolitical reality and a subject of international law has ceased to exist." All three agree. The text is quickly typed on the decrepit typewriter, and the three leaders sign the "Agreements establishing the Commonwealth of Independent States."

Yeltsin asks Kravchuk, "What are we going to do about Crimea and [Ukraine's] nuclear weapons?"

The latter replies, "Let's not discuss Crimea just now. First, we need to create a commonwealth, then deal with the borders."

The events in Belovezhskaya Pushcha catch everyone by surprise. Neither Kravchuk nor Shushkevich ever planned to disband the Soviet Union; they didn't even know that was an option. The new document frightens them. No one knows what the consequences will be. They fear being arrested as conspirators. Maybe the Soviet empire is, in fact, governed by some unseen, omnipotent force as yet unknown to them?

Yeltsin calls Soviet defense minister Yevgeny Shaposhnikov and informs him that he has been appointed, by decree of the three presidents, commander in chief of the armed forces of the newly created Commonwealth of Independent States. He has no objections, which means that the likelihood of another military coup to save the Soviet Union is minimal.

Everyone decamps to Yeltsin's suite, since his is the most spacious. They ponder the question of who will tell Gorbachev. The unenviable task is entrusted to Shushkevich, as the host of the meeting. He phones the Kremlin but can't get through: "Gorbachev is busy and cannot take your call. He will phone you back," comes the reply.

Yeltsin, meanwhile, is trying to get through to President George H. W. Bush. The White House cannot believe that Yeltsin is calling from some remote Belarusian village with such earth-shattering news. Yet Bush picks up the phone before Gorbachev does. Only after Yeltsin's conversation with Bush does Gorbachev ring back in a state of apoplexy: "What the hell have you done? You've turned the whole world upside down!"

That done, there is the important matter of dinner. During the meal, Yeltsin is informed that it may not be safe for him to stay in Belovezhskaya Pushcha—word is out that Gorbachev plans to arrest the leaders of the three republics and that KGB special forces are already moving in.

"Leonid Makarovich, I've been told we need to leave here as quickly as possible," Yeltsin says to Kravchuk. The Russian and Ukrainian delegations dash to the airfield. Bidding Kravchuk farewell, Yeltsin makes a characteristic gesture with his hand and says, "We've totally fucked

Mishka" (a reference to Gorbachev). But even back in Kyiv, Kravchuk fears arrest.

He goes to his country residence at Koncha-Zaspa, on the outskirts of the Ukrainian capital, climbs out of the car, and sees three men walking toward him. *The game's up*, he thinks. As they approach, Kravchuk sees they are Ukrainian paratroopers. They salute with the words: "Mr. President, we are here to protect you."

Years later, Kravchuk will describe his role in the creation of the Ukrainian state in the third person: "Independence came to Ukraine unexpectedly. Kravchuk flew in and brought it on a silver platter."

Comedian Instead of a President

The final collapse of the Soviet Union plays out on December 25, 1991, when Soviet president Mikhail Gorbachev announces his resignation, consigning the empire to history.

I interviewed Mikhail Gorbachev many times. In the years after his presidency, he largely reinvented his biography, forgetting that he was once perceived as a Soviet dictator. In his own memoirs, he always portrayed himself as a democrat-liberator whose goal was to give free rein to the peoples of the Communist bloc. Only his attitude toward Ukrainian independence was ambiguous: his wife, Raisa, who died in 1999, was Ukrainian. He himself was half-Ukrainian, on his mother's side, and all his life he spoke with a distinctly southern Russian accent, strongly reminiscent of Ukrainian. Gorbachev always struggled to see Ukraine as a separate country: "It's like tearing yourself in half," he would say.

On December 31, 1991, more than 200 million people across the defunct empire see in the New Year, the main Soviet holiday. The tradition of celebrating New Year instead of Christmas was introduced by the Bolsheviks. To begin with, however, they opposed New Year, too, as "clerical propaganda." But in 1935 Pavel Postyshev, Second Secretary of the Ukrainian Communist Party and then head of Kyiv, convinced Joseph Stalin that the country, especially children, needed new traditions, including a New Year tree. Just a few years before, Postyshev had been one of the drivers of the Holodomor, the man-made famine in Soviet Ukraine from 1932 to 1933 that killed millions. As a result of his efforts, the Soviet Union was able to fulfill its grain export plan and make a profit—at the cost of several million deaths from starvation. Postyshev himself had had a difficult childhood, and was always envious of children from wealthy families who had a Christmas tree, so he personally organized the first New Year celebration in the Soviet Union. The first city to put up a New Year tree was Kharkiv in eastern Ukraine, the former capital. Children and adults alike were delighted—those who had survived the Holodomor, that is.

The following year, New Year trees began popping up all over the country, and even Moscow held a big celebration, despite the religious undertones. Another novelty introduced at this time was the double act of Ded Moroz (Father Frost) and Snegurochka (Snow Maiden). These two figures, plucked from Slavic folklore, were chosen as the symbols of the new holiday: they wished everyone a "Happy New Year 1937!" Ironically, that same year saw the start of the Great Terror, the worst of the Stalinist purges. One of its many victims was the "bringer of New Year" himself: Postyshev was shot as a Japanese spy.

By 1991, the Soviet ritual of celebrating New Year was firmly entrenched (and continues across the post-Soviet space). It goes as follows: families and groups of friends spend the whole of December 31 cooking and preparing, before sitting down at the festive table close to midnight to "see the old year out"—that is, toast and drink to what's past. Another unwritten rule is that the television must be on during this last hour: there is always something interesting and humorous to watch. At five minutes to midnight, the joking stops and the head of state appears on the screen and delivers a New Year's address to the people. The camera then switches to the clock of Spasskaya Tower in the Moscow Kremlin, which chimes twelve times; some believe that if you make a wish during the chimes it will definitely come true. The truly superstitious write down a wish on a piece of paper, burn it, eat the ashes, and wash them down with champagne. How can that possibly fail to work?

The chimes are followed by a festive concert with comedy interludes between songs. Viewers watch and drink till dawn.

At the end of December 1991, the heads of Channel One, the main TV station in the Soviet Union, face a problem: The holiday is approaching, but who will deliver the address to the nation? Mikhail Gorbachev has departed, while Russian president Boris Yeltsin would not be suitable, because the broadcast goes out to all the now-ex-Soviet republics, not just Russia. Besides, as staff recall, he could not have recorded the New Year's address anyway, because he had started to celebrate early and was already "out of reach."

The host of the New Year concert in 1991 is Mikhail Zadornov, the most popular stand-up comic in the Soviet Union. On Soviet television, he is known as a "humorist." His background is controversial—until recently he directed the amateur theater of the KGB. However, few people know about this. With him now a regular fixture on television, audiences appreciate Zadornov for his jokes about politics and politicians. In the absence of an all-Union (and sober) leader, he is the one tasked with addressing the people before the clock strikes twelve.

"We may now live in different states, but no one, no one, can ever take away from us what we had . . . ," the comedian Zadornov says with unusual seriousness from the screen, clutching a glass of champagne. "Yes, the USSR is gone, but not the Motherland. They can divide the Motherland into states, but she is still one. Regardless of borders. I propose a toast to our Motherland."

This is not Zadornov's only appearance on television that night. He also does a satirical news sketch. Most of it is devoted to Ukraine, or rather to mocking its leaders. He tells long (and, let's be honest, unfunny) jokes about Ukraine's new currency, about the desire of the Ukrainian authorities to "privatize" the Soviet army, and about the fact that President Kravchuk mispronounced the word "imperial" in accusing Boris Yeltsin of having an "imperial mindset." One would like to think that the satirist Zadornov is parodying the shameful, colonial, arrogant statements of Russian politicians, but, unfortunately, not. Right now he is not joking.

Church Schism

One major difference between Soviet Ukraine and the other republics in the Union is the far stronger role of the Church there. Ukrainians are much more religious than other Soviet citizens. In Ukraine, the connection between clergy and parishioners is much closer, especially in the western regions, which only became part of the Soviet Union as a result of the Molotov-Ribbentrop Pact in 1939.

The breakup of the Soviet Union is not limited to state structures. The Russian Orthodox Church is also falling apart, and has been since the late 1980s, when émigrés who had fled from Soviet rule, including priests, started gradually returning to western Ukraine. Soon the Ukrainian Autocephalous Orthodox Church (UAOC) is reestablished and declares independence from Moscow. Its most ardent opponent is the Metropolitan of Kyiv, Filaret Denysenko, who has led the Church in Ukraine since 1966 in an extremely authoritarian manner. According to Archimandrite Kirill Govorun, a former bishop of the Ukrainian Church, in Soviet times Filaret behaved like a true Russian chauvinist, suppressing all signs of Ukrainianism and excommunicating dissenters.

However, the number of parishioners of the UAOC is rising, and in 1990 it even elects its own patriarch. He is Mstyslav Skrypnyk, who began his church career back in 1942, during the German occupation of Ukraine, and moved to Canada in the late 1940s. The newly elected patriarch is not a Soviet citizen, of course, and has long been denied a Soviet visa.

Filaret, after losing the election, nevertheless receives a consolation prize. The new patriarch of the ROC, Alexy II, creates the Ukrainian Orthodox Church–Moscow Patriarchate within the framework of the ROC—not independent, but with a certain degree of latitude. However, in 1991, after the coup in Moscow, everything changes, and in November of that year Metropolitan Filaret, yesterday a staunch fighter for church unity, now demands independence for this new Ukrainian church. According to Govorun, Filaret rushes from one extreme to another: from a Russian chauvinist, he turns into a die-hard Ukrainian nationalist.

The Moscow patriarch's entourage suspects that this is a continuation of the KGB's game: having lost control over the ROC, the Russian secret service wants to split off the Ukrainian church and create a hotbed of tension in which they can exert influence over everyone. At the same time, a scandal flares up in Moscow: Gleb Yakunin, a priest, gains access to the KGB archives and begins investigating Church hierarchs who worked for the agency. Based on his findings, Yakunin divides the clergy into three categories: those who collaborated with the KGB against their will; those who were more pliant, but still passive and showed no initiative; and those who proactively offered their services. It is in the third category that he places Filaret Denysenko. In March–April 1992, all ROC dignitaries, including Filaret and other metropolitans from Ukraine, gather in Moscow. There, one by one, the majority of the Ukrainian hierarchs renounce the demand for independence, claiming they were previously under pressure from Filaret and President Kravchuk. The Church officials accuse Filaret of every possible sin, including immoral behavior, specifically that he has a secret wife, which is prohibited under Church rules. Filaret promises to resign as soon as he returns to Kyiv, so that the Ukrainian clergy can choose a successor.

But on arriving back in his homeland, he declares that he rejects all the accusations and will head the Ukrainian Orthodox Church till his dying breath, since he was "given by God to Ukrainian Orthodoxy."

In May 1992, all the supreme Ukrainian Church hierarchs gather in Kharkiv and express a vote of no confidence in Filaret. Filaret again brands them "schismatics," describing the persecution against him as KGB intrigue. In June, in Moscow, the Church Council elects a new Metropolitan of Kyiv to replace Filaret—that same Volodymyr Sabodan who took second place in the recent patriarchal elections and lost out to Alexy in the second round.

President Kravchuk and the Ukrainian authorities, however, do not recognize Vladimir at first, calling him a protégé of Moscow, and Filaret retains control over all the Church's accounts. The net result is that Ukraine is home to no fewer than three Orthodox churches: the one subordinate to Moscow, headed by Metropolitan Vladimir, has the most parishes; the second is led by Filaret, and the third by Mstyslav, a Canadian citizen, who was finally issued a visa. All parties to the conflict blame the KGB for the schism, and there is plenty of truth in the charge. The Church curators-in-uniform find it easier to sow strife by playing on the internal contradictions, since they no longer have control over the whole Orthodox Church.

Army and Navy

Immediately after the collapse of the Soviet Union, a power struggle breaks out in Russia between the imperial and the liberal camps. President Boris Yeltsin, who has just dissolved the Soviet empire, is the leader of the democrats; supporters of the "Great Russia" idea are grouped around Vice President Alexander Rutskoy.

Rutskoy came to power largely by chance. A military pilot, he served in Afghanistan and was taken prisoner. During the 1991 presidential election, Yeltsin picked him as his running mate to secure the patriotic vote.

Rutskoy was deeply pained by the signing of the Belovezh Accords and even tried to get Gorbachev to arrest Yeltsin, Kravchuk, and Shushkevich.

Now in 1992, the vice president, who has little real influence within the Russian power structure, crosses swords with Yeltsin and his government of reformers. He is backed by members of the old Soviet elite: the military and others who want to preserve the empire. Rutskoy calls upon Yeltsin not to recognize Crimea as part of Ukraine, then pointedly visits the base of the Black Sea Fleet in Sevastopol, which provokes an international outcry: Kyiv is outraged that the Russian vice president entered Ukrainian territory uninvited and even inspected some warships.

Since the status of the fleet was not covered in the Belovezh Accords, it is a major bone of contention. In April 1992, first President Kravchuk, then President Yeltsin, sign two decrees, each of them claiming ownership of the Black Sea Fleet. To avoid aggravating relations, both presidents agree to withdraw their respective decree and start negotiations. The process of carving up the fleet will drag on for almost ten years. At one point, Kravchuk signs an agreement to concede the fleet to Russia in exchange for a gas debt write-off. But, on returning to Kyiv, he is accused of *zrada* (betrayal). He withdraws his signature, but his popularity is gone for good.

In May 1992, Kravchuk flies to Washington to complain about the Kremlin's increasing aggressiveness. He tells President Bush that Rutskoy has a map of "Great Russia" on the wall in his office, where even Alaska is marked as Russian territory. "Now you got my attention," Bush livens up.

November 1992 witnesses an event of crucial importance for the entire former Soviet Union, which occurs not in Russia or Ukraine, but in the United States. President George H. W. Bush loses the election to the young, charismatic Democratic candidate Bill Clinton. The two men are poles apart. Bush headed the CIA; then as president he oversaw the death throes of the Soviet Union. He has personal relations with Gorbachev, Yeltsin, and Kravchuk; he considers it vital to control the Soviet disintegration to keep it civilized. Clinton has no such foreign-policy experience and a completely different approach: he is focused on domestic issues, and has no wish to get bogged down in the affairs of the fifteen new states that have sprung up over the grave of the Soviet Union.

In 1992, the Russian government of reformers, led by Yegor Gaidar, hopes for significant economic assistance from the United States. They are counting on the West to initiate a kind of Marshall Plan for the defunct Soviet Union—an economic support program similar to that for post-war Western Europe in the late 1940s. But the Bush administration during the election campaign does not raise the issue, fearing it will be unpopular with voters, and Clinton's victory drives the final nail in the coffin of the idea.

Ukrainian president Kravchuk is at first delighted by Bush's defeat, feeling that he paid too much attention to Russia and too little to Ukraine. However, the Clinton administration's approach is even blunter: Washington will not discuss anything with Kyiv until Ukraine gives up its Soviet-inherited nuclear arsenal: 176 intercontinental ballistic missiles, able to carry 1,272 nuclear warheads and 2,500 tactical nuclear weapons. True, Ukraine cannot actually fire them: all the control systems are located in Russia. But Clinton and his diplomats echo the same mantra: any economic aid to Ukraine is contingent on all nuclear weapons being relocated to Russia. Kravchuk tries to resist, demanding compensation and security guarantees in return. In the end, Kravchuk gets the promises he wants.

At the end of 1992, the imperialists' struggle for power in Russia intensifies. In December, the so-called patriotic majority in parliament manages to force the resignation of Gaidar's pro-Western government, which Vice President Rutskoy describes as "boys in pink pants."

A War of Words

On October 30, 1992, Nobel Prize in Literature winner Joseph Brodsky speaks at the Jewish Center in Palo Alto, California. Two decades have passed since the great Russian poet immigrated to the United States.

"This is a bit close to the bone, but I'll read it to you anyway," Brodsky says, pouring himself a glass of water. "It's called 'On the Independence of Ukraine.'"

Brodsky has never read the poem in public before. A Jew born in Leningrad, in 1964 he was convicted of "social parasitism," since the Soviet authorities did not consider him a poet, and was sentenced just like Pushkin to five years' internal exile. Then, in 1972, he was expelled from the country. For the next twenty years, Brodsky built a reputation as one of the Soviet empire's most vehement opponents.

Now, two decades on, he is reading an "imperial" text of his own creation, full of anger, resentment, and misunderstanding: how did it happen that Ukraine seceded and became an independent state? The poem is strange and atypical for Brodsky, because it consists almost exclusively of insults and abuse. It begins with memories of Mazepa's alleged betrayal and the Battle of Poltava.

Dear Charles XII, the Battle of Poltava, thank God, you have lost.

Next, Brodsky mentions the "wevolutionary" (that is, Lenin) and "Kuzma's mother" (from Khrushchev's infamous threat to the Americans). Then he gets nasty:

Away with you [Ukraine],
Be gone to the four winds, to the sound of four-letter words.
There in a peasant hut,
let the Krauts and Polacks gang-bang your brains out, you piece of crap.

Brodsky ends his "poem" with yet another insult: this time directed not at the Ukrainian state, but at Ukrainian culture, declaring that the greatest Ukrainian poet, Taras Shevchenko, cannot hold a candle to Alexander Pushkin:

When it's your turn to die, meatheads,
You'll be grasping the edge of the mattress,
Croaking out lines from Alexander, not that Taras bullshit.

Is this really the same modest intellectual born and raised in Leningrad (St. Petersburg), who was awarded the Nobel Prize in Literature? As we can see, his protest against the Soviet empire did not translate into sympathy for Ukraine. He perceives Ukrainian independence as a personal insult, a betrayal, a breach of trust between the Russian and Ukrainian peoples.

That the poet accuses the Ukrainian people of betrayal is striking and symbolic. Brodsky was an enemy of the Soviet regime, suffered at its hands, slipped effortlessly into the world's intellectual elite, composed verses in English. The last thing you'd call him was a Russian imperialist.

In 1980, when mass protests broke out against the communist regime in Poland, Brodsky, from his home across the Atlantic, became one of the staunchest advocates of Solidarity. He spoke at rallies in the United States in support of the movement, urged his friends, American intellectuals, to support the Poles. And called on American banks not to deal with the Polish communist government, and on the West to prevent a Soviet military invasion.

Yet, for some reason, just ten years later, the separation of Russia and Ukraine provokes an entirely different reaction in Brodsky. He clearly feels justified in his attack, perhaps imagining himself as the successor of Pushkin, for whom Mazepa was a traitor.

The poem "On the Independence of Ukraine" is reminiscent of another poem by Pushkin, "To the Slanderers of Russia," which condones Russia's bloody suppression of the Polish uprising of 1830–31. In it, Pushkin talks disparagingly about the "jumped-up Polack"; Brodsky, then, seems to have taken his cue from Pushkin. The latter, however, wrote his lines in a moment of weakness, crushed by censorship, having had to burn the overtly political chapter 10 of his masterpiece *Eugene Onegin* for fear of the consequences. He hopes his latest patriotic verse will win over the authorities. Brodsky has no such excuse.

Oddly enough, the feeling of belonging to an empire comes naturally to Brodsky. It manifests itself in other poems of his. In "Letters to a Roman Friend," for instance, he advises: "If one happens to be born in the Empire, better to live in a remote province by the sea."

Growing up not far from the sea, but not in the provinces (rather in Leningrad), Brodsky hates the empire he was born into. Nevertheless, it is a part of him. At the same time, Brodsky himself clearly considers the poem "On the Independence of Ukraine" a provocation, an act of hooliganism, of which he is not proud. He intentionally does not include it in any collection or publish it anywhere, and reads it in public only twice.

According to those who knew him, while hating the Soviet Union, Brodsky is not against all empires per se; he believes in the notion of a good empire: for example, the United States, which he supports in every conceivable way. An acquaintance of the poet, literary critic Anna Narinskaya, recalls meeting Brodsky in the early 1990s. They clashed and fell out over his attitude to the wars in Vietnam and Iraq, which he considered to be righteous causes.

BALTIC
SEA

ESTONIA

St. Petersburg

LATVIA

LITHUANIA

RUSSIA

Moscow

BELARUS

R U S S I A

POLAND

Lviv

Kyiv

Kharkiv

U K R A I N E

Dnipropetrovsk

Donetsk

Kryvyi Rih

Zaporizhzhia

MOLDOVA

R O M A N I A

SEA
OF AZOV

CRIMEA

Sevastopol

BLACK SEA

TURKEY

**1994 UKRAINIAN
PRESIDENTIAL ELECTION**

Votes by regions, second round:

Leonid Kuchma (winner)

Leonid Kravchuk

200 miles

200 km

10

LANGUAGE AGAIN:
HOW LEONID KUCHMA SADDLED
THE DEVIL AND FLEW TO MOSCOW

Riding Satan

In 1991, along with the collapse of the Soviet Union comes the collapse of the entire Soviet economy. In each of the fifteen independent states that replaced it, 1992 is a time of wretched poverty. Inflation is out of control; people's savings are wiped out; banditry flourishes.

The president of Ukraine is Leonid Kravchuk. His government launches a series of reforms. The former ideology secretary of the Communist Party sincerely and wholeheartedly accepts Ukrainian independence, but the idea of a market economy is harder to swallow—it would go against his life philosophy to allow foreign companies to privatize Ukrainian enterprises. Therefore, his economic policy does not follow the path of, say, Poland, which opened its markets to Western investment, but rather the path of Russia, which did not let foreigners in, but put its enterprises in the hands of its own nouveau riche, who would later be dubbed "oligarchs." Many Ukrainians now have to spend most of their day at the market searching for affordable food and goods. To carry home whatever they find, they use a ubiquitous two-wheeled trolley, which soon becomes known as a *kravchuchka*.

On October 13, 1992, President Kravchuk appoints a new prime minister tasked with reforming the Ukrainian economy. He comes from the industrial lobby, the director of one of the biggest Ukrainian enterprises, the Yuzhmash plant in Dnipropetrovsk. His name is Leonid Kuchma. He is the new leader of the all-powerful Dnipropetrovsk clan. Yuzhmash isn't your average enterprise: it produces rocket and missile technology, including the fearsome Satan nuclear intercontinental ballistic missile, capable of destroying the world and then some. This missile holds a special place in Kuchma's heart.

Kuchma has been in office for less than a year when, in June 1993, the miners of the Donetsk basin (Donbas) region, who first started protesting back in 1989, go on indefinite strike, demanding the resignation of the president and parliament. Kravchuk replaces Prime Minister Kuchma, the head of the Dnipropetrovsk clan, with a member of the rival Donetsk clan. He is Yukhym Zvyahilsky, hitherto the boss of the largest mine in Donbas. A significant part of the Ukrainian economy at this moment is concentrated in two eastern regions: Donetsk and Dnipropetrovsk; Kravchuk wants to play them off against each other.

But it doesn't help him. Kravchuk's main conflict is with parliament. He is accused daily of being incompetent and wrecking the economy. This is a typical scenario at that time in the post-Soviet space: in September 1993, a similar mutual loathing arises between Russian president Yeltsin and the Russian parliament. The Russian parliament, together with Vice President Rutskoy, accuses President Yeltsin of betraying the national interests: they want to see Russia as an empire. Somewhat ironically, like Kravchuk, Yeltsin was the chairman of his country's parliament only a year earlier.

Both Moscow and Kyiv are considering the so-called zero option: the resignation and reelection of both parliament and president. But in Russia the talks break down and, in October 1993, a civil war breaks out on the streets of Moscow: parliament sends armed supporters to storm the Ostankino TV tower in the north of the city, in response to which the president orders tanks to shell the parliament building—that same building that in 1991 served as a bastion of democracy and Yeltsin's headquarters. Now with the building in flames, Rutskoy and the rebel parliamentarians are arrested and taken to prison. By force of arms, Yeltsin has managed to stop the aspiring imperialists. According to official figures, 158 have been killed.

After these events, a new constitution is adopted in Russia, granting the president almost unlimited powers. Its authors draft a new basic law specifically for the "democrat" Yeltsin, so that no parliament, whatever its composition, will be able to prevent him from reforming and liberalizing Russia.

In less than a decade, this same constitution will become a tool in the hands of the next president, Vladimir Putin, to push Russia in the opposite direction, turning it into an authoritarian empire.

In Kyiv, meanwhile, a deal is struck without a shootout: both parliament and Kravchuk agree to the early termination of their powers. After the new parliament opens, Kravchuk tries to postpone the presidential elections, but his own security services and the Ministry of Interior resist, asserting that they will not fire on the people.

Kravchuk's main rival in the fight for the presidency is his recent prime minister, Kuchma. They represent opposite ends of the political spectrum. Kravchuk, a former Communist Party secretary for ideology, is considered pro-Western by his supporters, or a nationalist by his opponents; Kuchma, the former director of the plant that builds Satan, is seen as an experienced manager and pro-Moscow: Russia, as the core of the former empire, still plays a special role in Ukrainian politics, which both Kyiv and Moscow accept as the norm.

Kuchma, who barely speaks Ukrainian, does indeed advocate rapprochement with Russia and special status for the Russian language; he also promises to sort out the economy. Russia, of course, supports Kuchma. Once again, there are echoes of Gogol's "The Night before Christmas": a Ukrainian from Dnipropetrovsk, riding Satan, flies to Moscow, secures a credit line, returns to his homeland, and wins the hearts and minds of voters.

It is the first competitive election campaign in the history of Ukraine. President Kravchuk is confident that "administrative resources" (that is, string pulling) will see him through: he does not even set up a campaign headquarters, believing that governors and other local officials are on his side. But he miscalculates: the regional heads have their own elections to win, so they take care of themselves, not the president.

The mass media, on the other hand, does work for Kravchuk: Kuchma is given practically no airtime on Ukrainian television. However, Kuchma gets plenty of coverage on Russian TV stations, which are still broadcast in Ukraine and are very popular. Kuchma's campaign messages even get played during the prime-time sketch show *KVN*.

The first round takes place on June 26. Kravchuk wins with 38.36 percent, followed by Kuchma with 31.17 percent. Neither has a majority, so a second round beckons. Moreover, Ukraine is split down the middle: Kravchuk wins in all the western regions; Kuchma sweeps up in the east and south.

The second round on July 10 turns into a clash of "administrative resources": officials from western Ukraine are working for the incumbent president; those from eastern Ukraine support Kuchma. The morning after polling day, radio and television announce that Kravchuk has won. But this is wishful thinking. In the end, the gap between the two candidates is too wide to pretend otherwise, and the Central Election Commission, after a lame attempt to fudge the result, is forced to recognize Kuchma's victory: 14.66 million votes (52 percent) versus 12.1 million (45 percent).

Kuchma himself does not believe he has won until the last moment. On polling day, he returns to Dnipropetrovsk and, when in the morning his campaign chief of staff calls to congratulate him on his victory, he thinks it's a joke. After all, it's already been announced on television that Kravchuk won.

However, the first president of Ukraine admits defeat and, to his credit, does not challenge the result. Later he will say that his main mistake was in having an overly servile team: "I was surrounded by people I'd long known and trusted. But they all had a Communist Party background. That meant they were incapable of acting outside the box. The Soviet mindset is the boss knows best. . . . So, during the campaign, they basically sat and listened to me in silence."

After stepping down, Leonid Kravchuk looked nothing at all like the founding father of the state. We met several times in Kyiv. There was no theatricality or arrogance about him. He joked and laughed like a wily old man. I once talked to him while strolling along Kyiv's Sofia Square, and the first president felt perfectly at ease among ordinary passersby.

He passed away in May 2022. So too, almost simultaneously, did two other architects of the Belovezh Accords: Stanislav Shushkevich and

Gennady Burbulis. Knowing the penchant of Putin's secret services for "show poisonings," I cannot help feeling that the deaths of three of the gravediggers of the Soviet Union in quick succession in the third month of the war are no coincidence.

Crimea and the KGB

The Ukrainian presidential campaign of 1994 saw the first flare-up over Crimea in the post-Soviet era.

Crimea in 1994 is a Russian-speaking part of Ukraine. After the collapse of the Soviet Union, the peninsula's authorities mulled the idea of seceding and becoming an independent state. Back then, Crimea was governed by the head of the local Communist Party, Mykola Bahrov. He initially supported his former party mate Kravchuk but later realized he could pursue a more independent line.

Two years before, in May 1992, the regional parliament had adopted the Constitution of the Republic of Crimea, which declared the peninsula to be a sovereign state and established the post of president. However, Crimea did not dare to go for full secession. All around, other post-Soviet republics were in the process of disintegrating; separatist movements were sprouting like mushrooms.

On January 1, 1992, war had broken out between the former Soviet republics of Armenia and Azerbaijan over the region of Karabakh, which both states claimed. Then, in March of that same year, armed conflict had erupted in Moldova. And since August 1992, full-scale hostilities had been ongoing between Georgia and its autonomous republic of Abkhazia. Therefore, viewing the chaos in the post-Soviet space, Crimea's leader, Bahrov, decided not to up the ante and risk a fight with Ukraine.

Just as the first president of Ukraine, Kravchuk, is losing his grip on power and his conflict with parliament is escalating, the situation in Crimea becomes tense. In January 1994, presidential elections are held there. Since the peninsula is predominantly Russian speaking, there is strong support for rapprochement with Moscow. Shortly before the vote, they unite in the "Rossiya" ("Russia") bloc. Their candidate is former prosecutor Yuri Meshkov, an inexperienced politician but an impressive orator. He advocates the introduction of Moscow time and the ruble, and a political and economic alliance with Russia. He does not openly talk about a union, but many voters want precisely that. In the second round, Meshkov crushes the former communist leader Bahrov, receiving 72.9 percent of the vote.

Having won, Meshkov goes to Moscow with his begging bowl. After defeating the rebellious parliament, President Yeltsin is taking a breather, hitting the bottle even more than usual; almost all power passes to the head of his security details, the former KGB officer Alexander Korzhakov. Korzhakov has a very different outlook from Yeltsin. In particular, he is drawn to the idea of returning Crimea to Russia.

Meshkov is desperate to see Yeltsin, but Korzhakov won't let him: maybe Yeltsin has had a bit too much to drink, or maybe Korzhakov believes he can handle it himself, without involving his boss. He selects a team for Meshkov, including economist and former deputy prime minister of Russia Yevgeny Saburov, who recently drafted a reform program in Moscow. He is dispatched to Crimea to head the government. Many other members of the new Crimean government are also Russian.

Inevitably, problems arise. First, Kyiv is adamantly opposed to the "Moscow government" in Crimea. Second, Saburov draws up a program of privatization and economic reform that local businessmen view with hostility: they fear that the Muscovites will buy up all the property in Crimea. "We are for Russia, but without Muscovites," says a local member of parliament, not mincing his words. And third, President Meshkov himself is not prepared to take orders from the Moscow economists. Prime Minister Saburov announces the liberalization of prices, which the president cancels a few days later: "There's economics, and then there are living people," Meshkov says.

Meshkov establishes Moscow time in Crimea but cannot fulfill his other promises. He is at loggerheads with parliament, despite his own Rossiya bloc having a majority.

Then, in the summer of 1994, when the "pro-Russian" candidate Kuchma wins the presidency in Ukraine, Moscow's position changes. Korzhakov stops supporting the separatist Meshkov, believing he can soon take control of the whole country.

Nothing works out for the Moscow reformers in Crimea: the president throws a monkey wrench in every gear, and on the ground the economy is controlled by bandits. "Unfortunately, we couldn't find an Adenauer," Saburov complains to reporters, referring to the first chancellor of West Germany, who revived the country after World War II. An aide standing behind him who looks like a gangster intervenes in the conversation: "Who couldn't you find here? We'll find and deliver him shipshape." In October 1994, parliament removes Saburov. In his place, the father of Kuchma's daughter's husband is elected as the new prime minister.

In December 1994, Moscow embarks on a military misadventure when President Yeltsin orders troops into Chechnya, a secession-minded autonomous republic within Russia. Supporting separatism in Crimea now feels foolish, and, besides, all attention is directed elsewhere. In March 1995, Ukraine's parliament scraps the Crimean constitution and abolishes the presidency. The fact that Meshkov was elected by popular vote is a snag, but Kyiv insists that the presidential elections in Crimea were illegitimate to start with. Meshkov does not accept the decision. Holed up in his office, he insists that he is the real leader of Crimea. But the ex-Soviet KGBers maneuver behind his back. Kuchma appoints Yevhen Marchuk, the former head of the Ukrainian KGB, as prime minister of Ukraine, who gets along nicely with his former colleagues in Moscow. Meshkov is taken to Russia by military plane. From now on, Crimea is governed by the father of Kuchma's son-in-law. And Crimean independence is kicked into the long grass.

The Empire Strikes Back

While Ukraine is witnessing the first-ever democratic transfer of power from one president to another, the most famous and outspoken Soviet dissident, writer Alexander Solzhenitsyn, is returning to Russia after years of exile. On May 27, 1994, he and his family fly from the United States to Magadan in the Russian Far East, board a train, and journey westwards, getting off at every stop along the way, talking to ordinary folk. He arrives in Moscow only on July 21.

Curiously, Solzhenitsyn's return to Russia had been predicted almost ten years earlier by another Soviet dissident writer, Vladimir Voinovich. Back in 1986, he had published the dystopian novel *Moscow 2042*.

In Voinovich's futuristic world, the Communist Party has merged with the KGB and the ROC and pure communism has finally been achieved in the city of Moscow. But this joint dictatorship ends when the writer Sim Karnavalov (a parody of Solzhenitsyn) returns to Russia on a white horse as the country's savior. The people fall at his feet and proclaim him tsar. Russia is transformed into an empire, with all the former hallmarks of communist dictatorship still in place; even officials retain their positions, simply changing their names and titles in line with the new fashion.

In reality, Voinovich's prediction about the merger of the Church and the KGB, and even about Solzhenitsyn-style empire building, will come true a little later, under Putin in the 2020s. But back in 1994, Solzhenitsyn's messianic arrival is greeted with indifference. There are no adoring crowds lining the route of his train; the return of the Nobel Prize winner leaves Russians cold.

Meanwhile, the new democratic authorities of St. Petersburg are pressing another exile to return home: Joseph Brodsky. The city's elected mayor, Anatoly Sobchak, awards Brodsky the title of honorary citizen, and the relevant documents are prepared by his deputy, one Vladimir Putin. Sobchak flies to New York to meet with Brodsky, and invites him to St. Petersburg. Brodsky promises to think about it but is in no hurry to return: the news coming out of his homeland does not inspire him with confidence.

In 1995, the Polish journalist and human rights activist Adam Michnik, one of the founders of the Solidarity movement, conducts a long interview with Joseph Brodsky about politics. He knows about Brodsky's love for Polish culture and how he supported Solidarity in the 1980s. But he wants to know why Brodsky never became a dissident and fought against the dictatorship.

"I've never stooped so low as to shout: 'Down with Soviet power!'" Brodsky says.

"That power was never a problem for you? Didn't interest you?" Michnik tries to clarify.

"Perfectly true. But that may have been the biggest challenge of all to that power. At best, it was the subject of jokes and anecdotes. But to take it seriously . . . It was clearly evil incarnate. Everything was absolutely clear. Neither I nor my friends had a shadow of a doubt."

They also discuss Solzhenitsyn. Brodsky says, "In his opinion, Russia is the custodian of certain values that the West has betrayed. What Solzhenitsyn says is utter nonsense. The usual demagoguery. As a politician he is a total zero. In the twentieth century, the idea of the people as the bearer of some kind of truth is simply childish," states Brodsky.

"But he has very deep roots in Russian traditions."

"Be careful with these traditions. They are barely one hundred and fifty years old," replies Brodsky.

Brodsky and Solzhenitsyn lived side by side in the United States for almost twenty years but never saw each other. They are separated by not only a stylistic but also an ideological abyss.

Michnik has not read Brodsky's poem "On the Independence of Ukraine," because it was not published. So, in the interview, he asks only about his homeland: "Tell me, should the Poles be afraid of Russia?"

"Not anymore," Brodsky replied in 1995. "As a great power, I think Russia is finished. Russia has no future as a state seeking to exert forceful pressure; at least it won't be able to strong-arm its neighbors. Not for a long time. Russia's territory will shrink. I don't think there's a threat of Russian military or political aggression. There is, however, a demographic threat. For Poland. Basically, it's time to walk away from the casino table. It's game over."

A few months after this conversation, in January 1996, Brodsky will die of a heart attack in New York, without having visited Russia.

In 2022, after Russia's invasion of Ukraine, I will find Michnik specifically to discuss Brodsky and his poem about the independence of Ukraine. Michnik will defend his late friend: "Brodsky was not a Great Russian chauvinist, absolutely not. But he didn't feel the emotions of Ukrainians who considered themselves not Russian. This problem still exists: many Russians don't know how to retune their imperial mindset in respect of Ukraine."

Clan Warfare

As president, Leonid Kuchma continues his predecessor's economic policy. He is a more experienced economic manager than Leonid Kravchuk, but also a former member of the Communist Party who, moreover, ran a defense enterprise. In the Soviet Union, such people were known as "red directors." Kuchma likewise is not ready to let foreign investors in and buy up the largest enterprises—that is contrary to his convictions. Rather, he believes in the strength of the old Soviet managers, his fellow "red directors." As a result, a new economic system takes shape in which control over Ukraine's whole economy passes to the oligarchs. The fight for property goes hand in hand with criminal wars.

On the evening of October 15, 1995, a soccer game takes place between Football Club Shakhtar Donetsk, the home team, and Sports Club Tavriya from Crimea. There are about two thousand people in the stands. The game is only five minutes old when Shakhtar owner Akhat Bragin shows up at the stadium. He is going up to his box in the stand when an explosion rings out. "A terrible explosion, like during the war," is how a veteran sports reporter who lived through World War II will describe it.

Approximately 11.5 kilograms of TNT had detonated under Bagrin's feet. Only an arm bearing his Rolex wristwatch remained of the once influential regional businessman. Five bodyguards were also killed; no fans were hurt.

Ever since the mid-1980s, when Gorbachev allowed cooperatives and the first Soviet entrepreneurs appeared, Bragin had ruled the Donetsk region: he controlled the central market, all trade channels, plus several major enterprises. He lived in the Hotel Lux, which he owned, a former government residence built in the late 1980s specially for Gorbachev's arrival in Donetsk. It is not the first attempt on the life of Alik the Greek (as business associates call Bragin); on one occasion, his car was fired on with five grenade launchers.

Who could have dared to take out the regional boss? the whole city is asking. Public opinion points the finger firmly at the opposing Dnipropetrovsk clan. These two regions in eastern Ukraine are home to all the country's key enterprises, and all the big money.

The Dnipropetrovsk clan has been significantly strengthened by Leonid Kuchma's election as president. But its real leader is not the head of state, but the governor of the Dnipropetrovsk region, Pavlo Lazarenko. He activated all available "administrative resources" to get Kuchma into the president's chair. And in May 1996, he was appointed to the post of prime minister of Ukraine for his efforts.

Lazarenko is an odious individual. Many years later, Kuchma's son-in-law, businessman Viktor Pinchuk, will claim that during Lazarenko's governorship in Dnipropetrovsk "not a single business could operate without, how shall we say, a contribution to the personal funds of the owner of the region." As the new prime minister, Lazarenko establishes his own rules throughout the country: he introduces a new Ukrainian currency, the hryvnia, and makes several privatization deals. He also fills his government with regional allies. According to most Ukrainian businessmen and their associates who survived the 1990s, Lazarenko did not hesitate to eliminate competitors.

On July 16, 1996, Prime Minister Lazarenko goes to Kyiv's Boryspil Airport to catch a flight to Donetsk. While he is on the way there, a bomb planted under a sewer hatch explodes under his motorcade. His armored BMW withstands the blast, and Lazarenko escapes with just cuts from the broken glass. He still flies to Donetsk, where he steps off the plane in a bloodied white shirt and declares melodramatically that his opponents from Donbas are behind the assassination attempt. Some voices in Kyiv are saying that the attack seems stage-managed, but Lazarenko insists that criminal bosses want him dead, but he was saved by angels.

The showdown continues. With Bragin now out of the way, the most influential person in Donbas is Yevgeny Shcherban. He tries to structure his property by combining roughly 200 enterprises in the Donetsk and Luhansk regions into the so-called Industrial Union of Donbas, which he controls.

On November 3, 1996, Shcherban flies to Donetsk aboard his private plane after attending the birthday party of the singer Iosif Kobzon, popular since Soviet times. In the 1990s, Kobzon gained considerable prestige in the world of Russian organized crime. And in 1995, the US

State Department even denied him a visa over his alleged ties to the Russian mafia. The singer himself states repeatedly that he has nothing to do with the mafia but is simply on good terms with various criminal bosses, including Shcherban.

Shcherban and his wife disembark from the plane and head for the airport building. Right there on the airfield, two men in police uniform approach them. One shoots Shcherban in the back of the head; the other fires indiscriminately in all directions. Shcherban, his wife, the pilot, and several others are killed. As Donetsk businessmen recall, it is the Dnipropetrovsk clan who benefit most from the killing. They quickly succeed in compelling Donbas enterprises to sign gas supply contracts with the Dnipropetrovsk Oil Extraction Plant, controlled by Prime Minister Lazarenko. In 2001, the Prosecutor General's Office of Ukraine will state that it was Lazarenko who ordered Shcherban's killing—but by that time he will already be under arrest in the United States.

In 1996, Rinat Akhmetov takes the place of Bragin and Shcherban in the precarious role of most influential businessman in the Donetsk region. After years of keeping a low profile, he now becomes the new president of the soccer club Shakhtar Donetsk.

"On October 11, 1996, I became the club's president, and told reporters that Shakhtar would become champions of Ukraine," Akhmetov recalls. "They all laughed, I even got a little offended. Why were they laughing? Because at that time Dynamo Kyiv was the grandee of Ukrainian, even European, football. It was impossible to compete with Dynamo Kyiv back then. Kyiv is the capital, Donetsk is a province."

In addition, six months after the murder of Shcherban, Viktor Yanukovych is appointed head of the Donetsk regional administration. It is these two men, Akhmetov and Yanukovych, who will rule Donbas for nearly the next two decades.

KVN for Yeltsin

On May 23, 1996, another round of *KVN* takes place in Moscow. Russian president Boris Yeltsin and his family are in the audience. Approximately three weeks are left before the Russian presidential elections, and Yeltsin has every chance of losing, just as his colleague Leonid Kravchuk did in Ukraine. Therefore, Yeltsin's campaign team makes sure he is constantly on television and associated with popular things.

Onstage that night are the president's hometowners from Yekaterinburg, as well as teams from St. Petersburg and Yerevan (the capital of Armenia) and a combined team from two Ukrainian cities: Zaporizhzhia and Kryvyi Rih. Surprisingly, it is the Ukrainians who joke about Yeltsin most of all—and not in a nasty way. They wish him victory in the elections, ridicule his communist rival, and riff on the president's "Vote or Lose" campaign slogan. In general, the Ukrainians look much more pro-Russian, and even pro-Yeltsin, than the Yekaterinburgers.

When the dust settles, the Yekaterinburg team is in last place; the Armenians and Ukrainians progress to the next round. This is the start of a long journey for the combined Ukrainian team (whose full name is the tongue-twisting Zaporizhzhya–Kryvyi Rih–Transit, or Transit for short), which will see them reach the semifinals, only to go down guns blazing to a team from Belarus.

After their defeat, the team returns home to Ukraine, with the firm intention of winning next year's competition. Most of the team's sketches are written by the brothers Borys and Sergey Shefir. They are no longer students, both are on the wrong side of thirty, but *KVN* is in their DNA. They never go on stage, but manage the team from behind the scenes.

Back in their native Kryvyi Rih, they scour other universities in the city for fresh blood for the Transit team. At one of the rehearsals, their eye is caught by a second-year student of the Kryvyi Rih Institute of Economics, eighteen-year-old Vova Zelensky.

Initially, Vova and his comrades view the Shefirs as competitors and enemies. The invitation to attend a rehearsal in Zaporizhzhia and see the Transit team in action is accepted only by Vova. There his hostility evaporates immediately: "This is a completely different level! I thought you were all jerks, but you're head and shoulders above us," Borys Shefir recalls the young Zelensky's words. The sophomore joins the all-star team and in the spring of 1997 goes with them to Moscow.

I spoke to Borys Shefir at his home in Dresden. In the first days of the war, he left Ukraine together with his wife and small children. Their TV set is always on, tuned to a Russian-language Ukrainian news station. Borys loves to recall past sketches from *KVN*. He usually precedes their retelling with the phrase: "This one's an absolute scream!" From time to time, in the middle of a conversation, he asks himself, *Maybe I should have stayed?* And answers his own question: he is over sixty years old, recently underwent an operation, can no longer serve in the army. In Germany, meanwhile, he runs a charitable foundation, raising money to help the Ukrainian military.

Almost a Champion

Someone from the stage shouts, "You wretched *Moskalis*!" A second comments, "That was a summary of the new Ukrainian constitution." The hall erupts in laughter. This joke is typical for the Transit team during the 1997 season. All rounds are held in Moscow and broadcast on Russia's Channel One station, so the Ukrainian team plays to the audience. That means a lot of jokes about Ukraine too. Back then, it was called self-irony; twenty-five years later, some might find it distasteful.

Or here's a joke about the infamous fight between boxers Mike Tyson and Evander Holyfield, which ended when Tyson bit a chunk out of his opponent's ear:

"Did you know Mike Tyson is a *khokhol*?"

"No, why?"

"He, too, lives by the principle: 'What I don't eat, I'll take a bite from.'"

Nowadays, for the sake of verbal etiquette, such dialogue would not be permitted on prime-time television.

Transit does political jokes too. One of the skits is a conversation between Presidents Yeltsin and Kuchma, with Zelensky, ironically, as Kuchma:

"When will you give up Crimea?" asks Yeltsin, and thinks to himself, *He won't give it up; he has a dacha with a swimming pool and a yacht there.*

"Ukraine considers Crimea to be ancestral Ukrainian territory," replies Kuchma, and thinks to himself, *I won't give it up, I have a dacha with a swimming pool and a yacht there.*

No one watching in the former Soviet Union, where *KVN* is broadcast, is shocked by any of this. Transit is one of the most popular teams, loved in both Russia and Ukraine. Ultimately, the team makes it through to the finals to face the Armenians. In 1997, no one cares that the final competition of Russia's most popular show is between two non-Russian teams.

For the young Vova Zelensky, the final is his first moment of glory: he plays the lead role in many of the sketches; for example, he portrays James Bond in a music competition.

An interesting thing happens during the "captains' contest"—a battle between the leaders of the two teams in which they exchange improvised jokes. The captain of the Armenians asks his opponent how he feels about the Ukrainian president, Leonid Kuchma. The leader of Transit, Misha Gulikov, replies that they often hang out together in the evening. To which the Armenian advises: "I'll tell you one thing, but don't be offended. Never joke about the president, because tomorrow any of us could end up in his shoes." At this moment, the future President Zelensky is standing in the wings, waiting for his turn to go back onstage.

Going into the final contest ("Homework"), Transit is leading by a whole point—a comfortable margin according to the scoring system. The final sketch by the Ukrainians features a Gogol-esque story about New Year's Eve. The protagonist finds himself caught in a kind of time loop, able to turn back the clock, but only to half an hour before midnight on December 31. One of the characters is again Russian president Boris Yeltsin, who delivers his New Year's address from an ordinary Soviet apartment.

The audience is ecstatic, and Transit is sure that victory is theirs. According to sketch writer Borys Shefir, it is one of the best "pieces of homework" in the history of *KVN*. But the show's host, Alexander Maslyakov, is not happy. Even during the rehearsal, he had criticized the sketch and demanded that several scenes be cut; the team complied.

After the finale, Maslyakov unexpectedly says that the jury needs to confer, and takes the judges backstage. They are gone for forty minutes. The audience and the teams become fidgety.

When the jury returns, Maslyakov announces they have decided not to announce any marks for the "Homework" contest; both finalists have won.

The Transit team cries foul, outraged by such daylight robbery. A fight nearly breaks out backstage.

According to Borys Shefir, years later, the captain of the Armenians admitted in private that his team had bribed Maslyakov.

A Doomed City

According to *KVN* rules, the winning team is not allowed to take part in the next season. Because it was a tie, both Transit and the Armenians have to sit out the 1998 season. No one is more upset about it than the nineteen-year-old Vova Zelensky: no sooner has he made a splash in the *KVN* major league when he is immediately forced into retirement.

He decides to put together a new team. The Shefir brothers go to Maslyakov and ask if Zelensky and comrades can take part in the new *KVN* season. To their surprise, Maslyakov agrees. But on one condition: a rematch between Transit and the Armenians shall take place in six months.

At first, the Shefirs refuse out of pride: they believe they won fair and square, but Maslyakov railroaded them. But, for the sake of Zelensky, they eventually agree. So, in April 1998, the "95th Quarter" team, headed by the now-twenty-year-old Vova Zelensky, appears in the *KVN* major league.

One of the team's highlights of that season is a sketch about Steven Spielberg. On a visit to Russia, the sketch goes, he is taken to the old Soviet film studio Mosfilm. "I'll take one of your movies and remake it American-style," Zelensky's Spielberg explains his idea.

Suddenly he hears the theme tune from the Soviet crime-comedy film *Beware of the Car* by cult director Eldar Ryazanov. "What's that song?" asks Spielberg-Zelensky. "Sounds a bit old-fashioned. But that's okay: we'll add an arrangement."

"No, we don't need it," replies the "Russian" giving the tour of the studio, played by one of Zelensky's friends.

"Come on, we can make money from it," insists the American.

"No, we don't need it. . . . Try to understand. . . . No, you'll never understand," the "Russian" answers him.

The idea that Soviet-born people have higher values than Americans, who care only about money, runs through Russian comedy in the 1990s like a thread. The most popular comedian in Russia at the time, Mikhail Zadornov, jokes about nothing else: "stupid Americans" are the leitmotif of every single gag he does. Zadornov is especially popular in the most impoverished countries of the former Soviet Union that cannot recover from the economic collapse.

That said, the level of anti-Americanism in Russian society in the 1990s is still very low. The next couple of decades, however, will see the propaganda in this direction intensify.

The debut of 95th Quarter in the *KVN* major league is unsuccessful. The team performs badly in the quarterfinals and is eliminated. However, Zelensky reappears onstage in the summer of 1998 in the scheduled rematch between Transit and the Armenians.

As before, the "Homework" contest will decide the outcome. This time it is Zelensky who writes the final sketch. He borrows the idea from the mystical novel *The Doomed City* by Soviet sci-fi writers Arkady and Boris Strugatsky. In Zelensky's version, it is a story about a strange city where every day people wake up in new, unusual roles. For example, the protagonist, nicknamed Blind, assumes the role of city mayor and starts speaking in the voice of President Yeltsin.

Zelensky plays the role of the author of the work. He sits at the edge of the stage and composes the story, which the actors play out in real time. At the end, when Blind has become mayor and improved the quality of life for residents of the strange city, Zelensky the author walks onto the middle of the stage. The final monologue goes like this:

"Now I'll write such a book for which I'll never be ashamed. In it will be everything: friendship, love, and simple human happiness. . . . Spring ruled the world. Two lovebirds lay in the endless feather-grass steppe. It smelled of thyme and mint. They were happy. . . . Blind saw all of this through the slit of a telescopic sight. He still had a hot day ahead of him."

At these last words, the team members start to laugh happily.

Transit loses the round, and the Armenians win the game. "It's our own fault. The sketch was way too abstract; it didn't connect," Borys Shefir recalls. "It was Vova's idea; we got carried away by it."

Three Hundred Bucks

Vova Zelensky and the Shefir brothers part ways. He goes home to Kryvyi Rih, while the experienced writing duo along with Misha Gulikov are invited to work in Moscow. One of the most popular presenters and producers of the day, Ivan Demidov, plans to launch a comedy TV channel and invites the Ukrainians to write sketches for it. Each is promised a salary of $600 a month—big money in those days. The former *KVN*ers rent an apartment on the outskirts of the Russian capital, receive a $300 advance each, and get down to work.

But soon, in August 1998, Russia is hit by yet another economic crisis. This time, Prime Minister Sergey Kiriyenko declares a default on the country's sovereign debt. Many projects are scrapped. Demidov's comedy channel dies before it is born. The Ukrainians never receive their promised salary.

Ten years later, Ivan Demidov will become a Russian propagandist and even set up the state-funded Orthodox TV channel Spas (Savior), before heading the ideological department of the pro-Putin United Russia party. And in twenty years' time, Sergey Kiriyenko will be in charge of all domestic policy in the Putin administration, as well as responsible for Ukrainian territory occupied by Russian troops.

After working in Moscow for several months for nothing, the Shefirs decide to return home to Kryvyi Rih. But the former captain of Transit Gulikov persuades them to stay: "Another six months working under me," he suggests. "If we don't make it, we'll leave." But they do make it: the Shefirs first write material for various TV comedy shows, then land jobs as editors in the *KVN* system itself.

Meanwhile, Vova Zelensky continues his *KVN* odyssey, now in the newly formed Ukrainian league. The winner will go to Moscow to compete in the big-league finals. But in the 1999 season 95th Quarter loses. Zelensky himself then travels to Moscow to see his senior former comrades and ask for their help. Without their input, Transit is finished. True, Zelensky warns them there is no money in the enterprise. But he promises that if the team starts doing well enough to go on tour, the writers will get a cut of the profits.

The former captain of Transit refuses. He has a job at the real *KVN*, and the idea of doing something for free (and not even in the big league at that, but in Kyiv) holds no appeal. The Shefirs, however, agree to help out their young compatriot from Kryvyi Rih.

New Television

Having won the presidency thanks to the support of Russian television, Kuchma is well aware of the threat this medium can pose. Russian TV stations are very popular in Ukraine, since their output is much better than that of the domestic ones. The president recognizes the urgent need to make Ukrainian television more appealing; otherwise, come the next election, he will find himself in Kravchuk's shoes if Moscow decides to back a new candidate.

It just so happens that in 1994 the young documentary filmmaker Alexander Rodnyansky returns to Ukraine, after several successful years in German television. His old buddy the young Russian TV presenter Konstantin Ernst, the future head of Russia's main propaganda station, Channel One, invites him to Moscow. At the same time, however, he receives an offer to launch a new station in Ukraine. Rodnyansky decides to remain in Kyiv and develop the concept of a new Ukrainian Russian-language TV channel.

Nothing initially comes of it. Rodnyansky finds himself surrounded on all sides by officials from Kuchma's retinue, who, as he quickly realizes, just want to use him to get a hot product in exchange for a 12 percent stake, with the remaining shares divvied up among themselves. Rodnyansky is ready to ditch the whole idea and return to Germany when he receives a new offer: to launch a Ukrainian-language channel. And so, on

January 1, 1997, 1+1 goes live, and it will soon become the most popular TV station in Ukraine.

Its schedule includes high-quality foreign movies dubbed into Ukrainian and well-made entertainment programs and talk shows. A regular in 1+1's political broadcasts is the young reporter Georgy Gongadze, the creator and author of the as-yet-unknown online publication *Ukrainska Pravda*. He is highly critical of the current government and of Kuchma personally.

In 1994, Kuchma agrees to the removal of the remnants of Soviet nuclear weapons from Ukraine. All medium-range missiles were sent to Russia under Kravchuk. Now, US president Bill Clinton is trying to get Ukraine to give up intercontinental missiles as well, in exchange for a promise that the United States, Russia, and the UK will be guarantors of its security. After signing the so-called Budapest Memorandum, Kuchma meets with French president François Mitterrand. Already seriously ill, Mitterrand looks pessimistically at the fifty-six-year-old Kuchma and tells him: "You should not have signed this, young man, you will be deceived." In 2022, after the Russian invasion, Clinton will say that he regrets putting pressure on Ukraine in the 1990s and forcing Kuchma to sign the Budapest Memorandum.

Meanwhile, Kuchma is gradually changing his foreign policy. In the beginning of his presidency he was perceived as a pro-Russian politician, but now he is starting to turn toward the West. "After every visit to Moscow, the Ukrainian nationalist wakes up in me," Kuchma tells subordinates, unhappy that the Kremlin does not consider Ukraine a separate country and treats him like a younger brother. In July 1997, he signs the Charter on a Special Partnership between NATO and Ukraine. And in a few years he will even write a book with the eloquent title *Ukraine Is Not Russia*.

Coming to America

As prime minister, Pavlo Lazarenko is nothing if not hard-nosed: he brazenly demands a share from all big businesses operating in the country and openly favors his own people. United Energy Systems of Ukraine, a company created by his close friend, the young, attractive businesswoman Yulia Tymoshenko, is a prime example. The name gives the impression of a state-owned structure, but this is misleading. The prime minister himself is a shareholder, and through his efforts it quickly monopolizes the Ukrainian gas supply market.

Pavlo Lazarenko's rampant corruption is beginning to embarrass Western politicians. Kuchma, of course, is well aware of how much, and by what means, his head of government earns, and is forced to periodically defend him before foreign partners. First, Russian prime minister Viktor Chernomyrdin tells Kuchma: "I won't work with this man anymore." Then President Bill Clinton wonders out loud to Kuchma whether it's worth sticking with such a prime minister. In a few years, Kuchma will say this about Lazarenko: "He had a habit of falling on his knees in front of me and crying out: 'Father! Everything I do is for Ukraine; I will not spare my life.'"

However, the friction between president and prime minister is growing. In July 1997, Kuchma dismisses Lazarenko after just one year in the prime ministerial chair. A month later, Lazarenko presents the president with a Franck Muller watch worth $42,000.

Admittedly, say those close to Lazarenko, he owes Kuchma far more. A few years later, the former prime minister's business partner Petro Kyrychenko will testify in a US court that, when the prime minister was fired, he confessed in a private conversation to owing Kuchma $50 million, adding, however, that he "would rather spend it on removing Kuchma from office."

Having lost his post, Lazarenko goes into opposition and creates a party called Hromada. In the parliamentary elections of March 1998, Hromada polls 4.67 percent—enough to get several seats. Not only Lazarenko himself but also his associate the charming Yulia Tymoshenko become members of parliament.

Subsequent events unfold like a soap opera: as early as September 1998, the Ukrainian Prosecutor's Office initiates a criminal case against Lazarenko, accusing him of large-scale embezzlement of state property. But the leader of Hromada is abroad, where he somehow manages to buy a passport of the Republic of Panama. It doesn't save him from arrest, however, which happens on arrival in Switzerland in December. But he is released on bail, and on February 20 he flies to New York. There, right at John F. Kennedy International Airport, he is arrested once again, this time for visa violations. He requests political asylum and hopes to be allowed to move in to his new home—he recently bought himself an estate in California where actor Eddie Murphy used to live. But instead he is sent to a detention center for undocumented migrants.

In June 2000, the US Attorney's Office will charge Lazarenko with laundering $114 million. A Geneva court finds him guilty of the same crime. The trial in America drags on and on; the former prime minister cannot return to Ukraine. Meanwhile, Lazarenko's former "friends" behave as if he has ceased to exist—or as if a passing tornado has sucked the former boss of Dnipropetrovsk into its vortex. Yulia Tymoshenko leaves the Hromada party and embarks on a solo political career without so much as a backward glance at her recent patron. Witnesses to Tymoshenko's career development say she is a witch. This is only partly a joke: in Ukraine, a hundred and fifty years after Gogol, supernatural forces are taken very seriously.

Two Families

In 1997, an important person appears in the life of Leonid Kuchma. The president's daughter, Elena, divorces the son of the Crimean prime minister and starts dating Viktor Pinchuk. He is already a prominent businessman, but not yet a household name in Ukraine. In pursuing Elena, he is, of course, keen to make a good impression on his potential father-in-law. So he decides to run for a seat in the Verkhovna Rada, the Ukrainian parliament. Because of his political inexperience and fear of falling flat on his face in front of Kuchma, he hires a team of spin doctors from Russia, one of whom is Timofey Sergeytsev. The consultants do not let him down: Pinchuk wins a seat in his native city of Dnipropetrovsk. Pinchuk's star is rising: the company Interpipe soon becomes the largest pipe manufacturer in Ukraine, and he acquires the TV station ICTV with a view to making it the most influential media company in the country. Sergeytsev is brought on board to develop the

TV business. As for marrying Kuchma's daughter, that happens only in 2002.

In Russia, the presidential family plays a much more important role in the late 1990s. Boris Yeltsin's daughter, Tatyana, likewise parts with her first husband and begins a live-in relationship with journalist Valentin Yumashev. Friends, and later the general public, know them as "Tanya" and "Valya."

Yumashev's rise is meteoric. Already in March 1997, he is appointed head of the presidential administration. And since President Yeltsin is gravely ill, Valya and Tanya are effectively in charge of the country.

They themselves are not oligarchs in the full sense of the word, but they enjoy the patronage of billionaires, the closest of whom are Boris Berezovsky and his junior partner in the oil business, Roman Abramovich. Berezovsky is also the owner of Channel One, Russia's most influential TV station. And he keeps his eyes and ears open at all times, compiling enough dirt on opponents and allies alike to have them under his thumb, including the president's family.

The indefatigable Berezovsky fancies himself as a puppet master, running the country from behind the scenes, with Tanya and Valya at his beck and call. And he promotes the myth of his own power, demonstrating to all around that it is he who holds the levers of government, and no one else. In reality, of course, he is not a member of the Family (the inner circle of Yeltsin's inner circle). Tanya and Valya eye him with mistrust and apprehension; they suspect that Berezovsky's scheming will cause them more harm than good.

Ukraine has its own Berezovsky in Viktor Medvedchuk, an oligarch who has the ear of the president, from which position of advantage he derives political benefits. A former lawyer, he served as the public defender at the trial of dissident Vasyl Stus but did not help him. Quite the contrary, in fact.

The oligarchic systems of Russia and Ukraine are very similar. That said, the one built by Kuchma turns out to be more stable: every Ukrainian oligarch is basically a monopolist in their industry, which stops them warring with each other; each has their own allotment, which makes them more interested in cooperation than confrontation. And together they exert a vast influence on politics: they buy politicians and regional officials, and set their own rules of the game, while the president acts like a jury foreman, preventing them from quarreling. Russia in the 1990s knows no such stability: the oligarchs fight endlessly, the president is dysfunctional, and his family cannot maintain the balance and must rely heavily on one of the business groups.

TV Killers

The next presidential elections are scheduled for 1999 in Ukraine and for 2000 in Russia.

Russian leader Boris Yeltsin is no longer eligible to run, and, in any case, he is physically unable to. He is so sick, in fact, that it's hard to know whether he has any say at all in the running of the country, or whether everything is decided by his family and right-hand oligarchs.

At the same time, the Yeltsin clan's enemies are very strong. The clear favorite in the elections is Moscow mayor Yuri Luzhkov, who is openly hostile to the Yeltsins and Berezovsky and positions himself as a far more imperially minded politician. He promises to restore Russia to its former greatness, which the democrats (that is, Yeltsin and supporters) have thrown away. The Moscow mayor's hobbyhorse is the handover of Crimea to Ukraine, which became significant only after the collapse of the Soviet Union. Luzhkov talks a great deal about how the peninsula historically belongs to Russia, how it was conquered by Catherine the Great, and so Yeltsin did not have the right to give it away with "the stroke of a pen." The mayor uses the Moscow budget to assist Crimea financially, for which the flagship of Russia's Black Sea Fleet, the cruiser *Slava*, is renamed *Moskva*. It would be more appropriate to name the vessel *Luzhkov*, but that would be too much for the Kremlin, which views the Moscow mayor as a dangerous threat.

(In the spring of 2022, the cruiser *Moskva* will sink unexpectedly: the Russian military will claim that a fire broke out on board, denying categorically that it was hit by Ukraine's armed forces. Ukrainians say they managed to flood it with the help of the Neptune missile system.)

The jingoistic mayor seems a shoo-in for the presidency. The pro-Luzhkov media show endless coverage of scandals surrounding Yeltsin's family, writing that his entourage has sold out to the oligarchs. The Moscow mayor himself talks about it publicly.

In the spring of 1999, the Moscow mayor steps up his preelection preparations with the launch of two ambitious projects. The first is to build a bridge across the Kerch Strait, which would connect the Crimean Peninsula with Russia. The second is to restore the Cathedral of Christ the Savior, blown up by the communists in 1931. Its construction is slated for completion just in time for the start of the presidential election campaign.

The Kremlin tries every which way to stop Luzhkov. As he himself recalls, Yeltsin regularly calls him and strongly advises him not to build the church in such haste. But Luzhkov only speeds up the schedule to spite the president.

The situation over in Ukraine is far more favorable for the incumbent president than in Russia: Leonid Kuchma has a good chance of securing reelection, as he has no strong rivals.

Six months before the elections, on March 25, 1999, Vyacheslav Chornovil, one of the leaders of the Ukrainian opposition and a potential presidential candidate from the People's Movement of Ukraine (Rukh), dies in a car crash. Everything about the accident looks suspicious—Chornovil's vehicle slammed into a truck performing an unexpected turn on the highway. The investigation finds the deceased driver, Chornovil guilty. An eyewitness of the accident, who was in the truck cab, behaves in a very odd manner: without telling friends or family, he moves to the countryside, drinks nonstop for days on end, then dies suddenly of a heart attack. The crash investigation is soon closed.

Death by strange road accident is not uncommon around the world at that time. Eighteen months previously, for example, Princess Diana was killed in Paris, with a lot of conspiracy theories around it.

The whole world is transfixed by the events unfolding in the Balkans. The Clinton administration decides to take military action in Yugoslavia. NATO troops intervene in the conflict between the Kosovo Albanians and the Serbs and on March 24 launch a bombing campaign against Serbian cities. Russia's response is one of shock and outrage: Prime Minister Yevgeny Primakov is flying to the United States on an official visit when he is informed of the operation. He immediately orders the plane to turn around over the Atlantic and return to Moscow. This overt anti-American gesture unexpectedly increases Primakov's domestic popularity. In Russian society, it turns out, there is a craving for confrontation with the West. Many Russians have felt nothing but humiliation since the collapse of the Soviet Union and the overnight loss of national pride. So Primakov's démarche makes a pleasant change.

The bombing of Belgrade sparks the first public altercation between the United States and Russia since the end of the Cold War. And Prime Minister Primakov suddenly becomes the main contender for the role of President Yeltsin's successor.

However, the family of the elderly Russian leader has its own plans for the power handover. Neither Primakov, nor the also very popular Moscow mayor, Yuri Luzhkov, fits the bill. What the family needs is a president who is fully controllable and will provide security guarantees. The most suitable candidate is the then-unknown director of the FSB, Vladimir Putin. Oligarch Boris Berezovsky, representing the Yeltsin family, flies specially to Biarritz, where Putin is vacationing with his family, to offer him the post. According to Berezovsky's later memoirs, Putin hesitated at first, saying he would prefer to head the state gas corporation Gazprom, not the entire country. But in the end, he agrees.

When Berezovsky returns, Yeltsin dismisses the government and appoints Putin as prime minister, simultaneously naming him as his successor. All of Russia is in shock: the name Putin is completely unknown. At the same time, war breaks out once more in the North Caucasus when a group of Islamists from Chechnya attacks Dagestan. It will later transpire that this was a preelection operation orchestrated by the oligarch Berezovsky. The Second Chechen War is Putin's opportunity to show the people of Russia what a strong, effective, and all-round heroic leader he is.

In early September 1999, Putin delivers a decisive blow to his main rival in the struggle for the presidency, Mayor Luzhkov. Moscow is shaken by a series of terror attacks: two apartment buildings are blown up in quick succession. The federal authorities lay the blame squarely at the mayor's door, accusing him of neglecting security to such an extent that Chechen terrorists can freely enter the capital and plant explosives in residential buildings. In stark contrast, Putin at this moment is taking the fight to the Chechens. Who was really behind the attacks has yet to be proven conclusively. However, over the years evidence has come to light pointing the finger of blame at the FSB, which, until March 1999, was headed by Putin.

The decisive battle between the Yeltsin family and its opponents is expected to take place in December 1999 during the parliamentary elections, which are essentially a rehearsal for the following year's presidential ones.

In Ukraine, the next presidential ballot is scheduled earlier, for October 31. Kuchma's campaign is managed by the same political strategists hired by Pinchuk, including Timofey Sergeytsev. They are more "methodologists" than election experts—followers of the doctrine of Soviet philosopher Georgy Shchedrovitsky, the founder of the Moscow Methodological Circle, an academic community that sought to examine issues from an interdisciplinary point of view.

A hallmark of methodologists is their belief that reality can be constructed. As such, any problem can be stated in the form of a game. The ability to dress up psychobabble as a bespoke solution to any problem is hardly cutting-edge know-how, yet methodologists treat their method as sacred and are sure that they can find a way out of problems like no one else.

The project cooked up by Sergeytsev and company for Kuchma is known as "street television." In cities across Ukraine, tents are set up from which TV anchors interview passersby live on air. In fact, each participant is prepped in advance by an experienced psychologist-moderator to ensure they say only positive things about the incumbent president. Russian TV presenter Dmitry Kiselev helps Sergeytsev and the company. He moves to Kyiv, where he heads the news service of Pinchuk's ICTV channel. Kiselev will work on Ukrainian television for six years, and all these years he will give the impression of a patriot of Ukraine. And then he will return to Russia and become the most odious propagandist: he will head the state news agency RIA Novosti.

The TV propaganda works. The incumbent president and his government-controlled communist opponent make it through to the second round of the elections. Viktor Medvedchuk proposes to Kuchma a scheme that was tested in the Russian presidential elections in 1996: one of the candidates who successfully performed in the first round will call on his voters to vote for the incumbent head of state in exchange for promotion to the position of secretary of the Security Council. It's going to be the former head of the KGB and former prime minister Yevhen Marchuk: he places fifth in the first round. Kuchma agrees and confidently wins in the second round.

In Russia, the election campaign is far more aggressive and in-your-face: Channel One host Sergey Dorenko (dubbed the "TV killer" for his on-screen hatchet jobs on politicians) trashes Primakov, Luzhkov, and their party on a daily basis, claiming they want to turn back the clock, restore the Soviet Union, and establish a KGB dictatorship. Putin, by contrast, they present as a staunch supporter of democracy who can restore order in the country.

The agitprop has an effect. In the ensuing parliamentary elections, the now-puppet communists take first place, while the synthetic pro-Kremlin party created by Berezovsky, Unity, comes second by a slender margin. The star turn is Sergey Shoigu, Minister for Emergency Situations. Unity positions itself as a democratic association committed to stamping out the vestiges of the Soviet imperial past. In the presidential campaign, it supports Vladimir Putin. Yuri Luzhkov's Fatherland party, which for many symbolizes the imperial past, manages only third place. And fourth goes to the liberal Union of Right Forces, which stands for democracy and Russia's integration into the civilized world, led by Sergey Kiriyenko. Twenty-two years later, it is Putin, Shoigu, and Kiriyenko who will be the faces of Russia's military invasion of Ukraine, completely changing their political slogans.

New Year Magic and the Antichrist

On December 31, 1999, Russian president Boris Yeltsin, as expected, addresses the nation. And not just once, but twice, as in the *KVN* sketch by Transit. At noon, he announces he is stepping down prematurely and transferring power to Prime Minister Vladimir Putin. Then, at midnight, Yeltsin tearfully hands the power over to his self-assured successor. It is truly a night of magical transformation and, for the Yeltsin family, a brilliant political ploy: neither Luzhkov nor his allies will have time to prepare for early presidential elections.

Earlier, on the morning of that landmark December 31, 1999, Luzhkov, expecting nothing out of the ordinary, visits the Cathedral of Christ the Savior in downtown Moscow. With the reconstruction almost finished, the patriarch of the ROC, Alexy II, celebrates the first liturgy in the magnificent new building. When the service ends, a press secretary clutching a mobile phone rushes up to the mayor and reports the president's resignation.

"Do you understand what it means?" Luzhkov whispers in reverential awe. "Yeltsin is the Antichrist! As soon as we finished building the cathedral, the Antichrist fell!"

In the evening, Yeltsin solemnly departs from the Kremlin, handing over the nuclear briefcase to Putin, uttering a portentous, "Protect Russia," in parting. Three months later, Putin will win the presidential election in the first round. Neither Luzhkov, nor Primakov, nor any other real opponent will risk putting themselves forward.

And a few months after that, Putin will launch an attack on Boris Berezovsky for daring to think that he can control the president. In August 2000, the "TV killer" Sergey Dorenko, on Berezovsky's instructions, will repeatedly attack Putin on the air, just as he destroyed Luzhkov and Primakov before. But this time the outcome is different. A few weeks later, under pressure from the Kremlin, Berezovsky is forced to sell his stake in Channel One to his erstwhile friend and junior partner Roman Abramovich.

I interviewed Luzhkov several times, in his small office off Tverskaya Street in central Moscow. He was long retired and felt almost like an oppositionist. And he was adamant that he'd been unfairly targeted by the authorities. "Life to the Fatherland, honor to no one," he says with a mischievous smile, citing an eighteenth-century military saying. Such a sweet, kind old man. In December 2019, I called him to arrange another interview, and he agreed to talk in two days. The very next day he died during a routine medical procedure.

Headless Journalist

Kuchma, having won the Ukrainian presidential elections in the fall of 1999, holds a nationwide referendum on constitutional amendments that could allow him to run a third time. To many onlookers, Kuchma's grip on power feels unassailable.

Everyone knows from Kuchma's first presidential term that he is very picky about his choice of prime minister: he considers heads of his government as possible threats to himself.

He even dismissed one of them, Yevhen Marchuk, a veteran of Ukrainian politics, "for creating his own political image." After the election, Kuchma forms a new, pro-Western, reform-minded government. And he offers the prime minister's chair to the young head of National Bank of Ukraine, Viktor Yushchenko; the deputy prime minister is Yulia Tymoshenko.

But the president soon regrets his choice: the forty-five-year-old Yushchenko is obsessed with both the public and the press. "Again I've picked the wrong guy," Kuchma complains to his inner circle.

Another hater of Viktor Yushchenko is politician Viktor Medvedchuk, whose influence over the head of state at this very moment is on the rise. He is the Deputy Speaker of Parliament, a seemingly insignificant position, but everyone knows he has the president's ear and uses it to push his agenda. Medvedchuk does all he can to turn Kuchma against Yushchenko.

In late 1999, the president finds himself at the center of a more sinister intrigue. According to one widespread version of events, Kuchma's bodyguard, Mykola Melnychenko, starts to pay more frequent visits to his boss's office. In November 1999, according to his own recollection, he installs a voice recorder under the sofa. From these secret recordings, it will later become known that in 2000 Kuchma first learned about the existence of the online publication *Ukrainska Pravda* and its editor in chief, Georgy Gongadze, the same journalist who speaks his mind on political talk shows on Rodnyansky's station.

The president, of course, does not use the Internet—in 2000 in Ukraine it is still the preserve of techies. But he is supplied with printouts of articles. Judging by the transcripts of Melnychenko's audio files, Kuchma has trouble remembering the editor in chief's name, referring to him simply as "the Georgian." Gongadze's articles enrage Kuchma. Several times in conversation—be it with his interior minister, the head of the secret services, or the head of his administration—he suggests teaching Gongadze a lesson: letting the Chechens kidnap him, strip him, take him to Georgia, and demand a ransom.

If the recordings are to be believed, Kuchma's interlocutors—Interior Minister Yuriy Kravchenko and secret service heads—demonstrate amazing persistence: time and time again they mention Gongadze: "That fucking Georgian bastard is way out of line."

On September 16, 2000, after work, Georgy Gongadze goes to see his colleague, the editor in chief of *Ukrainska Pravda*, Olena Prytula. At 10:30 p.m. he leaves her place, but he does not make it home to his wife. He is detained by four police officers, bundled into a car, and taken to the forest. There they dig a hole seventy centimeters wide and a meter deep, or about two feet by three feet. The journalist is pulled out of the car, laid on the ground, and tied up. Gongadze begs for his life, to which one of the officers, the head of the Main Criminal Investigation Department of the Ministry of Interior of Ukraine, Oleksiy Pukach, stuffs a handkerchief into the reporter's mouth and tries to choke him to death. He does not succeed, so another of the men removes Gongadze's belt and Pukach strangles the journalist with it. It is around 1:00 a.m. when Georgy Gongadze dies. They douse his body in gasoline, set it alight, and bury the remains in the pit.

The police officers return from the forest and report to Interior Minister Yuriy Kravchenko that his order to "kill, burn, bury" has been carried out to the letter.

Six weeks later, the interior minister is suddenly struck by the fear that the corpse of the missing Gongadze will be found, so he orders its relocation. Pukach digs up the body, cuts off the head with an ax, and reburies the decomposing remains in two different places.

In mid-October 2000, Major Melnychenko calls one of the leaders of the Ukrainian opposition, the former speaker of the Ukrainian parliament and former presidential candidate Oleksandr Moroz, and hands the recordings over to him.

Then, on November 2, in a forest 120 kilometers (75 miles) away, passersby notice a hand sticking out of a mound. The police organize a dig and find a decapitated body, which Olena Prytula identifies as Georgy Gongadze.

On November 4, Mykola Melnychenko resigns from the presidential security service. And on November 26, together with his family, he flies to the Czech Republic. On November 28, Oleksandr Moroz holds a press conference where he speaks publicly about Major Melnychenko's recordings and President Kuchma's alleged involvement in Gongadze's murder.

Years later, members of Kuchma's inner circle will voice a quite different version of what happened: there's no way Melnychenko could have put a voice recorder under the sofa, never mind regularly change the tape in it. Instead, they claim, the secret service had been listening in: ever since Soviet times, the president's office on Bankova Street had been stuffed with bugs, when the building was occupied by Communist Party leaders and monitored by the KGB. The former head of the Ukrainian KGB, Yevhen Marchuk, was not just aware of these devices but oversaw the wiretapping process himself. And, having been appointed Secretary of the Security Council, he was able to exploit his new position. However, according to this version, the wiretapping was not Marchuk's personal initiative, but part of an operation cooked up in Moscow. Putin, it is said, on coming to power immediately sought to take Kuchma under his control and punish him for moving closer to NATO.

Ukraine without Kuchma

On December 15, a powerful protest under the banner "Ukraine with-out Kuchma" breaks out in central Kyiv. The young activists meticu-lously re-create the protest of 1990: they pitch tents on the capital's main square, which, however, has since been renamed Maidan Neza-lezhnosti (Independence Square). But these protesters lack a magnetic, charismatic leader.

Closer to New Year, the authorities manage to force the protesters off the square under the pretext that it needs to be landscaped in the run-up to the tenth anniversary of independence. A column, fountains, gates, and a nearby mall are what define Maidan (or the Maidan) these days. But back in 2000 none of this existed yet, and the redevelopment was seen by journalists as a sneaky way to drive the protesters away. The Ukrainian authorities borrowed the idea from their Russian counter-parts: in the late 1990s, Moscow mayor Yuri Luzhkov all but destroyed Manezhnaya Square next to the Kremlin: under it, he built a mall, and decorated the area with fountains and animal statues. Thus, Manezh-naya became wholly unsuited to mass rallies, after having been the site, in the early 1990s, of the biggest protests in the history of the Soviet Union, with up to a million participants.

New Year 2001 is fast approaching. Kuchma's associates are confi-dent they have defeated the protest and the scandal of the recordings will soon be forgotten. But in January, the demonstrations resume with renewed vigor. Opposition activists set up tents on Khreshchatyk street, Kyiv's main thoroughfare. All the same, the authorities remain confident that the threat is not too serious.

On January 19, Kuchma fires Deputy Prime Minister Yulia Tymoshenko. Unexpectedly, the thirty-nine-year-old politician from Dnipropetrovsk goes over to the opposition. She claims to have been actively fighting corruption in the gas sector during her time in gov-ernment, for which reason she made many powerful enemies among the president's entourage and influential oligarchs, and was dismissed as a result. The colorful Tymoshenko is exactly what the protest needs. In a matter of days, the "Ukraine without Kuchma" movement enjoys a new lease on life, and Ukraine gets its own fiery twenty-first-century Joan of Arc: Tymoshenko's transformation from government official to oppositionist politician is lightning fast and very impressive.

At first, the authorities do not react. Only in February do they finally realize the situation is out of control. Tymoshenko is duly arrested and accused of corruption: it is alleged that during Lazarenko's prime ministership she embezzled millions as the head of a gas company. But the criminal case against the out-of-favor Tymoshenko in the midst of the protests does not destroy but rather enhances her reputation, turning her into an icon of the protest movement.

The day after Tymoshenko's arrest, her former boss, Prime Minister Yushchenko, makes a joint address with President Kuchma to the people. "An unprecedented political campaign has been launched against our state, with all the signs of psychological warfare," they say, blaming unprincipled politicians, first and foremost Tymoshenko. Then, for the first time in Ukrainian political history, Kuchma and Yushchenko describe their political enemies as fascists: "Suffice it to take a closer look at their symbols and slogans, at the attributes that decorate their theatrical political shows, to know that we are facing a Ukrainian version of national socialism," the address continues. "We must never forget the lessons of history. Remember how and from what fascism began."

On March 9, the birthday of Ukraine's national poet, Taras Shevchenko, there are major clashes between protesters and police. Several of the protest leaders are detained. The action is not as effective as the students' hunger strike in 1990, because the authorities have no plans to make concessions. But President Kuchma's authority lies in tatters.

Twenty years later, Yuriy Lutsenko, one of the organizers of the "Ukraine without Kuchma" movement and the right-hand man of Oleksandr Moroz, will say that the whole "cassette scandal" was organized by Moscow to overthrow the Ukrainian president and the opposition took the bait; he will express remorse for acting as the Kremlin's poodle and bringing people out onto the square.

In March 2001, the 95th Quarter team appears in the *KVN* major league. One of the sketches imagines a situation in which anyone can turn into any celebrity. "I'll be Al Pacino," Vova Zelensky thinks out loud, then turns to his friend Pikalov, "and you, Sanya, will be Kuchma. What, you don't want that? No one does."

BALTIC
SEA

ESTONIA

St. Petersburg

LATVIA

LITHUANIA

Moscow

RUSSIA

BELARUS

RUSSIA

POLAND

Lviv

Kyiv

Kharkiv

Ivano-Frankivsk

U K R A I N E

Dnipropetrovsk

Luhansk

MOLDOVA

Kryvyi Rih

Donetsk

Mykolaiv

SEA
OF AZOV

ROMANIA

CRIMEA

Sevastopol

BLACK SEA

**2004 UKRAINIAN
PRESIDENTIAL ELECTION**

Votes by regions, second round re-run:

Viktor Yushchenko (winner)

Viktor Yanukovych

TURKEY

200 miles

200 km

11

BANDERA AGAIN:
HOW PUTIN SOWED THE SEEDS
OF THE ORANGE REVOLUTION

Legacy of the Soviet History

New Russian president Vladimir Putin himself has no Ukrainian links. He has no relatives there, has never worked or studied there. Although his circle of friends includes at least two families with Ukrainian surnames, their mentality is decidedly not Ukrainian.

Back in the late 1990s, Putin, together with some close buddies, created a dacha cooperative: a sort of joint-stock company that owned the land on which the cofounders built their own dachas. The land acquisition scheme was murky and potentially corrupt. As soon as Putin was elected president, his dacha neighbors found themselves on the list of Russia's most influential politicians and/or businessmen.

Take, for example, Andrey and Sergey Fursenko. In the early 2000s, Andrey will end up in the government and Sergey at Gazprom. The former will be appointed minister of education and science, the latter as the head of the Russian Football Union. Despite their Ukrainian surname, the Fursenko brothers have never felt any connection with Ukraine. Both they and their father are natives of St. Petersburg; their grandfather was born in Crimea but spent most of his life in Russia's northern capital.

Another cofounder of the cooperative is Yuri Kovalchuk. He and his elder brother, Mikhail, were friends with Putin back in the 1990s. In the 2000s, Yuri will become a major banker and media mogul, while Mikhail will head the Kurchatov Institute, Russia's leading nuclear research institution.

Their family history does have a Ukrainian connection. Grandpa Kovalchuk was originally from the Mykolaiv region in southern Ukraine. In the late eighteenth century, this territory was annexed to Russia by Prince Potemkin. Grandpa moved to St. Petersburg before the revolution, and his son, Valentin, carved out a brilliant career in Soviet Leningrad as a military historian. During World War II, the latter taught at the Naval Institute in Sevastopol; the topic of his dissertation was "The Defense of the Sea Lanes of the Besieged Sevastopol."

The military history of Crimea is one of Valentin Kovalchuk's two areas of specialization. The other is the Siege of Leningrad, a topic he researched from the 1960s until the end of his life. Interestingly, one of Valentin Kovalchuk's colleagues and friends was none other than Aleksandr Fursenko, the father of Andrey and Sergey. The elder Kovalchuk and Fursenko worked side by side for most of their lives at the Leningrad branch in the Institute of History of the Soviet Academy of Sciences. True, Fursenko Sr. specializes in the history of the United States, which in the Soviet years is intermixed with ideology: an academic who studies America is duty bound to stigmatize the West's imperialism and aggressive militarism and expose the machinations of the CIA. Fursenko's doctoral dissertation is titled "The Expansion of American Imperialism in China in 1895–1900." Fursenko clearly adheres very closely to the party line: he is made an academician, which speaks of an impeccable ideological position.

Vladimir Putin hails from a far simpler family of factory workers. But he loves talking to his friends' Soviet historian-parents, and they have a great influence on him both in the 1990s and after his election as president. In 2006, he will award Kovalchuk Sr., and in 2007 Fursenko Sr., the Order for Services to the Fatherland.

It is their Soviet approach to history that will guide Putin's policies: Americans are enemies; Sevastopol is sacred for Russians; Ukrainians are not a separate nation; the Ukrainian language does not exist.

Exactly the same sentiment will prevail in the administration of President Vladimir Putin in the early 2000s. Officials there believe that the Ukrainian language is merely distorted Russian.

A top Kremlin official recalls how he once went to Kyiv on an official visit and was accommodated in the reception house on Bankova Street, next to the building of the presidential administration. One morning, President Kuchma himself drops by to see the guest from Moscow. On entering, the Ukrainian president instructs the servants to "set the table." It is 11:00 a.m., and the vodka is already flowing. What perplexes the Kremlin official most of all is Kuchma's remarks about Ukrainian nationalists. "They, of course, are more Ukrainian than we are. The future belongs to them; we still have a lot to learn from them," is how the guest from Moscow recalls the president's words.

Kuchma is referring primarily to his own poor command of the Ukrainian language and lack of knowledge of his country's history. But the Russian official is irritated by such deference, as he sees it, to the Ukrainian language. He cannot refrain from swearing when talking, for example, about the Ukrainian custom of "translating" all first names: every "Nikolay" in Russian turns into "Mykola" in Ukrainian; "Dmitry" into "Dmytro"; "Alexander" into "Oleksandr"; "Vladimir" into "Volodymyr"; and so on. "Why the hell do you have to translate first names? Who came up with this bullshit?" I listen to this senior politician and at first do not even notice the logical fallacy in his words. Only years later will I realize that in exactly the same way, only in the opposite direction, Russians have been translating Ukrainian names for centuries, turning Prince Volodymyr of Kyiv into Vladimir.

Indignation about "Ukrainization" was common even back in the Soviet Politburo. Questions as to whether Ukrainian is a separate language or just "wrong Russian," as well as Ukraine's alleged violation of the rights of the country's Russian-speaking inhabitants, can be found in the minutes of meetings of the Central Committee of the Communist Party. But in Soviet times, Ukraine and the Ukrainian language often had support at the very top from successive heads of state. In the Putin years, however, there are no more "Ukrainophiles" in power. All those with Ukrainian roots consistently behave like the "Little Russian" courtiers under Catherine II or Nicholas I: they claim that the Ukrainian language does not exist at all.

Two Viktors

Ukrainian president Leonid Kuchma manages to survive the months-long protests. Finally, in the spring of 2001, they gradually fizzle out. "The reins of power were lying on the floor, waiting to be picked up," recalls media manager Alexander Rodnyansky, head of the most popular Ukrainian TV channel, 1+1, "but no one did." Prime Minister Yushchenko is hesitant to challenge Kuchma, saying, when interviewed, that he "sees him as a father."

But the idyll does not last long. On April 26, 2001, the Verkhovna Rada (Ukraine's parliament) delivers a vote of no confidence in the government of Viktor Yushchenko. This is clearly the work of the president's right-hand man, Viktor Medvedchuk. "I'm leaving in order to return," Yushchenko declares suggestively, but says nothing about his erstwhile "father."

The president is still of two minds: Should he run for a third time—the ambiguous interpretation in the new constitution is still there—or is it better to find a successor as Russian president Boris Yeltsin has done?

Over in Russia, in just one year in power Putin has cracked down on his political opponents rather harshly. The country's two main TV stations that were once critical of him have now changed ownership: Boris Berezovsky's Channel One has been acquired by Roman Abramovich; and in April 2001 NTV passes into the hands of Gazprom. Then, in December 2001, Yuri Luzhkov's opposition party, Fatherland, merges with the pro-Putin Unity to form the new ruling party: United Russia. The party is headed de facto by the presidential administration.

Kuchma seeks to learn from Putin. He creates a Ukrainian equivalent of United Russia in the shape of the political bloc For United Ukraine, led by Vladimir Litvin, the head of Kuchma's administration, mirroring the situation in Moscow. In Ukrainian, the party's name, Za Yedinuyu Ukrainy, is abbreviated as Za YedU, which comically means "For Food."

However, whereas United Russia has no real opposition, a formidable adversary is taking shape right under Kuchma's nose: Viktor Yushchenko's Our Ukraine bloc. In the parliamentary elections of March 2002, Our Ukraine receives 23.57 percent and takes first place, with its ally Yulia Tymoshenko with 7 percent in fourth position. The party of power, Za YedU, can only manage third place, while the party of Medvedchuk, Kuchma's wingman, slumps to sixth. But that doesn't stop him. Instead of entering parliament, Medvedchuk becomes the new head of the presidential administration. It is he who sets out to rebuild Ukraine along the lines of Putin's Russia.

As ever, it all starts with television. The station 1+1 suddenly finds itself at the center of a lawsuit and comes close to losing its broadcasting license. The channel's management is told that it needs to curtail its criticism of the country's leadership and start supporting the authorities if it wants to survive. Its owner, Alexander Rodnyansky, accepts these terms. Today he recalls that the pressure on 1+1 became so intense he decided to leave for Moscow and work in entertainment television there, just to avoid having to dance to Medvedchuk's increasingly authoritarian tune.

Meanwhile, the head of the presidential administration forces almost all TV stations to obey: he sends out instructions on what can and cannot be discussed, known in Ukraine as *temniki* (topic lists). There are two main rules: never show or mention Viktor Yushchenko; always show and quote Viktor Medvedchuk at length. The journalists draw the obvious conclusion that the head of the administration is already grooming himself as Kuchma's successor.

Yushchenko is the antipode of Medvedchuk: the latter is the archetypal pro-Russian politician, and was even born in Siberia; the former is the ideal pro-American politician. He has fairly close ties to the US establishment, and his wife, Kateryna, was born in Chicago in an émigré family from Ukraine. In the 1980s she worked at the State Department, then at the White House, in the administrations of Ronald Reagan and George H. W. Bush, then at the Treasury Department. The US administration of George W. Bush sees Yushchenko as a man they can do business with. All the while, their faith in Kuchma and his entourage is collapsing.

Love Actually

On September 11, 2001, the United States is hit by a series of terror attacks that will change the world. Terrorists hijack four planes that crash into the towers of the World Trade Center in New York and the Pentagon building in Washington, D.C. The whole world is in shock. The first international leader to call US president George W. Bush to offer his support and condolences is Russian president Vladimir Putin.

The Bush administration immediately begins planning a military operation in Afghanistan with the support of almost all countries of the world, including Russia and Ukraine. That is followed by the war in Iraq. Putin is against it, causing the first cracks in his relationship with Bush to appear. But things for Kuchma are far worse.

The American media, citing intelligence reports, write that several Ukrainian-made Kolchuga radar installations were found in the possession of the Iraqi army. They analyze the Melnychenko tapes and find that, back in 2000, Kuchma seemingly discussed with the head of the Ukrainian military-industrial complex, Valery Malev, secret deliveries of Kolchuga systems through Jordan to Iraq—and even instructed him to keep it under wraps and take care that intermediaries did not leak anything. The press labels the scandal "Kuchmagate."

A scandal erupts. Kuchma publicly declares that no Kolchuga systems were sold to Iraq. Then, in March, Malev suddenly dies in a car accident: his vehicle smashes into a truck, just like the oppositionist Chornovil's had a couple of years before. The US State Department officially accuses Ukraine of selling weapons to Iraq, and even withholds financial aid promised to Kyiv.

In 2002, the Bush administration begins preparations for a military operation in Iraq. This war will permanently alter the whole system of international relations. Russia, France, and Germany oppose the offensive, their leaders Vladimir Putin, Jacques Chirac, and Gerhard Schröder form a kind of anti-war alliance, but Bush ignores them. British prime minister Tony Blair supports the United States, despite anti-war protests numbering in the hundreds of thousands.

No Kolchuga systems will be found in Iraq.

The war in Iraq becomes a springboard for the global anti-Americanism that Putin will soon champion. Curiously, in the run-up to Christmas 2003, the romantic comedy *Love Actually* (written by Richard Curtis) is released in Britain, in which the British prime minister, played by Hugh Grant, delivers a fiery anti-American speech: "I fear that this has become a bad relationship, a relationship based on the president taking exactly what he wants and casually ignoring all those things that really matter to Britain. We may be a small country, but we're a great one too. The country of Shakespeare, Churchill, the Beatles, Sean Connery, Harry Potter. David Beckham's right foot. David Beckham's left foot, come to that. And a friend who bullies us is no longer a friend. And since bullies only respond to strength, from now onward I will be prepared to be much stronger. And the president should be prepared for that." These words could have come from the lips of Putin, and indeed, just a few years later, he will make a similar speech.

In March 2003, the US operation in Iraq begins. Saddam Hussein's regime falls in the blink of an eye, but then the real battle commences: a protracted and bloody civil war that tears the country to pieces. This is unexpectedly countered by a triumph of US foreign policy six months later. But not in Iraq, rather in a country that most Americans never knew existed. In November 2003, the so-called Rose Revolution takes place in the former Soviet republic of Georgia. The incumbent government attempts to rig the elections, but opposition supporters gather in front of the parliament building and demand a rerun of the vote and the resignation of the president. The protesters, carrying red roses, are financed by former Russian oligarch Boris Berezovsky.

On the wave of popular discontent, power changes hands: the president's chair is taken by opposition leader Mikheil Saakashvili. He is the first cast-iron pro-American leader in the former Soviet Union. Ironically, it is Vladimir Putin who pushes him into the arms of the United States by stubbornly refusing to recognize the revolution and supporting the overthrown president, Eduard Shevardnadze.

The Bush administration hails the change of power in Georgia as a triumph for democracy. This irritates Putin even more. The Rose Revolution is the first in a series of events that will lead to a new schism between Russia and the West.

"You Don't Love Us, Russia"

In 2002, the 95th Quarter team finally gets to compete in the *KVN* big league. Vova Zelensky is now living in Moscow with his friends, the Shefir brothers. As Borys recalls, they rent a two-room apartment in the north of the city, near the Voikovskaya subway station. Also living with them are Shefir's mother and a huge Rottweiler named Fairy. There are not many beds, so Vova sleeps on the couch with Sergey, while Borys curls up with the dog. The mother of the Shefir family considers Vova her third son.

Despite its past failures, 95th Quarter is finally gaining popularity, and front man Zelensky is one of the brightest stars of the show. But so far this has not helped him financially in any way. The Ukrainian team, as always, jokes about politics: in the quarterfinals of 2002, Zelensky parodies Putin for the first time. It goes down well with the audience and the jury, and the team makes it through to the semifinals.

On October 20, 2002, 95th Quarter faces the highly fancied Moscow team. One of the most memorable sketches of the show is about a clearing of the air between Russia and Ukraine.

"It's high time that you, Russia, and we, Ukraine, had a heart-to-heart," Zelensky begins the skit. "You don't love us *khokhols*, Russia. You don't love us, but more fool you! Go to Tverskaya Street and look around—there's no one else to love besides us *khokhols*!"

The audience chuckles. The gist of the joke is that in the early 2000s

Moscow's central thoroughfare, Tverskaya Street, is full of prostitutes. Mostly from Ukraine.

"We were overjoyed, you might say," continues another of the comedians, "when you got Putin. But our joy was short-lived—he turned out to be a decent guy.

"So, Russia, here's the thing: either we become friends, or you lend us more money."

There the self-irony ends and the nostalgic jokes about the Soviet Union begin. "We're all stable companions, so to speak, from the same graduation class. Just remember our old school photo," says one of the comedians, and a huge poster is unfurled on the stage: in the center, where the teachers should be, are portraits of the creators of the communist ideology, Vladimir Lenin, Karl Marx, and Friedrich Engels; and all around, instead of the faces of school leavers, are the flags of all the former republics of the Soviet Union.

Zelensky takes the floor once more: "It was a tight-knit class, quite combative. . . . Back then the whole school was afraid of us." (A reference to the world's fear of the Soviet Union.) The audience shouts and applauds. "It's true: school is the best time of your life," sums up one of the 95th Quarter team.

The sketch plays well with the jury too, and the Ukrainians win the section comfortably.

But in the following sections, 95th Quarter's luck runs out. And the Muscovites make it through to the final. To this day, the Shefirs are sure their team was robbed—a sign of their long-standing feud with Maslyakov. Borys Shefir insists that "they stiffed us, so we decided enough is enough, we're outta here." However, Vova Zelensky tells the Shefirs he is not yet done with *KVN*. The Quarter team is still in play.

Freewheeling

In the 2003 season, the situation repeats itself: Quarter reaches the quarterfinals, where it faces two Russian teams, from Moscow and Pyatigorsk in southern Russia, and loses.

They could have given it one more go, in theory, but, during a summer tour in Crimea, another incident occurs. During the final song, the show administrator asks all the teams to take the stage. He sees that some players are not present.

He runs backstage and finds several 95th Quarter members there. They have already changed after the performance and refuse to go back onstage, saying that Captain Zelensky is there with other team members. But the administrator is not happy and ejects the team from the show for disobedience. This is the last straw: the Shefirs and Zelensky declare they will no longer do *KVN*.

A couple of months later, Maslyakov sends some truce envoys to Zelensky, including his friend, the former captain of Transit, Misha Gulikov. Zelensky is offered a position as a supervisor of the show, responsible for regional leagues. Everyone knows the offer is lucrative: *KVN* is a massive enterprise; competitions are held in every corner of the former Soviet Union under Maslyakov's license. But Zelensky unexpectedly turns it down, saying he will not return without his team. Later Zelensky is informed that success in *KVN* is determined by money and even the price of getting through each round is named. He feels cheated and insulted: What was the point of trying so hard then, if they had no chance of winning?

In the fall of 2003, the 95th Quarter team moves to Kyiv en masse: Zelensky and the Shefirs from Moscow, the rest from Kryvyi Rih. They rent two apartments: one three-roomer in the city's Osokorky neighborhood for the team and one two-roomer on Prospekt Peremohy (Victory Avenue) for the team leaders. The Shefirs live in one room, Zelensky and his wife, Olena (or Lena), in the other. Vova and Lena's very first night is disturbed by bedbugs on the couch. After that, they move to the three-room apartment in the suburbs.

The money quickly runs out, and no new jobs are forthcoming. So the *KVN*ers decide to put on a show of old sketches and take the idea to Rodnyansky, whom they know better than anyone else. After all, it is his 1+1 station that broadcasts the Ukrainian *KVN* league. Rodnyansky's reaction is overwhelmingly positive and he agrees to film and air the 95th Quarter show.

It is a smash-hit success, and immediately covers the cost of renting the two apartments. Rodnyansky wants to produce a series of shows: one per month, for at least a year. The Shefirs and Zelensky doubt they can write enough material for twelve original programs, and promise a maximum of four per year. Rodnyansky is even more pleased: it shows the guys are not prepared to sacrifice quality for the sake of money. They all shake hands on it.

Zelensky and the Shefirs come up with the structure of the new program. According to Borys Shefir, they observe that the Ukrainian audience, unlike the Russian, does not care much for obscene jokes: in Moscow everyone laughs if they hear the word *zhopa* (ass), but in Kyiv they wince. In the coming years, Ukrainian society will experience a kind of linguistic emancipation: in 2022, one of the main slogans of the resistance to Russian aggression will be the phrase "Russian warship, go fuck yourself." It will be uttered in the first days of the war by a Ukrainian border guard on Snake Island in the Black Sea, when the cruiser *Moskva* approaches and orders the Ukrainians to surrender.

The four programs are aired, and the ratings are excellent. At the same time, Zelensky lands a job on the neighboring station Inter, as the host of a culinary show; his fame is growing. 95th Quarter looks forward to an even juicier offer from 1+1 for the next year.

In the fall of 2004, the Shefirs themselves phone the channel but are told that Rodnyansky has left for Moscow and his deputy is not taking calls. They quickly realize that the TV station has no time for fun and games: a revolution is brewing.

Godfather

In late 2003, Ukraine unexpectedly faces a border clash with Russia in the Kerch Strait, which separates the Ukrainian Crimea from the Russian Krasnodar Territory. Russia starts reinforcing the coastline on its side of the water. Ukraine's Tuzla Island in the Black Sea finds itself under threat of becoming part of Russia.

The start of the work coincides with Kuchma's big visit to Latin

America, for which the Ukrainian authorities have high hopes. But the president is forced to return home ahead of schedule. From his plane he calls Putin—but the Russian president gives assurances that he's not aware of any activity; nothing serious is happening. Then Kuchma arrives in Tuzla and declares that he will give the order to the Ukrainian military to open fire if the works on the Russian side continues. And the rapid construction activity off the coast of Tuzla ceases. And soon Putin and Kuchma even meet in Crimea and sign a border treaty.

The conflict off the coast of Crimea is resolved and will soon be forgotten—but only for ten years.

"It was an act of political wisdom and political courage," reflects the president's son-in-law, Viktor Pinchuk, today. "Many in his shoes would have just called Putin, heard it was a case of local high-handedness, calmed down and continued their visit with a clear conscience. And during this time the dam would have been completed for sure. But Kuchma turned around and flew to Tuzla, because he clearly recognized the level of the threat. Kuchma was the first—and for almost twenty years the only—person to stop Putin."

President Kuchma's second term ends in 2004.

Meanwhile, Ukrainian media are gripped by the clash of the two Viktors: Yushchenko and Medvedchuk. As it happens, both their wives are pregnant. The political press jokes that whoever has a child first will win the political struggle.

In the end, it's not even close: Yushchenko's son Taras is born on March 25, and Medvedchuk's daughter Dasha on May 20. However, the head of the presidential administration proves that you can come in second and still win. Medvedchuk manages to find a common language with Russian president Putin, to the extent that the latter becomes his daughter's godfather. Dasha is baptized at Kazan Cathedral in St. Petersburg; the godmother is Svetlana Medvedeva, wife of the head of the presidential administration of Russia, Medvedchuk's opposite number.

For Putin, Medvedchuk is not just the father of his godchild, but a kindred spirit. The two men have a common KGB background (although Putin was a career officer and Medvedchuk was not officially on the payroll). They also share a cynical approach to politics and have a similar sense of humor and a dismissive attitude toward Ukrainian culture.

Kuchma's chief of staff, Medvedchuk, becomes Putin's eyes and ears in Kyiv. Under the influence of his friends the Kovalchuks, Putin has long believed that holding on to Ukraine is a political priority. His confidants recall how, in the early years of his presidency, he stated at almost every single meeting: "We must deal with Ukraine, or we'll lose it." (Eighty years earlier, these same exact words had been uttered by Stalin when he was drawing up his plan to suppress Ukraine.)

Formally, the Ukrainian question is handled by the head of the presidential administration, Dmitry Medvedev (since 2003). Ironically, his Ukrainian counterpart has a similar-sounding last name: Medvedchuk.* After a while, no one in the Kremlin seems to know who exactly is responsible for Russia's Ukraine policy: Putin's chief of staff or Kuchma's chief of staff.

In the meantime, Medvedchuk concocts a scheme to help President Kuchma's team hold on to power. He proposes political reform that would turn Ukraine into a parliamentary republic: all levers of influence would be transferred to the prime minister, thus making the presidency a ceremonial post. That way, Kuchma can head the government as prime minister and retain power, no matter who the next president is. True, this maneuver requires the loyalty of parliament. But Medvedchuk is well aware that most parliamentarians are controlled not by their parties, but by the oligarchs who "sponsor" them. These custodians of democracy would vote for Mickey Mouse if someone paid them to. Striking a deal with the oligarchs will be child's play. "There is no Ukrainian politics, only Ukrainian business" is how Medvedchuk, according to acquaintances, describes the situation in the country.

Successor from the East

Knowing he has to choose a successor, Leonid Kuchma is feeling the strain. As with prime ministers, all the candidates again seem unreliable, too weak or too uncontrollable. He even sends them to Moscow to be

---

* Both names are derived from the Russian word *medved* (bear).

vetted, as was the practice in Soviet times. But he has no faith in any of them. Medvedchuk is eager to put himself forward, and Putin is ready to consider his candidacy. But Kuchma insists that Medvedchuk is "unelectable."

Kuchma's son-in-law, Viktor Pinchuk, proposes the Dnipropetrovsk banker Serhiy Tihipko, but Kuchma, as ever, does not trust him. Kuchma also rules him out on a technicality: Tihipko was born in Moldova, which means he is not Ukrainian.

Kuchma and Medvedchuk come to a decision as follows: In Ukraine there are two economic poles, two centers of power: Dnipropetrovsk and Donetsk. The president has learned to balance between them, to act as a guarantor of stability, which he can now exploit. If he transfers power to a member of the Donetsk clan, the latter will not be able to govern the country without the "Dnipropetrovskians." He will need the patronage of an experienced politician from the Dnipropetrovsk region, that is, Kuchma himself. The only question is which of the Donetsk leaders to nominate. In the end, Kuchma and Medvedchuk go for the most inept— the one who, in their opinion, will not be able to tie his own shoelaces without Kuchma. He is the governor of Donetsk, Viktor Yanukovych.

Yanukovych has one other advantage: the president's wife, Lyudmila Kuchma, finds him attractive: he is tall and stately. No one else likes him, however, including the head of state himself.

Viktor Yanukovych is an atypical politician. During the Soviet years, he was twice in prison. First, in 1967, at the age of seventeen, he was arrested for robbery as part of a gang of juvenile delinquents. He received three years, but was released after six months for good behavior. When he turned twenty, Yanukovych was imprisoned for a second time: for "causing grievous bodily harm" during a fight. This time he served a full two years in an adult jail.

It is not the most auspicious biography for a future president. True, Yanukovych claims that his criminal record was wiped clean in 1978, when a Donetsk court allegedly ruled both sentences unlawful and annulled them. However, no supporting documents to confirm this have survived. Later the press will insinuate that Yanukovych lied about his convictions being quashed.

Viktor Yanukovych governed Donetsk for five years, from 1997 to 2002. A year before the next presidential election, in November 2002, Leonid Kuchma appoints him prime minister, and hence his successor.

In April 2004, American philanthropist George Soros comes to Ukraine. His organization Open Society has planned a congress of its international structures in Crimea, in the Livadia Palace, which once belonged to the Russian emperors. In Russia, Soros is usually accused of financing the opposition, but in Ukraine his activities are not prohibited. Unexpectedly, Medvedchuk strongly opposes the congress. On his command, fire drills are announced in the palace, and the Open Society event is banned. At the last moment, the family of the president finds out about the scandal. Pinchuk, who is familiar with Soros, goes to Kuchma, who calls his subordinates in the middle of the night and cancels Medvedchuk's decision.

In July 2004, in the same Livadia Palace, a meeting of the presidents of Russia and Ukraine takes place. The oligarchs of the two countries are also invited. Putin informs everyone that they are obliged to support Yanukovych; other options are excluded.

Berezovsky Again

The appointment of the odious Yanukovych as Kuchma's successor is a gift for the opposition. Surely this will make it easier for everyone to unite against him. That said, no Ukrainian oligarchs are rushing to openly stand up against the ruling authorities. The opposition has a leader, Viktor Yushchenko, but he has no money.

The drive to raise money for Yushchenko's campaign is led by an associate of his, the businessman Davyd Zhvania. In the nineties he recently moved from Georgia to Ukraine and enjoys close ties with the country of the victorious Rose Revolution. Zhvania goes to see Georgian president Saakashvili to persuade him to support Yushchenko's candidacy—if the latter wins, he says, he will become a lynchpin in the confrontation with Russia. Saakashvili is sold by the idea and takes Zhvania to see Boris Berezovsky. The Russian businessman who brought Putin to power and then helped Saakashvili become president of Georgia enthusiastically climbs aboard the undertaking. On the one hand, he is passionate about politics; on the other, he expects to acquire some Ukrainian enterprises as a reward, allowing him to become not just a Russian dissident, but a European businessman.

However, the more he finances Yushchenko's campaign, the less he likes working with his team. They gladly take his money but do not listen to his advice. Moreover, they fear publicity—God forbid that anyone find out that Berezovsky is sponsoring Yushchenko! That would only anger Putin and scare off voters. The oligarch is disgruntled about this state of affairs: the scheme "give money and don't interfere" does not suit him in the slightest. For Yushchenko to win, concludes Berezovsky, he needs a broad coalition, which means that he, Berezovsky, should give money not only to Zhvania but to other Ukrainian politicians too.

Berezovsky reaches out first to Oleksandr Volkov, Kuchma's former aide and the architect of his victory in the 1999 presidential election. Volkov eagerly joins the campaign. He introduces Berezovsky to Yulia Tymoshenko, the Joan of Arc of the Ukrainian protests and Yushchenko's former colleague in government. Tymoshenko turns out to be a very shrewd political player: she understands that Berezovsky, as the campaign sponsor, needs to feel appreciated. That means consulting him on a regular basis. Of course, she does not listen to his advice, but the main thing is to create the impression that his opinion matters.

Tymoshenko succeeds where both Zhvania and Yushchenko failed: she makes Berezovsky believe that he is not only the campaign's sponsor but also its brains. It is then that the oligarch puts forward a new condition: he pledges more money to Yushchenko only if he enters into a public alliance with Tymoshenko and promises to make her prime minister after winning the election.

Outraged, Zhvania and his people make an alliance with another sponsor—Ukrainian businessman Petro Poroshenko, owner of several chocolate factories. He is close to Yushchenko, who, in 2000 as prime minister, became the godfather of Poroshenko's two daughters. He also knows Medvedchuk well, having been a member of his party and even run for parliament on the party's lists. In 2004, Poroshenko joins Yushchenko's team and brings with him a very important asset—a small news channel that he owns. This is the only media that covers Yushchenko's campaign: all other TV stations follow Medvedchuk's orders and promote only Yanukovych.

The team that gathers around Yushchenko is nothing if not eclectic. Many do not trust, or even actively loathe, each other. But they understand the need to work together for the sake of the common cause and the goal of defeating Kuchma.

Terror and Elections

In August, Viktor Yushchenko's campaign headquarters announces that an attempt was made on his life: during a trip in the Kherson region, three times a truck tried to ram Yushchenko's car off a cliff. The press recalls previous occasions when a wayward truck interfered in Ukrainian politics. The candidate himself is sure that someone wants him dead.

On September 1, 2004, the worst attack in modern Russian history takes place when a group of terrorists seizes a school in the southern town of Beslan. More than eleven hundred people, mostly children, are taken hostage. Putin and the Russian authorities refuse to negotiate. On the third day, the school is stormed by special forces: 333 people are killed, among them 186 children.

President Putin's reaction to this tragic outcome is unexpected and far-reaching. He lays the blame at the door of outside powers who "want to tear juicy bits off Russia" and announces the scrapping of regional elections to better manage the country. Henceforth, the governors of all regions of Russia will be appointed by the head of state, that is, Putin himself.

The reform has consequences for Ukraine as well: Russian political strategists suddenly lose a lucrative source of income and head to Kyiv to feed off Ukraine's upcoming presidential elections. A unit of Russian intelligence services and a group of advisers from the presidential administration are also relocated there. The so-called Russian club is set up in Kyiv—a permanent team of spin doctors who hold endless, pointless roundtables.

Moscow's lobbying of Viktor Yanukovych is blunt but effective, the Kremlin is sure. Putin meets with him regularly, about once every two months, and doesn't shy away from voicing his support in the upcoming elections. Yanukovych travels twice to Sochi and three times to the Russian president's Novo-Ogaryovo residence outside Moscow. Putin calls to congratulate him on his birthday and hops over to Crimea, where he stays at Medvedchuk's dacha. The Russian advisers on the ground report to Moscow that a Yanukovych victory is in the bag.

All of a sudden, the campaign routine is interrupted by an extraordinary event: Viktor Yushchenko disappears.

Even eighteen years later, those close to his campaign headquarters have highly contradictory recollections. Suddenly, the candidate's health deteriorates, as can be seen from his now monstrous appearance: his face is swollen and disfigured. The word on everyone's lips is poison. At the same time, some campaign sources still claim the presidential candidate underwent some kind of cosmetic procedure that caused an acute allergic reaction.

Vladimir Putin's practice of poisoning opponents is not yet common knowledge. The first proven victim will appear only two years later, in November 2006, when former FSB officer Alexander Litvinenko is poisoned with polonium in London. Before that, however, in September 2004, just a week after the Yushchenko incident, Roman Tsepov, a former crime boss and close acquaintance of the Russian president, will die mysteriously in St. Petersburg. He will show obvious signs of poisoning with an unknown substance.

But whatever the cause of Yushchenko's health problems, the main question is what to do. The whole headquarters is in shock. Aide Oleksandr Volkov knows a clinic in Vienna that might be able to restore their candidate to health. Most importantly, he needs to be restored psychologically. After all, this handsome ladies' man has lost his looks overnight.

Meanwhile, Volkov and Zhvania develop the line that Yushchenko has survived yet another assassination attempt. In this regard, Yanukovych's criminal past and the sinister Putin lurking behind him are extra factors to convince the public.

On September 17, 2004, Yushchenko's headquarters announces that their candidate has been rushed to the Rudolfinerhaus clinic in Vienna due to poisoning. On September 18, Yushchenko returns to Kyiv and speaks at a rally on European Square in the center of the city. Onlookers are horrified by what they see: his face is swollen; he can barely speak.

Medvedchuk, stunned by the change in Yushchenko's appearance, decides to move in for the kill. Having ignored his campaign thus far, Ukrainian TV stations are now instructed to show the opposition leader's new face. His political opponents do not miss the chance to mock him, saying he was poisoned by bad sushi or too much vodka. They "advise" him to avoid foreign food and to eat only Ukrainian potatoes and pig fat.

The sneering continues until Yushchenko comes to parliament. There, in the well-lit chamber, everyone can see with their own eyes how the dashing young prince has turned into an ogre: his face is monstrously scarred and disfigured. In a matter of days, he has become an utterly different human being.

"Look at my face; listen to my words. This is just one hundredth of the problems I've had. See that it doesn't happen to you too! This problem is not to do with food. It is to do with power," enunciates Yushchenko. "Have any of you seen me drunk in the last twenty years? Raise your hands." No one stirs a muscle.

Viktor Medvedchuk realizes that the situation is turning against him. "We didn't touch him!" he shouts at a meeting with loyal media managers. Television reports that Yushchenko's blistered face is the result of low-quality Botox or stem cells, but no one believes this. The pro-government media's attempt to humiliate the opposition leader has backfired spectacularly. All of Ukraine now believes that the authorities wanted to murder Yushchenko.

Yushchenko's headquarters reports that dioxin, a poison that destroys the immune system, was found in his blood. Davyd Zhvania recalls that on September 5, five days before his emergency hospitalization, he and Yushchenko had dinner with the head of the SBU (the Ukrainian security service) and his deputy. President Kuchma knew about the meeting, and it was discussed whether Yushchenko should be provided with extra bodyguards to reduce the risk of assassination. Yuschenko's team insinuates that it was during that dinner that their man could have been poisoned.

A few years later, Davyd Zhvania will say that there was no poisoning and all the gruesome details were invented by Yushchenko's campaign team. In 2022, Zhvania will be killed during an air raid on the territory occupied by Russian troops. However, a version will appear in Kyiv that Zhvania is actually alive—and all those previous years he was an agent of the Russian secret services. Yushchenko himself, however, will continue to maintain that people wanted him dead and he knows who but cannot say it openly.

Whatever the truth, what matters most is that Yushchenko's own attitude has changed going into the elections: he now believes he is a martyr who has sacrificed himself for his own people. And he is ready to fight, knowing that his enemies will stop at nothing.

Gleb Pavlovsky, a Russian political strategist and the "Kremlin's enforcer" inside Yanukovych's campaign headquarters, believes that Yushchenko's alleged poisoning altered the course of the entire campaign. The carnival atmosphere ended, replaced by one of fear. From then on, it was no longer a political game, but a matter, literally, of life and death.

In late September, Viktor Yanukovych goes on a preelection tour of western Ukraine. In Ivano-Frankivsk, he is greeted by a crowd of students who have been herded in to rally in his support. They stand with posters reading "For Yanukovych" but chant: "Yushchenko! Yushchenko!" As the prime minister gets off the bus, one student throws an egg at him. Yanukovych clutches his chest and falls to the pavement as if shot through the heart. For some time afterwards, Yanukovych's campaign team claims their man was the victim of an assassination attempt. But the video footage shows otherwise. Half of Ukraine laughs out loud at the ridiculous PR stunt.

Military Parade in Kyiv

Russia employs all available means in the fight for a Yanukovych victory: it introduces preferential treatment for Ukrainian migrants working in Russia and lowers energy prices.

The closer the elections, the more comical Russia's support for Yanukovych becomes. On October 7, 2004, he attends Putin's birthday party. On October 28, three days before the vote, a parade is held on Khreshchatyk street, Kyiv's central thoroughfare, to mark the sixtieth anniversary of the liberation of the city from the Nazis. In fact, Kyiv was liberated on November 6, but the Ukrainian authorities shamelessly move the celebration forward a week to turn it into a preelection show for the government's candidate. Actors dressed in World War II military uniforms parade along Khreshchatyk, and the Banner of Victory—the iconic red flag that Soviet troops hoisted over the Reichstag building in Berlin in May 1945—is flown in specially from Moscow.

Standing on the VIP podium are Ukrainian president Leonid Kuchma, his chief of staff, Viktor Medvedchuk, and his successor, Viktor Yanukovych, as well as Russian president Vladimir Putin and his chief of staff, Dmitry Medvedev. No one back then could have imagined that Dmitry Medvedev was a future successor, who a few years later would keep Putin's seat warm for one presidential term.

The main thrust of the patriotic revelry is that Russians and Ukrainians defeated the Nazis together, a theme that runs through Yanukovych's entire election campaign. As a corollary of that, at the instigation of the Russian spin doctors, Yushchenko is accused of harboring nationalist and pro-fascist views. This 2004 campaign will prove to be a rehearsal for all the propaganda wars to follow.

Kremlin propaganda will use the Soviet victory in World War II as the basis of state ideology, a symbol of national pride. Liberal media will even coin the term *pobedobesie* (victory mania) to describe the exploitation of World War II and the hyperbolic celebration of victory over Germany in 1945. Recalling the "great victory" over fascism, the Kremlin will cultivate patriotism in the Russian people, sowing the seeds of a domestic brand of fascism.

Moscow is behaving as if Putin himself were running for the presidency of Ukraine. As if he, not Yanukovych, is Yushchenko's main rival. On the very cusp of the first round, the Russian leader gives interviews on Ukraine's top three TV stations. Stanislav Belkovsky, a Russian political strategist working for Yushchenko and Berezovsky, recalls that Putin strikes terror in the hearts of the opposition. Before the interviews, most Yushchenko supporters believed they had a great chance of winning. But seeing the imposing, self-assured Putin everywhere on Ukrainian television is terribly demoralizing. Now the majority opinion is that Putin is the most popular politician in Ukraine; challenging him is futile.

"Don't resist the inevitable," Yanukovych aide Pavlovsky tells Belkovsky in a head-to-head debate. His opponent seems to agree that a Yanukovych victory is inevitable and becomes defensive, snapping angrily that the prime minister's voters are all "ghouls and werewolves."

Orange Maidan

Unexpectedly, the first round of elections is practically a tie: Yushchenko leads Yanukovych by half a percentage point: 39.87 percent versus 39.32 percent, to be precise. But none of Yanukovych's Kremlin fan club doubts that victory is theirs. What happens next will be the worst defeat for Vladimir Putin in his first ten years in power.

On November 2, 2004, I arrive at the Spaso House residence of the American ambassador to Russia. It is the day of the US presidential election. George W. Bush is running against Senator John Kerry, trying to get reelected, and Moscow is having a diplomatic reception on the occasion. That evening I meet all the Russian political spin doctors who are hired by the Kremlin to serve Yanukovich. They are back in Moscow for a holiday after the first round, drinking expensive whiskey and radiating optimism and calmness. "Poor Americans, they have elections today and we still do not know who will win. By contrast, in Ukraine, we're still three weeks away from the second round, and we already know that our candidate Viktor Yanukovich will win," smiles Vyacheslav Nikonov, a member of Putin's Duma and grandson of Stalin's prime minister Vyacheslav Molotov.

On the eve of the second round, Yulia Tymoshenko urges opposition supporters to take to the main square in Kyiv to express their will. Several thousand people wearing orange symbols, in the color of Yushchenko's campaign, heed the call and gather on Maidan Nezalezhnosti (Independence Square), the scene of the previous mass protests.

Putin at this time is on an official visit to Brazil. When the polling stations close in Ukraine, he calls Kuchma, who informs him that the exit polls are saying Yanukovych has won. After that, Putin calls Yanukovych and congratulates him on his victory.

Meanwhile, Yushchenko's supporters are pitching camp on the Maidan, demanding the annulment of the second-round result, which they believe was falsified. Several tens of thousands of them will endure the bitter cold under orange flags for almost all of the next month.

There on the Maidan, it is announced that Yushchenko has won, according to independent exit polls. But Medvedchuk instructs the head of the Central Election Commission to name Yanukovych as the winner by midnight, as per the results of the preliminary count.

Kuchma does not dare to disperse the protest camp: he is still the president, so any bloodshed will be on his hands, not Yanukovych's. Kuchma has no intention of risking his own future for the sake of his successor. Moreover, US senator Richard Lugar, who is in Kyiv, warns the president that any use of force could put him in the dock of an international tribunal in The Hague, as happened with Serbian president Slobodan Milošević. "Putin tries to pressure Kuchma to use force against the Maidan," recalls Viktor Pinchuk. "If that had happened, Ukraine would have turned into a rogue state and become easy prey for Russia."

On the night of November 23, Leonid Kuchma calls Polish president Aleksander Kwaśniewski, promising that no blood will be spilled and asking his colleague to come to Kyiv. He also invites British prime minister Tony Blair. But Blair, who at this moment is trying to mend relations with Vladimir Putin, refuses: he says the Europeans should not interfere in Russia's zone of influence.

The Ukrainian parliament convenes on November 23. Yushchenko takes the floor and declares himself the winner of the elections. True, the speaker of parliament, the leader of the Za YedU bloc, turns off his microphone, but Yushchenko takes the oath on the Bible and the constitution anyway.

Putin demands a swift resolution to the impasse. But Kuchma is now holed up in his out-of-town residence. Yanukovych is totally at sea. The building of the presidential administration is practically empty: only Medvedchuk remains inside; he is in constant contact with Moscow.

The crowd on the Maidan continues to swell. Yulia Tymoshenko urges the people to storm the presidential administration: "Either they give us power, or we take it ourselves." It is explained to her that casualties will be unavoidable. "Then they'll die like heroes," Tymoshenko retorts.

Demyan Kudryavtsev, then Berezovsky's representative in Kyiv, recalls trying to train the opposition leaders in the right revolutionary techniques, based on his experience of Georgia's Rose Revolution. He advises blocking the subway to show that the authorities have lost control of the city.

"But how will everyone get to the Maidan tomorrow?" they ask him.

"What, are you planning to disband them? If they leave, they won't come back!" shouts the Russian political strategist. "You need to keep them on the Maidan, let them live there!"

But the Ukrainian oppositionists disagree: "No, they should be allowed to go home, sleep, wash, get warm, eat, then come back in the morning."

Kudryavtsev is horrified. He says it doesn't work like that, that it contradicts all the laws of mass psychology. In the end, the people disperse for the night and do come back the next morning. And in even greater numbers.

Yanukovych's Moscow aide Pavlovsky will later recall how difficult it was for him even to leave his hotel in Kyiv, which was located just off the Maidan. To get through the crowd of protesters, he had to don an orange scarf. Then, on arriving in Moscow, he discovered that the Kremlin had no clue what was going on: all were quaffing champagne and congratulating each other on a successful campaign. *Job done*, they thought: *Yanukovych is president; the Maidan protests can be ignored.* For a very long time, Moscow cannot get its head around the Ukrainian protests. That they represent the genuine feelings of Ukrainian society, and are not a game funded by the oligarchs or the West, is an untenable idea. Russian society has no voice of its own, which means that Russian journalists and politicians cannot imagine anything otherwise. And so their focus of attention remains squarely on the behavior of the elites.

Not a Place for Discussion

At last, on November 24, the Central Election Commission officially declares Yanukovych the winner. Putin congratulates Yanukovych for a second time. US secretary of state Colin Powell states that, due to reports of widespread election fraud, he does not recognize Yanukovych as the legitimate president.

Vladimir Putin is incensed by the reaction of world leaders to the events in Ukraine. He accuses the international community of bias, since it recognized the results of the blatantly undemocratic elections in Afghanistan, Kosovo, and Iraq. But different standards apply to Ukraine. On November 25, Putin arrives in The Hague for a meeting with EU leaders, where he openly accuses the United States of interfering in the internal affairs of Ukraine: Yushchenko's campaign, he claims, was directed from start to finish by US senator Richard Lugar.

The head of the TV station 1+1, Alexander Rodnyansky, now based in Moscow, returns to Kyiv to find the city engulfed in protest, yet his reporters are still required to follow Medvedchuk's "topic lists" and not mention Yushchenko's name on the air, although they themselves wear orange scarves to work. The team is disheartened as a result, and the best professionals leave. Rodnyansky goes to see Kuchma and says that 1+1 can no longer keep up the pretense. The president remains silent.

On November 25, Rodnyansky, surrounded by his leading reporters, announces that 1+1 is changing its editorial policy. Henceforth, it will not bow to political pressure, but only report the truth. It is a major precedent and a powerful blow to the regime, whose pillars of support are visibly crumbling.

On November 26, an EU mission headed by Polish president Kwaśniewski arrives in Kyiv. At the same time, supporters of Yanukovych from the Donbas region set off on a march to the capital under blue-and-white flags (the colors of Yanukovych's campaign), promising to disperse the Orange Maidan movement by force. A bloodbath is brewing. Kwaśniewski warns Kuchma that, if violence breaks out he will get the blame for starting a civil war. Yanukovych orders the marchers to turn back.

The mediators hold a roundtable to find a way out. The Ukrainian president calls Putin and asks him to send a Russian representative. He suggests Boris Yeltsin. Everyone knows Putin is mocking the process: the aged, infirm Yeltsin will only hinder the negotiations. "I can't take this seriously. I liked working with Yeltsin and respect him, but these talks are not a show," opines Kwaśniewski.

In the end, Putin sends former interior minister and now speaker of the Russian Duma Boris Gryzlov, a man famous for the phrase "Parliament is not a place for discussion." He is clearly well qualified for the task, which is to block any negotiations.

Gryzlov immediately sets out his stall: Yanukovych is the president; the reports of election fraud are false; there is nothing more to say. Someone at the meeting says that no more than 10 percent of the vote was falsified. "In that case," jokes Kwaśniewski, "just amend your constitution to say that elections shall be considered legitimate if the vote rigging is no more than 10 percent."

Gryzlov, in the finest traditions of Russian propaganda, recalls the 2000 US presidential election, when the Florida recount was stopped for the sake of stability. He proposes doing the same thing: recognizing Yanukovych as president, then going home.

Kwaśniewski calls the only person able, in his view, to influence Putin, German chancellor Gerhard Schröder, and asks him to explain to the Russian president that it is not the conniving Europeans or Americans trying to put "their boy" Yushchenko in the presidential chair; it is the multitudinous Maidan protesters refusing to disperse and demanding fair elections. Schröder comes back to Kwaśniewski empty-handed. The Russian president told the chancellor that he, Putin, understands the situation in Kyiv far better than Schröder and Kwaśniewski put together.

I spoke with Kwaśniewski after Russia's invasion of Ukraine. The Polish former president frequently recalled dealing with Putin, back in the days when they were colleagues. He said he should have guessed what he was up to even then. After all, during many hours of talks at the Kremlin, Putin made it clear that his three historical idols were Peter the Great, Catherine the Great, and "Iosif Vissarionovich." "I was struck by how he referred to Stalin, very respectfully, using his first name and patronymic, Iosif Vissarionovich," Kwaśniewski underscored.

"The Trend toward Disintegration"

The Russian media coverage of the Kyiv events is extremely one-sided: a Western-instigated, anti-Russian coup is taking place in Ukraine. Then, at the end of November, Russian television suddenly starts talking about separatism.

On November 26, in the city of Luhansk in eastern Ukraine, regional council deputies vote for the creation of a "Southeastern Republic" and appeal to Vladimir Putin for support. Then, on November 28, in the small town of Severodonetsk, also in the east of the country, the so-called Congress of Deputies of All Levels is convened—a gathering of opponents of the Orange Revolution from seventeen regions of Ukraine. Yanukovych keeps quiet; the tone of the meeting is set by the governors of Kharkiv and Donetsk, who propose a referendum on the creation of a "Southeastern Federal State with its capital at Kharkiv." On the executive committee, as a guest of honor, is Putin's special envoy, Moscow mayor Yuri Luzhkov, a longtime supporter of Crimean secession. However, his speech makes it clear that Moscow is not yet serious about Ukrainian separatism but is merely trying to scare Kyiv into accepting Yanukovych. "There are now two polar forces at work in Ukraine," Luzhkov argues. "On the one hand, there is gross interference in the affairs of Ukraine; on the other, there is Russia, which has full respect for the sovereignty of the country," he says, adding enigmatically: "As mayor of Moscow, I am ready to take off my favorite cap to be like Viktor Yanukovych."

The candidate himself, as ever, is hesitant: "Just a little longer and everything will collapse. Let's try to find a solution without resorting to drastic measures. If just one drop of blood is shed, there'll be no stopping the flood." The meeting breaks up without any resolutions being passed, and for the next ten years the Southeastern Republic will be forgotten.

Putin continues to press Kuchma to disperse the Maidan protesters.

The Ukrainian president understands that it's impossible, but he is not ready to lock horns with the Russian president. So he flies to Moscow to meet with Putin right at the government airport, Vnukovo. According to witnesses, Kuchma "examines his own shoelaces" and repeats, "You don't understand Ukraine, Vladimir Vladimirovich."

Kuchma proposes to annul the elections and hold new ones, with other candidates. Putin is not opposed to the idea but threatens that Ukraine could split into two parts: one western under Yushchenko, one eastern under Yanukovych: "We are very concerned about the trend toward disintegration. We are not indifferent to what's going on. . . . It's a Russian-speaking country, both in the east and the west. It's no exaggeration to say that one in two, if not more, families in Ukraine has family and personal ties with Russia."

But the idea of holding new elections from scratch has no support from anyone. Officially, no one disputed the legitimacy of the first round, but both sides challenged the second. After complex legal wrangling, the Supreme Court of Ukraine effectively sided with the Maidan protesters. Under pressure from civil society, it annulled the results of the second round and scheduled a third for December 26.

Round Three

On December 8, after a long debate, the Verkhovna Rada passes several compromise laws. First, at Yushchenko's suggestion, the electoral law is amended: rules are introduced that make falsification significantly harder. Second, the composition of the Central Election Commission is changed, which marks a clear victory for Maidan. Third, at Kuchma's suggestion, amendments are made to the constitution: a large portion of the president's powers are transferred to the government, which shall have a parliamentary majority. The changes mean that, if Kuchma becomes prime minister under a Yanukovych presidency, he and Medvedchuk will control parliament and wield other levers of influence.

On December 26, when most Europeans are feeling the aftereffects of Christmas Day, Yushchenko is declared the winner of the third round by a comfortable margin. This is no Christmas miracle, but the result of the willingness of a great many officials to go against the authorities and take the side of the protesters. The Maidan sings and dances all night long.

That night I am also on the Maidan—I have never felt such a festive atmosphere anywhere, not at any rock concert, not at the FIFA World Cup. People around are hugging me, crying with happiness and asking, "When are you going to have such a revolution in Moscow?" And at that moment I definitely believe that there will be one soon.

The result of the vote is a sucker punch for the Kremlin. Its Kyiv-based battalion of political strategists, spin doctors, and parliamentarians have been sending report after report to the Kremlin assuring that the situation is under control, that the people "are not infected by the Orange plague," and that "the pro-Western candidate has next to no chance." They cannot put the intelligence failure down to their own incompetence. Admitting that the huge sums they were paid were wasted (or stolen) would be tantamount to suicide. All they can do is blame the West: "We did our best, but the Americans paid their guys more." Putin, too, is in denial, unable to admit even to himself that he overplayed his hand, acted clumsily, misread the true intentions of Kuchma and Yanukovych, relied too heavily on his friend Medvedchuk.

I met Kuchma in Kyiv after the end of his presidential term. We'd arranged the interview sometime in advance. He sat in his huge, intensely gloomy office, looking demonic. Right off the bat, he flummoxed me with these words: "Only I won't give you an interview. This isn't an interview. We didn't actually meet, got it?" After that we had a long and very insightful conversation.

The Orange Revolution is a watershed moment for Vladimir Putin. It marks the start of his paranoia, his all-consuming fear that the Americans will stop at nothing to tear Ukraine away from Russia. "We must deal with Ukraine, or we'll lose it," he used to say even before this debacle. Having lost the country in Maidan-2004, Putin concludes that the best way to "deal with" Ukraine is to reconquer it.

BALTIC
SEA

ESTONIA

LATVIA

LITHUANIA

RUSSIA

● Moscow

BELARUS

R U S S I A

POLAND

● Lviv

● Kyiv

● Kharkiv

U K R A I N E

● Donetsk

MOLDOVA

● Kryvyi Rih

ROMANIA

SEA
OF AZOV

● Bucharest

**2010 UKRAINIAN
PRESIDENTIAL ELECTION**

Votes by regions, second round:

Viktor Yanukovych (winner)

Yulia Tymoshenko

BLACK SEA

TURKEY

200 miles

200 km

12

PROSPERITY AGAIN:
HOW VIKTOR YANUKOVYCH OVERCAME
THE ORANGE REVOLUTION

Komsomol Members at the Helm

In 2004, after the victory of the Orange Revolution, there is a generational shift in Ukrainian politics. Power falls into the hands of those who had no chance of advancing through the Communist Party ranks. When the Soviet Union collapsed and the party ceased to exist, they were still young and had only managed to carve out a career at the Komsomol level. The All-Union Leninist Young Communist League, or Komsomol for short, was created in USSR after Lenin's death, in 1924. Membership is mandatory for all high-school students in the Soviet Union.

Of all the members of the new Ukrainian government, the highest placed in the Komsomol was Oleksandr Zinchenko, who becomes Yushchenko's chief of staff after the elections. Yulia Tymoshenko, Petro Poroshenko, and his university course mate who would become the Georgian president, Mikheil Saakashvili, were also active Komsomol members in their Soviet youth.

Incidentally, many of Russia's new breed of oligarchs were also active Komsomol members. For example, it was through Komsomol connections that oil tycoon Mikhail Khodorkovsky built his first business. He, too, strove for power and dreamed of turning the country into a parliamentary republic. And it was mainly due to his political ambitions that the state seized his business in 2005 and locked him away for ten years. Thus, power in Russia eludes the former Young Communists: Yeltsin, an ex-communist himself, is replaced by KGB officer and communist party member Putin, which, if nothing else, ensures intergenerational continuity.

Orange Plague

Vladimir Putin finally congratulates Viktor Yushchenko almost a month after the latter's third-round victory: on January 20, 2005. That very same day sees the inauguration of George W. Bush, reelected for a second term, in Washington, D.C.

Bush's decisive victory makes a great impression on the Kremlin. He gains full control of both houses of Congress. Putin eyes Bush with a mixture of envy, respect, and fear, describing him as a "military emperor" and seeing him as the absolute master of the planet.

In his inaugural address, Bush states: "[I]t is the policy of the United States to seek and support the growth of democratic movements and institutions in every nation and culture, with the ultimate goal of ending tyranny in our world." These words trouble Putin deeply. He views the American president as a global policeman bent on imposing his own rules everywhere under the guise of platitudes about democracy and human rights. Both Putin and his inner circle are seriously worried that the next US-sponsored "color revolution" will take place in Moscow. "Orange Kyiv" was just a rehearsal, they fear.

"The Kremlin believed we'd soon see Mr. Bush in Russia. It was a panic reaction," recalls political strategist Gleb Pavlovsky, a recent adviser to Yanukovych. "Sure, it was based on a reassessment of the role and impact of George W. Bush. We had a strong feeling that Bush was here to stay. He'd been elected for a second term and wasn't going anywhere. That was the global mood at the time, so it wasn't surprising. We just knew we had to consolidate and strengthen our forces."

Pavlovsky at the time works for Vladislav Surkov, the "gray cardinal" of the Kremlin. Together, they make preparations to defend Russia from the "Orange plague" and prevent the revolutionary fever from spreading across the border from Ukraine. The coming year will see the closure of the largest Western NGOs in Russia, while domestic ones will be banned from receiving funding from abroad; the anti-revolutionary, pro-government youth movement Nashi (Ours) will appear, and television will talk endlessly about the "threat of exported revolution."

On top of that, Russia does everything it can to prevent Ukraine's new democratic authorities from succeeding. If the "Oranges" manage to implement reforms and improve people's lives, it will show that revolution is an effective mechanism for societal development. Putin needs to prove the opposite to the Russian public: he must demonstrate that the desire for political change leads only to chaos, instability, and poverty. Thus, the primary goal of Russian foreign policy is to teach Ukraine a lesson and scare the Russian populace.

"Then We'll Fuck Him Together"

Problems in Ukraine arise even before Vladimir Putin starts plotting his revenge for the recent humiliation of Yanukovych's electoral defeat. The Orange coalition, cobbled together in 2004, is already coming apart at the seams. It all starts with sunshine and smiles, however, on January 23, 2005, with Yushchenko's inauguration.

Throughout January 2005 the Orange camp waits with bated breath to see whom Yushchenko will appoint as prime minister. In the end, he offers the post to Petro Poroshenko. When the news reaches Berezovsky in London, he is terribly offended. He calls Yushchenko personally to remind him of their agreement:

"The government must be headed by Tymoshenko," says the fugitive oligarch, "otherwise I'll send this tape to Putin," whereupon he plays a recording of a conversation they had a few months earlier.

"I'll help you to fuck Putin," Berezovsky says on the tape.

"Then we'll fuck him together," the then presidential candidate Yushchenko replies.

The next day, the now-president Yushchenko formally nominates
Yulia Tymoshenko as prime minister, which parliament approves. These
are the same parliamentarians whom Kuchma and Medvedchuk considered their own until very recently. But Yushchenko's victory has, of course,
turned them all into ardent "Oranges."

The demoted Poroshenko ends up with the less significant post of
Secretary of the Security Council, to which the bad blood between him
and Tymoshenko can be traced.

Having blackmailed the president, Berezovsky is shunned by the new
Orange authorities. He had expected the winners to thank him for his
sponsorship by at least allowing him to participate in a privatization tender
for control of a state-owned telecommunications company or some other
valuable asset. According to his assistant Demyan Kudryavtsev, the Russian
businessman invested $50 million in the Orange Revolution. He does not
demand any special privileges, but simply for the new government to treat
him like an ordinary entrepreneur and let him pay the market price. But his
erstwhile partners do not answer the phone. Only Yulia Tymoshenko, as
before, hears him out and promises to do something, but never calls back.

Yushchenko and Tymoshenko quickly come to blows. First, there is a
national shortage of sugar. The prime minister claims that a cartel around
the chocolate magnate Poroshenko is to blame. Then Ukraine is hit by
gasoline problems. Yushchenko publicly reproves the prime minister. Tymoshenko says the crisis was artificially orchestrated by the oil companies.

Already by September the Orange coalition is falling apart.
Zinchenko, Yushchenko's chief of staff, accuses Poroshenko of corruption and conspiracy, and pointedly resigns. On September 8, 2005, Yushchenko makes the decision to fire both Tymoshenko and Poroshenko.

Night Vision

Ukraine's previous government is initially poleaxed by its defeat at the
hands of the "Oranges." The day after the third round of the presiden-

tial elections, December 27, 2004, Transport Minister Heorhiy Kirpa, a close friend of Kuchma, is found dead. The official verdict is suicide. On March 4, 2005, the corpse of ex–interior minister Yuriy Kravchenko is also discovered—that day he was due to testify in the Georgy Gongadze murder case. Kravchenko's death is also recorded as suicide, although how he managed to shoot himself twice in the head is never explained.

The Orange Revolution is also a kick in the stomach for Viktor Yanukovych. After his defeat, he feels like a political corpse. He himself told the following story to his closest circle. In 2005, on Epiphany (January 19, according to Russian and Ukrainian Orthodoxy), he decides to shoot himself at his Mezhyhirya residence outside Kyiv. When night falls, he takes a gun and goes out to the lake. Staring into the distance, he notices a moonlight cross on the icy surface. He takes it as a sign from above. He calls some staff and tells them to make an ice hole in the shape of a cross. Then, according to the Orthodox tradition of bathing in icy water on Epiphany, Yanukovych takes the plunge and returns home. By now, the estate is practically empty—after the lost elections his once large retinue has dispersed, leaving only a cook and a waitress. Despite the late hour, Yanukovych has dinner and decides to start afresh. In this new life, this waitress will soon become his common-law wife. It is hard to judge the plausibility of this story, for Yanukovych has a habit of telling shocking stories about himself to anyone who will listen.

Big business in Donbas understands that it was wrong to place its chips on Yanukovych. The oligarchs associated with him and Kuchma face hard times. Six months before the Orange Revolution, Kuchma's son-in-law Viktor Pinchuk and Donbas overlord Rinat Akhmetov created a consortium to buy Krivorozhstal, the largest metallurgical enterprise in Ukraine. It is located in Zelensky's hometown of Kryvyi Rih, about a half-hour walk from his school.

The terms and conditions of the tender are worded in such a way that no other bidder has a chance of winning: the enterprise duly goes to Pinchuk and Akhmetov for roughly $800 million.

Yulia Tymoshenko's first act as prime minister is to announce the annulment of this tender and the reprivatization of the enterprise. Without pausing for breath, she promises to seize other assets from Viktor Pinchuk as well. But her dismissal puts an end to this process.

On October 24, a new privatization tender for Krivorozhstal is held, won by Indian businessman Lakshmi Mittal of Mittal Steel, which pays $4.8 billion, that is, six times more than Pinchuk and Akhmetov the year before. But the privatization overhaul goes no further, which suggests to Donetsk big business that the new government is not so strong after all, and that perhaps Yanukovych should not be discarded just yet.

The sale of Krivorozhstal to a foreign company marks a precedent for Ukraine. It seems for a moment as if the country is about to do away with the old economic nationalism of Kravchuk and Kuchma, progress to the next stage, abandon the Russian-style oligarchic system, and let Western investors in. But there is no follow-up. Meanwhile, Ukraine's banks are being injected with capital. Former deputy head of the National Bank of Ukraine Vladyslav Rashkovan estimates that, since the Orange Revolution, Western investors have brought more than $40 billion into the country. But it doesn't last long: after the 2008 crisis, almost all foreign banks will leave.

Gas Mafia

For a couple of months after its defeat in the Orange Revolution, the Kremlin has no idea how to approach Ukraine. Moscow believes that Ukrainian politicians cannot be relied upon—they are fickle, irresponsible creatures. The unforgiving Russian president is convinced he was taken for a ride. It is now his turn to be in the driver's seat, he believes.

There is only one person Putin trusts in Kyiv: his friend Viktor Medvedchuk.

"There is no Ukrainian politics; there is Ukrainian business" is a phrase attributed to Medvedchuk. Since the new government is very weak, business soon begins to dictate its own rules. An informal committee of Ukraine's main oligarchs is effectively set up to manage Ukrainian politics. It is headed by Medvedchuk, who also acts as an intermediary between the oligarchs and Putin.

Many years later, in the 2020s, Russian business will wonder: in the 2000s and 2010s, Putin had enough cash to simply buy up Ukraine. He could have instructed Russian entrepreneurs to take control of various sectors of the Ukrainian economy. That would have met with resistance from the Ukrainians, but by acting gradually, with no sudden movements, Putin could have acquired a controlling stake in the Ukrainian economy through intermediaries. Yet, for some reason, he rejects the "creeping privatization" of Ukraine. He prefers to apply pressure by targeting the industry most dependent on Russia: natural gas. The effects of the appalling corruption in this business will be felt even in 2022, when Putin cuts off the gas to Europe in the midst of the war in Ukraine.

The bizarre and highly opaque scheme for exporting Russian gas to Europe through Ukraine took shape in the early 1990s. Russia's prime minister back then was Viktor Chernomyrdin, the creator of the Russian gas monopoly Gazprom and a former Soviet gas minister. With no way to pay salaries and pensions, he realized the only reliable source of foreign currency was from gas exports. So Chernomyrdin tasked Gazprom with making money from gas exports to Europe and paying it into the budget.

In the 1990s, the only route to Europe for Russian gas lay through Ukraine. And it was then that the horrendous corruption schemes were conceived. It all started with the manipulation of gas supplies from Turkmenistan, one of the former Soviet republics in Central Asia. It, too, produced gas for export to the West through Gazprom's pipelines, also through Ukraine. In 1992, the head of Gazprom told the president of Turkmenistan that the company would not share the foreign currency proceeds with him, because Turkmen gas did not go to Europe: it was separated off and left in Ukraine. The head of Turkmenistan was taken aback: "How do you know which gas is which in the pipeline?" "We know," snapped the head of Gazprom. After that, Turkmenistan had no choice but to try to collect money from Ukraine. Ukraine had no money, so it paid for gas in kind: clothes, food, household goods made in Ukraine.

All sorts of people got involved in the trade. By the end of the 1990s, the scheme became craftier: Gazprom decided to feather its bed even more by pumping Turkmen gas. There appeared intermediary companies that bought gas in Turkmenistan, sold it in Ukraine or even in Europe, and paid kickbacks to those who let them board the gravy train, that is, Gazprom and the Ukrainian authorities.

One such intermediary on the Russian side was the company ITERA. Many years later, it would become known that Gazprom top managers were its secret shareholders. And until the end of the 1990s Yulia Tymoshenko's company United Energy Systems acted as the Ukrainian intermediary. Tymoshenko, who found herself in the prime ministerial chair in 2005, understood the business better than anyone else. In particular, how and how much gas was being stolen, and by whom.

She also knew that the head of the gas mafia controlling all the flows was a certain Semion Mogilevich, a Ukrainian-born crime boss with connections to the Russian secret services. Mogilevich-affiliated structures acted as intermediaries in the gas trade between the three countries of Russia, Ukraine, and Turkmenistan. In the mid-2000s, this colossal corruption scheme ceased to be a secret: the FBI placed Mogilevich in second place on its international wanted list, behind only Osama bin Laden. However, all of Mogilevich's companies were registered to straw entities with a murky shareholding structure, which at first glance had nothing to do with him.

Three months before the Orange Revolution, Russia and Ukraine signed a new gas deal that was intended to feign an end to the dirty schemes. At Gazprom's behest, the role of intermediary was assigned to RUE, whose shareholders also lurked in the shadows.

Having become prime minister, Yulia Tymoshenko publicly calls the new gas scheme corrupt and begins to fight it. Tymoshenko's closest ally, the new head of Ukraine's security service, Oleksandr Turchynov, expresses the belief that RUE's other secret shareholder, besides Gazprom, is none other than Mogilevich.

However, during her six-month tenure as prime minister Tymoshenko does not have time to renegotiate with Gazprom, which insists on keeping the scheme in place.

Only in April 2006 is the owner of the other 50 percent stake in RUE named as the then little-known Ukrainian businessman Dmitry Firtash. What's more, he admits to having owned the previous shady intermediary as well. Where did he come from? Why did Gazprom and the Russian state cede half of a multibillion-dollar-a-year scheme to some guy called

Firtash? And who was behind Firtash? According to sources, the true beneficiary was Mogilevich after all and Firtash was just a hired hand.

Gas Attack

On September 8, 2005, the very day that President Yushchenko fires his two most powerful allies, Tymoshenko and Poroshenko, another historic event takes place in Berlin. Ten days before the parliamentary elections in Germany, in the presence of Vladimir Putin and German chancellor Gerhard Schröder, an agreement is signed on the construction of a new gas pipeline. It will run along the bottom of the Baltic Sea from Russia to Germany and supply all of Europe with gas. It will become known as Nord Stream. Everyone sees the agreement as a boon for German business, whereby Putin is helping his friend Schröder in the elections. But Schröder fails to retain power; the opposition, led by Angela Merkel, wins by a small margin.

Western Europe believes that the new pipeline from Russia will guarantee its energy security when the North Sea deposits run dry. Eastern Europe, by contrast, views the deal as a threat. Polish president Aleksander Kwaśniewski dubs the contract the "Putin-Schröder pact," alluding to the Molotov–Ribbentrop Pact of 1939, which carved up Poland and the Baltic countries between the Third Reich and the Soviet Union. Back in 2005, the leaders of the Baltic countries and Poland are sure the aim of the project is to bypass Ukraine, as well as Belarus and Poland, to have leverage over them. And it's true—Putin has not forgotten that it was Kwaśniewski who mediated the negotiations in the midst of the Orange Revolution and did everything possible for a Yushchenko victory.

New gas talks between Russia and Ukraine begin in Moscow. The Ukrainian delegation is received personally by Putin. The managers from Kyiv are amazed at his in-depth knowledge of the topic and how readily he sketches out a proposed gas price formula on a piece of paper. The fact is that he is now managing Gazprom personally, having realized that it's not just a business, but a potent foreign-policy weapon.

Sensing that his interlocutors are far less versed in the issue, Putin begins to sneer. He makes a bombastic speech about not letting the "Orange revolutionaries" steal from the Russian people and insisting that Ukraine immediately accept Gazprom's terms, otherwise tomorrow the price will be much higher.

Gazprom demands $90 per thousand cubic meters, with a gradual price increase. The Ukrainian gas delegation is horrified. The next day, just as he threatened, Putin appears on television and announces that Gazprom now requires $230 per thousand cubic meters. Even Gazprom employees are shocked.

Unsurprisingly, no agreement can be reached before New Year. Russian state channels broadcast propaganda pieces about how Gazprom is rehearsing scenarios to cut off gas supplies to Ukraine, which are allegedly being siphoned off there. European partners are sent warning letters to expect interruptions starting New Year's Eve, as Russia is preparing to cut gas supplies by the exact amount that Ukraine consumes, and hence Kyiv will presumably steal gas destined for Europe.

To Putin, such a move is a logical step in the energy security concept. It visibly demonstrates to Europe how dangerous it is to rely on erratic transit countries like Ukraine. The logical way out, in his view, is to build new bypass pipelines: Nord Stream through the Baltic Sea, and South Stream through the Black Sea.

On January 1, the pipeline pressure drops; on January 2, gas supplies to Austria are reduced by a third and to Slovakia and Hungary by 40 percent. On January 3, a team of negotiators from Kyiv flies to Moscow, where they are not taken to Gazprom's headquarters, but, ironically, to Hotel Ukraine. That is where Semion Mogilevich has his office. The Russian side proposes a compromise: the price can be lowered only if the trade goes through RUE. Firtash appears from the next room and joins in the negotiations.

As a result, a remarkable deal is struck: Gazprom will sell gas to RUE for $230, but Ukraine will buy it for $95. And RUE's losses will be covered by Gazprom, by allowing it to sell Russian gas to Europe at the market price.

After this deal, both Putin and Yushchenko continue to publicly state they have no idea who exactly owns RUE. Only in 2011 will it become known that Dmitry Firtash is also linked to the Rotenberg brothers, childhood friends of Vladimir Putin, who back in the 1960s trained with him at the same judo club.

The New Year gas war has a huge impact on the European public. The hypnosis they fell under after hearing the words "energy security" from Putin's lips seems to be wearing off. If anything poses a threat to Europe and needs fending off, it is Gazprom, European officials and politicians state after the Christmas break in January 2006. Dependence on Russia is already too high, they say, now viewing Nord and South Stream as a pair of pincers ready to squeeze Europe.

Zrada Everywhere

On the day of her dismissal, September 8, Tymoshenko shows up in Yanukovych's office for a long chat. After her departure, say members of his staff, when asked if she made an impression on him, Yanukovych answers: "She's so sleazy. Even if I wanted to, I couldn't fuck her."

Supporters of Yushchenko also go to see Yanukovych and find common ground, seeing in him someone they could control.

Yushchenko and Yanukovych agree on the following: the authorities will drop all criminal cases against the Donetsk clan and its allies for election fraud, separatism, and corruption, in exchange for which Yanukovych's parliamentary faction will vote for Yushchenko's choice of prime minister to replace Tymoshenko. Yushchenko effectively reneges on all of his campaign promises to investigate crimes committed before he became president. The press can only say that it's par for the course in Ukrainian politics: to tear chunks off each other before the elections, then go for a drink together afterwards. But this betrayal (*zrada* in Ukrainian) of the ideals of the Orange Revolution will live long in voters' memories.

There are parliamentary elections in 2006. The Orange coalition has a majority but for six months is unable to form a government. This opens the door to the rejuvenated opposition leader Yanukovych, who pieces together a coalition and becomes prime minister—for the second time.

The Kremlin is more than happy to see its protégé rise from the ashes. Putin immediately concludes a new gas contract with Yanukovych, and on much more favorable terms. The new prime minister then goes to America, where he announces that Ukraine wants to join the EU but is categorically against NATO membership.

In 2007, Yushchenko dissolves parliament. And more elections are held. Tymoshenko's bloc performs so well that the president is forced to reappoint her as prime minister. But Yushchenko's camp does not try to hide the fact that this former ally is now his worst enemy. Decades later, one of the leaders of the Orange Revolution, Yuriy Lutsenko, who served as minister of the interior in the Tymoshenko government, will recall how he tried to reconcile the parties: "I said to Yulia: 'Listen, Yushchenko's probably still a better bet than Yanukovych.' She was dead set against it: 'I don't even want to talk about it. He's an asshole.' I went to see Yuschenko: 'Viktor Andriyovych, Tymoshenko is no Yanukovych. Find a common language; at least agree on the economic issues.' 'No, she's worse than Yanukovych,' he replied."

I have interviewed a lot of prominent Ukrainian politicians, but probably no one has impressed me as much as Yulia Tymoshenko did in the first decade of the 2000s. She was at the peak of her political shape—she could hypnotize any listener. Even if you understood that she was lying, you could not help but admire her. Once, during an interview, she charmed me so much that I forgot the time and missed my train to Moscow.

Ukrainians and Little Russians

Yushchenko is very unlike his presidential predecessors. He sees himself not as a politician, but as the ideologist and educator of the nation, the guardian of its cultural traditions. Friends of the Yushchenko family say such a mindset is clearly influenced by his wife, Kateryna. Born in the United States to Ukrainian immigrants, she views her historical homeland completely differently than Soviet-born Ukrainians. She does not understand Soviet jokes, does not share the cultural code common to former Soviet citizens, and does not approve of the Russification of Ukraine, believing that the country should revive its old traditions, promote the Ukrainian language, and celebrate its own history.

In fact, Yushchenko is the first truly Ukrainian president: his predecessors were more comfortable in Russian than in Ukrainian. For Yushchenko, speaking Ukrainian is a matter of principle. This goes down very badly in Moscow. In the eyes of Kremlin officials, for a Ukrainian to speak their native tongue at talks in Moscow, for example, on gas, is the height of incivility.

Ukrainian history is also very important to Yushchenko. In particular, he studies the Holodomor, the great famine orchestrated by the Soviet authorities in Ukraine in the 1930s. On his personal initiative, parliament passes a law recognizing the Holodomor as a genocide of the Ukrainian people. Russia's attitude to this event, naturally, is very different: Russian historians argue that the Holodomor was part of the Stalinist terror, not a campaign against Ukrainians; other peoples suffered from famine, too, including Russians themselves. "We do not raise contrived issues such as the Holodomor, politicizing common problems of the past," declares Putin. The Holodomor is the first historical bone of contention between post-Soviet Russia and Ukraine, and an aggravator of the ideological differences between the two countries.

Next, Yushchenko signs a decree on Ukraine's celebration of the 350th anniversary of the Battle of Konotop. This engagement took place in 1659 during the period of Ukrainian history after the death of Bohdan Khmelnytsky known as the Ruin, which saw the Cossack Hetmanate gradually disintegrate. Bohdan's successor, Ivan Vyhovsky, tried to resist the Muscovite onslaught. The Battle of Konotop was one episode in this struggle and a rare success for the Cossacks. However, the victorious Vyhovsky was overthrown three months later. Unsurprisingly, the move to celebrate the anniversary of the battle irritates Russian officials, who accuse Yushchenko of "artificially contriving a confrontation with Russia."

During Yushchenko's presidency, the political culture of Ukraine experiences a kind of reawakening. The word *maloross* (Little Russian) reappears in the Ukrainian language, having fallen out of usage in the twentieth century. Significantly, before the revolution of 1917 it was synonymous with the word "Ukrainian," just as the name Malorossiya (Little Russia) referred to Ukraine. Now, in the twenty-first century, it has a completely different meaning: a *maloross* is a Russified Ukrainian who speaks Russian, probably doesn't know Ukrainian, and, most importantly, considers Russia as an elder brother and Ukraine as a borderland of the empire ("Ukraine" could be translated literally as "on the edge").

Years later, after Russia launches its full-scale war, people in Ukraine will say that Yushchenko was way ahead of his time in laying the foundations of national self-consciousness. However, the disillusionment in him over mistakes made will be so great that, despite all his merits, he will never acquire cult status as the founding father of the new independent Ukraine.

New Year Musketeers

Another consequence of the Orange Revolution is that the 95th Quarter team leaves the TV station 1+1. Having been unable to contact Rodnyansky, Zelensky and the Shefirs receive an offer from the rival channel Inter, which hires out a venue for four thousand spectators, twice the previous capacity. Thus, the show *Evening Quarter* is born, which will become the most popular comedy program on Ukrainian television in the 2000s.

Concurrently, Zelensky and the Shefirs try their hand at cinema. First, they are approached with an offer to "humorize" a ready-made script for a New Year film for Russian television. It is a movie adaptation of the classic Ukrainian comedy *Chasing Two Hares*, written by playwright Mykhailo Starytsky in 1883 in Ukrainian and adapted for the screen in the Soviet Union in 1961. In 2003, Russia's Channel One decides to produce a remake in time for New Year's Eve.

By this time, Channel One is already turning into a propaganda mouthpiece; its news and political talk shows pour vitriol over the "Ukrainian nationalists"—the term applied to the Yushchenko administration. But this doesn't yet apply to entertainment. The main roles in the comedy are played by the most popular pop diva of the Soviet Union, Alla

Pugacheva, Russian comedian Maxim Galkin, and Ukrainian drag queen Verka Serduchka.

The Shefirs want to decline the offer, saying they prefer to write their own material; adding jokes to others' scripts is small-fry. But Zelensky explains that they simply don't know how to negotiate and demands $50,000 for the task. "Volodya, are you nuts? Who'll pay that much?" Borys Shefir wonders. But the producers of Channel One agree.

In eight years after filming Maxim Galkin and Alla Pugacheva will marry, and in 2022 they will be the only Russian celebrities to openly oppose the war in Ukraine.

Chasing Two Hares is Zelensky's and the Shefirs' debut in the film genre. They relish the challenge. Inspired by the experience, they decide to write their own script for a New Year musical—a riotous adaptation of Alexandre Dumas's classic *The Three Musketeers*. In their version, the musketeers are all women, played by popular Russian and Ukrainian actresses. Cardinal Richelieu is also a lady, again played by comic diva Verka Serduchka. Only d'Artagnan remains a man. He is played by Zelensky himself. The film is aired on New Year's Eve 2004.

In the 2000s, Ukrainian show business enjoys a dominant position in Russia. Almost no popular TV project is without Ukrainian stars. Ukrainian media manager Alexander Rodnyansky runs the Russian entertainment channel STS, and many successful TV projects are shot on location in Kyiv. Russia's artistic circle is mixed: around half of all show business stars in Russia hail from Ukraine, which audiences are often unaware of, since they perform almost exclusively in Russian.

In 2007, however, the first crack appears. Verka Serduchka represents Ukraine in the Eurovision Song Contest with the song "Dancing Lasha Tumbai"—a meaningless title in any language. But the presenters hosting the broadcast in Russia are under the impression that "Lasha Tumbai" is code for "Russia, goodbye." A major scandal flares up. Russia's Channel One demands to know why an artist who has performed and earned so much in Russia would suddenly decide to offend his audience with a hidden political message. Verka Serduchka denies it, insisting that the song has nothing to do with bidding Russia farewell. But it's too late. The

Russian stage is closed to the transvestite singer. Other Ukrainian acts, however, including 95th Quarter, which is just embarking on its journey in Russian cinema and show business, are unaffected by the ban.

A World with One Master

In 2007, the situation in Russia is becoming increasingly tense. Vladimir Putin's second presidential term is nearing the end, and his inner circle is hatching a plan to maintain power.

Meanwhile, George W. Bush, the American "military emperor" who promised to promote democracy throughout the world, suddenly loses his aura. The president's sky-high rating is literally blown away by Hurricane Katrina and the White House's inept handling of the disaster. Putin's fear of Bush begins to fade, but the Russian president is deeply indignant about the West's double standards and prejudice against his country. Why, for example, have sanctions that were imposed against the Soviet Union back in the 1970s for preventing Jewish emigration (the "refuseniks") still not been lifted? The Soviet Union is long dead, the Jews have left, some have even returned, but the sanctions are still in place. Why has Russia not been accepted into the WTO? Why is NATO expanding eastwards, despite the president of the Soviet Union, Mikhail Gorbachev, being given a verbal promise in 1991 that this would not happen? Finally, why is he, Putin, not respected and considered as an equal partner?

Putin brings up all these grievances and more in his keynote speech at the Munich Security Summit in February 2007. He accuses the United States of building a unipolar world: "[a] world with one master, one sovereign," in which democracy plays no part. And of disregarding international law. Putin proposes a new global security architecture that will take Russia's voice into account.

His glaringly anti-American speech ruffles plenty of feathers. Putin is fast becoming the world's most vocal anti-Americanist and even gets named *Time* magazine's Person of the Year. That is, universal recognition comes to him not for any achievements, but purely for his anti-American rhetoric.

That said, in 2007 he did succeed in carrying out a complex and delicate internal political operation. Instead of amending the constitution and running for a third term, he decides to transfer power to a successor. Naturally, he selects the weakest and most pliable member of his inner circle: his chief of staff, Dmitry Medvedev. Putin needs a loyal placeholder who will be totally under his thumb.

On Ukraine, however, Medvedev is no different from Putin. He was involved in Yanukovych's campaign and is thus still shaken by the Orange Revolution. In the words of media manager Rodnyansky, it was with Medvedev's arrival on the scene that his problems in Russia started. Before, the founder of Ukraine's 1+1 station was calmly running the Russian entertainment channel STS. But when Medvedev becomes president, he recalls how 1+1 journalists sided with the revolution. This he cannot forgive, and he demands the immediate dismissal of the station's Ukrainian head.

Ukraine in NATO

Bush's second presidential term also expires in January 2009. As his time in office draws to a close, the American president wants to make a contribution to promoting democracy in Georgia and Ukraine. His aim is to pave the way for their NATO membership. Bush knows full well this is a red line for Putin but expects to break his resistance.

In early 2008, at the World Economic Forum in Davos, President Yushchenko meets with US secretary of state Condoleezza Rice and asks her to resolve the NATO issue before Bush leaves office. Ukraine, he says, is very keen to join.

The next NATO summit is scheduled for April 2, 2008, in Bucharest, where Georgia and Ukraine are due to receive candidate member status. Granting a Membership Action Plan (MAP) to a country means that its accession to NATO is a done deal—after a few loose ends have been tied up.

Georgian president Mikheil Saakashvili will recall that he was in Washington a few weeks before the Bucharest summit. In the morning,

German chancellor Angela Merkel calls him: "Whatever Bush promises you, know that I won't allow Georgia and Ukraine to be granted a MAP," she says. Saakashvili retells the conversation to Bush, who reassures him: "Do what you have to do; I'll take care of that woman."

The world flocks to Bucharest, including now prime minister Vladimir Putin, since Russia is a member of the alliance's Partnership for Peace. Angela Merkel is ready to fight to the death, and is supported in her stance by French president Nicolas Sarkozy. They are sure that Ukraine and Georgia are not ready to join the alliance: the former because most of its population is against NATO and the latter because, first, Mikheil Saakashvili does not look like a real democrat and, second, Georgia has two unresolved border conflicts: in Abkhazia and South Ossetia. NATO countries will not agree to send in troops if ever these "frozen" conflicts should turn hot, Germany and France believe.

The position of these two heavyweights angers the Eastern European countries. Merkel and Sarkozy are accused of being pro-Russian because Putin has bribed them with gas.

Evening dinner on the opening day of the summit turns into a war of words. The argument continues the next day. According to eyewitnesses, Angela Merkel and Condoleezza Rice have the most curious exchange: the two women stand in the hall away from the men and talk loudly to each other in Russian, which they both speak fluently. It is during this morning's discussion that the German chancellor proposes a compromise: no MAP for Georgia and Ukraine, but the final statement will say they will definitely "be members of NATO." Without specifying when.

This fudge suits neither Georgia, nor Ukraine, nor Russia. Putin is outraged. "Ukraine is not even a country!" he exclaims. "Some of it is Eastern Europe, and some of it, a significant part, was gifted by us!" Putin ends his short speech with the phrase: "If Ukraine joins NATO, it will do so without Crimea and the East—it will simply disintegrate."

Few people at the time pay attention to Putin's threat. Even as the world watches the confrontation between Russia and Georgia unfold, no one believes for a minute that a hot conflict could break out between Russia and Ukraine.

War in Georgia

On August 8, 2008, the Summer Olympic Games open in Beijing. The leaders of more than seventy countries arrive in the Chinese capital, including Vladimir Putin and George W. Bush.

On this day, Russian tank columns roll through the Roki Tunnel and into South Ossetia, a region of Georgia that declared itself an independent state back in the early 1990s, though no country in the world has recognized it.

At 3:00 p.m. on August 8, Russian TV stations broadcast an address by President Dmitry Medvedev in which he announces the start of an operation to "enforce peace"—at this moment, there is fighting in South Ossetia. He does not consider what is happening to be a war and so does not ask for approval from the Federation Council. Under the Russian Constitution, acts of war must be approved by the upper house of parliament.

Putin meets with Bush in Beijing. The US president demands that Georgia's territorial integrity be respected, but Russian tanks continue to move toward the Georgian capital.

French president Nicolas Sarkozy tries to mediate. He asks Putin not to start a war with Georgia, but to give him forty-eight—or at least twenty-four, or perhaps just twelve—hours for diplomacy, as France currently holds the presidency of the Council of the EU. Putin answers no three times.

Condoleezza Rice is on vacation in West Virginia. On August 10, Russian foreign minister Sergey Lavrov calls to inform her of Moscow's demands, one of which states that Saakashvili must go. Rice yells back that the US secretary of state cannot discuss with a foreign minister the overthrow of a democratically elected government.

"Your third condition just became public, because I'm going to call everyone I can and tell them Russia is demanding the overthrow of the Georgian president," she says.

"I told you this is only between you and me," says Lavrov, perplexed.

"No, it's not between you and me. Now everyone will know about it," retorts Rice, and hangs up. A few hours later, the US ambassador to the UN relates the conversation between Rice and Lavrov to a meeting of the Security Council.

Putin accuses the United States of cynicism. It was not Russia that attacked Georgia, he asserts, but Georgia that attacked South Ossetia, and Russia simply came to its aid. By August 11, Russian tanks are already nearing Tbilisi, the Georgian capital. There is panic in Saakashvili's office. Officials urgently pack up their stuff and burn documents. Saakashvili calls Bush with the words: "Look at the clock and note the time of the Soviet Union's return."

The president of Ukraine, Viktor Yushchenko, and leaders of Poland, Estonia, Latvia, and Lithuania fly to Tbilisi in support of their beleaguered colleague.

Sarkozy is still trying to mediate. He is set to fly to Moscow on August 12, and then on to Tbilisi. The French president's plane is in the air when Dmitry Medvedev appears on Russian television and declares that the "peace enforcement operation" has achieved its goals and is officially over. Sarkozy arrives in Moscow feeling like an idiot: the main goal of his visit has been achieved without him. But worse is to come.

As soon as the talks between him and Medvedev begin, Putin joins them and says that he plans to "hang Saakashvili by the balls." Sarkozy will later recount that during that meeting Putin strode up to him, grabbed him by the tie, and started shaking him to show how serious he was.

The Bush administration finally decides to act. "Russia has invaded a sovereign neighboring state and threatens a democratic government elected by its people. Such an action is unacceptable in the twenty-first century," Bush says on the White House lawn. Sixteen transport aircraft are sent to Georgia; the US Sixth Fleet sails into the Black Sea through the Bosporus.

In Beijing, meanwhile, the Olympics continue. On the day the war ends, swimmer Michael Phelps wins a gold medal (his third of these Games, the ninth in his life), and tennis sisters Serena and Venus Williams start their doubles campaign that will end in victory. Surprisingly, fourteen years later, in 2022, Russia will go to war right after the end of the Winter Olympics, also in Beijing.

One might think that the war in 2008 would have cast a long shadow over Russia–West relations for many years to come. But exactly three months later, America goes to the ballot box and elects Democrat Barack

Obama as their new president. And another three months later, his vice president, Joe Biden, arrives in Munich for the annual security conference, where he states that Russia and the United States should "press the reset button" on their relations. Then secretary of state Hillary Clinton even presents Sergey Lavrov with a huge red button labeled "Reset" and, laughing together, they press it. The recent war, Lavrov's words that Saakashvili must go, and Putin's promise to hang the Georgian president by the balls are all forgotten.

Broad Coalition

In early October 2008, Prime Minister Tymoshenko goes to Moscow for gas talks to settle Ukraine's $2 billion debt. Yushchenko tries to prevent her visit, even commandeering the plane on which her delegation is to fly to Moscow. But Tymoshenko gets around the obstacles.

During the meeting, Putin does not hide his dislike for Yushchenko. "Some pilferer dragged the plane away," he says dismissively. Tymoshenko, who's sitting next to him, giggles. Much of the talk is not about gas, but about Georgia. On the very eve of her visit, the Russian newspaper *Izvestia* publishes an article alleging that Ukraine supplied weapons and military specialists to Georgia during the August war. Putin is outraged once again: "A few months ago no one could have imagined that Russians and Ukrainians would fight each other. But it's happened. The person who did this made a huge mistake."

"I know the situation with Georgia is complex, but we want a peaceful settlement of this conflict. We want peace to prevail," Tymoshenko justifies herself. Her main aim is to get a gas agreement and exclude the hated RUE from the scheme, which means proving to Putin that she is "onside" and capable of negotiating.

For Putin, politics is always a personal vendetta. For him, Yushchenko has long been a symbol of everything hostile in Ukraine. Faithful adviser Medvedchuk offers him a plan: Tymoshenko and Yanukovych should be persuaded to form an alliance, and the president should be eliminated. Putin likes the idea.

Yulia Tymoshenko and Viktor Yanukovych should create a ruling coalition in the Verkhovna Rada, impeach Viktor Yushchenko, and occupy the posts of President and Prime Minister themselves. The date for announcing the new coalition has already been chosen: December 4. But at the crucial moment, Yushchenko's faction does everything to thwart the "Kremlin coalition." Plan A fails. So the Kremlin switches to plan B: a gas war.

On December 26, 2008, Gazprom warns European consumers of potential interruptions in supplies through Ukraine. On New Year's Eve, Gazprom cuts off the gas flow to Ukraine. Austria, Romania, Slovakia, and Poland announce that their deliveries are completely suspended. For the next three weeks, Europe is in a state of panic. Unsurprisingly, the parties to the conflict have different versions of what happened.

According to the Ukrainian authorities, Gazprom simply deceived President Yushchenko: he was promised a gas price of $250, "if Putin agrees." But it was a trap. Prime Minister Putin did not agree to anything, and, on December 31, President Medvedev announced on television that the price for Ukraine was now $450. And since no new agreement was signed, the taps were turned off.

The Russian version of events, which Yulia Tymoshenko also adheres to, is almost the exact opposite. Russia says that President Yushchenko simply could not agree on a price and called off the talks, believing that Gazprom would not dare cut off the gas.

The crisis ends only on January 18, when Tymoshenko again flies to Moscow to meet with Putin. The most striking detail of these talks is the long vertical zipper up the back of Tymoshenko's spectacular black dress, which, reporters joke, is designed to be removed with one swipe of the hand. In the end, the new agreement does away with intermediaries: Tymoshenko fulfills her long-standing election promise and gets rid of RUE, and the average annual gas price for Ukraine is set at slightly under $250.

Five days later, Semion Mogilevich, the "godfather" of the gas mafia, whom Tymoshenko described as RUE's "underground beneficiary," is arrested in Moscow. And a couple of days later, the nominal co-owner of RUE, Dmitry Firtash, is put on Russia's federal wanted list. The secret patrons of the gas mafia, without whom the company could not have operated so long and so successfully, most likely turned them in, preferring to deal with Tymoshenko.

The Ukrainian prime minister describes the agreement with Putin as a personal triumph, while Yushchenko calls it high treason, because of the huge price and the crippling terms. Relations between Yushchenko and Tymoshenko will never recover from this gas crisis. She again enters into negotiations with the archenemy Yanukovych to form a so-called broad coalition, which Putin insists upon. Yushchenko's opponents must unite and impeach the president, Putin believes. This will be the ultimate symbol of his victory over the Orange Revolution.

The "broad coalition" agreement means that Yanukovych and Tymoshenko must amend the constitution so that the president is elected by parliament, not by popular vote. That done, Yanukovych and Tymoshenko will become president and prime minister, respectively, and rotate in these positions until 2029. Viktor Medvedchuk, who has now morphed into Putin's special envoy in Ukraine, oversees the deal. He understands how vital it is for the Russian president to defeat "pimple face"—as the Kremlin calls Viktor Yushchenko.

But the plan is thwarted. On June 9, 2009, the Day of the Holy Trinity, Viktor Yanukovych goes to pray at the Kyiv-Pechersk Lavra, an important center of Orthodox Christianity, after which he tells reporters that he is walking away from the "broad coalition." The Kremlin is sure that Yushchenko is to blame. He must have persuaded Yanukovych that electoral victory will be his even without Tymoshenko. Meanwhile, Tymoshenko's camp believes that Yanukovych was led astray by their main enemy, Firtash, a major sponsor of the Party of Regions, to which Yanukovych is affiliated.

Patriarch of Kyiv

In the summer of 2008, President Yushchenko, unable to handle the schism in his own Orange coalition, tries to resolve the religious one.

Since the declaration of Ukrainian independence, the churches have continued to fragment. After breaking with Moscow, Metropolitan Filaret tried on several occasions to head the rival UAOC but succeeded only in splitting it. Now, as the head of just part of it, he proclaims himself Patriarch of Ukraine. Hence, as things stand in 2008, the picture looks as follows: the Ukrainian Orthodox Church–Moscow Patriarchate, headed by Metropolitan Vladimir, is the largest in the country, with around 11,300 parishes. Filaret (Ukrainian Orthodox Church–Kyiv Patriarchate) has 4,000, and the UkAOC 1,200. Yushchenko's plan is to unite all the churches that exist in Ukraine, excluding the one that is subordinate to Moscow.

To achieve his goal, Yushchenko invites the so-called "Ecumenical" Patriarch of Constantinople, one of the supreme authorities of the Orthodox Church. In world Orthodoxy, there are nine patriarchs in total: of Constantinople, Alexandria, Antioch, Jerusalem, Moscow, Georgia, Serbia, Romania, and Bulgaria. The first four posts, as a rule, are held by Greeks, the fifth by a Russian. As per tradition, Ukraine is considered a "canonical territory" of the Moscow Patriarchate, but Yushchenko wants to break the mold by persuading the Patriarch of Constantinople to take Ukraine under his wing.

Under a suitable pretext (the 1,020th anniversary of the Baptism of Rus), Yushchenko invites Bartholomew to Ukraine on a state visit. But according to Church protocol, Bartholomew cannot enter the territory of the Moscow Patriarchate without the consent of Moscow. This is where Metropolitan Volodymyr Sabodan of Kyiv comes into play. He has always been quite loyal to Moscow and Patriarch Alexy, but now, tired of all the games and intrigues of the secret services, he decides to help Yushchenko unify the churches. Two delegations, from Moscow and Greece, meet in Kyiv for talks. According to eyewitnesses, Metropolitan Vladimir uses a move more typical of the Middle Ages: he seats the priests at the table and suggests that they eat first, then negotiate. The food and vodka are plentiful, and Vladimir does not let the parties rise from the table until they agree. As a result, Moscow's emissaries give the green light to the rival patriarch's visit to Ukraine. On one condition: Moscow Patriarch Alexy shall also attend the feast.

I was there in Kyiv at these celebrations. The rally-type concert organized by the ROC on Maidan Nezalezhnosti made a major impression on me: Metropolitan Kirill, future Patriarch, ran onto the stage like a rock star and shouted: "Hey, Maidan!" He was so keen to please the Kyiv public. "Russia, Ukraine, Belarus—they are Holy Rus!" he shouts, expecting the audience to pick up the refrain and start chanting. But the people of Kyiv stare back at him in bewilderment. "Holy Rus is not an empire! Holy Rus is an ideal of beauty, goodness, and truth!" the future patriarch continues. In 2022, in his sermons, he will support the war and justify the killing of fellow believers.

The visit of the Patriarch of Constantinople in July 2008 is due to end on a triumphant note: Yushchenko, Bartholomew, and the heads of two Ukrainian churches: Filaret and Methodius, are set to sign a unification agreement, which has already been agreed upon and printed. But at the decisive moment, Filaret does not arrive.

Then, unbeknownst to the general public, Metropolitan Vladimir takes the initiative in unifying the churches. In October 2008, he flies to Istanbul and asks Bartholomew to recognize the autonomy of the Ukrainian Church. This is nothing short of a revolution: the head of the Moscow Church is rebelling against Moscow. His predecessor, Filaret, was removed from his post and excommunicated for doing likewise back in the early 1990s.

But the ROC cannot fight the influential Metropolitan Vladimir, especially after the elderly head of the Russian Church, Alexy II, passes away in December 2008. The latter's right-hand man, Metropolitan Kirill, sees himself as his successor, but not all the Church hierarchs trust him. There is little doubt that if the Metropolitan of Kyiv puts himself forward, he will win. So Kirill needs to convince Vladimir to step aside in his favor and guarantee him the votes of the Ukrainian delegates, who make up almost a third of all the electors. True, he cannot simply order Vladimir to do this; he has to find another reason.

Metropolitan Vladimir of Kyiv arrives in Moscow with his retinue for a meeting of the Local Council. Soon the candidate for patriarch Metropolitan Kirill, together with businessman Viktor Nusenkis, coal oligarch and the main sponsor of the Ukrainian Church, come to his hotel. They explicitly say that further funding will directly depend on how the Ukrainian delegates vote. In addition, Nusenkis reminds him that he is paying for not only the Church's needs but also the expensive treatment of the elderly Vladimir. The Kyiv metropolitan has cancer, Parkinson's disease, and diabetes, but his mind is as sharp as ever. The threats are successful. Vladimir agrees but in return demands autonomy for the Ukrainian Church, to which Kirill assents. The latter duly secures all the votes of the Ukrainian Church hierarchs, and wins the election comfortably.

True, he is in no hurry to repay the debt to Vladimir. His plan is different: wait for the gravely ill Kyiv metropolitan to die, not appoint a successor, and occupy the Kyiv throne himself, thereby uniting the patriarchates and assuming the title Patriarch of Moscow, Kyiv, and All Rus.

However, Patriarch Kirill's patience quickly runs out: he decides to organize a coup in the Ukrainian Church. On learning that Metropolitan Volodymyr has suffered a fall and broken his hip, the Moscow patriarchate decides it is time to act. The Holy Synod of the Ukrainian Church assembles in Kyiv and tries to depose Volodymyr on health grounds. But without success. Sabodan, though weak, refuses to leave.

The attempted church coup shocks Yanukovych the most: he considers the Ukrainian Church to be under his control, yet Patriarch Kirill nearly replaced the metropolitan right under his very nose. So, the president conspires a coup of his own—through oligarch Vadym Novynskyi, whom he appoints to oversee the Church. To put pressure on the elderly metropolitan, his secretary, the person closest to him, is arrested. That done, Novynskyi issues an ultimatum to Volodymyr Sabodan: his favorite assistant will be released only if the metropolitan retires. Still, the terminally ill archpriest refuses point-blank.

In 2022, after the outbreak of war, this story will be told to me in Europe by one of the former hierarchs of the Ukrainian church, close to Volodymyr Sabodan. By then he will have left Ukraine, changed his name, and even moved to another church—because he will be shocked that his former colleagues cannot dare to condemn the Russian invasion.

Life in Manhattan

Around 2008, the Shefir brothers and Zelensky start making a movie inspired by *Sex and the City*. The US series about women from Manhattan breaks all records in the post-Soviet space; both women and men, in Russia and Ukraine, want to be like the main character, Carrie Bradshaw: free, ironic, self-assured, living it up in New York. So 95th Quarter decides to make their own version for a Russian-speaking audience.

Zelensky and the Shefirs adapt their version to the more rugged, more masculine reality of post-Soviet life: three Russian-speaking young men live in New York. They have everything, including money, a great life, and, of course, sex. But then they happen to bump into Saint Valentine, who casts a terrible spell on them: they can no longer have sex without love. And so the characters spend the rest of the film searching for their true love.

The script falls into the hands of Russian producer Sergey Livnev, who specializes in intellectually lightweight but popular youth comedies. He is ready to start shooting straightaway: the Russian economy is booming, audiences are pouring into theaters to see Russian-made movies, filming in America is relatively cheap, and a homemade version of *Sex and the City* sounds like a recipe for success. But there's a problem. The authors have one condition: Zelensky must play the lead role.

Livnev did not watch *KVN* and does not consider Zelensky a star. He insists on professional, popular actors. But the Shefirs do not budge.

On a budget of $3.5 million, *Love in the Big City* makes $9 million at the Russian box office alone. The success is obvious, and the producers demand a sequel. Zelensky suddenly finds himself in the ranks of Russia's most popular movie stars. He still lives in Kyiv, where he is also a superstar, having won, in 2006, the very first season of the Ukrainian edition of the international franchise *Dancing with the Stars*.

In Ukraine, as in Russia, the second half of the 2000s is a period of growth and prosperity, accelerated by the Internet, smartphones, blockbusters, TV shows, and social media. The feeling of belonging to Western culture is palpable. Ukrainian young people, and not only them, want to dress as in the West, to feel like they're in Manhattan, no matter where they actually live. As for the oligarchs, both Ukrainian and Russian, finally they feel on top of the world, able to do absolutely anything.

Viktor Pinchuk, son-in-law of former president Leonid Kuchma, remains one of the richest men in Ukraine. According to him, back in the spring of 2004 he decided to focus on business, charity, and cultural projects. He created the Pinchuk Art Center, the largest contemporary art museum in Kyiv, and hosts "Ukrainian Davos," the annual Yalta European Strategy conference (YES).

At one of the first YES conferences, a plan is developed for the step-by-step integration of Ukraine into the European Union by 2020. "At first, I didn't think that the pro-European discourse, the idea of Ukraine's promotion to the European Union, could cause bitterness in Moscow," Pinchuk argues. "And the further, the harder. Only later did I realize that modern Russia does not accept the very philosophy of 'win-win' at all. The principle 'who is not with us is against us' is a strategy of the entire Putin rule. For him, any pro-Western actions are synonymous with anti-Russian ones. This is absolutely false, but he sees the world in this way. The Russian message to most neighbors is simple: 'You can't decide anything without us.' Russia does not need equal partners, it needs satellites and vassals."

The Pinchuk family owns a house in London. Ironically, their neighbor in Kensington is former Moscow mayor Yuri Luzhkov, once an advocate of annexing Crimea to Russia.

In the summer of 2008, Pinchuk organizes a Paul McCartney concert on the Maidan in Kyiv. Its slogan is "time to be together." The TV broadcast audience is more than 13 million. There were more than half a million spectators on the Maidan and on the squares of the main cities of the country, where huge screens are installed. McCartney is waving the Ukrainian flag from the stage, thanking the audience in both Ukrainian and Russian. The host of the broadcast is the country's most popular showman, Volodymyr Zelensky.

In August 2008, Kuchma celebrates his seventieth birthday. By his refusal to disperse the Orange Revolution, and ultimate acceptance of it, Kuchma got what he wanted: he is not an outcast, but a respected retired heavyweight politician. He plans to celebrate his birthday in style. The two key organizers are political strategist Timofey Sergeytsev, a longtime employee of Pinchuk's holding company, who handles the pomp and the politics, and showman Volodymyr Zelensky, who, as the host of the evening, is in charge of the entertainment program and fun. The main guest star is none other than Elton John, whose rendition of "Rocket Man" is the highlight of the event, largely because everyone remembers that Kuchma is the former director of Yuzhmash, a plant that makes rockets and missiles, including with nuclear warheads.

After that Timofey Sergeytsev will go to live in Russia. In 2022, he will write an article titled "What Russia Should Do with Ukraine"—one of the most overtly fascist propaganda texts written after the invasion. It will be published on the website of state news agency RIA Novosti. In the text, Sergeyev will call for the "de-Ukrainianization" of the Ukrainian people: "Besides the elite, a significant portion of the mass population, who are passive Nazis, accomplices of Nazism, are also guilty. They supported and encouraged Nazi power. Just punishment can be meted out to this part of the population only through the inevitable hardships of a just war against the Nazi system, waged as carefully and prudently as possible in respect of civilians. Further denazification of this mass of the population consists in re-education, which is to be achieved through ideological purging (suppression) of Nazi attitudes and strict censorship: not only in the political sphere, but necessarily in the sphere of culture and education, too."

Ukraine's richest person in the late 2000s is Rinat Akhmetov of Donetsk. He owns the soccer club Shakhtar Donetsk. He recalls that back in 1999 he attended a football match in Paris between French and Ukrainian national teams. He liked what he saw: a grand stadium, an electric atmosphere, thousands of fans cheering in one voice, an incredible celebration. So he decided to build a similar stadium in Donetsk.

The project takes three years and $400 million. Finally, the opening of the Donbas Arena is slated for August 2009. An elaborate show is planned. Akhmetov's twenty-year-old son, Damir, present during the consultations, makes a suggestion of his own:

"If you want to make a splash, invite Beyoncé."

"Who?" they ask in unison.

Come the opening of the stadium, President Yushchenko delivers a speech, followed by his rival, Yanukovych, the former boss of Donbas. But both are overshadowed by Beyoncé, who has interrupted her world tour to appear in Donetsk for a reported fee of $1.5 million.

The show feels more like the opening ceremony of the Olympic Games. One of the more bizarre elements is a short theatrical soccer match between Shakhtar players and aggressive aliens who arrive aboard a flying saucer.

No one can guess that in just five years' time other aliens—from Russia—will turn up here for real. But not for a game of soccer. Instead, the stadium will be destroyed.

Washington Specialist

As Yushchenko's presidency nears the end, his popularity sharply declines. Likewise, his image undergoes a great change: from a young, progressive politician, he turns into a dull patriarch who talks about history and appears divorced from real life. My first interview with Yushchenko was when he was still president. His office was reminiscent of an ethnographic museum: it was littered with all kinds of memorabilia, pictures, statuettes.

Yushchenko took offense at me twice during our initial conversation. First, because I did not drink his favorite coffee, but preferred tea. Then I asked him a harsh question about the oligarch Dmitry Firtash and the murky gas trading scheme. Before that, the president had spoken to me in Russian; after the question about Firtash, he switched to Ukrainian.

The president's eccentricity often surprises even his entourage. According to aides, on the way to an important meeting Yushchenko would suddenly stop his motorcade in the middle of the road, climb out, and start examining the exposed roots of a tree by the curb.

Virtually all his former allies in the Orange Revolution have turned their backs on him, their places filled by bureaucrats who idolize the president.

Yushchenko has not given up the idea of running for a second term, but he approaches the 2010 presidential election with a rock-bottom rating. Meanwhile, his former rival Viktor Yanukovych's star is rising. Since five years ago, the former petty crook has undergone a transformation. Gone are the rough manners and inarticulateness; he now looks like a model European politician.

This is the work of spin doctors and image makers. One team consists of Russian PR experts led by Timofey Sergeytsev, a Kremlin-aligned political strategist. The other team is managed by the American lobbyist and political consultant Paul Manafort, who has worked on the election campaigns of several US presidents, including Ronald Reagan and George H. W. Bush. True, he also worked for several dictators, such as the Philippines' Ferdinand Marcos and the Congolese Mobutu Sese Seko.

Paul Manafort was hired back in 2005 by Rinat Akhmetov, the main sponsor of Yanukovych's 2004 presidential campaign. To begin with, Manafort was asked to analyze Yanukovych's performance as a politician, and he wrote a thirty-five-page report in response. It sounded like a judge passing sentence. "Yanukovych's inability to lead the campaign against the current administration will result in failure," writes Manafort, "and to the demise of the Party of Regions." So the obvious solution is to replace him with someone else.

But Akhmetov cannot simply replace Yanukovych, who has long been his own man and, besides, has many other sponsors. He is a compromise figure for a great many oligarchs. Yanukovych himself hires Manafort and sets him the task of getting him back into politics. The American spin doctor rebuilds the old campaign but in a new way. Ukraine's future, he believes, lies in alliance with Russia. All Ukraine's problems stem from the fact that Yushchenko and Tymoshenko do not see eye to eye with Putin, but Yanukovych does.

Manafort brings with him to Kyiv his longtime deputy Rick Gates, as well as Adam Strasberg, who worked for Democrat John Kerry in 2004, and also Tad Devine, who will become Democrat Bernie Sanders's presidential campaign manager in 2016. Their efforts produce the desired effect: Yanukovych is in the lead after the first round, with 35 percent versus Yulia Tymoshenko's 25 percent. For the incumbent President Yushchenko, the election is a total wipeout; he polls a measly 5 percent.

Tymoshenko went into the elections confident of Moscow's support after her agreement with Putin. However, Putin's go-between in Ukraine, Medvedchuk, prefers Yanukovych, and he is the one in receipt of campaign funding from Ukraine's biggest oligarchs, primarily Rinat Akhmetov and Dmitry Firtash. As a consequence, Yanukovych wins the second round by a margin of 1 million votes.

After the results are announced, Yanukovych holds a celebratory dinner where, as a token of gratitude, he presents Manafort with a huge can of black caviar, estimated to be worth $30-40,000.

Prison Term, Presidential Term

After taking office, Viktor Yanukovych behaves like Moscow's long-lost best friend. In 2010, he signs a whole series of bilateral agreements with President Dmitry Medvedev: Russia lowers the gas price, and in return Ukraine prolongs the lease of the Black Sea Fleet for twenty-five years and agrees to an increase in the maximum number of Russian troops stationed in Sevastopol.

Yanukovych also begins criminal proceedings against his sworn enemy Yulia Tymoshenko. Even his inner circle is opposed to the move, but the president is convinced that this is the only way to prevent another Maidan and a new revolution. If he doesn't topple Tymoshenko, sooner or later she will topple him.

Already in 2010, several charges are brought against her, but the case quickly falls apart. The new prosecutor general, Viktor Pshonka, is a longtime friend of Yanukovych and nothing if not dogged. In 2011, he formulates a new charge: the 2009 gas agreements that Tymoshenko signed with Putin were unfavorable for Ukraine. In doing so, she exceeded her powers and harmed the national interest. Even the now-ex-president Yushchenko testifies against her. In the fall of 2011, she is sentenced to seven years in prison, which is deliberately longer than Yanukovych's presidential term, meaning that she will not be able to run against him in the next elections.

In jail, Tymoshenko fears for her life: she eats and drinks only what her family brings her. The prison authorities do what they can to delay the deliveries, forcing the prisoner to go on a "dry" hunger strike.

The West unanimously condemns Tymoshenko's sentence. Angela Merkel is especially worried. Every meeting she has with Yanukovych starts and finishes on this topic. Tymoshenko constantly complains about her deteriorating health. At Merkel's request, German doctors are admitted to the prison hospital in Kharkiv. A thorough examination does not reveal any serious illnesses.

In 2011, Ukraine is due to conclude an association agreement with the European Union. However, the Tymoshenko affair pushes it back. There are repeated calls in the West to impose sanctions on Ukraine due to Yanukovych's indecent treatment of his former rival. The president again turns to Manafort—to help clean up his image and mend relations with the United States and the European Union.

The American political strategist creates a network of Yanukovych lobbyists, which he calls the Hapsburg Group: it consists of prominent, retired politicians who defend Yanukovych in face-to-face meetings, write articles in respectable Western publications, and convince Western leaders not to impose sanctions over the persecution of Tymoshenko. According to US media, the Hapsburg Group includes former Austrian chancellor Alfred Gusenbauer, former Italian prime minister Romano Prodi, and, reportedly, former Polish president Aleksander Kwaśniewski, although he denies the allegation.

Manafort's work starts bearing fruit. Over the next two years, the Tymoshenko case is gradually forgotten, and the European Union becomes more tolerant of Yanukovych, talking less of sanctions on Ukraine and more about its European integration.

Sasha the Dentist

After his inauguration in 2010, Viktor Yanukovych, surrounded by friends, makes a toast: "No guzzling for two years! Everyone must work for the good of the country!" Ironically, when these two years are up, it turns out that Yanukovych has been the primary guzzler, enriching himself beyond imagination.

Having come to power with the support of the biggest Ukrainian oligarchs, Yanukovych decides to end his dependence on them. The only way to ensure complete freedom from Ukraine's business magnates is to become one of them, and the biggest at that.

Yanukovych is essentially repeating what Putin did in Russia, that is, enabling the rise of a new group of oligarchs loyal to him, who seize all the juiciest assets for themselves. Putin's "wallets" under this scheme are his old friends, the Kovalchuk brothers and the Rotenberg brothers. Yanukovych's "financial guard" is formed by his thirty-seven-year-old son, Oleksandr, known as "Sasha the Dentist" because of his medical background. The position of First Deputy Prime Minister, for instance, goes to his friend, thirty-four-year-old Serhiy Arbuzov, whose mother previously headed the Yanukovych family bank. Other friends of the son also get government posts. Being independent of the oligarchs and reporting only to the president, they launch an attack on big business, snatching significant chunks from it. Ukrainian media dub them "the Family" by analogy with the name for the group of oligarchs that surrounded Russian president Boris Yeltsin in the late 1990s.

The Dentist's aggressive high-handedness shocks even the hard-boiled business sharks. He seizes not just businesses that are small or unfriendly but also those of friends and sponsors of his father. One of Sasha Yanukovych's victims is Vladimir Yevtushenkov, a major Russian business figure, who considers himself a friend of the Ukrainian president.

Russian big business is shocked by the behavior of Yanukovych Sr. as well. By the 2010s, those of them who lived through the turf wars of the 1990s have come to feel like civilized Europeans. They have taken their companies public and made them transparent and now hobnob with global celebrities. But Yanukovych—in real life, not in the role prescribed for him by Manafort—seems like a bygone of the gangster era. One Russian businessman recalls how he met with the Ukrainian president at his Mezhyhirya dacha. As they strolled around the residence, the head of state boasted about his good physical shape. He proceeded to go up to a security guard and, with all his might, smacked him hard in the stomach, as if it were a punching ball. The guard collapsed onto the lawn, and the president, having demonstrated his strength, walked on with a satisfied smile.

A member of the Ukrainian government in the Dentist's inner circle says that Yanukovych had some strange habits. For example, the president liked to play tennis for money. It went like this: The head of state chose an opponent and placed a bet on who would win (usually around a million dollars). The spectators, made up of major businessmen, also contributed to the "prize fund"—another million each. All the money went to the winner of the match, that is, the president.

Tensions are rising between the old oligarchs and Yanukovych's young wolves. One of the Family's "wallets" is the young entrepreneur Sergey Kurchenko, who is not yet thirty. He started out as a friend and business partner of the son of Prosecutor General Pshonka, but then the president decided to make use of him.

In 2012, Kurchenko buys Football Club Metalist Kharkiv. A few months later, he invites Yanukovych and Akhmetov to his stadium, which is hosting the finals of the Ukrainian Cup. The president praises the young Kurchenko, saying in earshot of his entourage how good it is that the owner of Shakhtar Donetsk has a rival. Everyone interprets this as a challenge to Akhmetov.

At the same time, a conflict flares up over the Lysychansk oil refinery—in 2022 this territory is occupied by Russian troops. Back in 2013 it belongs to the Russian oil company Rosneft, which plans to sell it. It is assumed that Dmitry Firtash, the longtime sponsor of Yanukovych, is the main contender. However, he is unexpectedly bypassed by the twenty-seven-year-old wunderkind Kurchenko. The oligarchs, already simmering, begin to boil over.

Napoleonic Failure

Zelensky and the rest of *Evening Quarter* are very popular figures at the court of Yanukovych. They are not shy about cracking jokes about politics and the president, but he doesn't mind. On the contrary, he takes pride in being parodied and recommends the show to his cronies. True, the parodies are lighthearted, nothing offensive.

In December 2010, Zelensky is appointed general producer of the

TV station Inter. The channel is owned by businessman Valeriy Khorosh-kovsky, a friend and partner of Dmitry Firtash. But after Yanukovych's election as president, Khoroshkovsky is made the head of the Ukrainian security service. The setup is a little strange: the head of the security service of Ukraine appoints as the head of his TV station Zelensky, who satirizes the Ukrainian authorities.

According to the Shefirs, 95th Quarter felt no pressure from the authorities: only once, when a joke about the president's son is heard during filming, the team is asked "not to touch the family."

Zelensky himself recalls that he got invited to countless corporate soirées: as a master of ceremonies or to perform with his Quarter buddies. One evening, for example, the comedians give a private show to just two spectators: Ukrainian president Yanukovych and Russian president Medvedev. Dressed in bathrobes, the two heads of state nip to the bathhouse in between sketches.

Zelensky's film career is also taking off. Producer Livnev recalls seriously discussing the idea of creating a large film company, its cofounders being Zelensky, the Shefirs, Livnev, and Inter owner Khoroshkovsky. Livnev even travels to Kyiv for talks, which take place at the headquarters of the Ukrainian security service.

The year 2011 sees the release of a remake of the cult Soviet comedy *Office Romance*. Zelensky plays the lead role: a shy office worker who has an unexpected love affair with his hard-nosed female boss. Critics trash the new film. The 1977 original, directed by the great Eldar Ryazanov, is still adored in the Russian-speaking world forty years later, while the remake is flat and lackluster.

In 2012, Zelensky takes on the role of Napoleon. The director of *Love in the Big City* fame this time makes a trash comedy on the theme of Russian history, *Napoleon versus Rzhevsky*. In 1812, two hundred years before the film's release, Napoleon's army invaded the Russian Empire, encountered fierce resistance, including guerrilla warfare, ultimately took Moscow, but was then forced to retreat. One of the fictional folk heroes of this war is Lieutenant Rzhevsky, the subject of a 1962 film, again by Eldar Ryazanov, *The Hussar Ballad*, and a popular character in Russian jokes. In Soviet folklore, stories about the lieutenant are usually intertwined with the plot of Leo Tolstoy's *War and Peace*, and for some reason he is often depicted as the suitor of the novel's main protagonist, Natasha Rostova.

Now Zelensky, the Shefirs, and the screenwriters mix everything up even more: they concoct a tale about Russia's war against the French in which Rzhevsky appears in drag as a countess, causing Napoleon to fall in love with him, while Natasha Rostova is Miss Europe 1810 and the pacifist Leo Tolstoy himself is the leader of the people's militia.

Zelensky's Napoleon is a ridiculous, cowardly, clueless commander who, to the jeers of the victorious Russians, shamefully flees the battle-field.

All in all, the film is the pinnacle of low-budget kitsch, rather typical of Russian movies in the late 2000s. Slammed by the critics, *Napoleon versus Rzhevsky* also bombs at the box office. For some reason, the producers decide to release the film in 3-D, and it does not break even.

Bolotnaya Square

Yanukovych's efforts to mend relations with the West do not bother Moscow at all. For one thing, Putin is convinced Ukraine does not intend to join NATO. And for another, the Kremlin is pushing Yanukovych to take more repressive measures against Tymoshenko and other opposition figures, knowing this will further hinder Ukraine's European integration.

The powerful anti-American paranoia that gripped the Kremlin in the late 2000s subsides a little, especially after the Obama administration cancels Bush-era plans to deploy a missile defense system in Europe, with bases in Poland and the Czech Republic.

However, Putin's conviction that the Americans are plotting to depose him somehow lingers on. The more he looks, the more Putin sees proof of this everywhere. In late 2010, the Arab Spring breaks out—the much-feared "color revolutions" that Putin is desperate to contain in the post-Soviet space are now engulfing the Middle East. People in Tunisia, Egypt, and Libya, armed with smartphones and social media, are taking to the streets and overthrowing their dictators.

The Arab Spring even causes Prime Minister Putin to fall out with his protégé, President Medvedev. The president does not use Russia's UN veto to stop the NATO operation in Libya, which the prime minister views as stepping out of line. It feels like a threat, a local revolution: the younger Dmitry Medvedev, a lover of social media and iPhones, is planning his own "Kremlin spring" and will soon dare to disobey his master. So Putin moves to nip the rebellion in the bud: in September 2011, it is announced that Medvedev will not seek a second term; instead, Putin will run for a third.

In October 2011, in Libya, a mob brutally murders the deposed dictator Muammar Gaddafi, whom Putin knew well. The footage of Gaddafi's death leaves a lasting impression on him. He becomes even more convinced that he must defend his power, or else the same fate beckons.

Then, in December 2011, first on Moscow's Bolotnaya Square, then throughout Russia, mass street protests erupt. People are angered by fraud in the parliamentary elections, but Putin is sure that the rallies are the result of Western intrigue. What's more, he believes it to be a conspiracy orchestrated by US secretary of state Hillary Clinton. He is told that the US State Department has given a hefty sum to Golos, an NGO that monitors elections. It was American money, Putin is convinced, that spurred Russians to protest. Washington is trying to prevent his reelection and carry out a "color revolution" in Russia, for which Putin will never forgive either the United States or Hillary Clinton personally.

Putin's next move is to fire his former strategist Vladislav Surkov, who has seemingly failed to prevent the "Orange plague" from spilling over into Russia. He is replaced by the far more conservative political strategist Vyacheslav Volodin, who alters the vector of the Kremlin's electoral policy: there is no point in flirting with the intelligentsia, or in trying to please the middle class. The focus must shift to the ordinary masses from the provinces, those who want to make Russia great again, who are nostalgic for the Soviet Union, who dream of living in a great empire feared by the whole world.

At this time I am heading the Dozhd television channel, the most popular opposition media outlet in Russia of that period. We cover all the protest rallies—or, as the officials would say, we help the US State Department to organize them. In the winter of 2012 I am absolutely certain that Putin has only a few months left in power: civil society in Russia is getting stronger, and he will not be able to crush it. I think I am already experiencing the same feeling I first felt in Kyiv on the Maidan on December 26, 2004.

BALTIC
SEA

ESTONIA

LATVIA

LITHUANIA

RUSSIA

BELARUS

RUSSIA

Moscow

POLAND

Lviv

Kyiv

Kharkiv

U K R A I N E

Slovyansk
Kramatorsk

Luhansk

D
O
N
B
A
S

Debaltseve

Dnipropetrovsk

Donetsk
Ilovaisk

MOLDOVA

Zaporizhzhia

Mykolaiv

Kherson

Odesa

SEA
OF AZOV

ROMANIA

CRIMEA

Simferopol

Sochi

**RUSSIAN OCCUPATION OF CRIMEA
AND EASTERN UKRAINE IN 2014–2015**

BLACK SEA

_____ State borders

Crimea occupied by Russia in 2014

Self-proclaimed Donetsk People's Republic
and Luhansk People's Republic

Territories controlled by the self-proclaimed Donetsk People's Republic
and Luhansk People's Republic in February 2015, according to the BBC

TURKEY

200 miles

200 km

13

CRIMEA AGAIN:
HOW PUTIN UNLEASHED WAR ON UKRAINE

Full Steam Back

In the summer of 2013, Putin makes an official visit to Kyiv. The formal occasion is the celebration of the 1025th anniversary of the Baptism of Rus. It is not quite a round date, but everyone knows that Putin can't resist historical allusions. The trip for him is symbolic. He feels like the unifier of Russia and Ukraine. To impress Putin, the Yanukovych administration organizes a grand prayer service on so-called Volodymyr's Hill, the steep right bank of the Dnieper River, home to Kyiv's monument to Prince Volodymyr, who baptized Rus in 988. The liturgy is performed by Metropolitan Volodymyr of Kyiv, the namesake of both the prince and the Russian president.

Immediately after the solemnities, the first emergency happens: the elderly metropolitan's pacemaker goes haywire. Volodymyr is immediately taken to the Kyiv-Pechersk Lavra, where, in almost domestic conditions, he undergoes a highly delicate medical procedure: the doctors stop his heart and start it again. The metropolitan's entourage is sure it was an assassination attempt: someone "shone some kind of beam at him," which disabled his pacemaker, they allege.

The head of the Ukrainian Church, which is subordinate to the Moscow Patriarchate, has long had serious issues with Yanukovych. In recent years, the Ukrainian president has paid him regular visits at the Lavra and urged him to step down in favor of the younger generation. Yanukovych has his own candidate in mind for the post of Metropolitan of Kyiv. The president is keen to use the Church in his campaign for the forthcoming presidential elections. But the seventy-seven-year-old Volodymyr resists. Despite all his ailments, he has no intention of retiring and even less of handing the Church over to Yanukovych.

However, to murder the metropolitan right in the midst of the anniversary of the Baptism of Rus would be a step too far even for Yanukovych. Volodymyr comes round, his heart is restarted, the pacemaker is working again, and so the metropolitan goes to his next meeting—with Moscow Patriarch Kirill.

The program of Putin's visit is extensive but, as Kyiv officials note, built entirely around the Lavra. The Russian president is indeed fond of this ancient Kyiv monastery: he meets with Ukrainian clergy, lays flowers on the grave of Prime Minister of the Russian Empire Pyotr Stolypin (assassinated in Kyiv in 1911 and buried at the Lavra), descends into the ancient caves containing the relics of Orthodox saints, and drinks vodka with the abbot. He spends far less time with Ukrainian president Yanukovych. According to the priests, there in the Lavra Putin gets some kind of mystical experience that affirms his idea that he must fight for Ukraine.

Despite being a pro-Russian president, Yanukovych describes Ukraine's integration into the European Union as his main goal. This is pure rationalism: he and his inner circle understand that Ukrainians want to live like Europeans and the EU vector is so popular that it could easily guarantee him reelection for a second term in 2015.

On September 17, 2013, the Ukrainian government unanimously backs EU integration. Yanukovych's entourage is sure it's a done deal. When, for instance, in January 2013, a pro-Russian parliamentarian for the (likewise pro-Russian) Party of Regions criticizes Ukraine's EU course and advocates rapprochement with Russia, he is expelled from the party, stripped of his parliamentary mandate, and even put on trial—for some minor offense committed back in 2007. The message is clear: don't cross the president.

There is just one step left before the signing of an agreement with the EU, and only then does Vladimir Putin intervene. Officials close to him say he never once mentioned his disapproval of Ukraine's European integration to Yanukovych. On the contrary, Putin always publicly stated that he had nothing against Ukraine joining the EU; his objections were confined solely to NATO membership.

In reality, however, Putin harbors a deep resentment against Yanukovych that he didn't express publicly until the very last minute. It is rumored in the Russian presidential administration that, in the midst of the Orange protests, Yanukovych was issued a Russian passport so that he could quickly leave Ukraine if threatened. This has never been openly acknowledged, but, if true, it gives Putin a trump card that will immediately delegitimize Yanukovych's tenure as president (under Ukrainian law one cannot hold dual Russian and Ukrainian citizenship).

In October 2013, Putin invites Yanukovych to a meeting in Sochi. The Russian president spooks his Ukrainian counterpart into thinking that the Europeans are plotting to free Tymoshenko and overthrow him. He also offers a $15 billion loan. Yanukovych flies to Russia several more times after that.

Birthday Knockdown

On October 5, 2013, a historic event takes place at Moscow's Olympiyski Stadium: a title fight for the crown of heavyweight world boxing champion. The winner will pick up every single belt under the sun: IBF, IBO, WBO, WBA. The contenders are Ukraine's Wladimir Klitschko, Olympic champion in 1996, and Russia's Alexander Povetkin, Olympic champion in 2004.

Klitschko is sponsored by the Ukrainian company Interpipe, owned by Viktor Pinchuk. Povetkin's sponsor is the Russian oil state corporation Rosneft, headed by another right-hand man of Putin, Igor Sechin. This lends the fight a strong political overtone. All the Russian and Ukrainian political and business elites are there in the stadium.

October 7, two days later, will be Putin's birthday. A friend has told him that everything is under control: Klitschko has been given $50 million to go down. So Putin watches the fight firmly expecting an early birthday present.

In the second round, Klitschko knocks down his opponent. In the sixth, Povetkin's eye swells up and closes. The Russian hangs on for the full twelve rounds, despite falling over a couple more times. The judges unanimously award victory to the Ukrainian, Klitschko.

The atmosphere inside the stadium is like a war zone. Fans scream insults at Klitschko. Sechin, on his way to Povetkin's dressing room, runs into Klitschko and Pinchuk in the corridor, but instead of congratulating the winner, he looks away and walks on.

Even though Klitschko didn't take the money, Putin will later be told that he did, but flaked out; after all, Ukrainians always flake out.

Iron Maidan

All of a sudden, on November 21, the Ukrainian government votes unanimously against EU integration. None of the ministers understands why, but they have been ordered by Yanukovych to do a massive U-turn, and it is folly to disobey. Ukrainian society is shocked.

That same evening, Mustafa Nayyem, a journalist for *Ukrainska Pravda*, posts on Facebook: "Who's ready to go to the Maidan before midnight tonight? Likes don't count. Only comments under this post with the words 'I'm ready.' As soon as we have over a thousand, we'll organize it." A little later, after seeing the reaction to the post, he adds: "Meet at 10.30 p.m. at the Independence Monument."

Mustafa Nayyem was born in Afghanistan but moved with his family to Kyiv in 1991 at the age of nine. He is one of the country's most renowned reporters and my old friend and colleague. Back in the 2000s, he started working in the Kyiv office of the Russian newspaper *Kommersant*, and I worked there as a war correspondent and international observer.

By midnight, around fifteen hundred people have taken to the square: they are mostly Kyiv-based liberal journalists but are later joined by opposition politicians, including boxer Wladimir Klitschko and his elder brother Vitali, also a boxer, but who went into politics and now heads the opposition faction in parliament.

Both the authorities and the opposition start to mobilize supporters. Students from western Ukraine go to Kyiv. Lviv University, for example, lets them go, without any punishment for truancy. Meanwhile, busloads of Yanukovych supporters arrive in the capital from Donbas; the media report that they are paid 200 hryvnia a day, or about 25 dollars.

On Sunday, November 24, the opposition organizes a large procession along Kyiv's main street, Khreshchatyk, and a rally on European Square. Then the protesters go to the government building, demanding the continuation of European integration. The police disperse them with tear gas. At the same time, Yanukovych's supporters hold their own rally, calling it "anti-Maidan," on Mykhailivska (St. Michael's) Square.

Other cities organize their own "Euromaidans," but in the eastern regions those who take part are often beaten by police or local hooligans paid by the authorities to disperse them: these thugs for hire are known in Ukraine as *titushki*.

On November 28, the so-called Eastern Partnership Summit starts in Vilnius: the plan was for the EU to sign an association agreement with three former Soviet republics: Ukraine, Georgia, and Moldova. As now expected, however, Yanukovych signs nothing. At the general meeting, he sits at the corner of the table, exchanging barely a word with anyone. Later footage will appear online of the Ukrainian president pleading with Angela Merkel: "I want you to listen to me. I've been alone for three and a half years. On a very uneven playing field and facing a very strong Russia one-on-one," says Yanukovych, punching the palm of his hand with each word.

Also in Vilnius, besides Yanukovych and his delegation, is Petro Poroshenko, who does not currently hold an official post in Ukraine, although he did have a spell under Yanukovych as minister of economy. He is there as a special guest of the EU.

The Vilnius summit ends on November 29. Moldova and Georgia have signed agreements with the EU; Ukraine has not. A large rally takes place on the Maidan in Kyiv. From the stage, the singer Ruslana, winner of Eurovision 2004, reads out a resolution demanding Yanukovych's resignation. Then most of the protesters disperse. After midnight only a few hundred remain on the Maidan, mostly students singing songs.

But at 4:00 a.m. officers from the Berkut, Ukraine's riot police, appear on the square, tasked with clearing the area of unauthorized persons: ostensibly because a New Year's tree is to be installed there. The dispersal is violent. The security forces use tear gas, batons, and stun grenades. The students flee from the Maidan up the street to St. Michael's Monastery; the monks open the doors and grant them refuge. The Berkut does not dare to break into the monastery. Come the morning, this almost medieval turn of events will shake the whole country.

There are many different versions as to who gave the order to install the ill-fated New Year's tree and disperse the Maidan rally. The opposition believes it was initiated by Andriy Klyuyev, a longtime friend of Yanukovych and secretary of the Security Council. But Yanukovych himself will claim a few years later that the Maidan crackdown was secretly organized by the head of his administration, Serhiy Lyovochkin, a business partner of Dmitry Firtash. According to Yanukovych, he only found out himself about the nighttime dispersal during a game of tennis the following morning. Lyovochkin, for his part, writes a letter of resignation in protest at the crackdown, but Yanukovych does not accept it. He himself expresses outrage at what has happened.

The strong-arm tactics against students shock Ukraine. All TV stations, including Inter, owned by Firtash and controlled by Lyovochkin, reiterate that the authorities deployed force at night against "unarmed children."

The next day, Sunday, December 1, many thousands of people gather on Kyiv's main thoroughfare. This time the police are the ones who disperse, abandoning the equipment brought in to install the New Year's tree. Around 1:00 p.m., a group of nationalists, who will later become known as Right Sector, separates from the crowd and seizes the Mayor's Office, the building being not far from the main square. An hour later, opposition parliamentarians occupy the House of Trade Unions on the Maidan itself.

At the same time, a group of unidentified individuals fire up a bulldozer that was left on the Maidan by construction workers. They ride the bulldozer to Bankova Street to storm the building of the presidential administration. Later the opposition will claim they were provocateurs or even plain-clothed "Berkutists." Petro Poroshenko rushes to Bankova to try to prevent a massacre. The day of chaos ends with the Berkut beating up the crowd around the administration building. However, the Maidan and the buildings seized nearby remain in the hands of the protesters.

Hundreds of casualties are taken to hospitals around the city; dozens are arrested. Miraculously, no one is killed.

The protesters hastily erect barricades on the main square. In a matter of days, the Maidan will turn into a city-in-a-city, reminiscent of the Zaporizhian Host, which all Ukrainians have read about in the history books: a self-governing community of free men and women, ready to fight and die for their liberty.

Cookies or Gas

The clashes in Kyiv come as a huge shock to everyone, including the oligarchs sponsoring Yanukovych. The next day, Rinat Akhmetov meets with the president and tries to persuade him to dismiss his interior minister and punish those responsible. But Yanukovych thinks this would be seen as a sign of weakness. More importantly, the president does not believe that the Maidan is a spontaneous protest of citizens. He is sure it is a conspiracy led by Tymoshenko, directing operations from her prison cell.

Instead of concessions, he seeks support abroad. On December 3, Yanukovych flies to China, stopping over in Sochi on the way back, on December 6, to see Putin.

Putin tells him that Kuchma's main mistake in 2004 was being too soft. The Russian leader sees President Islam Karimov of Uzbekistan as a model of correct behavior: in the spring of 2005, a few months after the Orange Revolution in Ukraine, similar protests broke out in Andijon, one of Uzbekistan's biggest cities. Karimov ordered troops to fire on the protesters, nipping the "color revolution" even before the bud. Putin presents this as an example to Yanukovych, demanding no less resolute action from the Ukrainian leader in exchange for the promised $15 billion loan and a gas discount. Both Putin and Yanukovych are confident the protests will go away.

The day after their meeting in Sochi, Sunday, December 8, protesters in Kyiv demolish the Lenin monument on Khreshchatyk. Unveiled in 1946 by the then leader of Ukraine, Nikita Khrushchev, the statue is highly symbolic, as is the act of tearing it down. It demonstrates once again that the Euromaidan movement aims to be a revolution not only against Yanukovych but also against Russian colonialism, which Lenin represents. Putin is no fan of Lenin, but he likes the signal even less. This only increases the pressure on Yanukovych.

On December 10, US assistant secretary of state Victoria Nuland arrives in Kyiv. For Vladimir Putin, who is already convinced that Washington has a hand in all the protests, it is another poke in the eye.

On the night of December 11, the Berkut attempts once again to disperse the Maidan, but this time the "massacre of the innocents" does not succeed. The square is barricaded. There are few people there at night, but the Maidan leaders learn of the impending crackdown and summon people to the square on social media. At 2:00 a.m., the bells of St. Michael's Monastery ring out to warn the people of Kyiv of the approaching trouble—just like in the Middle Ages. People from all across Kyiv come to the square on foot. The war of attrition continues through the night: the two crowds push against each other. The black-helmeted Berkut police try to push the protesters off the square, but the latter—having got hold of symbolic orange construction helmets from somewhere—stand their ground. Come dawn, the Maidan is still in the hands of the opposition.

The next morning, Victoria Nuland goes to the square. Petro Poroshenko called her the night before to explain what was happening. Nuland takes with her a huge bag of cookies and sandwiches, which she hands out to both the protesters and the police. The footage of her on the square is broadcast everywhere, but especially in Russia: Kremlin propagandists will say that the Ukrainian opposition feeds on American money and the Maidan protesters have sold themselves to the US Department of State "for a handful of cookies." That is exactly what Putin thinks is happening.

On October 17, Yanukovych flies to Moscow to discuss what "cookies" Putin is ready to give Ukraine: even cheaper gas and the first tranche of the loan: $3 billion of the promised $15 billion.

Both the Kremlin and the Yanukovych administration on Bankova Street firmly believe they have turned the tide and the Maidan will soon fizzle out. Winter, cold, the New Year holidays—the protesters are bound to get disheartened and go home.

Baptism of Fire

Late 2013 is a triumphant moment in the life of Vladimir Putin. The Winter Olympic Games in Sochi are approaching and, as an act of reconciliation, or rather as a demonstration of self-confidence, he decides to pardon some of his political opponents. Shortly before the New Year, the former oil oligarch Mikhail Khodorkovsky is released from prison, having served ten years. Also set free are members of the punk band Pussy Riot, whose performance of the song "Virgin Mary, Chase Putin Away" in Moscow's Christ the Savior Cathedral caused a huge scandal and resulted in a two-year prison sentence.

Yanukovych follows big brother's example and, in December 2013, announces an amnesty for protesters detained on the Maidan.

The New Year period is calm, save for a traditional torchlight procession by members of the radical political party Svoboda through central Kyiv on January 1—to mark the 105th anniversary of the birth of Stepan Bandera, the hero of Ukrainian nationalists. On the eve of the march, Vitali Klitschko says it has nothing to do with the Maidan. But Russian TV stations will repeatedly broadcast the footage as proof that power in Ukraine is falling into the hands of die-hard fascists.

On January 1, 2014, the Russian state TV channel Rossiya broadcasts a New Year's show, hosted by two of the country's most popular comedians: Maxim Galkin and Volodymyr Zelensky. They crack lighthearted jokes, and Zelensky optimistically invites the audience to spend the whole coming year watching Rossiya. It is this station that will become Putin's main mouthpiece in 2014: it is here that his two most aggressive propagandists, Dmitry Kiselyov and Vladimir Solovyov, air their views.

Vladislav Surkov, the same Kremlin ideologue who, post-2004, was supposed to protect Russia from the "Orange plague," goes to Kyiv. After the 2011–12 protests in Moscow and other major cities, he was fired from the administration but was then recalled and assigned to the Kremlin's Ukraine section. True, he denies the very existence of the country he is now responsible for: "There is no Ukraine. There is only Ukrainianism. That is, a specific mental disorder. A pathological obsession with ethnography and blood-soaked local lore," he explains later.

It is he who is assigned the job of shepherding Yanukovych and helping him to handle the new revolution. Surkov brings a package of laws developed by the Russian presidential administration aimed at pacifying the Maidan protests. The Ukrainian parliament is expected to adopt it forthwith. This creation of Surkov will later become known in Ukraine as the "dictatorial laws." They include a variety of measures: the actual banning of all online media; equating any opposition activity with extremism; criminal liability for defamation; and the introduction at the legislative level of the "foreign agent" concept. Many of these laws were adopted in Russia after the protests of 2011–12, but for Ukraine in 2013 they seem excessive in the extreme.

On January 16, the speaker of the Ukrainian parliament, Party of Regions member and longtime Yanukovych friend Volodymyr Rybak, familiarizes himself with Surkov's laws. He quickly understands their adoption will be a disaster, and asks the opposition to lock him in his office so that parliament cannot sit. The deputy speaker from the Communist Party is also locked in, but he has no idea what laws are to be considered. Risking his life, he climbs out through the window onto the roof and then back inside via a different route. He occupies the speaker's chair in the latter's absence. The attempt to disrupt the session has failed.

The other members of the Party of Regions arrive at the parliamentary session on January 16 believing they will be asked to approve next year's budget. Electronic voting is blocked by the opposition, so the deputy speaker proposes a simple show of hands. In one day, amid complete chaos, a parliamentary majority passes all eleven laws. Someone raises both hands, not even realizing what they are voting for.

In the evening, Rinat Akhmetov calls Viktor Yanukovych and asks him not to sign the laws. The president is silent. Later that night, he puts his signature to the legislative package.

Another big Maidan gathering is slated for January 19. The "dictatorial laws" have demoralized many, and this time the crowd's discontent is directed at all politicians. The leaders of the three opposition parties in parliament, Vitali Klitschko, Arseniy Yatsenyuk, and Oleh Tyahnybok, are accused of indecision and internal squabbling. Hence, the protesters will have to take the initiative themselves. The most radical among them move from the Maidan toward European Square, where Berkut riot police are stationed. They plan to break through the cordon, walk along Mykhailo Hrushevsky Street to the building of the Verkhovna Rada, and force it to repeal the "dictatorial laws." Klitschko tries to stop the radicals, but someone sprays a fire extinguisher in his face—the activists no longer feel any deference toward their leader, even if he is a former heavyweight boxing world champion.

The battle commences. There, on Mykhailo Hrushevsky Street, Right Sector grunts set fire to a bus, pull up the cobblestones, and hurl them at the security forces, who turn on the water cannon. It is ten degrees Celsius below zero (14°F). The protesters shout: "Baptism!"—for January 19 is a major Orthodox feast, Epiphany. That is followed by a hail of rubber bullets and stun grenades. The clashes on Mykhailo Hrushevsky Street last two days. On January 22, the first fatalities are reported: three Maidan activists die from gunshot wounds. Who fired at them, and from where, is not known.

All across the country, opponents of the authorities seize regional administration offices and buildings. They encounter very little resistance, since the security forces have all been called to Kyiv. Yanukovych is about to declare martial law but then hesitates. It is explained to him that if he brings in the army the casualty figures will be in the hundreds. The Maidan cannot simply be dispersed by force.

On January 24, the Gifts of the Magi are brought to Kyiv from Moscow. These ancient Christian relics are on loan to Russia from their home at St. Paul's Monastery on Mount Athos in Greece, paid for by Russian businessman Konstantin Malofeev, a dedicated ultra-nationalist and imperialist.

Accompanying the relics is Malofeev's security chief, former Russian FSB officer Igor Girkin, known by the alias Igor Strelkov (which sounds like "shooter" in Russian). He spends several days in Kyiv, where he goes to the Maidan and talks with supporters of the protests. Then, on January 30, he flies to Crimea, taking with him the precious gold, frankincense, and myrrh.

Meanwhile, Yanukovych is negotiating with the three Maidan leaders: Klitschko, Yatsenyuk, and Tyahnybok. He even invites Yatsenyuk to form a government, and he refuses. The oppositionists already understand they have lost control of the crowd. To make things worse, the protesters consider the negotiations with the tyrant Yanukovych a betrayal.

On January 28, parliament dismisses the government and repeals most of the "dictatorial laws." As his new acting prime minister Yanukovych appoints Serhiy Arbuzov, a friend of his son Oleksandr, which greatly irritates the Ukrainian elite, including the Party of Regions. The president is glad when the time comes to fly to Sochi for the Winter Olympics.

Let the Games Begin

On February 7, 2014, Sochi stages the opening ceremony of the Winter Olympic Games. Everything goes according to plan, apart from a technical hitch that causes the last ring of the Olympic symbol not to open. Only one scene, which the CEO of Russia's Channel One, Konstantin Ernst, had insisted on, is cut from the show at the request of the International Olympic Committee (IOC). As conceived by the head of the propaganda station, Ernst, each spectator in the stadium should be given a photograph of someone who had died during World War II. At some point, the host would announce a minute's silence and the spectators would lift up the photos. But the IOC wants to keep politics out of the equation.

Almost forty world leaders descend on Sochi for the opening of the Games, including five from the G20, as well as Viktor Yanukovych. The events in Kyiv dampen Putin's mood. He urges Yanukovych to accept assistance, including security personnel. But the Ukrainian president repeats that "everything is under control." Putin does not believe it, and does not authorize the next tranche of the loan until Yanukovych puts his house in order.

On February 14, Putin chairs a meeting of the Security Council in Moscow to discuss the events in Ukraine. He returns to Sochi the day after to watch a hockey match between Russia and the United States. The game ends in scandal. With the score tied at 2–2 in overtime, Russia scores a third goal, but the American referee rules it out, because the net was dislodged. Russia loses the shootout.

Putin, like all Russian fans, is furious. Why was an American refereeing a match featuring the United States? It's an anti-Russian conspiracy. This dovetails perfectly with Putin's world view: the events in Kyiv are likewise orchestrated by the Americans; they are financing the protests and have all the opposition leaders dancing on puppet strings.

Immediately after the controversial hockey game, Putin meets with veterans of the Soviet–Afghan War to mark the twenty-fifth anniversary of the withdrawal of Soviet troops. Until now, this war was considered a shameful page in the history of Russia, one that led to the collapse of the Soviet Union and plunged Afghanistan into endless civil war for decades. Putin, however, says that he understands the motives behind it: the Soviet leaders were guided by national interests.

On February 16, the Berkut and internal troops in Kyiv are given live ammunition. Then war breaks out in Kyiv. First, the protesters hold a peaceful march to parliament, which the Berkut tries to disperse. They are aided by *titushki*. There are casualties. Then the protesters set fire to the central office of the Party of Regions.

Yanukovych summons opposition leader Oleksandr Turchynov, the former head of Ukraine's security service. The president paces around the office, yelling: "I'll destroy you all! I'll bury everyone! You won't escape abroad, don't even hope. I already gave the order to set up cordons! You're all finished!" Turchynov describes the situation to Sonya Koshkina in an interview for the book *Maidan: An Untold Story*.

Yanukovych and Turchynov come to some sort of agreement: the Berkut will stop shooting; the protesters will return to the Maidan. But it's a trick on the part of the authorities: in fact, the security forces plan to storm the Maidan.

Tires are set alight around the square so that the Berkut police's vision is obscured. Many oppositionists propose retreating once again to St. Michael's Monastery and defending themselves from behind its walls. But Turchynov convinces everyone that the Maidan is a symbol. There must be no retreat.

On the night of February 19, in the midst of the Games in Sochi, more than thirty people are killed on the Maidan. Law enforcement officers seize and set fire to the House of Trade Unions. The whole area is blanketed in smoke—only this prevents the Berkut from completely dispersing the Maidan. A man of deep faith, Turchynov believes this is the work of Divine Providence: the black smoke from the fire does not go up but toward the advancing Berkut police, stinging their eyes so they cannot see.

At night, Putin calls Yanukovych, followed by US vice president Joe Biden. German chancellor Merkel, and the head of the European Commission, José Manuel Barroso, also try to call the Ukrainian president, but he does not pick up the phone.

Polish foreign minister Radek Sikorski is skiing in Italy on the morning of February 19. On seeing the images from Kyiv, he calls his colleagues and, together with the German and French foreign ministers, flies to the capital of Ukraine. Their appearance prevents a fresh nighttime assault on the Maidan. Yanukovych agrees to negotiate with the international mediators.

Taking the Knee

On the morning of February 20, the foreign ministers of the three EU countries go to St. Michael's Monastery, which has been converted into a field hospital and mortuary. Medical operations are performed in the refectory; the last rites are read for the dead in the church.

From there, the diplomats go to Bankova Street, to see Yanukovych. Sikorski notices snipers on the rooftops and hears distant shots. No one realizes that at this moment, just off the Maidan, the bloodiest episode in all the months of revolution is about to unfold.

This gunfire is one of the most mysterious events of Euromaidan, as the 2014 protests become known. The greatest number of people die just when a solution is about to be found: Yanukovych is in talks with the European mediators. That is, the carnage is beneficial only to those forces that want to stop Yanukovych, the opposition, and the Europeans from reaching an agreement. A year later, the Ukrainian security services will claim the shots were fired by Russian snipers on the personal instruction of the Kremlin's envoy Vladislav Surkov. But no evidence is presented and no further investigations are made into the shootings.

The European diplomats are not yet aware of the Maidan massacre when they sit down at the table and shake hands with Yanukovych. In his customary manner, he starts shouting excitedly on entering the room, but German foreign minister Frank-Walter Steinmeier interrupts him: "Mr. President, you should shorten your term in office." Yanukovych falls silent.

At one point during the meeting, Yanukovych interrupts the conversation and goes into another room, saying he must call Moscow. From there, he returns with two pieces of news: first, he will agree to early elections at the end of the year; second, the talks will continue in the presence of Putin's representative, Vladimir Lukin, a well-known Russian politician, a former ambassador to the United States, and a founder of the liberal party Yabloko. The European diplomats breathe a sigh of relief.

The negotiations are joined by Lukin, the Klitschko-Yatsenyuk-Tyahnybok trio of opposition leaders, and several Yanukovych supporters from the Party of Regions. Sikorski is greatly surprised to see that, behind the scenes, these political foes—the opposition and the ruling party—are cordial with each other and on first-name terms. "If our government used weapons against protesters, the distance would be far greater," remarks the Polish foreign minister.

The talks go on all night. Dozens of private jets are already taking off from Kyiv's airports: Party of Regions members are evacuating their families and valuables; everyone senses that Yanukovych is living on borrowed time.

At 7:00 a.m. February 21, the negotiations finally come to an end. Yanukovych agrees to constitutional reform, a curbing of presidential powers, and early elections in December 2014. In the past twenty-four hours, seventy-seven people have been shot near the Maidan, more than in the preceding two months of protests.

In the afternoon, Yanukovych, the trio of opposition leaders, and the European ministers conclude a "peace treaty." Lukin does not attend because Putin has forbidden him to sign any agreement that does not stipulate the federalization of Ukraine.

Klitschko, Yatsenyuk, and Tyahnybok go to the Maidan. Employees of the Yanukovych administration look out the window and see that the Berkut officers guarding the building are hastily loading up trucks ready to depart. A government member will later sum up: the security forces are demoralized; the heads of the Interior Ministry know they will be punished for the violence, and so have given the order for everyone to go home. Without informing anyone, Yanukovych himself leaves for Mezhyhirya.

An even greater drama is unfolding on the Maidan. Vitali Klitschko reads out the agreement with Yanukovych, and tries to explain that this is the best that could be achieved. One of the activists, Volodymyr Parasyuk, rushes onto the stage: "They shot my comrade!" he shouts. "He left behind a wife and small child, and our leaders are shaking hands with the killer. Shame on them!"

At this moment, coffins carrying the dead are brought into the square.

"Let me tell you," continues Parasyuk. "We, the ordinary people of Ukraine, are defending our rights. And we, the ordinary people, say to our politicians standing behind me: there will be no Yanukovych in office for another year. By ten a.m. tomorrow he must be gone!"

The coffins are brought up onto the stage. Everyone standing there, including the politicians, kneels down. Vitali Klitschko, who considers himself a unifying presidential candidate, casts a searching glance at the crowd and also drops to his knees.

In total, the last month of the standoff in Kyiv cost around one hundred lives. They will soon be immortalized as the "Heavenly Hundred."

Border Incident

At his Mezhyhirya estate, Yanukovych is having dinner with the last people loyal to him: his chief of staff, Klyuyev, and the speaker of parliament, Rybak. Just then Surkov calls him with news of an impending assassination attempt, saying he must leave Kyiv at once or face certain death. Surkov surely knows how to scare people. Rybak immediately pens a letter of resignation. And they all decide to fly to Kharkiv, where a separatist congress is planned for the following day, the so-called congress of deputies of all levels, which aims to challenge the Maidan victory and, potentially, demand federalization or even secession of Ukraine's eastern regions. Yanukovych's previous such attempt, at the height of the Orange Revolution in 2004, ended in failure. But now Surkov instructs as follows: go to the congress, declare Kharkiv the new capital of Ukraine, and fight against the Maidan by any means.

Later, Russian officials will claim they tried to persuade Yanukovych to stay until the very end: a livid Putin is said to have told Surkov to prevent the flight of the Ukrainian president, expressing his opinion of Yanukovych in no uncertain terms: "Who'd have thought he was such an asshole, and such a coward." In fact, Yanukovych is acting strictly according to instructions.

Meanwhile, the evacuation from Mezhyhirya of Yanukovych's valuables continues apace. Suitcases full of cash are removed—$2 billion, according to Ukrainian media, plus paintings, statues and other luxury items that the president so adores. He himself goes to Kharkiv.

That same evening, the Verkhovna Rada votes for a new package of liberal laws, including decriminalization of the Criminal Code article under which Yulia Tymoshenko is imprisoned. Several members of parliament immediately go to collect her from the prison hospital in Kharkiv, to which Yanukovych is also flying.

Kharkiv governor Mikhail Dobkin, on meeting Yanukovych at the airport, is surprised to see him behaving as if nothing has happened, as if he is still in control of the situation. Yanukovych is determined to separate the east and the south from the rest of Ukraine:

"Think up a new name for the country," Yanukovych asks one of his longtime associates.

"China," he replies.

"Stop jerking around," snarls the president.

Meanwhile, the news from Kyiv reaches the Kharkiv prison hospital. The warden takes Tymoshenko from her hospital bed to a small, windowless room and orders her to sit quietly. He is clearly afraid that Yanukovych supporters could exploit the chaos to try to kill the prisoner. Tymoshenko spends most of the day there in the back room. Unlike the jailers, she is not aware of what is happening.

In the morning, Yanukovych learns that protesters have taken over his beloved residence, Mezhyhirya. The president is very much attached to his dacha. Since 1935, Mezhyhirya, north of Kyiv on the banks of the Dnieper River, had been used as a residence for leaders of Soviet Ukraine, including the instigators of the Holodomor and later Nikita Khrushchev. Yanukovych himself moved there in 2002, and in 2007, as part of his agreement with Viktor Yushchenko, he was able to privatize it.

The 140-hectare (345-acre) complex is enclosed along the perimeter by a five-meter-high fence. Inside is a zoo, an equestrian club, a shooting range, a tennis court, a marina for yachts, and hunting grounds. The Maidan supporters who storm the estate find there a golden toilet bowl and a loaf-shaped paperweight made of solid gold.

The morning news is a huge blow to Yanukovych. Surkov calls him again with more scary assassination rumors: Maidan supporters have allegedly penetrated the congress and are ready to "deal with" the president. At the same time, Governor Dobkin tries to dissuade him: "I was afraid they'd boo him at the very least. He was a fish out of water," he says in an interview with Sonya Koshkina. The governor adds that he cannot guarantee Yanukovich's safety. All these telephone conversations take place literally on the doorstep of Kharkiv Sports Palace, where the congress is to be held. At the last moment he turns around.

Next, Yanukovych records one last televised presidential address, in which he describes the opposition as Nazis, vows never to sign the new laws adopted by the Rada, and promises not to leave the country. He also makes up the story that the speaker of parliament, Rybak, was shot during the night.

Back in Kyiv, the Verkhovna Rada holds another session. Since Speaker Rybak has resigned, Oleksandr Turchynov is elected to replace him. The parliamentarians, including former supporters of the president, watch Yanukovych's address and vote to remove him from office. Under the Constitution of Ukraine, Turchynov, as head of parliament, becomes interim head of state. New presidential elections are scheduled for May 25.

Yanukovych arrives at the Donetsk airport; his voluminous luggage is loaded onto two planes bound for Moscow. But the border guards, obeying the command of the new government from Kyiv, do not let Yanukovych and his entourage through. They offer a bribe but get flatly refused. So Yanukovych's belongings are loaded back into the cars, and the motorcade drives off.

At this same time, the now-released Yulia Tymoshenko is being taken to Kyiv. There, in the evening, she appears on the Maidan stage in a wheelchair and promises to run for president.

Yanukovych visits his old friend Rinat Akhmetov at his Donetsk office. The latter suggests that he write a letter of resignation but urges him not to leave the country. Yanukovych does not reply. Surkov's words really did scare the hell out of him. The motorcade moves on to Crimea. Yanukovych is afraid he will be killed. Once, on Mount Athos in Greece, when he was having his fortune told, it was predicted that his "journey would be cut short" in 2014. He demands to be evacuated. Finally, he is taken away from Ukraine aboard a Russian military vessel.

His close associates also flee the country: his son Oleksandr, Acting Prime Minister Arbuzov, the young oligarch Kurchenko, and others. Later they will claim the turmoil was the result of a conspiracy among the old cast of oligarchs: Akhmetov, Firtash, and others dissociated themselves from Yanukovych at the right time, gave him up, and sponsored Euromaidan.

"This crisis was wholly engineered by the Kremlin," Viktor Pinchuk says confidently. "Starting with Yanukovych's abrupt rejection of an association with the European Union, through his total refusal till the very last day to compromise with the protesters, to the shootings on the Maidan. I'm sure

Yanukovych was kept on a very short lead. Which isn't surprising, given that the three heads of our law enforcement agencies under Yanukovych were citizens of the Russian Federation."

The revolution draws to a close. In Ukrainian history, it will become known as the "Revolution of Dignity." True, this is not quite the end. On February 27, a soccer match takes place in Donetsk: a Europa League round-of-sixteen clash between the local Shakhtar and the Czech Republic's Football Club Viktoria Plzeň. In the middle of the match, the stadium announcer invites the crowd to honor the memory of those killed in Kyiv. The fifty-thousand-strong stadium begins chanting in unison: "Berkut! Berkut!" Donbas is not at all pleased with the victory of the revolution.

Little Green Men

The Olympic Games in Sochi come to an end. Although Team Russia tops the gold medal table, Vladimir Putin is not at all happy. He is certain that he was duped by the Western mediators, who only two days before shook hands with Yanukovych and agreed that he would remain president until the end of the year.

On February 23, Putin spends the night at his Novo-Ogaryovo residence outside Moscow, along with Defense Minister Sergey Shoigu, Security Council secretary Nikolay Patrushev, FSB head Alexander Bortnikov, and Chief of Staff Sergey Ivanov. It's the final day of the Olympics, and Putin decides to annex Crimea to Russia, something he threatened George W. Bush with back at the NATO summit in 2008.

The topic of Crimea's annexation has never really been popular in Russia. It has never stirred public opinion, and only rare firebrands ever mention the peninsula. One of them was Moscow mayor Yuri Luzhkov. But he was fired back in 2010 after falling out with then-president Medvedev. However, Luzhkov then became friends with Igor Sechin, head of state oil company Rosneft and one of Putin's closest and most influential associates. It is Sechin who becomes obsessed with the idea of conquering Crimea. He talks endlessly about it, including with Putin, knowing the latter's contempt for Ukraine's new government.

The Kremlin does not prepare in advance for the annexation. In 2013, the Russian General Staff has several plans for operations in Ukraine, but the seizure of Crimea is never plan A. However, on the night of Yanukovych's getaway, Putin decides to act. He believes the chaos in Ukraine will provide the ideal conditions for a swift takeover.

The participants in the meeting at Novo-Ogaryovo react with varying degrees of enthusiasm: Patrushev believes Russia must strike without delay. Shoigu, on the other hand, is extremely cautious. He knows he will be responsible for the operation, so he lists the arguments against it.

The FSB, citing various secret polls, assures Putin that the population of Crimea will jump at the chance to join Russia. There can be no resistance: the Ukrainian state is in disarray; there is no one to give the order to defend it. In the end, it is decided to go ahead with "Operation Return Crimea" but with care, reacting to events on the ground.

The Kremlin needs a new prime minister to govern the peninsula. All the current politicians seem too unreliable, that is, too independent, so a more malleable leader is required. The short list is whittled down to just one candidate: a businessman with a criminal past by the name of Sergey Aksyonov, the leader of the Russian Unity party, known in the 1990s as the bandit "Goblin."

On February 26, riots begin in the Crimean capital, Simferopol. Two opposing groups gather outside the building of the Supreme Soviet: one of Crimean Tatars, the other of Russians. A rumor spreads around the city that the Supreme Soviet intends to ask Putin to admit Crimea into Russia. The Russians come out in support of the motion, the Crimean Tatars against.

Historically, the Crimean Tatars made up the majority of the local population. However, from the mid-eighteenth century, Crimea was actively settled by Russians, and in 1944 Stalin ordered the deportation of the Crimean Tatars, accusing them of collaborating with the Nazis. According to various sources, between 190,000 and 420,000 people were resettled in Uzbekistan, during which many died. Only in 1989 were the Crimean Tatars allowed to return to their homeland, and in 2014 the prospect of rejoining Russia does not fill them with joy.

A scuffle breaks out in the square. There are already fatalities: one person is crushed; another dies of a heart attack. But the leaders of the

Russian and Crimean Tatar parties manage to separate the crowd. At this very moment, a new government is being formed in Kyiv, headed by Arseniy Yatsenyuk. Crimea is currently off the radar of Ukraine's politicians.

On the night of the twenty-seventh, the Russian paratroopers are transferred to Crimea. They seize the buildings of the Supreme Soviet and the Crimean government and close the airspace. Their mission is formulated as follows: establish control over the buildings, without even knowing in which city or country. The troops have no insignia; locals refer to them simply as "little green men." The Russian authorities deny any involvement, of course. This is a basic principle of Putin: he does not consider deception to be shameful; on the contrary, hoodwinking an opponent, for him, is a sign of skill.

In a matter of days, Russian forces, backed by pro-Russian militias, will seize control of Ukraine's military bases in Crimea.

A group of FSB and GRU officers is already in Crimea, as well as Igor Strelkov, a veteran of the secret services who brought the Gifts of the Magi to Crimea and remained there. Their task is to organize an emergency sitting of parliament to dismiss the previous, unreliable prime minister and elect a new, pro-Moscow one. Some members refuse to attend, so plain-clothed operatives take them to the parliament building by force.

On the afternoon of February 27, the speaker of the Crimean parliament puts the election of Aksyonov as the new prime minister to the vote. According to official data, there are sixty-four parliamentarians in the chamber, sixty-one of whom are in favor. Putin will say that legally everything is shipshape and deploy a Russian idiom to make his point: "A mosquito won't eat away the nose," meaning that it can't be faulted.

Special Tourists

On February 28, Il-76 military cargo aircraft deliver several hundred veterans of Afghanistan and Chechnya, along with athletes, bikers, and members of patriotic clubs, to Sevastopol. All these "tourists" simply want Crimea to return to Russia and are full of nostalgia for the Soviet imperial past. They would quite happily wage war for the cause, but their role is not military, but as extras. They play the part of protesters: agitated Crimeans demanding the annexation of Crimea to Russia. In a way, it is similar to the Maidan, and the emotions are just as sincere as in Kyiv. The difference is that most of the participants are Russians, that is, foreign citizens. Appearance-wise, however, they are indistinguishable from the locals. They are accommodated in military sanatoriums in Crimea.

On the evening of February 28, Verkhovna Rada member Petro Poroshenko arrives in Crimea on a fact-finding mission. But he is met by an enraged mob shouting: "Russia!," "Berkut!," "Get out of Crimea!" He is put in a cab and taken back to the airport.

On March 1, Putin seeks the approval of the upper house of the Russian parliament to deploy the Russian army in Ukraine, a mere formality. A native of the Khmelnitsky region in Ukraine, Speaker Valentina Matvienko urgently assembles the senators, who vote unanimously in favor. That same evening, the Russian Ministry of Defense delivers an ultimatum to Kyiv: all Ukrainian military in Crimea must lay down their arms and surrender by midnight. Acting President Turchynov tries to contact Putin, but the Russian president does not consider him a legitimate head of state and so refuses to talk. But the State Duma speaker, Sergey Naryshkin, does agree. "Tell Putin I've given the command to shoot to kill in the event of an attack," Turchynov informs him.

That evening, showman Volodymyr Zelensky arrives at the studio of a popular TV news station and, unexpectedly for many, makes the first political statement in his life, entirely devoid of jokes. First, he appeals to the new Ukrainian authorities: "If people in the east and in Crimea want to speak Russian, let them. Get off their backs. Let them be legally entitled to speak Russian." Then he addresses Putin: "Dear Vladimir Vladimirovich, do not allow even a hint of a military conflict on your part. Because we, Russia and Ukraine, are indeed fraternal peoples. If you want, I am ready to beg you on my knees, but do not bring our people to their knees." This appeal, of course, gets drowned out in the deluge of words and is soon forgotten.

Having elected a new prime minister of Crimea, the peninsula's parliament decides to hold a referendum on May 25, to coincide with Ukraine's presidential elections. The wording of the question is, at first, unclear: everyone thinks it is about declaring independence; that is, Crimea will share the fate of other "unrecognized republics," such as Abkhazia and South Ossetia, which separated from Georgia.

The "systemic liberals" In Putin's entourage, that is, pro-Western officials who initially opposed the Crimean adventure but then bowed to pressure, believe the Abkhazia/South Ossetia scenario to be optimal. President Medvedev recognized them as independent in 2008 but did not annex them to Russia so as not to violate international law, thereby avoiding major sanctions. In the same way, Crimea must simply be recognized as independent, say West-leaning officials.

On the night of March 2, Vladimir Putin and Barack Obama speak over the phone for an hour and a half. The US president threatens Russia with isolation. Moreover, he promises not to attend the next G8 summit, which is due to be held in Sochi. A day later, speaking from the White House, he condemns Russia's actions, but the word "sanctions" does not fall from his lips. At the same time, Angela Merkel puts pressure on Putin. But the Russian president does not believe that the United States or Europe will dare to impose major sanctions. *So what if they don't come to Sochi? It's no big deal, not after how they ruined my Olympics*, muses Putin, according to the top bureaucrat from the Kremlin. What's more, he remembers the consequences of the Georgian war, or rather the near total absence thereof.

On March 6, the Crimean parliament moves the date of the referendum from May 25 to March 16, leaving only ten days' preparation time. More importantly, the question of the peninsula's annexation to Russia is put to the vote. On March 7, a patriotic rally is held in Moscow under the Kremlin walls, where the slogan *Krym nash* (Crimea is ours) sounds for the first time. This will be the main slogan of Russian imperialists in the following years.

On March 16, polling stations do not even open in areas populated predominantly by Crimean Tatars, who are against joining Russia. But in Simferopol, people with both Ukrainian and Russian passports can vote freely. According to official data, 96.77 percent support accession to Russia.

Two days later, March 18, Putin ceremoniously signs an agreement in the Kremlin on the admission of Crimea into the Russian Federation.

It is one of the most triumphant moments of his presidency. As the editor in chief of an opposition TV channel, I am invited to the Kremlin for the first and last time—to witness with my own eyes the collapse of our dream of a free and democratic Russia and the triumph of the empire. Gathered in the historic palace interiors of the Kremlin, officials and propagandists rejoice, interrupting Putin's speech dozens of times with applause. The head of Chechnya, Ramzan Kadyrov, is sitting right in front of me. During the president's speech, he sings the Russian anthem in an undertone. At the end of the event, everyone stands up, and Kadyrov, along with everyone else, sings it again. I don't get up and I don't sing.

The propaganda media is buzzing with excitement. The president's approval ratings are through the roof. The internal opposition—including those ardent protesters of just two years ago—is demoralized and no longer dares to voice an opinion. The Kremlin's political strategists are convinced that patriotic hysteria is the best cure for all domestic political problems.

True, Putin is mistaken about the sanctions. The G8 ceases to exist altogether: Russia is expelled from the club, and the Sochi summit never happens. At the same time, the United States and the European Union begin imposing individual sanctions on Russian officials. But at this Putin licks his lips: the greater the sanctions, the more united the elites in Russia—they have nowhere to run.

In Crimea itself, meanwhile, a wave of repression comes crashing down on locals who oppose joining Russia. In the coming months, between 35,000 and 50,000 people who oppose the occupation will move from Crimea to other parts of Ukraine.

Throughout almost all of the Revolution of Dignity, 95th Quarter has been off the air. Only in April does another show appear on the TV station 1+1. In it, Zelensky delivers a long monologue: "We heard Putin's speech, in which Vladimir Vladimirovich said the following phrase, which sticks in the mind, and in the soul: 'Kyiv is the mother of Russian cities.' Mother. Motherfucker. Of Russian cities. So, I now have a question for Russians. Her kids. Why, then, do you say all sorts of nasty things about your mother in the news? Your birth mother. You say she won't survive without you, her kids. That she'll be living hand to mouth. Actually, she's happy to live hand to mouth. Only without you! Normal children generally want to live without their mother. You, however, need to stay with us in our apartment. You even snatched a room the other day, one with a sea view."

Thank You, Donbas

On March 12, in Vienna, at the request of the FBI, Dmitry Firtash, one of Ukraine's biggest oligarchs, for many years the main partner of Gazprom and a sponsor of Viktor Yanukovych, is arrested. It is not an attack against Ukraine, but against Russia: the FBI has long been hunting for Russian crime boss Semion Mogilevich, who, it believes, is Firtash's *krysha*, that is, protection. The United States wants to get Firtash to spill the beans on Russian gas corruption.

But this is not the end for Firtash. On March 21, a sympathetic Russian oligarch close to Gazprom bails him out. Besides, Firtash still wields enormous influence in Ukrainian politics: wisely, he put his eggs in several baskets, supporting not only Yanukovych but his opponents too. On March 27, Firtash is paid a visit in Vienna by some interesting figures: his business partner Serhiy Lyovochkin, Yanukovych's chief of staff prior to Euromaidan, as well as opposition politicians Vitali Klitschko and Petro Poroshenko. The topic of discussion is who will be the next president of Ukraine. The main thing for Firtash is to prevent Yulia Tymoshenko, the spoiler of his business interests, from ruling the country. In the end, they agree that Poroshenko, who has a higher rating, will run for the presidency and Klitschko for the Kyiv Mayor's Office.

Until quite recently, it was Klitschko who was considered the country's most popular politician and an obvious presidential candidate. But after the months-long Euromaidan and tortuous negotiations with Yanukovych, his popularity has slipped. Meanwhile, the experienced Poroshenko seems to many voters the best choice at a time of conflict with Russia: he has connections both in the West and in Moscow and will surely negotiate with all sides. Even the revelation that the alliance with Klitschko was arranged by Firtash does not hurt Poroshenko's rating.

The politicians in Kyiv, busy with their own political struggles, do not have the time or energy to keep a close eye on Ukraine's eastern regions. There, unlike in the now-pacified capital, the revolution is only just beginning.

The inhabitants of eastern Ukraine have long-standing grievances against the Kyiv authorities. Conversely, the people of Kyiv have plenty of axes to grind with Donbas. During Yanukovych's time in office, the chant "Thank you, Donbas, for giving us President Shit-Ass," was very popular among soccer fans elsewhere in the country. In eastern Ukraine, such taunts always cause great offense—they believe the people of Kyiv and western Ukraine look down their noses at them as second-class citizens.

The rallies continue in many regions in the east and south of Ukraine. These are all mini-Maidans, the difference being that Kyiv underwent, to use Marxist terminology, a bourgeois revolution, while in the regions proletarian uprisings are brewing. The protesters are genuinely outraged that the new Kyiv authorities are deaf to their pleas when it is their regions that "feed the whole country," since Ukraine's industry is concentrated in the east.

At the very same time, lots of strangers are showing up in the major cities of eastern Ukraine: they are clearly not local but take a very active part in the rallies. Many are, in fact, from Crimea. After the referendum there, the paratroopers and other military returned to their deployment bases, while "tourist volunteers" went to eastern Ukraine to continue implementing Putin's threat that "if Ukraine joins NATO, it will do so without Crimea and the east."

At first, no one is in charge of the operation in Donbas; there is no single decision-making center. Vladislav Surkov formally remains the Russian president's Ukraine adviser, but after Yanukovych's flight he was very nearly fired. He goes abroad on vacation in March, expecting to be soon relieved of his civil service duties. But Surkov's career is dramatically rescued by the European Union, which names him in its sanctions list. Putin cannot now punish someone already punished by his enemies, and so Surkov retains his position. His new task is to exploit the seething resentment in Donbas and find leaders for the new Maidans.

The political and business elites of Donbas meet to discuss a common course of action. One of the oligarchs, Viktor Nusenkis, a major sponsor of the Ukrainian Church, suggests a more pro-Russian stance. Rinat Akhmetov prefers acting as mediators between the opposing sides with a view to reconciling everyone, while former prime minister Zvyagilsky insists on the need to accept the new reality and support the new Kyiv authorities. His idea includes hiring the now jobless Berkut officers as private security contractors to smash the separatist mob. But he is alone: most of the Donbas leaders are against the use of force.

Kyiv politicians realize they've lost control and try to shift the responsibility to local oligarchs. Turchynov appoints the owner of PrivatBank, Ihor Kolomoyskyi, as governor of the Dnipropetrovsk region, and Serhiy Taruta, head of the Industrial Union of Donbas, as governor of the Donetsk region.

The general feeling inside the Kremlin is that Ukraine as a state has ceased to exist: there is no more central power; the eastern regions are ready to fall into Russia's arms one by one, as Crimea did; the Ukrainian military will not resist; the local populations will vote for annexation.

One of the main proponents of Russia's actions in eastern Ukraine is economist and Putin aide Sergey Glazyev. It is he who brings up the concept of *russkiy mir* (Russian world), under which the Russian lands must be regathered. Ironically, he himself comes from Zaporizhzhia.

Glazyev is the most active promoter of the "Novorossiya" project. This toponym has not been used since the time of Potemkin and Catherine the Great, but now it is resurrected. As envisioned by Glazyev, Novorossiya should be the next region to join Russia after Crimea.

However, Putin is not yet ready for such drastic action. Let the people of eastern Ukraine take the first step, he says; then Moscow will support them.

In early April, the situation changes. Protesters storm regional administration buildings in Donetsk, Kharkiv, and Luhansk and raise the Russian flag over them. This prompts Ukraine's acting president, Turchynov, to announce that the time has come to launch an anti-terrorist operation in the east of the country. But his words are not immediately converted into action.

The situation in the rebellious regions varies greatly. Dnipropetrovsk, for example, stays out of separatist hands: for one thing, it is far from the border with Russia, and for another, the new governor, oligarch Ihor Kolomoyskyi, creates his own powerful private army there, the Dnipro battalion, which is capable of fighting off any militias. In Kharkiv, the regional administration is recaptured in twenty-four hours. Ukraine's new interior minister, Arsen Avakov, was born in the city. He controls the local security forces, so order is quickly restored. In Donetsk, however, things are more complicated. The security forces there have been run by Yanukovych's son Oleksandr for the past few years, so neither the Kyiv authorities nor the Donetsk oligarchs have control over them. But they are easy to manage from Moscow, where Yanukovych Jr. is now located.

On April 7, on the steps of the building of the Donetsk administration, the creation of the Donetsk People's Republic (DPR) is announced, along with its intention to become part of Russia. Surkov's new recruit, Denis Pushilin, who had a hand in the infamous MMM financial pyramid, becomes cochairman of the interim government of the DPR. The next day, Rinat Akhmetov, the city's most respected businessman, attempts to negotiate with the rebellious citizens on Kyiv's behalf.

"I went there on my own, without security, and tried to convince them to come out of the administration building and lay down their arms," says Akhmetov. "My message to them was clear: only in a united Ukraine can Donbas be happy." He talks mainly with roughneck Donetsk inhabitants, whose minds are made up—they seem almost zombified. The rebels propose that he should lead the DNR. Akhmetov replies that the common goal should not be to secede, but to live better. The long conversation produces no result.

Akhmetov recalls how after the meeting he tried to convince his compatriots in other ways: by putting up billboards all over Donetsk, recording a video message and showing it on the TV station Ukraina, which he then owned: "I tried with all my might to persuade them. But when I realized they weren't independent, but puppets of the Russians, I publicly labeled them as chancers and terrorists." Tensions are rising.

The Shooter Pulls the Trigger

On April 12, a group of armed men crosses the Russian-Ukrainian border and seizes a police station in the city of Slovyansk in the Donetsk region. They are led by the "shooter" Igor Strelkov. It marks the start of the war in eastern Ukraine.

In 2022, the main question on the lips of Russian propagandists will be: "Where have you been these past eight years?" Its meaning: Why did no one care about Donbas before, which has been fighting Ukraine for eight years now? The vast majority of Russians who believe the propaganda, of course, do not suspect that it was not Ukraine that attacked Donbas, but a group of Russian terrorists headed by Strelkov. According to sources, Strelkov's raid is financed by his former employer, the prominent Russian businessman Konstantin Malofeev.

"[I]t was me who pulled the trigger of war," Strelkov boasts in an interview with the nationalist newspaper *Zavtra* in November 2014. "If our unit hadn't crossed the border, it would all have ended like in Kharkiv, like in Odesa. There would have been dozens killed, burned, arrested. And that would have been the end of it. It was our unit that set the flywheel of war in motion, which is still spinning. We shuffled all the cards on the table. All of them!"

After working as an adviser to Aksyonov in Crimea, Strelkov recruited a squad of fighters, fifty-two in total, and went to fight for Donbas. "Crimea as part of Novorossiya is a colossal acquisition, a diamond in the crown of the Russian Empire. But Crimea alone, cut off by the isthmuses of a hostile state, is not the same thing," he will argue later.

Hesitating to target the regional center straightaway, he chooses instead Slovyansk, with a population of around 100,000. Next in line is Kramatorsk, with about 150,000 residents. The route is likely dictated by how loyal the local security forces are to the invaders: Kramatorsk is the hometown of former prosecutor General Pshonka, who fled to Moscow with Yanukovych; the local authorities are still under his control.

Slovyansk and Kramatorsk are now controlled by militias, as Strelkov's people call themselves. Russian television claims they are local Ukrainians. At first, people in the captured cities believe that Russia's "little green men" have arrived and everything will be fine, like in Crimea. But no. Inhabitants of the Donetsk region watch in horror as people in Slovyansk are shot without trial for disobedience. The Kyiv authorities launch the promised anti-terrorist operation but cannot liberate the city.

Vladislav Surkov, meanwhile, unfolds another trademark PR campaign, called the Russian Spring, making a mockery of the Arab Spring wave of revolutions in the Middle East, supported by the West. This time, it is a wave of revolutions in the cities of eastern Ukraine, supported by Russia. It is also revenge for all the previous times when the Kremlin felt humiliated. The time has come to play with the West by its own rules. That is, no rules.

Surkov portrays Strelkov as a folk hero: already on April 26, the former FSB colonel gives his first interview with the Russian propagandist press, and he soon acquires a taste for it. This media project is overseen by Moscow political strategist Alexander Borodai.

At the same time, terror is being unleashed in Donbas against those residents who do not want to join Russia. For example, on April 17, Volodymyr Rybak, a member of the Horlivka city council, attempts to remove the flag of the self-proclaimed republic and hoist a Ukrainian one in its place. His body, showing signs of torture, will be found in a nearby river a few days later. A similar fate awaits many Ukrainian activists in Donbas: those who take to the streets with Ukrainian flags are harassed, detained, and tortured.

Putin has not yet deployed troops, but the idea of a "Russian spring" is growing on him. On April 17, he uses the term "Novorossiya" for the first time in public. He states that Kharkiv, Luhansk, Donetsk, Kherson, Mykolaiv, and Odesa (in a word, Novorossiya) were never historically a part of Ukraine, but a gift from Lenin. He will repeat the same legend again when declaring war on Ukraine in February 2022.

On April 21, US vice president Joe Biden arrives in Kyiv to show support for the Ukrainian authorities. The main topics for discussion are the situation in Donbas and the country's energy security.

At this moment in time, the Ukrainian business elite from the entourage of the ousted President Yanukovych are concerned about their safety. One of them is entrepreneur Mykola Zlochevsky, who for a long time has combined a job as an official with a successful business. When Yanukovych first became prime minister, in 2003, he appointed Zlochevsky to head the State Committee for Natural Resources. Under Yanukovych as president, Zlochevsky assumes the post of Minister of Environmental Protection, at the same time as owning the large gas-producing company Burisma. After the fall of the Yanukovych regime, Zlochevsky is seeking new business patrons. In early May 2014, shortly after Biden's visit, he invites top-ranking foreigners to join Burisma's board of directors. For example, Aleksander Kwaśniewski, the former president of Poland, as well as Hunter Biden, son of the US vice president.

The appointment of Biden Jr. is unexpected, despite his extensive experience in public service and in business: he was a director in the US Department of Commerce in the Clinton administration, then served on the board of directors of the railroad company Amtrak, appointed by President George W. Bush. All the same, many link Hunter Biden's appearance on the board of directors of Burisma not to his merits, but to Zlochevsky's desire to be closer to the White House, especially after Joe Biden's recent visit. A mini-scandal erupts in the American media, forcing the vice president's office to release an official comment: Hunter Biden is a private individual; his activities are not connected to his father's work in any way. A few years later, the appointment will have dramatic consequences.

The End of Donetsk

On May 2, the Surkov-instigated confrontation in Ukraine reaches a new level. Armed clashes between pro-Russian and pro-Ukrainian activists flare up in Odesa, a city in the south of the country that has been relatively calm thus far. There are sporadic shootings throughout the day. The denouement, when it comes, is tragic: local criminal groups decide to do away with these "agents of Moscow" and smash the anti-Maidan tent camp that has been set up. Its inhabitants take refuge in the nearby building of the House of Trade Unions, which the attackers set on fire. Forty-two people die in the blaze. For Russian anti-Ukrainian propaganda, the victims will be what the Heavenly Hundred are to Ukrainians—heroes who gave their lives for the cause.

Putin arrives in Sevastopol for the Victory Day parade on May 9, the day when Russia marks the end of World War II. The city is buzzing, chanting: "Russia, Russia!"

After the parade, the Russian president goes to Viktor Medvedchuk's dacha in Yalta to celebrate. He has not lost touch with his old friend.

On May 11, the Donetsk and Luhansk regions hold "independence" referendums. The Ukrainian authorities do not recognize them, calling the whole process a sham. But the Moscow-appointed leaders of the DPR and the LPR (Luhansk People's Republic) announce that the majority of residents voted for independence. The life goes on pretty much as normal. Even after the referendums, nothing seems to have changed: trains still run between Kyiv and Donetsk, and Ukraine's most popular rock band, Okean Elzy, plays a concert there.

Ever more strangers keep arriving in the city: some Chechens, some dressed up as Cossacks, who are usually found in southern Russia. At the same time, Surkov's colleague Moscow political strategist Borodai is appointed prime minister of the DPR, and Strelkov defense minister.

On May 25, 2014, new presidential elections are held in Ukraine. Petro Poroshenko wins in the first round, but largely because the Donbas region did not take part. On May 20 Rinat Akhmetov leaves Donetsk for several days, planning to return soon. "I packed my suitcase for one week only," he recalls. But on May 25 the militias seize his house. The next day, the fight for the Donetsk airport begins.

The airport was built for the UEFA Euro 2012 soccer championship, which Ukraine cohosted with Poland. Officially called Donetsk Sergey Prokofiev International Airport, it was named after the great composer, whose works include the ballet *Romeo and Juliet*. Few people associate Prokofiev with Donbas, for he spent most of his life in Moscow. But he was born near Donetsk.

On the night of May 26, DPR militiamen try to seize the airport. Ukrainian troops repel the attack, but in a matter of hours the shiny new terminal is transformed into a smoldering heap of metal. No plane will ever land there again. Nor will Akhmetov ever return to Donetsk.

At the same time in Slovyansk, Strelkov holds press conferences and records video messages. In them, he calls on the Russian authorities to come to his aid. One can hear a note of reproach in his voice, even a challenge to the Kremlin. However, the Russian army does not arrive. Moscow is already facing sanctions over Crimea, and Putin is not about to annex eastern Ukraine. Yet.

Instead, he sets a different task. Putin does not need a new unrecognized state on his hands. What he does need is leverage over Ukraine. So Surkov's new mission is to turn Donbas into a problem, a suppurating sore that will prevent Ukraine from ever joining NATO or any other alliance. At any moment it chooses, Russia will be able to poke this sore and the pus will seep out all over Ukraine.

In July, the Ukrainian army advances and almost encircles Strelkov's militia. Surkov gives the order not to surrender Slovyansk under any circumstances—to fight to the bitter end. Perhaps the plan is to furnish Donbas with yet more dead heroes, in addition to the activists burned alive in the Odesa House of Trade Unions. Strelkov reports back that he will attempt to break the encirclement and leave Slovyansk. Moscow categorically forbids such a move. But on July 5, 2014, with Slovyansk almost fully surrounded by Ukrainian troops, Strelkov and his men make a hasty escape.

Russian propaganda continues to insist it was the Ukrainian army that attacked Donbas and the militias are only defending themselves. On July 12, Russia's Channel One airs a news item in which an alleged resident of Slovyansk says that the Ukrainian army carried out a show execution in the city: the crucifixion of a three-year-old boy, the son of a militiaman. This propaganda image will become iconic and is proven a fake almost immediately. But Russian television will continue to fabricate story after story about atrocities by Ukrainians, who are known in Russia as "Banderites."

On leaving Slovyansk, Strelkov's column heads for Donetsk. Residents track the advance of this veritable army online as it travels almost 150 kilometers (about 90 miles) along the highway from Slovyansk to Donetsk. Natalya Yemchenko, a board member of the Rinat Akhmetov Foundation, recalls: "It was startling to see your home being taken over, and nothing being done about it." That same day, she leaves the city.

"When we entered Donetsk, everything was wonderful," Strelkov will say later. "The mayor and the police were still subordinate to Kyiv. It was a classic case of dual power. The city was wholly unready to defend itself. The checkpoints were poorly equipped; the roads were not blocked; you could get in any way you pleased. . . . Donetsk back then was so peaceful. People sunbathing and swimming, athletes training, people drinking coffee in cafes. Just like Moscow in the summer."

In the coming months, Donetsk, a city of millions, will turn into hell. Strelkov's first move is to blow up a string of nine-story buildings on the edge of the city to make it easier to defend. Personal vehicles will be commandeered for military purposes. A 5 percent "war tax" will be imposed on businesses. A *torture chamber* housed in a crumbling factory will operate quite openly, and extrajudicial executions will become commonplace.

This bustling European city is captured by terrorists—and almost no one in the world knows or cares about it. But not for long.

Evil Empire

On the evening of July 17, Igor Strelkov posts the following online: "In the vicinity of Torez, we just downed a plane, an AN-26. It's lying somewhere in the Progress mine. We warned them not to fly in 'our sky.' Here's video confirmation of the latest 'birdfall.' The bird fell on a waste heap. Residential areas were not hit. No civilians were hurt. There's also information about a second downing, reportedly a Su[khoi]." An hour later, news breaks that a Boeing 777, Malaysia Airlines Flight 17 from Amsterdam to Kuala Lumpur, has been shot down over Ukraine, killing all 283 passengers and fifteen crew members on board.

The whole world is in shock. Until this moment, few people were aware of what was happening in eastern Ukraine, but now everyone is finding out. It is no less of a shock for the Kremlin. It marks a turning point, after which the lifting of sanctions is no longer possible: the most hard-line stance is now taken not by Poland or the Baltic countries, but by the Netherlands. In 1983, a Soviet fighter jet shot down a South Korean Boeing airliner after it mistakenly entered Soviet airspace. It struck a terrible blow to the country's image: US president Ronald Reagan dubbed the Soviet Union an "evil empire." Now Vladimir Putin faces the same situation. He understands there is no way to restore the previous relationship with the West.

The separatists do not admit their guilt; rather, they shift responsibility to the Ukrainian side. But inside they are utterly demoralized. In time, Russian propagandists will figure out how to properly respond to incontrovertible accusations: denying everything is not enough; you need to advance as many insane and contradictory versions as possible. Why try to persuade people, when you can blow their minds. Let them think the truth can never be known because it doesn't even exist. The theories propounded by Russian television multiply: MH17 was shot down by a Ukrainian jet, or maybe it was a Buk missile system, after all, but fired by the Ukrainians. Or perhaps there was a kamikaze terrorist on board. Was it a passenger plane at all, or a dummy aircraft loaded with corpses, which the Europeans themselves set up to discredit Russia? An international investigation will ultimately prove it was the Russian military assisted by Strelkov's troops who downed the plane using a Buk missile system.

At the end of July, the Ukrainian army's offensive becomes more successful and rapid, while the morale of the militias hits rock bottom. Strelkov continues his active public life online, asking Putin for urgent military backup. Meanwhile, the Ukrainians surround Donetsk on both sides, as in the case of Slovyansk, and are close to cutting it off from the Russian border.

Also in late July, the Ukraine security services publish a recording of a wiretapped telephone conversation between the DPR prime minister, Alexander Borodai, and the militia's main sponsor, businessman Konstantin Malofeev. "If nothing changes militarily, we won't last two weeks," says Borodai, confirming that the DPR's forces are at breaking point. He also complains to his sponsor that the money has run dry. The latter promises to give more.

Malofeev, for his part, reports that he "is on a trip with Father Tikhon," meaning Putin's "personal confessor" Metropolitan Tikhon Shevkunov, and conveys the latter's request that Strelkov should publicly declare his allegiance to the Russian president in a symbolic interview. "I finally made it to Donetsk," Malofeev suggests what Strelkov should say. "Some people online are alleging that I oppose the supreme commander. . . . This is my response. I am an officer; I have a supreme commander. At the moment I am not following his direct orders because I am in another country. But I have the utmost respect for him. I consider him the most dazzling leader of our time, who raised Russia from her knees. We all look at him with hope, not in the sense of 'when?' or 'how much?,' but in the sense that we love, we believe, he is our ideal, and no matter what decisions he makes, we will fulfill them, for he is the much-wise leader of the Russian world."

Father Tikhon and Putin himself are concerned because Strelkov's online popularity is snowballing rapidly. Public opinion, which only yesterday applauded Putin for annexing Crimea, is already demanding new victories. And Strelkov's calls to send troops to Ukraine resonate with many. More and more people are starting to publicly reproach Putin for indecision.

In August, the situation in the DPR becomes critical. The separatist-controlled territory shrinks to a quarter of its original size. Any more and Russia will have no leverage over Ukraine. Petro Poroshenko will have won, and will have no reason to listen to Moscow. It is then that Putin decides to send in the army. But, as in Crimea, below the radar.

Army on Leave

To support Strelkov, Sergey Shoigu dispatches the same paratroopers who seized Crimea in the winter. The DPR immediately goes on the counteroffensive. Soon, in an interview with *Zavtra*, Strelkov will describe the Russian military as "vacationers," since, according to the official version, they all took leave to go and fight as volunteers for Novorossiya. "We held Donetsk for forty days until the 'vacationers' arrived. The last few days have been desperate," he says. Both Strelkov and Borodai are recalled from Donbas to Moscow as soon as the Russian troops enter. Their mission is accomplished. Plus Strelkov talks too much, which irritates the Kremlin.

In late August, the Russian army encircles the Ukrainian troops near the city of Ilovaisk. Even Putin comments on the fighting, proposing a humanitarian corridor to allow the Ukrainian military to escape the encirclement. But when Ukrainian columns begin to move along it, the Russian military opens fire. The "Ilovaisk cauldron" is Ukraine's most terrible defeat of 2014: about a thousand people are killed.

The Russian army also suffers its first casualties—fresh graves of paratroopers killed in eastern Ukraine appear in a cemetery at Pskov in western Russia. It is no longer possible to cover up the Russian military's involvement, but Putin continues to deny the obvious. In a telephone conversation with Angela Merkel, he assures her that only soldiers on leave are in Donetsk.

"Okay, but do your soldiers usually go on leave with weapons and military equipment?" the chancellor retorts.

"Oh, you know, there's so much corruption in our country. It must have been stolen from a depot," Putin replies without batting an eyelid. Merkel hangs up.

Putin takes pride in how skillfully he twists the truth so that no one can contradict him. The Russian audience is not offended by such lies. On September 10, a week after the Battle of Ilovaisk, the president goes to church to "light candles for those who suffered defending the people of Novorossiya." The families of killed soldiers are promised compensation—on condition that they do not talk to journalists.

Strelkov, a war criminal who unleashed hell in Donbas and shot down a passenger plane, is initially seen in Moscow as an up-and-coming politician of an ultra-nationalist, imperialist persuasion. He unashamedly gives interviews in which he expresses regret that Russia did not immediately accept the Donetsk and Luhansk regions as its own. "No one was making the case for the Luhansk and Donetsk republics. To begin with, everyone was for Russia. A referendum was held for Russia; people went to war for Russia. They wanted to join Russia. Russian flags were everywhere. I flew the Russian flag at my headquarters, and so did everyone else. The population associated us with the Russian flag. We thought a Russian administration would be set up, the rear would be organized by Russia, and there would be one more republic within Russia. State building wasn't even on my mind. When I realized Russia wasn't going to take us in, it came as a shock for us," Strelkov says in 2014. Only in eight years' time will Putin finally decide to annex Donbas. And that will require another war.

Back in Moscow, Strelkov seeks to expose Surkov, who is directing the Kremlin's policy in Donbas. He calls his former handler a "great schemer [. . .] who is using all available means to drive Novorossiya back into Ukraine as an autonomous region in exchange for recognizing Crimea as Russian." He also accuses Surkov of theft: all the money allocated to Donbas, complains Strelkov, is siphoned off by Surkov and his team.

Lastly, Strelkov condemns Putin for limiting himself to Crimea and not annexing Kharkiv, Dnipropetrovsk, Odesa. And Kyiv as well. Thereupon, the Kremlin instructs the federal media to stop interviewing the former hero of Novorossiya, and he quickly turns into a half-forgotten, marginal figure.

No Laughing Matter

The occupation of Crimea and the war in Donbas do not lead to an immediate severing of ties between Russia and Ukraine—the inertia is too great. Planes continue to fly between Russian and Ukrainian cities; performing artists continue to tour.

On May 7, Volodymyr Zelensky arrives in Moscow for filming and, against the backdrop of the Kremlin, shoots a comedy sketch for the show *Evening Quarter*, a news parody: "I am now in the heart of Russia. If, of course, she still has a heart. All the reports that Russia is waging an anti-Ukrainian information war are untrue. I've been here for two days now, and I have to say I'm starting to dislike you Banderites," he addresses Ukrainian viewers back home, before proceeding to joke at length about Putin, Medvedev, and other Russian politicians.

Gradually, however, the jokes of Zelensky and other comedians about Russia and Putin on Ukrainian television become more biting. On May 17, 2014, *Evening Quarter* airs a sketch about "the young family of

Vladimir Putin and Alina Kabaeva." Zelensky plays the role of Kabaeva, an Olympic rhythmic gymnastics champion, whom Western media describe as the unofficial wife of the Russian president.

The story line is as follows: Putin returns home late; his young wife ticks him off. He tries to justify himself:

"Shoigu and I were discussing sending troops to Crimea."

"Do I look like a fool?" replies Kabaeva-Zelensky. "I watch Russian news. There are no troops in Crimea."

Putin asks her not to watch any more of the nonsense bandied around on Russian television.

It then transpires that Yanukovych lives in their closet. Putin explains that he took pity on him because he "was sitting by the door, looking so sad, surrounded by all his valuables." Kabaeva complains that Yanukovych has eaten all the food in the fridge and painted the toilet bowl gold. She orders Putin to kick him out with the ultimatum: "It's him or me." Putin meekly goes to the closet and says to Yanukovych, "Here's the thing, you understand. Alina is going to be the next president of Ukraine."

No comedian in Russia would ever dare to write such a sketch, still less a TV station show it. Jokes about Putin have long been unacceptable in Russia, especially about his personal life. That is a no-go area. This is the general rule for all media. Only once, back in 2008, did the tabloid *Moskovsky Korrespondent* write that Putin was getting a divorce in order to marry Kabaeva, and the newspaper was immediately shut down. Since then, not a single Russian media outlet has dared to touch on the president's family life. True, in 2014 one joke was popular among high-ranking officials and businessmen that they would tell each other in a half whisper: Putin invaded the Ukrainian city of Luhansk because its name reminds him of the Swiss city of Lugano, where Alina Kabaeva bore him two children.

Playing Kabaeva is a turning point in Zelensky's life, although he doesn't know it yet. This is when Putin first learns of the existence of this Ukrainian comedian. Sure, when 95th Quarter performed at various private events, for example, at informal CIS summits in Crimea, Putin was in the hall, but he never noticed Zelensky. Now in Putin's mind's eye he singles him out from the crowd on the stage, and the sketch itself becomes etched in his memory, according to a presidential administration source.

It is in June 2014, according to Zelensky's partner Sergey Shefir, that 95th Quarter learns that legal action has been brought against Zelensky in Russia. He decides not to go to Moscow anymore. True, no one at the time connects this news with the Kabaeva sketch.

In October 2014, 95th Quarter again enters dangerous territory. News anchor Zelensky announces a headline: "The head of Chechnya, Ramzan Kadyrov, has reacted to the demolition of the Lenin monument in Kharkiv." Viewers are then shown footage of Kadyrov weeping during a memorial prayer. But a different voice has been superimposed, that of a pensioner from Kharkiv genuinely distraught over the fate of the monument.

Poking fun at Kadyrov is another red line that neither Russian comedians nor journalists ever cross. The Chechen leader is believed to be behind many contract killings in Russia, including, for example, that of journalist Anna Politkovskaya. Laughing at Kadyrov, and Chechens in general, is out of the question. There have been cases when Chechens have forced comedians to publicly apologize for the most innocent jokes about people from the Caucasus.

The day after the broadcast, Zelensky does indeed publicly apologize to Kadyrov. To resolve the situation, Zelensky has to meet with representatives of the Chechen community in Kyiv. In the fall of 2014 his car is set on fire in Kyiv, and later the Ukrainian Interior Ministry states that an attempt on his life, organized by "Kadyrovites," has been prevented. Zelensky hires bodyguards until the storm passes.

(In 2019, after being elected president, Zelensky will once again ask for forgiveness from Muslims. And, in 2020, Kadyrov will demand another apology. During the 2022 war, Kadyrov himself will suddenly start doing skits, in which he humiliates the actor playing President Zelensky.)

In the summer of 2014, Ukraine imposes its first ban on Russian performers who supported the occupation of Crimea. Zelensky speaks out against the move. "Why should someone decide for us who we can listen to, who can visit us, whose concerts we can go to?" he writes on Facebook.

At this very moment, 95th Quarter is touring Ukraine, performing for Ukrainian troops fighting the Russians.

Before long, the Kremlin's youth organization calls for Zelensky to be declared persona non grata in Russia for being "a fundamental and systemic anti-Russian propagandist who has given free concerts to the National Guard of Ukraine and personally donated one million hryvnia to fight the separatists." Seeking allies, they turn to Ramzan Kadyrov.

Despite all this, in December 2014 the romantic comedy *8 Best Dates*, starring Zelensky, opens in Moscow movie theaters. He himself does not come to Moscow for the premiere, but Russia's culture minister, Vladimir Medinsky, unexpectedly stands up for him, in a way: "We shall not deprive our viewers of the right to choose what to watch because of someone's ill-considered buffoonery," he says. (It is Medinsky who will head the Russian delegation in the spring of 2022 at the talks in Istanbul after Russia's attack on Ukraine. The negotiations will end in failure.)

Minsk Agreements

In the summer of 2014, Metropolitan Volodymyr of Kyiv dies. Politically he managed to outlive President Yanukovych. At the height of the war in Donbas, all of Moscow Patriarch Kirill's former plans to head the Ukrainian Church now seem hopelessly unrealistic.

Yet in 2022, after the Russian invasion, the new Metropolitan of Kyiv, Volodymir's successor, will not find the courage to condemn the war. The prevarication displayed by him and other hierarchs of the Ukrainian Orthodox Church (Moscow Patriarchate) will effectively sign their own guilty verdict: the last head of this church to have any principles, it turns out, was the now-deceased Metropolitan Volodymyr.

Despite the fact that the Russian and Ukrainian armies have been fighting since August 2014, Moscow and Kyiv have not lost contact. Putin's godfather, Medvedchuk, President Poroshenko, and the Kremlin's

Ukraine curator, Surkov, are in constant touch. Poroshenko and Surkov have known each other for a long time and well: back in 2004, the chocolate tycoon was a frequent visitor to the Kremlin as a bridge builder on behalf of the Orange team. Unlike President Yushchenko, he maintained constructive relations with Russia. Besides, one of Poroshenko's largest confectionery factories is located there, in the Lipetsk region, which makes the president of Ukraine a Russian taxpayer.

After the terrible defeat at Ilovaisk, Ukrainian society is downbeat. Everyone wants peace quickly, and Poroshenko is working hard to stop the fighting. In early September, the first truce, the Minsk Protocol, is signed. The architects of the agreement are Surkov and Medvedchuk, although it is formally signed by Russian ambassador to Ukraine Mikhail Zurabov and former president Leonid Kuchma, representing Ukraine. But the war does not stop. On the contrary, hostilities resume with renewed vigor in January 2015: first in the area of the Donetsk airport, then near the key railway junction of Debaltseve, which is controlled by the Ukrainian army. In early February, Putin claims that the Ukrainian troops in Debaltseve are surrounded, but Poroshenko refutes all talk of an encirclement. Nevertheless, to avoid more carnage, Poroshenko agrees to the signing of a peace treaty.

On February 11, Petro Poroshenko and Vladimir Putin, together with German chancellor Angela Merkel and French president François Hollande, meet in Minsk. Ukraine insists on dialogue with Russia. Putin asserts that he himself is merely a mediator in Poroshenko's negotiations with the leaders of the DPR and LPR. In the end, European diplomats come up with a stratagem that suits everyone: the document is signed by representatives of Russia, Ukraine, and the OSCE, while the heads of the unrecognized republics sign the same sheets a little lower and without specifying their positions.

The agreements themselves were drawn up by Surkov and lobbied by Medvedchuk in the form that Putin wanted. The parties are to cease fire, and Ukraine shall undertake to amend its constitution at a later date, recognize the autonomy of Donetsk and Luhansk, and retain the local armed formations—the people's militia.

In fact, the matter has to do with restoring Ukraine's integrity, but

Donbas is granted special status and its own army. At the same time, the region will be able to block the country's accession to NATO and the European Union. Russia now has a legal lever of influence over Ukraine. In addition, the population of Donbas will again participate in Ukrainian elections, and, given Russia's total control over the local authorities, the Kremlin will significantly increase its ability to directly interfere in the voting process.

Poroshenko understands, of course, that he will not be able to fulfill these agreements: the Ukrainian public will never accept them. The DPR and LPR themselves, meanwhile, violate the agreements from day one. The fighting around Debaltseve continues with increased intensity. More than three hundred people die in the Debaltseve pocket. Yet Poroshenko apparently hopes that the Minsk agreements are not permanent, and that he will be able to somehow strike a deal later, with the help of that same Medvedchuk.

The new president has a very businesslike relationship with Putin's godfather. In 2022, already during the latest Russia-Ukraine war, Medvedchuk, under interrogation by the Ukrainian security services (SBU), will say that his links to Poroshenko were, first and foremost, business related. In 2014, for example, they set up a scheme to supply coal from Donbas to the rest of Ukraine. The fact is that, when the war started, Ukraine officially banned the import of raw materials from the occupied territories, with the shortfall to be covered by supplies from South Africa. However, according to the SBU, Poroshenko and Medvedchuk fiddle the paperwork to register Donbas coal as South African. The deals are settled in cash. If the accusations are true, it means that the head of state is making direct payments to the separatists fighting his country's army.

Later, in 2016, Medvedchuk will testify that he and Poroshenko created another joint business to take control of the Samara–Western Direction pipeline, which pumps petroleum from Russia to Europe.

Essentially, the Minsk agreements are a victory for Putin. He is closer than ever to his goal of turning Ukraine into a failed state. He now has two options: either implement the agreements or leave everything as is. As the smoldering military conflict continues, Russian propaganda maintains the necessary level of patriotic hysteria among viewers. They are convinced their country is not the aggressor, but the victim, that Russia did not attack Ukraine, but that it was the United States that "captured" Ukraine and is now using it as a battering ram against Russia, which must defend itself.

**RUSSIAN INVASION OF UKRAINE
IN 2022–2023**

——	State borders
– – –	Crimea occupied by Russia in 2014
	Occupied by March 2022
	Occupied by March 2023

Occupied territories according to the *Financial Times*

200 miles
200 km

14

LENIN AGAIN:

HOW VOLODYMYR ZELENSKY

STOPPED JOKING

New Yalta

After the occupation of Crimea and the downing of the Malaysian Boeing jet, Vladimir Putin suddenly finds himself an international pariah, rather than the respected leader of a superpower he dreamed of becoming. The G20 summit in Brisbane, Australia, in the fall of 2014 is especially symbolic. In the traditional head-of-state "school photograph," he is positioned not in the center, but on the very edge. And at the business dinner, he sits alone at the table. No other leader wants to be seen near him.

However, this isolation does not last long. After signing the Minsk agreements, Putin finds a great way to regain his former standing. In September 2015, he travels to New York for a meeting of the UN General Assembly, where he delivers a keynote speech. In it, he recalls the Yalta Conference of 1945 and also claims that "the Yalta system was hard-won through suffering, paid for by the lives of tens of millions of people."

He further accuses the West of demolishing this stable system by supporting the "color revolutions" and the Arab Spring: "Instead of the triumph of democracy and progress, there is violence, poverty, social catastrophe, and disregard for human rights, including the right to life itself. It's tempting to ask those who created this situation: 'Do you at least realize now what you've done?'"

Putin then moves swiftly from reproaches to the main course: he proposes to create a "new anti-fascist coalition"—this time in Syria, against Islamic State.

There is no formal response from the West, of course, but Putin does not need one. He has already decided to send troops to Syria to help out the local dictator Bashar al-Assad; the first detachments arrive in August 2015. Putin is true to his principle of supporting dictators the West wants to topple. In essence, he is honing the same strong-arm tactics as before, only what failed last time with Yanukovych must succeed this time with Assad.

The Russian Ministry of Defense is happy: the military budget is growing, as are the opportunities to pilfer, and no one cares how the money gets spent. It is in Syria that the Russian military acquires the brutish habits that will later manifest themselves in Ukraine: disregard for civilian lives; the belief that war crimes will go unpunished; war as an opportunity to steal from the federal budget with impunity.

Involvement in the Syrian war puts Putin back on the world's political map; he is an outcast no more. Until this moment, he has shown total indifference to the Middle East and has not participated in any peace initiative in the region. Now the problems of the Middle East cannot be discussed without him.

Syria almost helps him to pull off the same trick that worked in 2008 after the war in Georgia. One year later, Crimea and Donbas are off the agenda. Even German chancellor Angela Merkel, one of the West's most principled politicians, is moving toward rapprochement and approves the construction of the second stage of the Nord Stream gas pipeline. Likewise in America, Ukraine is almost forgotten, and in 2017 only a hacking scandal prevents Donald Trump from pursuing a second "reset" of relations with Russia.

Master of the East

After parts of Donbas are snatched from Ukraine in 2014, the long-standing oligarchic balance in the country shifts dramatically. Since the time of Kuchma, the two most powerful clans, from Donetsk and Dnipropetrovsk, have set the tone. Now, however, the Donetsk oligarchs have been dealt a blow, and some of their enterprises have fallen into separatist hands. This means that Dnipropetrovsk's clout has risen significantly.

The effective ruler of Dnipropetrovsk is PrivatBank owner Ihor Kolomoyskyi: he was appointed governor of the region in March 2014 and proceeded to form his own private army, the Dnipro-1 Regiment. He comments on his position in an interview: "Who controls Dnipropetrovsk controls the entire East." Kolomoyskyi's sphere of influence includes other regions, too, such as Odesa, where the local governor is his longtime business partner.

For Petro Poroshenko, also an oligarch, and now also president, such a powerful competitor is a serious challenge. Not just he, but the whole of Ukraine, is well aware that Kolomoyskyi is a man with a nasty streak, and not just one.

The Poroshenko–Kolomoyskyi conflict goes public as early as March 2015. It is triggered by the question of who controls the country's largest oil company, Ukrnafta, and the oil pipeline operator, Ukrtransnafta. The state has more than a 50 percent stake in both, but Kolomoyskyi controls the management and can block government efforts to change it. The authorities go on the offensive, introducing laws to make it easier to replace company heads.

On March 19, 2015, a new CEO, accompanied by armed guards, arrives at the office of Ukrtransnafta and kicks his predecessor out. That night, Kolomoyskyi turns up to defend his manager, accompanied by gunmen of his own. Reporters are waiting for him outside when he leaves. One of them is a correspondent for Radio Svoboda (Liberty). Kolomoyskyi has unpleasant memories of this media outlet. In October 2014, it was Svoboda that found out that the Dnipropetrovsk governor had dual citizenship, although Ukrainian law prohibits this for civil servants. Asked directly by Svoboda journalists, Kolomoyskyi replied that he had three passports:

Ukrainian, Cypriot, and Israeli, adding that, unlike dual citizenship, the law says nothing about triple citizenship, so he has violated no law.

In March 2015, a Svoboda journalist asks Kolomoyskyi a more innocent question: What is the governor doing at a state-owned enterprise in the middle of the night, surrounded by armed men? The oligarch goes ballistic in response, spewing a five-minute stream of invective at the correspondent. "We were freeing the building from Russian saboteurs, and you're sat here with your fucking Svoboda like some chick lying in fucking wait for her cheating man. Well, are you gonna shut your trap or do you want to ask about passports? Let's talk about Russian saboteurs; why haven't you caught any? Radio Svoboda, you bitches . . . Cat got your tongue? Or did you stick it up your ass? You're the celebrated Radio Svoboda. Broke the Soviet Union, overthrew the Bolsheviks . . ."

There were no Russian saboteurs in the building, of course. It is simply that, after the war, it became customary in Ukraine, during internal conflicts, to label opponents as agents of Moscow. The video, which shows the oligarch swearing at the reporter, is watched by the whole country. The day before, Kolomoyskyi was a folk hero, the savior of Dnipropetrovsk from Russian aggression. Now public opinion changes dramatically.

The conflict unfolds rapidly: the president reprimands Kolomoyskyi; PrivatBank blocks the president's accounts, citing a "technical malfunction." There is another night skirmish, too, outside the building of the oil company Ukrnafta. This time Kolomoyskyi is confronted by Mustafa Nayyem, the *Ukrainska Pravda* reporter famous for sparking Euromaiden, who is now a member of parliament for Poroshenko's party. The oligarch is more polite on this occasion, although in response to Nayyem's request to be let inside the company's office, he tells him to "remember his Afghan past" and to smash the gate with his head.

The deputy governor of Dnipropetrovsk, Kolomoyskyi's right-hand man, adds fuel to the fire by declaring that "Kyiv is run by thieves, and it's time for them to leave." On March 24, Poroshenko signs a decree dismissing Kolomoyskyi as governor.

But even after his removal, Kolomoyskyi remains a dangerous opponent for Poroshenko. The oligarch controls 1+1, the most popular TV station in the country. And he co-owns the Evening Quarter studio, whose eponymous show is broadcast on the channel. The next episode of the show features a sketch titled "Poroshenko and Kolomoyskyi. Who Fired Who?"

The action takes place in Poroshenko's office. Kolomoyskyi (played by Zelensky) is sitting at the table. The president comes in and tries to persuade the Dnipropetrovsk governor to resign.

"Why was there no coverage on 1+1 about you swearing at that unfortunate journalist?" Poroshenko asks.

"You think you're smart? Tell me, when you screw up, do you release a cake in honor of the event?" Kolomoyskyi answers him, referring to Poroshenko's confectionery business.

Supporters of the president accuse Zelensky of making Kolomoyskyi seem more likeable and persuasive than Poroshenko. "The only positive political character on the show is the owner of the channel that hosts *Evening Quarter*. We each have a boss, and we each decide how much to serve. Zelensky clearly lacks all sense of moderation," Oleg Medvedev, a Poroshenko aide, writes on Facebook.

According to Kolomoyskyi's entourage today, that was when the battle for control over the station began in earnest: the president wants 1+1 for himself, believing that without a popular media resource he will not win a second term in office. The head of the National Bank of Ukraine, Valeria Hontareva, suggests a way to target 1+1, pointing out that some of its shares are pledged as security with PrivatBank, the largest private bank in Ukraine, owned by Kolomoyskyi. And the bank itself has been balancing on a fiscal knife-edge since the crisis of 2008.

According to Poroshenko supporters, 1+1 had nothing to do with PrivatBank's financial position—even international credit organizations were demanding that the unreliable bank be sanitized. A protracted struggle ensues.

Servant of the People

In November 2015, for the first time since the show started, *Evening Quarter* is not aired. The audience is worried. Some suspect chicanery on the part of the disgruntled Poroshenko team. In fact, however, it is a publicity stunt: a week later, 1+1 broadcasts the first episode of a new series, *Servant of the People*, with Zelensky in the title role.

Borys Shefir recalls that back in Moscow 95th Quarter once came up with an idea for a comedy talk show: to gather a group of witty individuals who have nothing to do with politics and to ask them what they would do if they suddenly found themselves in government. Over time, the idea morphs into a TV series about an ordinary guy far removed from politics who suddenly becomes president.

The series begins with a quarrel between a school history teacher, played by Zelensky, and a colleague. The angered historian utters an extended, highly obscene monologue about the political situation in Ukraine: "There's no one to choose from. Of two shit sticks, we choose the slightly less shitty. It's been like that for twenty-five years. And you know what? We'll choose another shit stick again. . . . When these assholes come to power, all they do is talk shit, shit, shit, then more cunting shit. The words are different, but the meaning's the same: Fuck everyone. Fuck you, fuck me, fuck us all. A big flying fuck to all of us. If I were in charge for one week, I'd sock it to those douchebags. I'd stick their motorcades and privileges up their bitching ass. Fucking let a simple teacher live like the president, and the bitch-ass president like a simple teacher!"

A student secretly films this outpouring on their smartphone and posts it on YouTube, where it gets millions of views. Just a few months later, the unsuspecting teacher is elected president of Ukraine. All subsequent episodes of the comedy series address the mind-boggling corruption and other problems faced by the new head of state.

When the show ends, Zelensky is approached by some business acquaintances with the words: "You should run for office!" According to Sergey Shefir, there were no such plans at that time, but many were genuinely fed up with President Poroshenko. Zelensky brushes the idea aside.

Servant of the People attracts fans from unexpected quarters too. Zelensky is contacted by Mikhail Zadornov, the same comedian who addressed the now-defunct Soviet Union on New Year's Eve 1991–92 in the place of the departed Gorbachev. The aged comedian, considered a Russian imperialist by many, thanks Zelensky for a good job.

The series is so popular in Ukraine that 95th Quarter immediately starts working on a second season, but then it changes plans and decides to make the series into a feature film.

It is then the studio runs into political problems. In September 2016, on tour in Latvia, Zelensky does a parody of Poroshenko. The skit begins: "Good evening, my name is Petro. I am fifty-two years old. Today I will tell you why you should give me money. I became president of Ukraine at a very difficult time. And for two years now I've ensured this time has remained very difficult." Next, Poroshenko-Zelensky opens an empty suitcase, places it at his feet like a street musician, and proceeds to urge the audience to be generous.

"What is Ukraine, and why should you throw your money into it? Sorry, I mean invest. We have succeeded in reaching a new economic level, called begging," continues the comedian. "Between you and me, Ukraine is like an actress in a German porn movie. That is, ready to accept any amount from either side, whatever's on offer."

Poroshenko-Zelensky concludes his monologue with the words: "How will I, as president, pay it all back? We'll take out a four-year loan, so it's not my problem, but my successor's."

This time, not only the presidential administration is indignant. In the Rada, Zelensky is accused of humiliating the country, with calls for him to be banned from performing in Ukraine.

In February 2016, the movie *8 Best Dates* is released in Moscow, another romantic comedy from 95th Quarter, the last in a trilogy that began with *8 First Dates*. Protesters gather in front of the movie theater holding banners, one of which reads: "Went to see *8 Best Dates*, murdered children in Donbas." Russian imperialists call Zelensky a fascist for his support of the Ukrainian anti-terrorist operation in eastern Ukraine, and demand that the movie be banned. In the end, it barely breaks even at the box office.

The Ukrainian premiere of *Servant of the People 2*, as the movie is called (the first part being the TV series), is scheduled for December 2016. That is the precise moment when the struggle between President Poroshenko and the oligarch Kolomoyskyi comes to a head. On the eve of the premiere, December 18, 2016, the National Bank of Ukraine declares that PrivatBank is insolvent and must be nationalized. It is a terrible blow to Kolomoyskyi's business empire, but not the coup de grâce that Poroshenko wanted: both his source of influence in the form of 1+1 and his main source of cash in the form of Ukrnafta remain under his control. In June 2017, Ihor Kolomoyskyi leaves Ukraine, living first in Switzerland, then in Israel, from where he declares his support for any presidential candidate who will run against Poroshenko in the next election.

President and Showman

At the same time that showman Zelensky starts to play the Ukrainian president on-screen, US tycoon and long-time *Apprentice* host Donald Trump launches his presidential campaign. He announces his intention to run in May 2015; by the fall, he is the Republican front-runner.

The US primaries get under way in February 2016. At this time, in Kyiv, member of parliament and *Ukrainska Pravda* journalist Serhiy Leshchenko receives a letter. It contains twenty handwritten pages: names and numbers. At first he doesn't understand the meaning of it. But a few months later he learns that it is the off-the-books accounts of the Party of Regions—an inventory of bribes paid to politicians and officials who supported Viktor Yanukovych during his presidency.

Leshchenko is one of the most famous investigative journalists in Ukraine. In 2014, he becomes a member of parliament, joining the pro-Poroshenko faction, but, in the two years that follow, his relationship with the new president, whom he accuses of corruption, deteriorates sharply. Kyiv is also on the receiving end of US criticism. Just then, in March 2016, the White House demands the immediate dismissal of Prosecutor General Viktor Shokin, explaining that he is not doing enough to fight corruption. The chief foreign-policy expert in the US administration happens to be Vice President Joe Biden, who insists that the prosecutor general must go. Shokin departs, to be replaced by Yuriy Lutsenko, an experienced oppositionist, organizer of the Ukraine without Kuchma movement in 2001, and one of the leaders of the Orange Revolution, who served several years in prison under Yanukovych.

Meanwhile, Leshchenko continues his investigation. On May 31, 2016, he holds a press conference at which he announces the discovery of the off-the-books accounts. In the same month, Trump won the Indiana primary and looks unstoppable in the race for the Republican nomination.

Soon afterwards, in June 2016, the Trump headquarters is headed by Paul Manafort, well known in Ukraine for his work with Yanukovych. The American press starts to explore the secret ties between Manafort and Ukraine. Leshchenko recalls that he met Manafort several times: in 2006 in Davos, then at Yanukovych's inauguration. Looking once again at the list of bribe takers, he spots Manafort's name staring back at him.

Meanwhile, the US elections are heating up. On July 19, Donald Trump is officially nominated for the presidency by the Republican Party. On July 22, three days before the Democratic National Convention, nineteen thousand emails stolen from the inboxes of Party functionaries are leaked. This operation against Hillary Clinton's campaign is orchestrated by Russian hackers. There is no love lost between Putin and Clinton: he still blames her for the protests that swept over Russia in the winter of 2012. It was she, as US secretary of state, who sponsored the Russian opposition, Putin is sure.

On July 26, Hillary Clinton is officially nominated as the Democratic candidate. And on July 31, the FBI begins an investigation code-named Crossfire Hurricane. Its purpose is to determine whether the Russian authorities interfered in the US election campaign. But the most important stage of the US election race is yet to come.

On August 19, Leshchenko holds another press conference in Kyiv. This time he claims that Paul Manafort may have received $13 million in cash for his work for the Party of Regions, which Manafort will deny. This is a clear case of fraud and tax evasion. On the same day, Manafort resigns as Trump's campaign manager. A scandal erupts over the Russian hacking, but on November 8 it is Trump who wins the presidential election.

Shortly after Trump's inauguration, Putin offers his own version of what happened. In February 2017, at a press conference in Budapest, Putin suddenly declares that Russia did not interfere in the US elections, Ukraine did. Thus, thanks to the Russian president, Ukraine finds itself at the epicenter of the US election scandal.

Various conspiracy theories circulate in the American conservative media in support of Putin's hypothesis. One of them concerns the company CrowdStrike, allegedly owned by a Ukrainian oligarch and hired by the Democratic Party to investigate the server hack. According to this version of events, the company removed the servers of the Democratic Party and hid them in Ukraine. The second conspiracy theory revolves around Burisma, that same gas company whose board of directors included Hunter Biden from 2014 to 2019. According to US conservatives, Ukrainian prosecutor general Shokin tried to investigate corruption linked to Biden Jr., for which he paid with his job.

These narratives have a key supporter in the shape of former New York mayor, now President Trump's personal lawyer, Rudy Giuliani. For him, incriminating Biden is the best way to protect Trump from accusations. He starts to spin this version and arranges a meeting with Ukrainian prosecutor general Lutsenko.

In January 2017, Leshchenko arrives at Manafort's former office in Kyiv, whereupon the new tenants of the premises hand him some documents they found in the safe. They include several advertising contracts, plus an agreement to wire the sum of US$750,000 to Manafort from Kyrgyzstan through Belize. Leshchenko is triumphant. At last, he has found the smoking gun that proves Yanukovych's off-the-books accounts are no fake. He passes all the materials to the FBI, then publishes them in *Ukrainska Pravda*. In October 2017, Manafort will be arrested.

The investigation of Russian interference in the US elections continues in parallel. In May 2017, a special counsel investigation is set up, headed by former FBI director Robert Mueller, to find out if the Russians helped to put Trump in the White House.

New Vladimir

After the occupation of Crimea, Russia sets about devising a new patriotic ideology. It is based on the version of Russian history espoused by Vladimir Putin. Russian minister of culture Vladimir Medinsky, history buff and author of several pseudo-history books, is responsible for developing the concept.

The key figure in the new historical doctrine is Grand Prince Vladimir (Volodymyr) of Kyiv, a legendary figure who lived in the late 10th–early 11th centuries, said to be a descendant of Rurik and a Viking by origin, and, of course, Putin's namesake. The most important episode in the life of Vladimir is the so-called Baptism of Rus. The chronicles describe how Vladimir became a Christian on being baptized in 988 in the Crimean city of Chersonesus, then forced his subjects to be baptized and destroyed their pagan idols. Moscow did not yet exist; it will be founded only a century and a half later. But that is of no importance to Medinsky and Putin, as the traditional concept of Russian history, created by Innokenty Gizel, makes Moscow the natural successor to Kyiv.

In 2016, as part of the new concept, the Kremlin decides to put up a statue of Vladimir in central Moscow, in addition to the monument to the prince that already stands in Kyiv, erected back in the mid-nineteenth century, during the reign of Nicholas I, at the very beginning of the Crimean War. In honor of the new conquest of Crimea, Putin sites his bronze Vladimir on Borovitsky Hill near the Kremlin. At the unveiling of the monument, standing next to Putin and Patriarch Kirill is Natalya Solzhenitsyn, widow of the Nobel-winning writer who suffered under the Soviet system. Her presence is intended to show that, by occupying Crimea, Putin is building on the cultural tradition expressed by Alexander Solzhenitsyn himself in his 1990 article "Rebuilding Russia," in which he wrote that Ukraine is an ancestral part of Russia.

Joking Aside

95th Quarter's problems start to mount up: in November 2017, the Ukrainian security service bans its most commercially successful project, the TV series *Matchmakers*. This family comedy is one of the studio's few shows that do not star Zelensky the actor; this time he is the creator.

The first season premiered back in 2008, and another five followed. Now season seven is banned by the Ukrainian authorities. And all because one of its stars, Fyodor Dobronravov, a Russian citizen, visited the occupied Crimea after 2014. According to a new Ukrainian law, he is now banned from entering Ukraine. His work is outlawed, and the entire series is stripped of its screening license. Outraged, Zelensky records some irate video appeals, but to no avail.

1+1 receives more and more calls from the presidential administration with demands to remove various sketches from the *Evening Quarter* show. On one occasion, the Quarter team is informed that the concert hall where the show is usually filmed is supposedly unavailable, being already booked up for that particular day.

Volodymyr Zelensky and Sergey Shefir set up a meeting with Petro Poroshenko. This is no easy task, not least because the president works at night and always keeps others waiting for him. The president says he has nothing personal against the studio. But others in his entourage whisper in their ears: "He's decided to shut you down."

The Quarter team, which consults with everyone, has many political acquaintances, including, for example, the influential Interior Minister Arsen Avakov. He gives some unconventional advice: the comedians should create their own party and try to get into parliament. Even with just a handful of seats, the studio will find it easier to protect its interests. So, in December 2017, 95th Quarter registers a party under the name Servant of the People. Avakov adds: "And to boost the party's ratings, Vova [Zelensky] should run for president."

The idea grows on Zelensky: "We have so many ambitions," he tells friends. "First, it was to prove we don't just do *KVN*, but also TV. Then, to prove we also make movies. And serials. And animated films. Now it's to win the elections and lift the country up. Cool or what?"

Andriy Yermak, then a lawyer and film producer, recalls hearing Zelensky's presidential ambitions in the winter when they are skiing together in the Swiss Alps. "What, you think we can't turn our country into Switzerland?" says Zelensky, laughing. "Why can't people in such a rich country live like this?" Yermak admits that his reaction to these words is surprisingly serious: "Well, you'll have to lay down your life. Are you ready?"

On New Year's Eve 2017–18, Zelensky begins the last *Evening Quarter* show of the year with a joke about his possible nomination: "After the success of the *Servant of the People* movie, everyone said I was, like, eyeing the presidency. Not really, but . . ." Instead of finishing the sentence, he starts analyzing the New Year's Eve addresses of all Ukraine's presidents to date: Kravchuk, Kuchma, Yushchenko, Yanukovych, and Poroshenko. He jokes about how they all traditionally blame their predecessor for the mess and all ask for help from "Ukraine's strategic partner": this is followed by video footage of the heads of state talking about God in their New Year's Eve speeches. Zelensky ends his stand-up routine with a nod and a wink: "Someday the time will come when we have a president for whose sake the whole of Ukraine will gather in the kitchen and say, 'Lord, you've no idea how long I've been looking for you.'"

New Faces

Gradually emerging in the Ukrainian political arena is a new generation of public figures who demand reforms. Former Komsomol member Petro Poroshenko finds himself being surrounded by younger politicians and activists whose world view is very much post-Soviet. In Ukraine, reforms of the police and the oil and gas industry get under way; work begins on setting up anti-corruption bodies.

However, Petro Poroshenko quickly disappoints his erstwhile supporters. Many of them realize that the old vices of Ukraine's economic and political system have not gone away. Journalist Svitlana Zalishchuk, elected to the Verkhovna Rada from the Poroshenko bloc, says the president's enforcers are inside every sector of the economy; it's just like it was under Yanukovych. Formally, new anti-corruption bodies have been set up. But through the efforts of the president and his appointed prosecutor general, Yuriy Lutsenko, a former political prisoner and people's champion, these structures are effectively paralyzed. Ukrainian media report ever more investigations into alleged corruption on the part of the president and his entourage.

The crowning moment of Poroshenko's presidency comes in the summer of 2018, when Patriarch Bartholomew of Constantinople visits Kyiv and finally recognizes the Ukrainian Church as independent from

Moscow. However, in the words of Archimandrite Kirill Govorun, the credit does not belong to Poroshenko: he "jumped on the bandwagon at the last moment," then appropriated all the laurels as the liberator of the Church.

All the same, everything could have gone wrong in 2018 as it did in 2008. Patriarch Bartholomew of Constantinople again lays out conditions. First, the various conflicting Churches in Ukraine must dissolve themselves so that a new structure can be formed that will be granted autocephaly, or independence from external patriarchal authority. Second, and no less fundamental, Filaret Denysenko must be sidelined. At this point, the patriarch of Kyiv, who over the years of independence has turned into a cult figure and a symbol of Church independence, tries again to derail the process. He arrives for the Synod, but at the crucial moment he informs President Poroshenko that he intends to boycott it. "Leave, then. There are tens of thousands of believers out there on the square," Poroshenko answers him. "Go and explain to them why you're fleeing." Filaret caves in, and his disciple Epiphanius is elected head of the new united Ukrainian Church.

There is no doubt that the old patriarch of Kyiv expects to continue to lead the Church—through the hands of his young protégé. But Epiphanius doesn't play ball and refuses to be a puppet. So Filaret tries to backpedal and withdraw his signature on the statement about the self-dissolution of his Kyiv Patriarchate. He begins to actively oppose the new united Church, giving interviews to Russian TV stations and repeating the slogans of Moscow propaganda, disappointing many of his supporters in the process. By contrast, President Poroshenko looks like a national hero.

In 2018, one year before the next presidential elections, President Poroshenko effectively launches his new campaign. He has undergone a major image makeover and now appears to be emulating Donald Trump: the same rhetoric, the same showmanship, a similar electorate.

For Ukraine, such transformations are nothing new. President Leonid Kuchma once said, "After negotiations with Russia, any president of Ukraine becomes a Ukrainian nationalist." So, having been quite close to Moscow at the start of his presidential term, Poroshenko looks increasingly anti-Russian toward the end of it.

He came to power in 2014 as the man who could achieve peace be-tween the two neighbors, but he, too, has turned into a military leader, the guardian and protector of traditional Ukrainian values. His new slogan is: "Army, Language, Faith." He is the leader of the Ukrainian army; he is the guardian of the Ukrainian language; he is a devout Christian. Poro-shenko supporters (also known as "Poroshenko bots") use classic bellicose rhetoric: the commander in chief is the leader of our warring country; any criticism of him is unpatriotic.

To many Ukrainian voters, this transformation of the oligarch-diplomat Poroshenko feels fake. And the more the president basks in his own glory, the more ground the quieter candidates make up.

Opinion polls in early 2018 show that most Ukrainian voters want to see the back of the current crop of politicians. The Komsomol generation has utterly discredited itself, and people are demanding someone new. They even name names: Svyatoslav Vakarchuk, the leader of Ukraine's most popular rock band, Okean Elzy, and comedian Volodymyr Zelensky.

Vakarchuk already has some political experience. In 2004, he was one of the symbols of the Maidan, performing multiple times in front of Yushchenko supporters. In 2007, he was elected to parliament as a mem-ber of then-president Yushchenko's party, but he resigned after just nine months. In 2013, he sang again at Euromaidan, after which he considered going into politics once more. In 2015, he went to study in the United States, enrolling in Yale University's four-month World Fellows Program. Incidentally, Moscow has long believed that this course is specifically tar-geted at pro-American politicians. Another graduate of the course, in 2010, was Alexei Navalny, the leader of the Russian protests of 2011–12 and Vladimir Putin's main enemy.

The ace up Vakarchuk's sleeve is his mastery of the Ukrainian lan-guage. He is the son of a rector of Lviv University and grew up speaking perfect Ukrainian. Zelensky needs to play linguistic catch-up as a matter of urgency.

Zelensky has a problem: he barely speaks Ukrainian. He grew up in the Russian-speaking east, in a Jewish family; nor could his parents speak Ukrainian. In *Servant of the People*, his character, Vasily Goloborodko, is a Russian speaker, who even after becoming president speaks only Russian in every situation. In real-life Ukrainian politics, however, this is impossible. Ukrainian is the only official state language, and the president is obliged to speak it. A few years ago, Yanukovych and his prime minister, Mykola Azarov, were constantly ridiculed for mangling the Ukrainian tongue. Now that language is part of Poroshenko's sacred triad, rivals who speak faltering Ukrainian will get burned.

Back in 2017, on registering his new party, Zelensky hired a private tutor. Together, during lunch breaks in the studio when his colleagues went out, they drilled his language skills.

The population of Ukraine in the early nineties was a little over 51 million people. In 1994, 62.3 percent said Ukrainian was their native language and 34.7 percent said Russian. In thirty years of independence, the situation has changed: the population will decrease to 43 million, at the beginning of 2022, 76 percent of citizens will consider Ukrainian as their mother tongue, and only 20 percent will speak only Russian.

Already in March 2022, during my Zoom interviews with Zelensky, he will occasionally forget a Russian word—and even ask his aides several times to help him translate from Ukrainian into Russian.

The oligarch Kolomoyskyi, who lives in Israel, likes the idea of Zelensky running for the presidency: he does not believe it will succeed, of course, but, as a gambler, he offers his backing. At the same time, he insists that Zelensky announce his candidacy as soon as possible—why waste time? But Zelensky, on the contrary, takes his time so as not to become the target of media smear campaigns. The later you declare, the less time your enemies have to attack you, he reasons. That, incidentally, was Vladimir Putin's path twenty years earlier: he, too, entered politics just months before the vote.

Other seasoned politicians also give advice. President Poroshenko's main rival, Yulia Tymoshenko, urges him on: "Vova, you need to run for the presidency. You have to save the country. Vakarchuk is Washington's candidate." What she is really counting on, of course, is for Zelensky to take votes from Vakarchuk, thus ensuring that she and Poroshenko go through to the second round, which she will win. At the time of the conversation, Tymoshenko is indeed on top of all the ratings.

"Yulia Volodymyrivna, but what if I win?" Zelensky asks. Tymoshenko sees that this political greenhorn is terrified by the prospect. Like a mother, she reassures him: "It's okay. In that case we'll create a coalition, you'll appoint me as prime minister, and we'll work it all out together."

Zelensky himself initiates talks with Vakarchuk and suggests uniting forces. But Vakarchuk rejects an alliance, and even decides to drop out of the race altogether.

I talked with Vakarchuk many times and saw him on stage many times. He is a brilliant musician, a real Ukrainian Mick Jagger, who simply realized that if he went into politics, he would never again be able to do his life's work—music. Zelensky, meanwhile, by the summer of 2018 has already decided to run for office, but so far only a narrow circle is privy to this information. He decides not to announce anything before the New Year.

No one in Zelensky's team has political experience, with the possible exception of parliamentarian and investigative journalist Serhiy Leshchenko, who likes the idea of completely new faces in power and so becomes an adviser to Zelensky's campaign headquarters.

Holiday Candidate

In late December 2018, all the stars of 1+1 go to Mezhyhirya. The legal status of the estate after Yanukovych's flight is still not settled. In the meantime, it has been turned into a makeshift museum, so it is easy and inexpensive to shoot there on location. There they prerecord videos wishing viewers a happy New Year. Among the stars sending their congratulations is the station's biggest name, Volodymyr Zelensky. But no one on the 1+1 staff has any idea what he is going to say.

On New Year's Eve, as per tradition, 1+1 airs a special festive edition of *Evening Quarter*. Five minutes before midnight, according to the ongoing Soviet custom, the entertainment program should be interrupted, whereupon the president appears on the screen to congratulate the country on the New Year. Then the singers and comedians return to the air. But on the evening of December 31, 2018, a different scenario unfolds on 1+1.

A few minutes before midnight, as planned, the first part of the entertainment show ends. But it is not President Poroshenko who appears on the screen, but the actor Zelensky: "Good evening, friends. Very soon we will celebrate New Year and continue with the show. In the meantime, while I have a short break, I have decided to speak openly with you, as Volodymyr Zelensky," he begins in Russian. The second, political part of his address he delivers in Ukrainian: the vast audience hears him speaking the official state language for the first time. He explains that every Ukrainian has three choices: the first is to live as you do now; the second is to go abroad to earn money for your family; the third is to try to change something yourself. He has chosen the third path for himself, and announces his intention to run for president.

It is a very brief address, just one minute. After, the clock strikes midnight, the New Year is ushered in, and only then does Poroshenko appear on the screen with his New Year's address to the nation. Later the head of the station will say that showing the president before midnight is a Soviet tradition and doesn't need to be rigidly obeyed.

Zelensky's declaration is the biggest event of the election race so far. In the first week of 2019, he immediately finds himself in first place in the ratings: ahead of the favorites, Yulia Tymoshenko and Petro Poroshenko. Thereafter, his popularity is on an upward curve; theirs only falls.

Zelensky's campaign is nothing if not unconventional. He hastily shoots a third season of *Servant of the People*, believing, as do all members of the Quarter team, that the show is the best possible campaign vehicle. On March 27, four days before the first round of voting, the first three episodes are broadcast.

This, of course, is no longer a sitcom, but an extended three-episode campaign commercial. The story is told from the future, from a prosperous Ukraine in 2049.

Retrospectively, the events of 2019–23 are called the Second Ruin—by analogy with the historical period in the latter half of the seventeenth century, when Ukraine was torn apart by war with Muscovy and Poland. In the previous season of the show, Goloborodko, Zelensky's character, lost power. Now, in the first episode of the new season, the new president bears a striking resemblance to Poroshenko, and monstrous corruption plagues the country. In the second episode, a Yulia Tymoshenko look-alike becomes president. She starts printing money; inflation goes through the roof. She is soon overthrown by the nationalists, and Ukraine breaks up into twenty-eight small "principalities." At this point, the hero Zelensky-Goloborodko returns to power and rescues the country.

On the eve of the first round, known as the "day of silence" because no campaigning is allowed, 1+1 airs only programs featuring Zelensky. Not just *Evening Quarter*, but other shows too. In the evening, it shows a BBC documentary about Ronald Reagan, the Hollywood actor who became president of the United States, in which he is voiced by Zelensky.

According to the results of the first round on March 31, Zelensky gains 30.24 percent of the vote and takes first place; Petro Poroshenko comes second with 15.95 percent. Yulia Tymoshenko fails to make the second round, scoring just 13.4 percent.

An Alcoholic and a Druggie

The election campaign, as Zelensky's team expected, involves a lot of dirt-digging, what in Russian is known as *kompromat* (short for "compromising materials"). The comedian is accused of having business interests in Russia. However, this is no secret for voters; everyone knows that after 2014 Zelensky stopped working there. As for Poroshenko, whether or not he sold his chocolate factory in the Russian region of Lipetsk remains a mystery to the public.

Before the second round, the accusations get nasty. Poroshenko's team spreads a rumor that Zelensky is a drug addict. It even reaches the point where Zelensky proposes that he and Poroshenko be tested for drug and alcohol addiction: after all, it's also said that Poroshenko likes his drink. Both rumors are picked up by Russian propaganda: henceforth, Moscow reporters and politicians will constantly refer to Zelensky as a drug addict. The topic will be seized upon during the 2022 war by former Russian president Dmitry Medvedev, who himself often gets accused of being an alcoholic.

In the end, the two candidates agree to a blood test. Both samples are clean. The next test is nonmedical: the preelection debates. Zelensky suggests holding them in a stadium: his campaign team thinks Poroshenko will refuse, because he, unlike Zelensky, has no experience speaking at such a large venue. But the president agrees.

"I'm not a politician; I'm a simple guy who came to break this system," Zelensky states. "I'm not your opponent; I'm your sentence." And he mentions his previous meeting with Poroshenko at which the latter tried to dissuade him from running for president. "It's really tough. You won't see your wife and kids; you'll earn less," Zelensky recalls the president's words. "There's only one question: Why are you sticking your nose [into politics]?"

Then the accusations and recriminations start flying. Zelensky alleges that Poroshenko has secret ties with Putin through Medvedchuk. Poroshenko retorts that Zelensky's film company received money from Russia, including from the state itself. And he brings up Zelensky's apologies to Kadyrov and promise to kneel before Putin, demanding that Zelensky ask forgiveness from Ukrainians for such demeaning behavior. Zelensky says he is ready to kneel before every mother who will no longer see her son, before every child who has lost their father, before every wife robbed of her husband by the war in eastern Ukraine. And he does indeed kneel down. Poroshenko must respond. He turns to a group of supporters behind him, which includes several Ukrainian army veterans and the widow of a dead soldier. He drops down on one knee before her and kisses her hand. It looks a little awkward, to say the least. By all accounts, Zelensky wins the debate: he looked like a normal person, while Poroshenko tried to crush him with pathos and patriotism.

April 21 is the second round. In the end, it is Zelensky who does the crushing, winning 73.22 percent versus Poroshenko's 24.45 percent. According to Sergey Shefir, there was no ballot-box fraud: Interior Minister Avakov played a key role in this. On the day of his inauguration, Zelensky dissolves parliament.

Sergey Shefir recalls that the team was used to putting their feet up after a long project. When filming is wrapped up, everyone celebrates, drinks, and takes a break. "This time it was like this: we got through the first round, had a drink, and let our hair down. Then in the morning we were told: 'Guys, time to get ready for the second round.' Fine. We won the second round. Then the Rada was dissolved. And that meant preparing for more elections."

Before the parliamentary elections, Zelensky decides to refresh the ranks of his Servant of the People party. The idea is to clear out all the old faces, so that not a single member has ever sat in parliament or held a civil service post before. Zelensky's team casts the recruiting net far and wide: hundreds of regional politicians, businesspeople, activists, journalists, doctors, and teachers are interviewed in drawing up the party list. In the elections, Servant of the People, made up of little-known faces, wins an absolute majority: 254 out of 450 seats. It marks a generational shift in Ukrainian politics.

Russian comedian Maxim Galkin recalls that his life changed the moment Volodymyr Zelensky becomes president of Ukraine. It all begins when Galkin starts joking onstage about how he would be the next president of Russia after Putin. Immediately after the performance, a local governor present in the hall approaches him.

"Very pleased to meet you," he says with fake servility.

"We've met before." Galkin is surprised. "But now we're meeting for the first time in your new capacity," the governor, who took the comedian's words at face value, says, smiling.

Galkin soon notices that many officials are starting to look at him warily, and the invitations to official state events gradually dry up.

Fateful Call

A few days before the first round of the presidential elections in Ukraine, it is headline news in the US media—but in no way because of the Zelensky–Poroshenko confrontation.

On March 20, 2019, Ukrainian prosecutor general Yuriy Lutsenko gives an interview to the political website *The Hill* in which he says that back in 2016 US ambassador to Ukraine Marie Yovanovitch gave him a list of US citizens whose activities cannot be investigated. Lutsenko does not explicitly name Biden, but it is clear to all that he is referring to the son of the former US vice president who served on the board of directors of the gas company Burisma. This means, according to Lutsenko, that the Americans helped Clinton's campaign and tried to interfere in Trump's. The interview with Lutsenko was organized by Giuliani and will soon be retweeted by Trump's son. President Trump himself is furious—he is sure that Giuliani has uncovered a conspiracy against him involving the Clintons, the Bidens, and Ukraine.

The timing of Giuliani's offensive is not coincidental: the Mueller team investigating Trump's connections with Russia is due to release their findings in April. The report is duly made public on April 18, 2019, three days before the second round of the presidential election in Ukraine. Mueller could not establish "collusion" between the Trump campaign and Russia but stated that Russia's illegal interference in the 2016 election was "sweeping and systematic," and that the Trump campaign welcomed this interference and expected to benefit from it.

On April 21, the night following Zelensky's victory, Trump calls to congratulate him. "We were guided by your example," the new Ukrainian leader thanks him. Trump, in turn, "praises" Ukraine: "When I owned the Miss Universe pageant, Ukraine was always well represented."

Already on May 9, Giuliani tells the *New York Times* that he intends to visit Kyiv, meet with President Zelensky, and pressure him to set up an investigation into Ukrainian interference in the 2016 US elections and corruption in the Biden family. Zelensky and his team are horrified. Only now does it sink in that they are embroiled in the political squabbles of the most powerful country in the world. Everyone realizes how precarious this is, that one misstep could be fatal. Helping Giuliani means falling out with the Democrats and losing the financial aid that the US Congress allocates annually to Ukraine, around half a billion dollars. "It's not our war," Zelensky's aides say to him.

The former mayor of New York feels that it won't hurt to apply the thumbscrews to the young Ukrainian administration. On May 10, he tells Fox News that he won't go to Ukraine to carry out his own investigation: "I'm convinced that [Zelensky] is surrounded by people who are enemies of the president, and one person in particular, who is clearly corrupt and involved in this scheme." And he proceeds to name Ukrainian investigative journalist Serhiy Leshchenko.

Leshchenko wakes up in the morning and sees a missed call from Zelensky. He phones back, gets all the details of Giuliani's speech, and tries to explain that it's all a response to the Manafort investigation. Leshchenko had hopes of joining Zelensky's team, but Giuliani's accusations have dashed them. Zelensky has yet to be inaugurated, but his relationship with Trump is already damaged.

Soon Giuliani's associate Lev Parnas, a Soviet émigré, now US citizen, arrives in Kyiv. He is received by Volodymyr Zelensky and Sergey Shefir, the newly appointed first aide to the president. Parnas is extremely frank: Zelensky must personally announce the start of an investigation into Hunter Biden's activities. Only then can the Ukrainians expect US vice president Mike Pence to attend the inauguration. Zelensky and Shefir listen to Parnas's demands and decide it's too risky to play games with this schemer. Shefir even blocks him on WhatsApp. Yermak, then presidential aide for international affairs, says they had no doubts at all about the correctness of the decision: "We're generally honest guys. We come from similar families, our parents are simple well-bred people who raised us this way."

"Okay, they'll see," Giuliani says to Parnas.

Zelensky's team cannot decide on the date of the inauguration—they're waiting for confirmation of the arrival of Vice President Mike Pence, but there's no clear answer. In the end, the inauguration is scheduled for May 20. Instead of Pence, the US delegation is led by Energy Secretary Rick Perry. This is the first sign of Trump's anger, but not the last.

Trump's attitude toward Ukraine is shaped by the conspiracy theories Giuliani feeds him: the president tells his subordinates that the Ukrainians are "horribly corrupt people" who tried to "take him down." In July 2019, Trump orders a freeze on US aid to Ukraine, even though Congress has already approved the allocation of US$400 million to Kyiv for the purchase of military equipment. But the president blocks the transfer.

On July 25, 2019, Trump and Zelensky speak on the phone. Trump congratulates Zelensky on his party's landslide victory in the parliamentary elections. Zelensky responds with flattery: "We worked hard, but I must admit I took the opportunity to learn from you. We applied your experience and knowledge as a model for our elections. . . . We're not typical politicians. We want a new format and a new type of leadership. You're our great teacher in this."

Trump turns the conversation to what matters most to him: "I would like you to do us a favor though because our country has been through a lot and Ukraine knows a lot about it. I would like you to find out what happened with this whole situation with Ukraine, they say CrowdStrike. . . . I guess you have one of your wealthy people. . . . The server, they say Ukraine has it. There are a lot of things that went on, the whole situation. I think you're surrounding yourself with some of the same people. . . ." Next, Trump promises that the US attorney general will call Zelensky and explain what the issue is.

On hearing the name CrowdStrike for the first time, Zelensky's aides google it. "Yes, everything you just mentioned is very important for us. . . . I can personally tell you that one of my aides recently spoke with Mr. Giuliani. We hope that Mr. Giuliani will come to Ukraine and we will meet. Let me assure you there are only friends around us. You, too, Mr. President, have friends in our country, and we can continue our strategic partnership. . . . And I guarantee, as president of Ukraine, that all investigations will be open and transparent."

Afterwards, Trump recalls a "very good prosecutor" of Ukraine (meaning Lutsenko) who "was shut down, and that's really unfair." The US president also promises that Zelensky will get a call from Giuliani: "Rudy very much knows about what's happening and he is a very capable guy." Then he switches straight to the topic of the Biden family: "There's a lot of talk about Biden's son, that Biden stopped the prosecution and a lot of people want to find out about that, so whatever you can do with the attorney general would be great. Biden went around bragging that he stopped the prosecution, so if you could look into it . . . It sounds horrible to me."

This phone call provokes a huge scandal, on September 24 Nancy Pelosi announces an impeachment inquiry, claiming he violated the Constitution and betrayed national security interests by urging a foreign leader to find dirt on a rival of the US president himself; the proceedings begin in December. Trump believes there was nothing untoward, and even orders the transcript of the conversation to be published. In his opinion, it proves that he did not exert pressure on Zelensky. But many, conversely, interpret the transcript as irrefutable evidence of Trump's guilt.

At that very moment, in the midst of the scandal, Zelensky touches down on his first visit to the United States. A huge crowd of reporters is invited to his first meeting with Trump, who all want to know if the American president put pressure on the Ukrainian. "Only my youngest son can put pressure on me," Zelensky replies with a smile.

Meeting with Putin

Already in the first months of his presidency, Zelensky understands that he cannot rely on help from the United States: he must try to deal with Putin one-on-one. President-elect Zelensky, according to those close to him, sincerely believes he can find a common language with Russia. The team of negotiators has had a makeover: now the talks with Vladislav Surkov will be conducted on the Ukrainian side by presidential aide Andriy Yermak.

The first face-to-face meeting between Vladimir Putin and Volodymyr Zelensky is due to take place on December 12 in Paris. French president Emmanuel Macron and German chancellor Angela Merkel are there as mediators. On the eve of the meeting, the Russian TV station TNT, owned by Gazprom-Media, gives Zelensky a gift: it shows the first three episodes of the new season of *Servant of the People*— a remarkable thaw in the bilateral relationship. True, a joke about Putin is cut out.

Volodymyr Zelensky believes in his superpower to charm and conquer people with his openness and sense of humor. But the Kremlin lord is made of kryptonite. At the Élysée Palace, despite his eternal habit of being late, the Russian president arrives on time. Zelensky speaks in Ukrainian, then switches to Russian.

As soon as he starts, recalls Yermak, Surkov and Lavrov pointedly put on their headphones and begin discussing something loudly. Zelensky interrupts his speech to ask them: "Am I disturbing you?" The longer it goes on, the more fidgety Surkov becomes. According to the Ukrainian negotiators, at the meeting he gets hot under the collar, hysterically shouting and hurling the pages of the agreement across the table.

But even after the Paris meeting, Zelensky's team still believe they can negotiate with Putin—they just need to find the right communication channel. Surkov is the enemy, they feel. But if he could be replaced by someone less hostile, Zelensky will be able to work his magic.

After the meeting, however, Zelensky is left with more questions than answers about how to find a common language with Putin. A few years later, during our first meeting, he will tell me that he even read my book *All the Kremlin's Men* so as to better understand Putin the man.

But in late 2019, there is nothing to negotiate. Putin firmly insists on the Minsk agreements. Zelensky, on the other hand, understands they cannot be implemented: Ukrainian society will never accept a change to the constitution to turn Donbas into a "state within a state." He even states frankly that if he were to try to legalize such a move, "the next round of negotiations will be with a different president." Fulfillment of Minsk will be seen back home as another *zrada* (betrayal). The ultra-patriotic camp of Petro Poroshenko is particularly zealous in this matter, as it continues to publicly accuse their man's successor of close links to Russia.

Putin does not understand such reasoning: How can this be when Zelensky won the election by a landslide and, unlike his predecessors, controls both parliament and the government? Putin considers the phrase "society will never accept" to be a ridiculous excuse.

Nevertheless, the meeting does produce some results. First, the parties agree on a prisoner swap: all for all. Second, Putin is generally satisfied by the lack of any agreement: the frozen conflict is a huge stumbling block for Ukraine on the road to new alliances. Third, Putin at last feels like a key international player, a partner the West must negotiate with. The Western sanctions imposed in 2014 remain in place, but the seizure of Crimea has been almost forgotten in the past five years; Putin is now perceived as a respected global leader, rather than as an aggressor who occupied part of a neighboring country.

Meanwhile, Putin's longtime friend Viktor Medvedchuk continues his political activities in Ukraine. His new party has a faction in parliament, and he owns several popular TV channels. They accuse pro-Western politicians, including members of the Zelensky team, of working for George Soros. Medvedchuk's media keep repeating that the *"sorosyata" (Soros's piglets)* are ruining Ukraine. Putin is regularly advised that Medvedchuk's ratings are breaking records, and that he is about to be ready to compete for power with Zelensky. This is a very serious exaggeration, but Putin is pleased.

No more episodes of the new season of *Servant of the People* are shown on Russian television. Yet Zelensky is still heavily criticized in Ukraine for allegedly receiving money from Gazprom, which owns TNT. 95th Quarter's managers try to explain that the international rights to the series were sold long ago, so the president doesn't earn a dime from its distribution in Russia.

Memory of the Holocaust

In late January 2020, Israel hosts a forum to mark the seventy-fifth anniversary of the liberation of Auschwitz, one of the most infamous Nazi concentration camps, in which more than a million Jews were killed. Israeli prime minister Benjamin Netanyahu invites more than forty heads of state; the event is set to take place at the Yad Vashem memorial complex, the world's largest Holocaust museum.

Ukrainian president Volodymyr Zelensky is among the invitees. And he has his own goals for the trip. First, he wants to make a speech, for not only is he one of the few Jewish heads of state; his relatives died in the Holocaust. But the organizers refuse: only the leaders and heads of delegations of the victorious countries of World War II will speak: Russian president Putin (as head of the official successor state of the Soviet Union), French president Macron, US vice president Mike Pence, and Prince Charles representing the UK. The Israeli press writes that Netanyahu deliberately organized it so that Putin would have center stage.

Zelensky's second goal in Israel is to get a face-to-face meeting with Putin during the summit. But the Russian side rejects the idea out of hand, and publicly announces this in the most humiliating way.

Polish president Andrzej Duda refuses to go to the forum in protest:

he has no desire to sit there in the hall and listen to Putin's speech. But Zelensky acts more diplomatically. He flies to Israel but does not attend Putin's speech. Meanwhile, his foreign-policy aide, Andriy Yermak, comes up with the idea of giving tickets to this event to Ukrainian survivors of the Holocaust.

Not for the first time, Putin's speech causes a furore. It showcases all his usual historical stereotypes. What's more, the Yad Vashem complex itself shows a video that is fully consistent with Putin's narrative about World War II: it makes no mention of Stalin's pact with Hitler; rather, it focuses on the liberating role of the Red Army and lays part of the blame for the Holocaust on the countries of Western Europe. A few weeks later, Yad Vashem will apologize for the video.

Zelensky, shortly after the forum in Israel, has another opportunity to speak on the personally important topic of the Holocaust. Poland holds its own event on the occasion of the seventy-fifth anniversary of the liberation of Auschwitz (Polish: Oświęcim) on the site of the actual death camp itself. Zelensky was not initially invited, but his foreign aide Yermak manages to come to a hasty agreement with Poland and the World Jewish Congress, whereupon the Ukrainian leader effectively headlines the event. In his speech, the Ukrainian president stresses the special role of the Ukrainian soldiers who liberated Auschwitz in the ranks of the Red Army.

It is a PR coup. Just a couple of weeks after the forum in Auschwitz, Yermak will be appointed Zelensky's chief of staff, that is, Ukraine's de facto number two. Soon Zelensky and Yermak will form a strong team of two. In this position Yermak becomes one of the most influential officials in the history of independent Ukraine.

Putin Forever

Zelensky's position on the Minsk agreements causes Putin to appoint a new Ukraine strategist. The cynical and unprincipled "Russian world" ideologist Vladislav Surkov is replaced with Dmitry Kozak, a technocrat and meticulous lawyer Putin has known since his youth in St. Petersburg. More importantly, Kozak is Ukrainian, a native of the Kirovohrad region.

He does not share Surkov's nihilistic attitude, and does believe in the existence of Ukraine.

Kozak is considered one of the most effective managers on Putin's team: he was the one in charge of organizing the Sochi Olympics, when it seemed that all deadlines would be missed, all budgets had been plundered, and nothing could be done. Moreover, Kozak has some experience in resolving frozen conflicts in former Soviet republics. In 2003, he came up with a plan to reconcile Moldova and the breakaway republic of Transnistria. Moldova was set to become a federation. But at the last moment the United States instructed the Moldovan president not to sign the Kozak-brokered agreement with the separatists—yet more proof of US meddling in Russia's backyard.

Now Putin offers Kozak a new assignment, this time without even demanding a peaceful settlement: if the status quo is preserved, that will do nicely.

The substitution of Surkov by Kozak is a watershed moment in Russian politics. For the two men are not rank-and-file lackeys, but the purveyors of opposing ideologies. Surkov believes the international sanctions are permanent, so there is no point in even trying to improve relations with the West. Kozak, however, is used to having an impact. In his view, the unresolved problem with Ukraine is hindering the normalization of relations with the West, which must be rectified.

The bohemian, decadent Surkov, who seems more like a Dostoyevskian anti-hero than a high-level official, has already got up the nose of Putin bureaucrats with his antics and snobbery. When news of his dismissal breaks, propagandist Margarita Simonyan cannot conceal her glee: "Let him go back to his favorite pastime—reading Allen Ginsberg aloud in the original," she posts on social media.

The first talks between Kozak and Yermak seem to be bearing fruit. The parties agree to set up a kind of "advisory council" that would include representatives of all sides, including the occupied territories of Donbas. However, stresses Yermak, he does not mean officials of the self-proclaimed republics. "The agreements signed by Poroshenko contain a time bomb. It was written that Ukraine would be required to coordinate its decisions with representatives of these territories," recounts Yermak.

"And I said in front of our entire delegation: we must explain who these 'representatives of the territories' are. If we're seen to be negotiating directly with LPR/DPR separatists, the idea will be buried. But representatives of the Church or public organizations are acceptable—basically anyone who isn't a terrorist from the so-called DPR/LPR."

However, when the Ukrainian delegation returns home from Minsk, it runs straight into a barrage of accusations. The cry of "*zrada!*" (betrayal) rings out on all sides, especially from the camp of Poroshenko, whose hand it was that signed the Minsk agreements. Direct negotiations with the separatists are a betrayal of national interests. Yermak buckled, Moscow won! shout critics of the Zelensky administration. There's no alternative: the Ukrainian representatives must withdraw their signatures. But, most important, the Zelensky administration does not agree with what, for Putin, is the key provision of the Minsk agreements: "They wanted to have a cancerous tumor inside the body—and to influence Ukrainian policy," says Yermak. "They demanded it in law. Zelensky replied plainly: 'That won't happen.'"

According to Yermak, Kozak believes he is a diplomatic guru who will push the Ukrainians through in the end. "He arrives in Moscow and tells Putin that they can't be trusted. He can't say they're standing their ground and arguing their case—that would be of no benefit to him," recounts Yermak.

For Putin, it's a case of déjà vu all over again—the Ukrainians keep leaving him in the lurch, for which they must be punished. Neither Surkov nor Kozak has any influence over Putin's views or decisions. They differ only in style, while being equally dutiful executors of the president's will. One person who does have a degree of influence over Putin is Russia's "number two"—the president's longtime friend Yuri Kovalchuk, son of historian Valentin Kovalchuk, who specialized in Sevastopol and the Siege of Leningrad. During Putin's presidency, Kovalchuk is the only Russian oligarch close to the levers of power; all other billionaires have no political influence. And they don't even fully own the property that is theirs by law. "I'll let them sit on their money for the time being," Putin says about them. Kovalchuk is a different story. He is now the only media tycoon in the country, the owner of practically every non-state TV station: Channel One, NTV, TNT, STS, RENTV, Pyatnitsa (Friday), Channel Five, RBC, and others. But his main asset is worth more than money can buy: access to "the body," that is, to Putin himself.

Kovalchuk finally established himself as the country's second most powerful person back in 2016, when his protégé Sergey Kiriyenko, a former prime minister and former head of the nuclear state monopoly Rosatom, was appointed chief supervisor of domestic policy in the presidential administration. On the instructions of Putin and Kovalchuk, Kiriyenko sets about developing what for them is the most vital strategy of all: how to cling to power.

Under the current Constitution of the Russian Federation, Putin's last presidential term is due to expire in 2024. This time, he is not prepared to temporarily transfer power to a Medvedev-type placeholder. So the basic law must be changed. In January 2020, he announces a string of amendments, without a word about his own position for the time being. Most of the innovations are of a defiantly anti-Western nature: Russian law is declared to take precedence over international law, plus several additional requirements are prescribed for presidential candidates, one of which is that they must have lived in Russia for twenty-five consecutive years.

For the sake of form, the amendments are discussed in the State Duma. The Duma at this moment is controlled by Kiriyenko's predecessor as domestic policy curator, Speaker Vyacheslav Volodin, who is keen to compete with his successor. The parliamentarians adopt a set of new amendments, all of them ultra-conservative and jingoistic. They include a ban on same-sex marriages, the repositioning of Russian as the "language of the state-forming nation" (and, by inference, Russians as the state-forming people), as well as a declaration of Russia as the successor of the Soviet Union.

However, the presidential administration leaves the most important change till last: Kiriyenko instructs the eighty-three-year-old Valentina Tereshkova, the first woman in space, to submit it to parliament. She proposes to reset Putin's presidential terms, so that in 2024 he will be elected for another first term.

Thus, in March 2020, it seems as though Putin has again kicked the successor question into the long grass: he can now rule unimpeded until 2036. It is at this moment that a new threat appears on the horizon, one that he seems, perhaps for the first time, unable to control: Covid-19.

Prisoner of the Pandemic

The new coronavirus almost derails the referendum that is due to approve Putin's constitutional amendments. The nationwide vote is organized at the very peak of the disease, when most other countries worldwide have already introduced a total lockdown. The referendum duly delivers the desired result for Putin, after which the Russian people, too, are confined to their homes.

Putin's way of life also changes dramatically as a result of the pandemic. He stops receiving visitors: only officials and businesspeople who have self-isolated for two weeks are granted access to "the body." Even his once close associate Igor Sechin, head of the state oil company Rosneft, is forced to quarantine for two to three weeks every month, all for the sake of a few periodic meetings with the president. And at the entrance to Putin's residence, a special disinfecting corridor is installed to spray visitors from head to toe with an antiseptic, so that they enter the room soaking wet.

During the pandemic, Putin lives at Valdai, between Moscow and St. Petersburg, one of his various residences. He is accompanied there by his faithful friend Yuri Kovalchuk. There they quarantine together. Their habits and philosophical outlook are in perfect harmony, consisting of a bizarre mix of Orthodox mysticism, anti-American conspiracy theories, and hedonism: palaces, haute cuisine, rare wines. Throughout the summer of 2020, Putin and Kovalchuk become almost inseparable, and together they hatch plans to restore Russia's greatness.

What topic is front of mind for Putin and Kovalchuk at a time when thousands of people are dying of the coronavirus in Russia and the lockdown is destroying the economy? The history of World War II, of course. In June 2020, Putin publishes an article titled "75 Years of the Great Victory: Shared Responsibility to History and the Future"—first in English in the international relations magazine *The National Interest*, and only then in Russian. In it, the president draws unambiguous parallels between the global political situation after World War I and the present. "The League of Nations and the European continent in general turned a deaf ear to the repeated calls of the Soviet Union to establish an equitable collective security system," writes Putin, reiterating that he has repeatedly proposed the creation of a new system of European security, but his initiative continues to be ignored.

He does not hesitate either to draw analogies between himself and Stalin, noting that "unlike many other European leaders of that time, Stalin did not disgrace himself by meeting with Hitler, who was known among the Western nations as quite a reputable politician and was a welcome guest in the European capitals."

Next, Putin explains in detail why, in his view, Poland only had itself to blame for the Third Reich's attack on it, because it had colluded with Hitler in the partition of Czechoslovakia. He accuses Britain and France of betraying Poland by not taking the fight to the Germans during the so-called Phony War, the relatively quiet first months of World War II (October 1939–March 1940). As a result, argues Putin, Stalin was forced to come to the aid of those Ukrainians and Belarusians living in Poland and protect them from Hitler—that was the only reason he occupied eastern Poland. "Obviously, there was no alternative," Putin notes.

Finally, he writes that if Stalin had wanted to, he could have pushed the frontier much farther west, away from the Soviet Union.

Much of the article castigates the West for always downplaying the Soviet Union's contribution to defeating fascism: "Desecrating and insulting the memory is mean." He also mentions Ukraine, immediately accusing Stepan Bandera: "There can be no excuse for the criminal acts of Nazi collaborators, there is no statute of limitations in such cases." At the end, he jumps on his favorite soapbox again, demanding to be reckoned with, protesting against the proposal to strip members of the UN Security Council of their veto, and insisting that Russia should have a weighty say in global affairs.

The historical part of the text, of course, was not penned by Putin. It was prepared by former culture minister Vladimir Medinsky, an amateur historian who heads the so-called Russian Military Historical Society. But it expresses Putin's own thoughts and reflections.

Revolution and Humiliation

Seclusion has a marked impact on Putin's psychology and worldview. He intentionally narrows his circle of contacts, almost never sees anyone, and only a small handful have access to him.

Another shock contributes to his growing paranoia. On August 9, 2020, presidential elections are held in Belarus, in which the long-incumbent President Alexander Lukashenko loses: the majority of votes, around 70 percent, go to the single opposition candidate: Sviatlana Tsikhanouskaya. The Belarusian dictator has no intention of relinquishing power. The Lukashenko-loyal electoral commission simply concocts the desired result—and awards him 80 percent.

The State Security Committee of Belarus (still known as the KGB) forces Tsikhanouskaya out of the country into Lithuania. But this only galvanizes her supporters. Massive street protests break out nationwide, with more than 1 million participants. Their leader is Tsikhanouskaya's head of staff, thirty-eight-year-old flutist Maria Kalesnikava.

The rallies strongly recall the Ukrainian protests against Yanukovych in 2014; it seems that the regime is about to fall. Putin immediately sends Russian security forces to Belarus to assist the local authorities. And Lukashenko cracks down on the uprising with an iron fist: thousands of people are arrested and thrown into jail, where they are beaten and tortured.

On September 7, the Belarusian special services kidnap Kalesnikava in central Minsk, take her by force to the Ukrainian border, and order her to leave, just as they did Tsikhanouskaya. But at the border she resists deportation, tearing up and throwing away her passport. The security officers have no choice but to put her behind bars.

Lukashenko, of course, would not have been able to stay in power if not for Russia's help. I met with the Belarusian president back in 2014. Then he did not hide how much he did not like Putin. He was emotional as he criticized the occupation of Crimea. He enjoyed gossiping about the personal life of the Russian president and his relationship with gymnast Alina Kabaeva. But in 2020, Lukashenko realized that Putin was his only chance to survive.

In the midst of the Belarusian protests, Putin, still in isolation, takes another radical step: to prevent the Ukrainian and now-Belarusian scenario from spreading to Russia, it is decided to remove the potential leader of the Russian protests. Alexei Navalny, oppositionist and anti-corruption activist, is poisoned in the Siberian city of Tomsk with an unknown substance and falls ill on the plane back to Moscow. The pilot decides to land at the nearest airport rather than continue the flight. Navalny, already in a coma, is taken to an intensive care unit in the Siberian city of Omsk. The pilot's quick thinking, as doctors will later say, saves Navalny's life.

By a strange coincidence, Navalny's poisoning occurs exactly eighty years after Leon Trotsky, Stalin's chief enemy, was murdered in Mexico City.

Two days after the poisoning, amid tremendous pressure from the international community, the Russian authorities allow the dying Navalny to be taken to Germany, where he emerges from his coma and undergoes several months of rehabilitation. Meanwhile, his team investigates the attempt on his life.

In December 2020, Navalny posts a YouTube video with the results of this investigation, which, together with the findings of the independent investigative organization Bellingcat, show that an FSB team of poisoners, having secretly followed him on all business and personal trips for several years, tried to assassinate him. The attack was carried out using the nerve agent Novichok, the same poison used by the Russian security services in the attempted killing of defector Sergei Skripal in the British city of Salisbury in 2018.

"If they'd wanted to poison him, they'd have poisoned him," is Putin's comment on Navalny's accusations voiced during a press conference.

Navalny's videos of his investigation into the failed attempt on his life take YouTube by storm, clocking up more than 20 million views. In early January 2021, the oppositionist decides to return from Germany to his homeland. He believes he is sufficiently recovered and must continue the fight against Putin on Russian soil. On January 17, as soon as the plane lands, he is arrested at the airport in Moscow. The official charge is laughable: while in a coma, he apparently went abroad illegally. And this despite the fact that Putin himself gave consent for the patient to be transported.

On January 19, Navalny's team releases the most scandalous video to date: about Putin's secret palace that has been under construction for many years on the Black Sea coast. This revelation strikes perhaps the most powerful blow to Putin during his entire reign. The video is watched by 120 million people, that is, almost the entire adult population of Russia. Mass protests spring up across the country, but they are suppressed Belarus-style: more than seventeen thousand people are arrested in the course of one week.

The damage to Putin's credibility is colossal. Seriously fearing he might lose control of the situation, he tasks his administration with taking action and mobilizing the electorate. Six years before, Putin had found himself similarly cornered, and the only cure for the protests had been patriotic hysteria over the annexation of Crimea. Under attack from Navalny and his supporters, the Kremlin once again turns to Ukraine to divert public attention.

Immediately after Navalny's arrest, the presidential administration decides to revive the Donbas question. A conference is hastily organized in Donetsk, at which the head of the DPR, Denis Pushilin, announces the "Russian Donbas" program. But the main news item is the statement by Russia's most influential propagandist, Margarita Simonyan, head of the TV station RT (formerly Russia Today). She ends her emotional speech with the phrase "Mother Russia, take Donbas home." Such rhetoric sounds strange to many: everyone has almost totally forgotten about Donbas; the topic of its accession to Russia has long died down. But Simonyan's speech in Donetsk symbolizes the next stage of the Kremlin's strategy: the preparations for a new war are beginning.

In March, a court sentences Navalny to nine years in prison, having come up with yet more new charges, as per the authorities' usual tactic against him.

Russia and Anti-Russia

Plans for a full-scale invasion of Ukraine were already in place at the very beginning of 2021, say sources close to the Kremlin. They are known to only a very narrow circle. Most high-ranking officials are completely in the dark, including Foreign Minister Sergey Lavrov, Ukraine curator Dmitry Kozak, and other senior figures who should, by virtue of their status, be kept informed of Kremlin policy. But this is Putin's style: he always makes decisions at the very last minute, keeping everyone guessing until the very end.

Another who isn't warned is Belarusian president Alexander Luka-shenko. According to a source close to the Kremlin, in the winter of 2020–21 relations between Moscow and Minsk are reconfigured. Putin saved Lukashenko from revolution, which means a de facto *Anschluss* between Russia and Belarus—the country ceases to exist as a separate polity.

Throughout 2021, the Russian Ministry of Defense handles the logistical preparations for the coming war. And Putin readies the Russian people psychologically and ideologically. In July 2021, he publishes a second article on history: "On the Historical Unity of Russians and Ukrainians."

The text is drafted by Vladimir Medinsky, a professional publicist and former minister of culture, who in recent years has served as court historian under Putin. Medinsky's political career began by writing popular books about Russian history. All unpleasant facts he declares to be myths and slander invented by Western historians. For example, Tsar Ivan the Terrible, according to Medinsky, was not a bloodthirsty tyrant at all, or at least no more so than his European contemporaries. And all the ghoulish details of his reign are Russophobic fiction.

Putin's article about Ukraine is in the same vein. The president sets Medinsky the task of showing that Russians and Ukrainians are one people. But other than the author's inner convictions, there is little in the way of argument. What's more, besides the main premise, there are a number of outlandish claims: that Ukraine within its current borders was the creation of Lenin; that Ukrainian nationalism was invented by Austria-Hungary; that the Russian Empire and the Soviet Union never infringed

upon the rights of Ukrainians; that the Americans are trying to manu-
facture an anti-Russian regime in Ukraine and turn it into "Anti-Russia."
The author is particular fond of this last motif, and repeats it several times.

The appearance of the article takes Russia watchers by surprise, because in 2021, seven years after the occupation of Crimea, many feel that
the Ukrainian question has long lost its relevance. But, once again, Putin
puts Ukraine back on the political agenda.

In Kyiv, Putin's work is closely scrutinized. Viktor Pinchuk recalls
that in September, at the annual Yalta European Strategy forum that he
organized, one of the panel discussions was dedicated to "deconstructing
this 'perversion of historical justice'"—Putin's article, which denied the
Ukrainian people's right to exist. Leading world historians—including
Timothy Snyder of Yale University, Serhii Plokhy of Harvard, and Niall
Ferguson of Stanford—trashed this anti-scientific nonsense from a historical point of view. There could be only one reason behind this article:
Putin's mind was hatching an imperialist war against Ukraine, as scary as
that sounds. Additional and disturbing proof of this is that Putin's "article
began to be studied at political classes in the Russian army," Pinchuk says.

Historical Moment

In 2021, the pandemic is slowly receding, but Putin is still rarely in Moscow. He spends most of his time in his secret bunker in the Urals. There
he finally loses all interest in the present: the economy, the social sphere,
the fight against Covid. It's all a major source of irritation for him. Caring
only for the past, he and Kovalchuk immerse themselves in history. It is
in the summer of 2021 that Putin senses a unique historical opportunity:
never before during his rule have Western leaders been so weak.

On August 15, 2021, the Taliban retakes Kabul. The whole world
watches the awful footage of desperate Afghans clinging to the sides of
moving military aircraft. For Putin, this means one thing: the power-
less US president Joe Biden has completely surrendered Afghanistan. For
twenty years, the Americans have waged war in Afghanistan against Islamic fundamentalists and sponsored a pro-Western regime. But now, in

the blink of an eye, all the blood and treasure invested in the country by previous US administrations is shown to have been in vain. Washington didn't even try to save face.

The fall of Kabul is a turning point in the mind of the Russian president. According to sources in his administration, Putin was constructing a plan along similar lines: the Ukrainian elites will flee in the event of a crisis, he is sure, and the Americans won't help them because they fear getting involved.

This idea is immediately picked up by Russian propagandists. State channels draw parallels between Afghanistan and Ukraine, stating mockingly that the Americans will abandon their Kyiv puppets in the same abject fashion, rushing to the exit door to save only themselves. No one ever mentions the exact scenario in which this may happen, but everyone knows: when Russian tanks roll into Kyiv.

An additional source of Putin's self-confidence is his very low opinion of all other world leaders. British prime minister Boris Johnson seems to him a fatuous airhead, French president Emmanuel Macron a bumbling amateur. Putin respects German chancellor Angela Merkel and even considers her a worthy opponent. However, it is no secret that she will step down in the fall of 2021. So, for Putin, Merkel is a lame duck.

In August, the German chancellor visits Kyiv, where she declares that Moscow, like Kyiv, is a party to the conflict in Donbas. Putin sees this as a great pretext to escalate.

Russian foreign minister Sergey Lavrov orchestrates a scene: he declares he will not return to the negotiating table until everyone recognizes the DPR, LPR, and Ukraine as the warring parties and Russia merely as a mediator. The real mediators, Germany and France, refuse to play by such rules. First, all "foreign armed formations, mercenaries and military equipment must be withdrawn from the territory of Ukraine," they say. So the Russian Foreign Ministry embarks on a maneuver unprecedented in diplomatic practice: it publishes all its correspondence with the French and German foreign ministers. "We're all human. You could say I've had it up to here with them," Lavrov tells reporters.

Things go from bad to worse. In October 2021, former Russian president/prime minister Dmitry Medvedev also takes it upon himself to pen an article about Ukraine, but far ruder and cruder than Putin's in July. It is titled "Why Contacts with the Current Ukrainian Leadership Are Meaningless." Medvedev begins by directly insulting Zelensky, calling him "an unfortunate man" with "no stable self-identity," who, "having particular ethnic roots," has become a "devout servant of the most rabid nationalist forces in Ukraine." "This state of affairs is just as insane as if members of the Jewish intelligentsia in Nazi Germany had enlisted in the SS out of ideological considerations," writes Medvedev. The text, of course, makes mention of Bandera and Shukhevych, calling them "terrorists and Judeophobes."

Medvedev continues: "It is pointless dealing with vassals. We must do business with the suzerain." What this means is that the Kremlin is ending all negotiations with Ukraine; henceforth, it will talk only to the Americans.

The article effectively signals Medvedev's return to politics, but in a new role. If in a previous life he was considered a liberal and a Westerner, now he seeks to cultivate the image of a hawk and a reactionary. He still has hopes of one day reoccupying the presidential chair, and understands that his only chance is to play the role of bogeyman even more brashly than Putin.

The article contains one other interesting phrase: "There has never been a leader [of Ukraine] willing to sacrifice himself for the sake of the country, and not try to monetize his time in power, and it seems like there won't be for some time to come," the former president firmly believes. In just six months, the Kremlin will find out how wrong he is.

Babyn Yar

In 2021, the Babyn Yar Holocaust Memorial Center is due to be unveiled in Kyiv. On the very spot where tens of thousands of Jews were murdered in 1941, there will now stand the largest Holocaust museum in Europe. For Zelensky, himself a Jew, the project is of great significance: he describes it as his duty as a politician to create such a memorial; it will form part of his legacy, he explains, using the English word. However, Ukrainian public opinion over the memorial is divided. Critics point out that the project's artistic director, renowned filmmaker Ilya Khrzhanovsky, is a Russian citizen. In the context of the war in eastern Ukraine, this is a problem for many. However, Zelensky actively supports the project.

The fact that there is no museum at the Babyn Yar (in Russian, Babi Yar) ravine itself has been an ongoing problem ever since Soviet times. In 1961, twenty years after the execution there of some thirty-five thousand Jews, the twenty-nine-year-old poet Yevgeny Yevtushenko, popular in the Soviet Union, visited the site of the massacre, where, instead of a monument to the dead, he found an industrial waste dump. The shocked Yevtushenko wrote the poem "Babi Yar" in response, which provoked a huge political scandal, since the topic of anti-Semitism was taboo in the Soviet Union.

The Soviet authorities claimed that not only Jews but also people of other ethnicities were killed at Babyn Yar. Yevtushenko's poem was immediately banned, and the editor in chief of *Literaturnaya Gazeta*, which had dared to publish it, was fired. Nevertheless, Yevtushenko had many supporters, staunch opponents of anti-Semitism. For example, in 1962, one of the most famous Soviet composers, Dmitri Shostakovich, wrote a symphony to the words of the poem.

In October 2021, the presidents of Ukraine, Germany, and Israel attend the unveiling of the memorial in Kyiv. Shostakovich's symphony is due to be performed at the ceremony. However, sixty years after Yevtushenko wrote the words in 1961, they now sound risky in the context of the war in eastern Ukraine. For example, one stanza reads:

O, my Russian people, I know you
Are international by nature.
But often those with hands unclean
Abused your name so pure.

The Ukrainian choir refuses to sing these lines, but a compromise is found: the symphony will be performed by an orchestra from Germany, with a German choir.

The memorial at Babyn Yar is quickly turning into one of the most important cultural centers in Kyiv. Artist Marina Abramović creates a "crystal wall" for him. Director Sergei Loznitsa makes several documentaries. Architect Manuel Herz build a unique synagogue.

Zelensky is satisfied. At this moment, of course, he has no idea that the Babyn Yar memorial will not, in fact, be the most important part of his legacy. A few months later, a Russian missile fired at Kyiv will explode right on the territory of the memorial complex, killing several people. "Now it is important for us that Babyn Yar becomes a memorial for the victims not only of World War II, but also of the current tragedy," Andriy Yermak, head of the presidential office, will tell me in 2023.

Anti-oligarchic Law

Open conflict with Putin is not Volodymyr Zelensky's only problem. In November 2021, he makes good on his long-standing promise and signs the so-called anti-oligarchic law. A special register of oligarchs is drawn up, including all those who satisfy two of the following three criteria: first, they have a fortune greater than 1 million times the living wage; second, they are active in the country's political life; third, they have media influence. Those in the register can no longer sponsor political parties or participate in privatization. And civil servants are required to declare all connections with them.

It is an attempt to finally move away from the oligarchic economy that formed under Kravchuk and Kuchma, toward an open market friendly to foreign investors. But the law strikes a blow to big business in Ukraine. It is not long before everyone unites against the president: major politicians, including sworn enemies of Petro Poroshenko and Yulia Tymoshenko, as well as big business players, including Rinat Akhmetov and Ihor Kolomoyskyi, and former allies, such as recent Rada speaker Dmytro Razumkov and former interior minister Arsen Avakov.

TV stations and top journalists and bloggers, who see the law as a power grab in disguise, also consolidate against Zelensky. According to polls, the Ukrainian president's approval rating drops to 23 percent.

All of Ukraine is stocking up on popcorn, waiting to see if the opponents of the president and his anti-oligarchic law will assemble a new Maidan. "Of course, Putin decided to seize the moment," Andriy Yermak is sure. It is then, late November 2021, that US intelligence reports show that Russian troops are concentrated along the Ukrainian border: around ninety-two thousand in total. An invasion, says US intelligence, can be expected in January–February of next year.

In the wake of the news, Zelensky declares he has information about a Moscow-planned coup d'état that involves dragging in oligarch Rinat Akhmetov. True, Zelensky states he does not believe Akhmetov will agree, adding: "It will be his big mistake. I am not Yanukovych; I will not run away."

The Kremlin is indeed plotting to overthrow Zelensky and believes that now is the time, since the Ukrainian government has no support. The CIA's disclosure of information about the buildup of Russian troops on the Ukrainian border angers Putin. As Medvedev forewarned, he issues an ultimatum to the suzerain.

In early December, the Russian Foreign Ministry sends drafts of two proposed new treaties to the United States and NATO. All of Moscow's demands are spelled out in detail: an end to NATO expansion and a return to its pre-1997 borders, that is, before the admission of the countries of Eastern Europe; neutral status for Ukraine; a withdrawal of all US nuclear weapons from Europe. The ultimatum is utterly infeasible—it's hard to imagine NATO abandoning Poland or the Baltic countries against their will. Knowing how unrealistic its demands are, the Kremlin makes the ultimatum public, in contravention of diplomatic tradition.

However, sources close to the Kremlin say that most officials there are sure the Americans will agree to hold talks, which will lead to a promise not to expand NATO. But Washington remains silent and doesn't react to Moscow's ultimatums in any way.

In essence, it is almost a declaration of war: the mask has slipped. But in early 2022, some final attempts are still being made to avert an attack. Negotiators for Russia and Ukraine, namely Dmitry Kozak and Andriy Yermak, as well as representatives of France and Germany meet twice, in Paris and Berlin. But to no avail both times. After the Berlin talks, there are no more illusions, say European diplomats: war is unavoidable. All the same, Yermak recollects, no one in the world at that moment had any inkling of how large the invasion would be. He also recalls the predictions of various politicians and diplomats: "We'll have three to ten days in the event of a Russian attack."

On February 4, Putin flies to Beijing for the opening of the Winter Olympics. It is already a tradition of his to go to war during the Olympics. A source close to the Kremlin claims that during this trip the Russian president warned Chinese leader Xi Jinping of his intention to attack Ukraine. The latter asked him to wait until after the Games.

On February 7, French president Emmanuel Macron arrives in Moscow and holds a six-hour talk with Putin late into the night. Or rather, according to a high-ranking French diplomat, he listens to Putin's six-hour history lecture.

At a joint press conference with the French president, Putin loses his cool, slamming Zelensky's unwillingness to abide by the Minsk agreements: "The current president recently stated he doesn't like a single point of the Minsk agreements. Like it or not, be patient, my beauty. There's no other way!"

Russian journalists are shocked: many recognize the source of this statement, from the punk band Krasnaya Plesen (Red Mold), popular in Russia in the 1990s. The song in question is about necrophilia. The full chorus, which Putin quoted from, goes as follows:

The beauty sleeps in her coffin.
I creep up and fuck.
Like it or not, sleep, my beauty!

George III

In early February, US intelligence reports make for grim reading. Top diplomats and officials in the White House admit privately that they believe the war will be quick, Zelensky will be killed, and the Russian army will take Kyiv and install a puppet government.

This is the Kremlin's plan to the letter. It looks flawless. On February 22, Putin calls Macron and Scholz and informs them of his decision to recognize the independence of the DPR and the LPR. Half an hour later he convenes an expanded meeting of Russia's Security Council—a strange body that is not mentioned in the constitution, but one that Putin has turned into a kind of Politburo. The only difference is that in the Soviet years the Politburo did make collective decisions: for example, the war in Afghanistan was supported by a majority, even though the head of the Soviet government was against it. This is not the case in Putin's Russia: the Security Council meets to publicly swear allegiance and sign off on decisions already made by the president.

It is reminiscent of a lesson in school: Russia's top officials go up to the blackboard and try to guess what Putin wants to hear from them. They all try to be on point, yet noncommittal, in case they say something wrong. On February 22, everyone, including former president Medvedev, Duma Speaker Volodin, and Foreign Minister Lavrov, knows what they must say: immediate action is required.

Only Sergey Naryshkin, head of the Foreign Intelligence Service, and a former chief of staff and Duma speaker, fluffs his lines. His exchange with Putin is broadcast on all state TV channels, and clearly demonstrates how things are done at Putin's court:

Naryshkin (nervously): "I would agree with the proposal that our Western partners, so to speak, can be presented one last chance to force Kyiv to choose peace and implement the Minsk agreements in the shortest possible time frame. Otherwise, we must take the decision that is being discussed today."

Putin (mockingly): "What do you mean by 'otherwise'? Are you suggesting we start negotiations?"

Naryshkin (horrified): "No, I, erm . . ."

Putin (mockingly): "Or recognize the sovereignty of the republics [in eastern Ukraine]?"

Naryshkin (stammering): "I w-w-w . . ."

Putin (firmly): "Speak plainly."

Naryshkin (with hope): "I would support the proposal for recognition. . . ."

Putin (irritated): "Would support or do support? Speak plainly, Sergey Yevgenievich."

Naryshkin (humiliated): "I support the proposal . . ."

Putin (acidly): "Just say yes or no."

Naryshkin (trying to assert himself): "Yes. I support the proposal to admit the Donetsk and Luhansk People's Republics into the Russian Federation."

Putin (laughing): "That's not what we're talking about. We're discussing whether to recognize their independence."

Naryshkin (almost fainting): "Yes. I support the proposal to recognize their independence."

In fact, however, Putin's inner circle is not united at all. Chief negotiator Dmitry Kozak, for example, a native of Ukraine, is against the war and does not stop trying to reach an agreement with Kyiv to the last. For this, however, he will soon lose favor and access to "the body."

In Kyiv, on February 23, President Zelensky gathers together all politicians and representatives of big business: those now labeled oligarchs whom he's been fighting these past months. They meet in the evening in the president's office on Bankova Street. Zelensky tries to sound upbeat, saying there will be no war.

At this moment, a Russian plane is already flying from Moscow to Minsk with Viktor Yanukovych on board, so that he can be quickly injected into Ukraine to fill a vacancy. Similarly, in 1979, having ordered the invasion of Afghanistan and the assassination of President Hafizullah Amin, the Soviet leadership immediately delivered his successor to the country aboard a military plane. Then, when the first coup attempt failed, they took him back. However, the Kremlin's plan in 2022 seems watertight: a landing at the Hostomel military airfield near Kyiv; a strike from the territory of Belarus through Chernobyl to the Ukrainian capital; a quick coup. Everything will be over before the West has finished its breakfast. But most of Putin's inner circle, including, for example, Foreign Minister Lavrov, are not aware of these plans: they still think the war will not go beyond Donbas.

It is late in the evening when Ukraine's business elite leaves Zelensky's office. Some fly out straightaway. These are the last flights to leave Ukraine before the full-scale invasion.

Others remain in Kyiv. A small group of entrepreneurs and politicians throw a party, unaware they are bidding farewell to a peaceful life. All evening they watch the American musical *Hamilton* on television and sing the aria of British king George III in unison: "I will kill your friends and family to remind you of my love. Da-da-da da-da."

At 4:00 a.m. February 24, full-scale war begins: Russia launches air strikes on Kyiv, Lviv, Rivne, and other Ukrainian cities. One of the most famous Soviet songs about World War II contains the following couplet:

On June twenty-second,
When the clock struck four,
Kyiv was bombed,
We were told it was war.

Remarkably, or perhaps deliberately, the World War II buff Putin follows this scenario to the minute.

Yermak remembers arriving at the presidential office building on Bankova Street at around 5 a.m. President Zelensky is already there.

Many world leaders are offering to help him evacuate. US President Biden calls Zelensky to discuss how to get him to Lviv. A legend has it that Zelensky replies: "I need ammunition, not a ride." Yermak does not remember such a phrase. But it doesn't matter anymore. Zelensky is already a legend himself. He has been preparing for this role all of his life and knows exactly how to play it.

EPILOGUE

The war changes everything. By remaining in Kyiv during the bombing, Volodymyr Zelensky sets an example of courage and fortitude for the whole world. He records daily video appeals to Ukrainians and other peoples. It seems as if he has been preparing all his life for this role, that of heroic leader.

For the first two months of the war, Zelensky mainly works out of a Soviet-built bunker under the building on Bankova Street. But already in May, his entire office moves upstairs: leading the country from a shelter is impractical.

In this, and in many other ways, he is the exact opposite of his enemy Vladimir Putin. As if their characters had been created by a Hollywood screenwriter. Putin looks like a grotesque dictator. He hides in his bunker, receiving visitors, ministers, and generals, at a long table: they at one end, he at the other. All footage of him is carefully stage-managed. While Zelensky, unshaven, in a khaki T-shirt, is constantly on the street, among the people. He records his selfie-style appeals on a mobile phone.

Zelensky is soon the most popular person in Ukraine, an icon of resistance.

He soon becomes the most popular politician in the world. US sociologists say that if a foreigner could run for president, Zelensky would have every chance of being elected.

An important feather in Zelensky's cap is that he constantly talks to his people. Every day he finds the right words, expresses universal emotions.

On September 11, 2022, Zelensky posts another appeal on the messenger app Telegram: this time addressed not to Ukrainians, but to Russians:

Do you still think we are one people? Do you still think you can scare us, break us, force us to make concessions? You really don't get it?

Don't you understand who we are? What we stand for? What we're about?

Read my lips: Without gas or without you? Without you. Without light or without you? Without you. Without food or without you? Without you. Cold, hunger, darkness, and thirst are not as terrible and deadly for us as your friendship and brotherhood. But history will sort things out. And we well have gas, electricity, water, and food . . . without you!

"Without you" means what exactly? To me, a writer from Russia, it makes perfect sense. "Without you" means without us, the great Russian people, as we used to call ourselves, while it was supposed that Ukrainians should call us the "fraternal Russian people."

To imagine a world "without us" is the main challenge facing Russia right now.

Putin philosophized on this topic back in 2018. In a documentary film by propagandist Vladimir Solovyov, he threatened: "Why do we need such a world if Russia is not there?" Many Russians at the time were amused, not appalled. The phrase, uttered in March 2018, was considered presidential bravado. Now, in October 2022, as I write this book, nuclear war no longer seems like a fantasy. It hasn't happened yet. And I hope it hasn't happened by the time you read this book.

But something else definitely has happened. Russia as an empire has been consigned to the past, as a direct and irreversible consequence of the war. Many of us born into that empire cannot yet grasp this evident fact.

On February 24, the first day of the war, around 140 million people woke up without the future they'd had the night before. All plans, all dreams, were destroyed that morning. And not at the whim of one man. They were devoured by the empire.

Not everyone realizes this yet. Many are still drugged up, intoxicated by the grandeur of imperialism.

We've been smoking this drug for centuries, feeding our own vanity. The myth of greatness was spooned down our throats, injected into our veins, and it made us high. We escaped reality, no longer saw what was happening around us, lost our empathy and human aspect. It's time to get off the needle. Because we're a danger to others and to ourselves.

Imperial history is our disease; it's inherently addictive. And the withdrawal symptoms will hurt. But this is inevitable. We have to return to reality and realize what we've done.

We have to learn this lesson. To stop believing in our own uniqueness. To stop being proud of our vast territory. To stop thinking we're special. To stop imagining ourselves as the center of the world, its conscience, its source of spirituality. It's all bunk.

We must strip the state of the right to impose its own view of the past on us. We have to roll up our sleeves and completely reinterpret our history, or rather the history of the peoples who fell victim to the empire. We have to look at the stories of those who have lived in Russia for centuries, who have been raped and killed for centuries, the pain blunted by imperial morphine. Administered by rulers who never hesitated to up the dose.

Looking back, we see a horrific sight: our ancestors, indoctrinated to believe they were victors, were themselves victims. They were forced to kill, to rejoice in the killing, to take pride in the killing. And they were good at it. They were proud; they got high; they wrote beautiful poems, songs, and books glorifying blood and violence, the crunching of bones. And they forgot it was their own blood, their own bones.

Sure, not only Russia is intoxicated by this drug. It affects all empires. But they have to sort themselves out. We cannot cure them; we must cure ourselves. We are the ones guilty in front of the Ukrainians, Poles, Finns, Georgians, Kazakhs, Kyrgyz, Uzbeks, Tatars, Kalmyks, Tungus, Yakuts, Buryats, the list goes on.

It's my fault that I didn't understand this earlier. I am guilty before Nadya, and also Mustafa, Seryozha, Anton, Sevgil, Kolya, Sveta, Nika, Natasha, and my other friends, as well as people I don't know who now live in Ukraine, under Russian bombs.

But now the empire is forever consigned to the past. Some might argue it's still too early to say. Oh no it isn't. Future generations of Russians will remember with horror and shame the war that Putin unleashed. They will marvel at how archaic hubris came to dominate the minds of twenty-first-century people. And they will not tread the same path if we, their ancestors, bear the punishment today.

ACKNOWLEDGMENTS

The author wishes to thank the following people for their contributions to *War and Punishment*:

Editorial consultants: Anna Afanasyeva, Thomas Hodson
Map designer: Olga Terekhova
Head of research: Pavel Krasovitsky
Researchers: Pavel Krasovitsky, Evgeniy Kalansky, Mikhail Malkin, Ivan Korneev

Special thanks to Anne Applebaum and Serhii Plokhy.

SOURCES

PART I

CHAPTER 1

Acts Relating to the History of Southern and Western Russia, Collected and Published by the Archeographic Commission: in 15 vols. [Akty, otnosyashchiesya k istorii Yuzhnoi i Zapadnoi Rossii, sobrannye i izdannye Arkheograficheskoi komissiei: v 15 t.] Saint Petersburg, 1863–1892.

Archive of Southwest Russia: in 34 vols. [Arhiv Yugo-Zapadnoi Rossii: v 34 t.] Kyiv, 1859–1911.

Belyakov, S. S. *The Shadow of Mazepa: The Ukrainian Nation in the Era of Gogol [Ten' Mazepy. Ukrainskaya naciya v ehpokhu Gogolya].* Moscow, 2016.

Bulychev, A. A. *History of a Political Campaign of the 17th Century: Legislative Acts of the Second Half of the 1620s Banning the Free Distribution of "Lithuanian" Printed and Handwritten Books in Russia [Istoriya odnoi politicheskoi kampanii XVII veka: Zakonodatelnye akty vtoroi poloviny 1620-kh gg. o zaprete svobodnogo rasprostraneniya "litovskikh" pechatnykh i rukopisnykh knig v Rossii].* Moscow, 2004.

Collection of State Letters and Treaties [Sobranie gosudarstvennykh gramot i dogovorov]. Vol. 3. Moscow, 1822.

Correspondence of the Hetmans of Left Bank Ukraine with Moscow and St. Petersburg, 1654–1764: A Collection of Documents [Perepiska getmanov Levoberezhnoi Ukrainy s Moskvoi i Sankt-Peterburgom, 1654–1764 gg.: sbornik dokumentov]. Vol. 1: The Hetmanate of Bogdan Khmelnitsky, 1654–1657 [Getmanstvo Bogdana Khmel'nickogo, 1654–1657 gg.]. Moscow, 2017.

Danilevskii, I. N., Tairova (Yakovleva), T. G., Shubin, A. V., and Mironenko, V. I. *A History of Ukraine [Istoriya Ukrainy].* Saint Petersburg, 2018.

Encyclopedia of Ukraine, vols. 1–5, edited by Volodymyr Kubijovyc and Danylo Husar Struk. Toronto: University of Toronto Press, 1984–1993.

Florya, B. N. *The Russian State and Its Western Neighbors (1655–1661) [Russkoe gosudarstvo i ego zapadnye sosedi (1655–1661 gg.)].* Moscow, 2010.

Gaida, F. A. "Ukraine and Little Russia: The Outskirts and the Center" [Ukraina i Malaya Rus: Okraina i Tsentr]. *Russkii Sbornik*, vol. 16 (2014), pp. 97–108.

Galashin, A. V. "Russia and the Beginning of B. Khmelnitsky's Uprising" [Rossiya i nachalo vosstaniya B. Khmelnitskogo]. *Slavyanskii almanakh*, Moscow, 1999.

Gayda, F. A. "'A Ukrainian' as Self-Identification in the Context of the Collapse of Empires in the Early Twentieth Century" ["Ukrainets" kak samoidentifikatsiya v usloviyakh raspada imperii v nachale XX veka]. *Historia Provinciae: The Journal of Regional History*, vol. 3, no. 3 (2019), pp. 845–883.

Gizel, Innokentii. *Kyiv Synopsis [Kievskii Sinopsis]*. Kyiv, 1823.

Grekov, I. B., Korolyuk, V. D., and Miller, I. S. *Reunification of Ukraine with Russia in 1654 [Vossoedinenie Ukrainy s Rossiei v 1654 g.]*. Moscow, 1954.

Keenan, Edward L. "Muscovite Perceptions of Other East Slavs Before 1654: An Agenda for Historians," in *Ukraine and Russian in Their Historical Encounter*. Edmonton, 1992, pp. 20–38.

Keenan, Edward L. "On Certain Mythical Beliefs and Russian Behaviors," in *The Legacy of History in Russia and the New States of Eurasia*. Armonk and London: M. E. Sharpe, 1994, pp. 19–40.

Kohut, Zenon E. "The Question of Russo-Ukrainian Unity and Ukrainian Distinctiveness in Early Modern Ukrainian Thought and Culture," in *Culture, Nation, and Identity: The Ukrainian-Russian Encounter (1600–1945)*, ed. Andreas Kappeler et al. Edmonton and Toronto: CIUS Press, 2003, pp. 57–86.

Kotenko, A. L., Martynyuk, O. V., and Miller, A. I. "'Maloross': The Evolution of the Concept before World War I" ['Maloross': evolyutsiya ponyatiya do Pervoi mirovoi voiny]. *Novoe literaturnoe obozrenie*, no. 2 (2011).

Krom, M. M. *The Birth of the State: Moscow Rus of the 15–16 Centuries [Rozhdenie gosudarstva. Moskovskaya Rus XV–XVI vekov]*. Moscow, 2018.

Magocsi, Paul Robert. *A History of Ukraine: The Land and Its Peoples*. Toronto: University of Toronto Press, 2010.

Miller, A. I. *"The Ukrainian Question" in Government Policy and Russian Public Opinion (Second Half of the 19th Century) ["Ukrainskii vopros" v politike vlastei i russkom obshchestvennom mnenii (vtoraya polovina XIX veka)]*. Saint Petersburg, 2000.

Miller, A. I. *The Ukrainian Question in the Russian Empire [Ukrainskii vopros v Rossiiskoi imperii]*. Kyiv, 2013.

Milyukov, P. N. *The Main Currents of Russian Historical Thought [Glavnye techeniya russkoi istoricheskoi mysli]*. Saint Petersburg, 1913.

Oparina, T. A. *Foreigners in Russia in the 16th–17th Centuries: Essays on Historical Biography and Genealogy [Inozemtsy v Rossii XVI–XVII vv.: Ocherki istoricheskoi biografii i genealogii]*. Moscow, 2007.

Pashuto, V. T., Florya, B. N., and Khoroshkevich, A. L. *Ancient Russian Heritage and the Historical Fate of Eastern Slavs [Drevnerusskoe nasledie i istoricheskie sudby vostochnogo slavyanstva]*. Moscow, 1982.

Peshtich, S. L. "'Synopsis' as a Historical Work" ['Sinopsis' kak istoricheskoe proizvedenie], in *Works by the Department of Old Russian Literature [Trudy Otdela drevnerusskoi literatury]*, vol. 15. Moscow, Leningrad, 1958, pp. 284–298.

Plokhy, S. *The Gates of Europe: A History of Ukraine*. New York: Basic Books, 2015.

Reunification of Ukraine with Russia: Documents and Materials in Three Volumes [Vossoedinenie Ukrainy s Rossiei. Dokumenty i materialy v trekh tomakh]. Moscow, 1953.

Reunification of Ukraine with Russia: 1654–1954. Collection of Articles [Vossoedinenie Ukrainy s Rossiei, 1654–1954. Sbornik statei]. Moscow, 1954.

Smolii, V. A. (ed.) *A History of Ukraine: Popular Scientific Essays [Istoriya Ukrainy: nauchno-populyarnye ocherki]*. Moscow, 2008.

Solovyov, A. V. "Great, Little and White Rus" [Velikaya, Malaya i Belaya Rus]. *Voprosy istorii*, Moscow, 1947, no. 7, p. 31.

Stepanov, D. Yu. "'Russian,' 'Little Russian' and 'Moscow' in the Views of the Hetmanshchyna Elite in the 50–60s of the 17th Century" ["Russkoe," "malorossiiskoe" i "moskovskoe" v predstavleniyakh elity Getmanshchiny v 50–60-e gody XVII veka]. *Slavyanovedenie*, no. 4 (2012).

Stepanov, D. Yu. *Ethno-confessional Self-Consciousness of the Orthodox Population of Rzeczpospolita and Hetmanshchyna in the Middle and Second Half of the 17th Century [Etnokonfessionalnoe samosoznanie pravoslavnogo naseleniya Rechi Pospolitoi i Getmanshchiny v seredine—vtoroi polovine XVII v.]*. Moscow, 2016.

Subtelny, Orest. *Ukraine: A History*. Toronto: University of Toronto Press, 1994.

Tairova-Yakovleva, T. G. *Incorporation: Russia and Ukraine After the Pereyaslavl Rada (1654–1658) [Inkorporaciya: Rossiya i Ukraina posle Pereyaslavskoi rady (1654–1658)]*. Kyiv, 2017.

Tarasov, S. V. "Bogdan Khmelnitsky in Russian Pre-revolutionary Historiography" [Bogdan Khmelnitskii v Rossiiskoi dorevolyutsionnoi istoriografii]. *Visnik Mariupolskogo derzhavnogo universitetu*, no. 20 (2018).

Tarasov, S. V. "Life and Activity of Hetman Ivan Vygovsky as Portrayed by Russian Pre-revolutionary Historiography" [Zhizn i deyatelnost getmana Ivana Vygovskogo v izobrazhenii rossiiskoi dorevolyutsionnoi istoriografii]. *Visnik Mariupolskogo derzhavnogo universitetu*, no. 16 (2016).

Tkachenko, V. V. "'Synopsis' and the Teaching of Russian History in the Eighteenth Century: On One Historiographic Myth" ["Sinopsis" i prepodavanie istorii Rossii v XVIII v.: ob odnom istoriograficheskom mife], in *Istoriya Rossii s drevneishikh vremen do XXI veka: problemy, diskussii, novye vzglyady*. Moscow, 2018, pp. 41–48.

The Western Fringes of the Russian Empire [Zapadnye okrainy Rossiiskoi imperii]. Moscow, 2006.

Zamlinskii, V. A. *Bohdan Khmelnytsky [Bogdan Khmel'nitskiy]*. Moscow, 1989.

CHAPTER 2

Acts Relating to the History of Southern and Western Russia [Akty, otnosyashchiesya k istorii Yuzhnoi i Zapadnoi Rossii]. Vols. 3–4. Saint Petersburg, 1861–1863.

Archive of Southwest Russia: in 34 vols. [Arkhiv Yugo-Zapadnoi Rossii: v 34 t.]. Kyiv, 1859–1911.

The Baturyn Archive and Other Documents on the History of the Ukrainian Hetmanate in 1690–1709 [Baturinskii arkhiv i drugie dokumenty po istorii Ukrainskogo getmanstva 1690–1709 gg.]. Compiled by T. G. Tairova-Yakovleva. Saint Petersburg, 2014.

Bushkovitch, Paul. *Peter the Great: The Struggle for Power, 1671–1725*. Cambridge: Cambridge University Press, 2001.

A Chronicle of Events in Southwestern Russia in the 17th Century. Compiled by Samoil Velichko [Letopis sobytii v Yugo-Zapadnoi Rossii v XVII vekė. Sostavil Samoil Velichko]. Vols. 1–4. Kyiv, 1848–1864.

Evarnitskii, D. I. *Sources for the History of the Zaporozhye Cossacks [Istochniki dlya istorii zaporozhskikh kazakov]*. Vol. 1. Vladimir, 1908.

Kostomarov, N. I. *Mazepa [Mazepa]*. Moscow, 2004.

Lappo-Danilevskii, A. S. *History of Russian Social Thought and Culture in the 17th–18th Centuries [Istoriya russkoi obshchestvennoi mysli i kultury XVII–XVIII vv.]*. Moscow, 1990.

Letters and Papers of Peter the Great: in 13 vols. [Pisma i bumagi Petra Velikogo: v 13 t.]. Saint Petersburg, Moscow, and Leningrad, 1887–2003.

Letters of Ivan Mazepa, 1687–1700 [Listi Ivana Mazepi. 1687–1700]. Vols. 1–2. Kyiv, 2002–2010.

Pavlenko, N. I. and Artamonov, V. A. *June 27, 1709 [27 iyunya 1709].* Moscow, 1989.

Pavlenko, S. O. *Ivan Mazepa [Ivan Mazepa].* Kyiv, 2003.

"Pylyp Orlyk's Letter to Stefan Jaworski (1721): A Self-Described Testimony of Mazepa's Apostasy" [List Pilipa Orlika do Stefana Yavorskogo (1721 r.): svidchennya samovidtsya pro Mazepine vidstupnitstvo], in Subtelnii, Orest. *The Mazepints: Ukrainian Separatism in the Early 18th Century [Mazepintsi. Ukraïnskii separatizm na pochatku XVIII st].* Kyiv, 1994, pp. 158–184.

Sources of Little Russian History: in 2 parts. Collected by D. N. Bantysh-Kamensky [Istochniki Malorossiiskoi istorii: v 2 ch. Sobrany D. N. Bantyshem-Kamenskim]. Moscow, 1858–1859.

Subtelny, Orest. *The Mazepists: Ukrainian Separatism in the Early Eighteenth Century.* New York, 1981.

Tairova-Yakovleva, T. G. *Ivan Mazepa and the Russian Empire: A History of "Betrayal" [Ivan Mazepa i Rossiiskaya imperiya: istoriya "predatelstva"].* Moscow, 2011.

Tairova-Yakovleva, T. G. *Mazepa [Mazepa].* Moscow, 2007.

Yakovleva, T. G. "Mazepa the Hetman: In Search of Historical Objectivity" [Mazepa—getman: v poiskakh istoricheskoi obektivnosti]. *Novaya i noveishaya istoriya,* no. 4 (2003).

CHAPTER 3

"About the Private Life of Prince Potemkin, About Some Traits of His Character and Anecdotes" [O privatnoi zhizni knyazya Potemkina, o nekotorykh chertakh ego kharaktera i anekdotakh]. *Moskvityanin,* no. 2 (1852).

Belyakov, S. S. *The Shadow of Mazepa: The Ukrainian Nation in the Era of Gogol [Ten' Mazepy. Ukrainskaya naciya v ehpokhu Gogolya].* Moscow, 2016.

Borinevich, A. S. *Empress Catherine II. Novorossiya and Odessa: A Public Essay [Imperatritsa Ekaterina II. Novorossiya i Odessa: Obshchedostupnyi ocherk].* Odesa, 1896.

Brikner, A. G. *Potemkin [Potemkin].* Saint Petersburg, 1891.

Catherine II and G. A. Potemkin. Personal Correspondence, 1769–1791 [Ekaterina II i G. A. Potemkin. Lichnaya perepiska. 1769–1791]. Moscow, 1997.

A Chronological Review of the History of the Novorossiysk Territory: 1730–1823 [Khronologicheskoe obozrenie istorii Novorossiiskogo kraya: 1730–1823]. Part 1: 1730–1796. Odesa, 1836.

Eliseeva, O. I. *The Geopolitical Projects of G. A. Potemkin [Geopoliticheskie proekty G. A. Potemkina].* Moscow, 2000.

Eliseeva, O. I. "Government Policy for Resettlement in the Crimea and Novorossia in the Second Half of the 18th Century" [Pravitelstvennaya politika po pereseleniyu v Krym i Novorossiyu vo vtoroi polovine XVIII veka]. *Istoricheskoe obozrenie,* no. 7 (2006).

Etkind, A. *Domestic Colonization: The Imperial Experience of Russia [Vnutrennyaya kolonizatsiya. Imperskii opyt Rossii].* Moscow, 2013.

Field Marshal Rumyantsev: Collection of Documents and Materials [Feldmarshal Rumyantsev: Sbornik dokumentov i materialov]. Moscow, 1947.

Gelbig, G. *Russian Chosen People and Random People [Russkie izbranniki i sluchainye lyudi].* Saint Petersburg, 1887.

Griffiths, D. *Catherine II and Her World: Articles from Various Years [Ekaterina II i ee mir: stati raznykh let]*. Moscow, 2013.

The History of Novorossia [Istoriya Novorossii], edited by V. N. Zakharov. Moscow, Saint Petersburg, 2017.

"Instructions of Catherine II to Prince Vyazemsky on His Assumption of the Post of Procurator General in February 1764" [Nastavlenie Ekateriny II knyazyu Vyazemskomu pri vstuplenii im v dolzhnost general-prokurora v fevrale 1764 goda], in *Sbornik russkogo istoricheskogo obshchestva*. Vol. 7. Saint Petersburg, 1871, p. 348.

Isabel de Madariaga. *Russia in the Age of Catherine the Great [Rossiya v epokhu Ekateriny Velikoi]*. Moscow, 2002.

Klyuchevskii, V. O. *Works: in 9 vols. [Sochineniya: v 9 t.]*. Vol. 3: A Course in Russian History [Kurs russkoi istorii]. Moscow, 1988.

Kotsur, V. A. "Contribution of Pyotr Kalnyshevsky, Koshev ataman of the Zaporizhian Sich, to Church Construction" [Vklad koshevogo atamana Zaporozhskoi Sechi Petra Kalnyshevskogo v tserkovnoe stroitelstvo. *Teoriya i praktika obshchestvennogo razvitiya*, no. 10 (2013).

Kruglova, T. A. "Methodological and Source Approaches to the Study of 'Notes on the Disorder in Malorossia' (1750s)" [Metodologicheskie i istochnikovedcheskie podkhody k izucheniyu "Zapiski o neporyadkakh v Malorossii" (1750-e gg.)] *Vestnik Moskovskogo universiteta. Seriya. 8. Istoriya*, no. 2 (2015), pp. 3–23.

Kruglova, T. A. "On the Question of the Time of Compilation of 'Notes on the Disorder in Little Russia': In the Reign of Elizabeth Petrovna or Catherine II?" [K voprosu o vremeni sostavleniya "Zapiski o neporyadkakh v Malorossii": v tsarstvovanie Elizavety Petrovny ili Ekateriny II?] *Vestnik Moskovskogo universiteta. Seriya 8. Istoriya*, 2011.

Kruglova, T. A. "On the Resignation of the Last Hetman of Little Russia K. Razumovsky (1764): A New Reading of Sources" [Ob otstavke poslednego malorossiiskogo getmana K. G. Razumovskogo (1764 g.): novoe prochtenie istochnikov]. *Vestnik Moskovskogo universiteta. Seriya. 8. Istoriya*, no. 1 (2010), pp. 3–25.

Kruglova, T. A. "Was G. G. Orlov a Real Candidate for the Little Russian Hetman in 1764?" [Byl li G. G. Orlov realnym kandidatom v malorossiiskie getmany v 1764 g.?]. *Istoricheskoe obozrenie*, no. 9 (2008).

"Letters of A. A. Bezborodok to Count Peter Alexandrovich Rumyantsov" [Pisma A. A. Bezborodka k grafu Petru Aleksandrovichu Rumyantsovu]. *Starina i novizna*, no. 3 (1900).

Letters of the Orlov Brothers to Count Peter Alexandrovich Rumyantsov (1764–1778) [Pisma bratev Orlovykh k grafu Petru Aleksandrovichu Rumyantsovu (1764–1778)]. Moscow, 2021.

Litvinova, T. *"Landowner's Truth": The Nobility of Left-Bank Ukraine and the Peasant Question at the End of the 18th Century and the First Half of the 19th Century. ["Pomeshchichya pravda": dvoryanstvo Levoberezhnoi Ukrainy i krestyanskii vopros v kontse XVIIIspervoi polovine XIX veka]*. Moscow, 2019.

Lyubavskii, M. K. *Historical Geography of Russia in Relation to Colonization [Istoricheskaya geografiya Rossii v svyazi s kolonizatsiei]*. Saint Petersburg, 2000.

Lyubavskii, M. K. *An Overview of the History of Russian Colonization [Obzor istorii russkoi kolonizatsii]*. Moscow, 1996.

Maksimovich, G. A. *Activities of Rumyantsev-Zadunaisky in the Governance of Little Russia [Deyatelnost Rumyantseva-Zadunaiskago po upravleniyu Malorossiei]*. Nezhin, 1913.

Markevich, N. *History of Little Russia [Istoriya Malorossii]*. Moscow, 1842–1843.

Miller, G. F. *The Origin of the People and the Name of Russia [Proiskhozhdenie naroda i imeni rossiiskogo]*. Saint Petersburg, 1749.

Miller, G. F. "Reasoning About Zaporozhets" [Rassuzhdenie o zaporozhtsakh], in *Historical Works on Malorossia and the Malorossians by G. F. Miller, a former historiographer of the Russian [Istoricheskie sochineniya o Malorossii i Malorossiyanakh G. F. Millera, byvshego istoriografa rossiiskogo]*. Moscow, 1846.

"A Note on Little Russia" [Zapiska o Maloi Rossii], in *Prince Vorontsov's Archive [Arkhiv knyazya Vorontsova]*. Vol. 25. Moscow, 1882, pp. 350–381.

"On the Disorder That Arises from Abuse of the Rights and Customs Confirmed by the Charters of the Little Russia" [O neporyadkakh, kotorye proiskhodyat ot zloupotrebleniya prav i obyknovenii, gramotami podtverzhdennykh Malorossii], in *Notes on Southern Russia [Zapiski o Yuzhnoi Rusi]*. Published by P. Kulish. Vol. 2. Saint Petersburg, 1857, pp. 169–196.

Pavlenko, N. I. *Catherine the Great [Ekaterina Velikaya]*. Moscow, 2006.

Petelin, V. *Field Marshal Rumyantsev [Feldmarshal Rumyantsev]*. Moscow, 2006.

Prokop, T. I. "Administrator and Military Commander Peter Alexandrovich Rumyantsev-Zadunaisky" [Administrator i voenachalnik Petr Aleksandrovich Rumyantsev-Zadunaiskii]. *Rusin*, 2015, no. 1 (39), pp. 69–82.

"Reforms in Little Russia Under Count Rumyantsev" [Reformy v Malorossii pri gr. Rumyantseve]. *Kievskaya starina*, no. 9 (1891).

Rigelman, O. I. *The Chronicle of Little Russia and Its People and the Cossacks in General [Litopisna opovid pro Malu Rosiyu ta ii narod i kozakiv uzagali]*. Kyiv, 1994.

Russian State Archive of Early Acts (RGADA), coll. 7, desc. 2, no. 2126.

Segyur, Lui-Filipp. *Notes on a Stay in Russia During the Reign of Catherine II [Zapiski o prebyvanii v Rossii v tsarstvovanie Ekateriny II]*. Saint Petersburg, 1865.

Seven Handwritten Letters and Notes of Prince G. A. Potemkin-Tavrichesky to Count P. A. Rumyantsov-Zadunaisky (1769–1788) [Sem sobstvennoruchnykh pisem i zapisok Knyazya G. A. Potemkina-Tavricheskogo k Grafu P. A. Rumyantsovu-Zadunaiskomu (1769–1788)]. Saint Petersburg, 1902.

Shubin, A. V. *The History of Novorossia [Istoriya Novorossii]*. Moscow, 2015.

Skalkovskii, A. *History of the Nova Sich or the Last Kosh of Zaporozhye [Istoriya Novoi Sechi ili polednego kosha Zaporozhskogo]*. Odesa, 1841.

Smirnova, A. S. "'The Origin of the People and the Name of Russia' (1749): Sources and Translation" ["Proiskhozhdenie naroda i imeni rossiiskogo" (1749 g.): istochniki i perevod. *Millerovskie chteniya—2018*.] Proceedings of the 2nd International Scientific Conference, May 24–26, 2018. Saint Petersburg, pp. 61–68.

Solovyeva, R. P. "The Resettlement Policy of Catherine II" [Pereselencheskaya politika Ekateriny II]. *Nauchnyi potentsial*, 2020, no. 3 (30), pp. 127–131.

Solovyov, S. M. *History of Russia Since the Earliest Times [Istoriya Rossii s drevneishikh vremen]*. Moscow, 1959–1966.

Solovyov, S. M. *Works [Sochineniya]*. Moscow, 1988–1995.

Vasilchikov, A. A. *The Razumovsky Family [Semeistvo Razumovskikh]*. Vols. 1–2. Saint Petersburg, 1880.

Vasilenko, M. "Teplov and His 'Note on Unrest in Little Russia'" [G. N. Teplov i iogo "Zapiska o neporyadkakh v Malorossii"]. *Zapiski Ukraïnskogo naukovogo tovaristva v Kievi*. Kyiv, 1911. No. 9, pp. 29–54.

Zygar, Mikhail. *Interview with Rinat Akhmetov*, 2023.

CHAPTER 4

Belinsky, V. G. *Collected Works [Polnoye sobraniye sochineniy]*, vol. 12: Letters of 1841–1848. Moscow, 1956.

Belinsky, V. G. *Complete Collected Works [Polnoye sobraniye sochineniy]*, vol. 4. Moscow, 1954.

Belinsky, V. G. "The Kobzar of T. Shevchenko" [Kobzar T. Shevchenka], in *Polnoye sobraniye sochineniy*, vol. 4. Moscow, 1954.

"Brief Biographical Sketch of N. I. Kostomarov" [Kratkii biograficheskii ocherk N. I. Kostomarova]. *Kievskaya Starina*, 1885, vol. 12, no. 5, pp. 2–9.

Chalyi, M. K. *Life and Works of Taras Shevchenko [Zhizn' i proizvedeniya Tarasa Shevchenko]*. Kyiv, 1882.

Chukovsky, K. I. The Resurrecting Shevchenko [Voskresayushchiy Shevchenko], in *Sochineniya*, vol. 2. Saint Petersburg, 1911.

"Circular of Minister of Internal Affairs P. A. Valuev to the Kiev, Moscow and St. Petersburg Censorship Committees Dated July 18, 1863" [Tsirkulyar ministra vnutrennikh del P. A. Valueva Kievskomu, Moskovskomu i Peterburgskomu tsenzurnym komitetam ot 18 iyulya 1863 g.], in Miller, A. I. *"The Ukrainian Question" in the Policy of the Authorities and Russian Public Opinion (Second Half of the 19th Century) ["Ukrainskii vopros" v politike vlastei i russkom obshchestvennom mnenii (vtoraya polovina XIX veka)]*. Saint Petersburg, 2000, pp. 240–241.

The Cyril and Methodius Society in Three Volumes [Kyrylo-Mefodiiivske Tovarystvo u Tryokh Tomakh]. Kyiv, 1990.

Dziuba, I. M. *Taras Shevchenko: Life and Works [Taras Shevchenko: Zhittya i tvorchist]*. Kyiv, 2008.

Hinkulov, L. F. *Taras Shevchenko [Taras Shevchenko]*. Moscow, 1960.

Konisskii, A. Ya. *The Life of Ukrainian Poet Taras Hryhorovych Shevchenko [Zhizn ukrainskogo poeta Tarasa Hryhorovycha Shevchenko]*. Odesa, 1898.

Kostomarov, N. I. *Autobiography of N. I. Kostomarov [Avtobiografiya N. I. Kostomarova]*. Moscow, 1922.

Kostomarov, N. I. "The Beginning of Rus" [Nachalo Rusi]. *Sovremennik*, no. 1 (1860).

Kostomarov, N. I. *Historical Works: Autobiography [Istoricheskie proizvedeniya. Avtobiografiya]*. Kyiv, 1990.

Kostomarov, N. I. "Letter to the editor of 'The Bell'" [Pismo izdateliu "Kolokola"], in *"Cossacks": Actual History of Russia [Kazaki. Aktualnaya istoriya Rossii]*. Moscow, 1995.

Kostomarov N. I. *Stenka Razin's Rebellion [Bunt Stenki Razina]*. Saint Petersburg, 1859.

Kostomarov N. I. "Thoughts on the Federal Principle in Ancient Russia" [Mysli o federativnom nachale v Drevnei Rusi], in *Collected Works: Historical Monographs and Research [Sobranie sochinenii: Istoricheskie monografii i izsledovaniya]*, , book 8, vol. 21. Saint Petersburg, 1903.

Litvak, B. G. "N. I. Kostomarov" [N. I. Kostomarov], in *Portraits of Historians: Time and Fate [Portrety istorikov: vremya i sud'by]*, vol. 1. Moscow, Jerusalem, 2000, pp. 52–64.

"Memories of an Old Teacher I. K. Zaitsev (1805-1887)" [Vospominaniya starogo uchitelya I. K. Zaitseva (1805–1887)]. *Russkaya starina*, April–June 1887, vol. 54.

Memories of Taras Shevchenko [Vospominaniya o Tarase Shevchenko]. Kyiv, 1988.

Naryshkina-Prokudina-Gorskaya, N. A. "Taras Shevchenko in St. Petersburg" [Taras Shevchenko v Peterburge]. *Terra Linguistica*, 2013, no. 1 (167), pp. 159–168.

Ostapenko, O. I. and Ryashko, V.I.T.G. "Shevchenko and the Repressive and Punitive Apparatus of Tsarist Russia" [Shevchenko ta represivno-karalnii aparat tsarskoi Rosii]. *Visnik Natsionalnogo universitetu "Lvivska politekhnika." Yuridichni nauki*, no. 810 (2014),pp. 206–212.

Palamarchuk, G. "New Information about T. G. Shevchenko: From the Diary and Memoirs of E. F. Junge (Tolstoy)" [Novoe o T. G. Shevchenko: iz dnevnika i vospominaniy E. F. Yunge (Tolstoy)]. *Sovetskaya Ukraina*, 1960, no. 3, pp. 169–171.

Pinchuk, Yu. A. *Mykola Ivanovych Kostomarov [Mikola Ivanovich Kostomarov]*. Kyiv, 1992.

Pogodin M. P. "Response to P. V. Kireevsky" [Otvet P. V. Kireevskomu]. *Moskvityanin*, no. 3 (1845), p. 57.

Polevoy, N. A. "Kobzar. T. Shevchenko" [Kobzar. T. Shevchenka], in *Taras Shevchenko v krititsi*, vol. 1. Kyiv, 2013.

Polonsky, Ya. P. *Memories of Shevchenko: T. G. Shevchenko, Kobzar [Spominky pro Shevchenka. T. H. Shevchenko, Kobzar']*. Prague, 1876.

Portraits of Historians: Time and Destinies [Portrety istorikov: Vremya i sudby]. Vol. 1: Domestic History [Otechestvennaya istoriya]. Moscow, Jerusalem, 2000.

Public Dispute Between Kostomarov and Pogodin on March 19, 1860, on the Beginning of Rus [Publichnyi disput Kostomarova i Pogodina 19 marta 1860 goda o nachale Rusi]. *Sovremennik*, vol. 80 (1860).

Rachev E. R. "Perception of N. I. Kostomarov in National and Foreign Historical Science: Transformation of Radical and National Trends" [Vospriyatie N. I. Kostomarova v otechestvennoy i zarubezhnoy istoricheskoy nauke: transformatsiya radikalnogo i natsionalnogo trendov]. *Gumanitarnye issledovaniya. Istoriya i filologiya*, no. 4 (2021).

"Response of N. I. Kostomarov to I. S. Aksakov" [Otvet N. I. Kostomarova I. S. Aksakovu]. *Kievskaya Starina*, no. 11 (1897), p. 51.

"Review of the Poem 'Trizna' by P. A. Pletnev" [Retsenziya P. A. Pletneva na poemu 'Trizna,' Sovremennik]. *Sovremennik*, vol. 34. no. 6 (1844), pp. 295–296.

Shcherbina, F. "On the Biography of N. I. Kostomarov" [K biografii N. I. Kostomarova]. *Kievskaya Starina*, 1895, vol. 49, no. 4, pp. 63–75.

Shevchenko, T. *Autobiography. Diary. Selected Letters and Documents [Avtobiografiya. Dnevnik. Izbrannye pis'ma i delovye bumagi]*. Moscow, 1956.

Shevchenko, T. G. *Collected Works in Five Volumes*. Vol. 5: Autobiography. Diary. Selected Letters and Business Papers. Moscow, 1956.

Shevchenko's Dictionary. In two volumes [Shevchenkivskii slovnik. U dvokh tomakh]. Kyiv, 1976–1978.

Smolii, V. A., Pinchuk, Y. A., and Yas', O. V. *Mykola Kostomarov: Milestones of Life and Creativity: Encyclopedic Handbook [Mykola Kostomarov: Vikhy zhyttia i tvorchosti: Entsyklopedychnyi dovidnyk]*. Kyiv, 2005.

State Archive of the Russian Federation (GARF), coll. 109, desc. 37, no. 230, part 38, p. 56 rev.

Teslya, A. A. "Variation on the Theme of Political Theology: 'The Book of Genesis of the Ukrainian People'" [Variatsiia na temu politicheskoi teologii: "Kniga Bytiia Ukrainskogo naroda"]. *Sotsiologicheskoe obozrenie*, vol. 14, no. 2 (2015), pp. 82–106.

Yunge, E. F. *Memories [Vospominaniya]*. Moscow, 1914, pp. 167–170.

Zhur, P. V. *The Labors and Days of Kobzar [Trudy i dni Kobzarya]*. Lyubertsy, 1996, pp. 389–431.

Zhur, P. V. "Shiryaev's First Draftsman" [Pervyi risovalshchik u Shiryaeva]. *Neva*, no. 3 (1961), p. 205.

Zimin, I. V. "'Doctors and Autocrats': The Mystery of the Death of Nicholas I" ['Mediki i samoderzhcy': zagadka smerti Nikolaya I]. *Otechestvennaya istoriya*, 2001, no. 4. pp. 57–66.

CHAPTER 5

Andreev, A. R. *Symon Petliura: "I was born in Poltava, and I believe in Ukrainian statehood..."* [Simon Petlyura. *"Ya rodilsya v Poltave i ya veryu v ukrainskuyu gosudarstvennost . . ."*]. Kyiv, Minsk, and Moscow, 2010.

"Autobiography of Mykhailo Hrushevsky from 1906 and 1926 as a Source for Studying His Life and Work" [Avtobiografiya Mikhaila Grushevskogo z 1906 i 1926 rokiv yak dzherelo do vivchennya iogo zhittya i tvorchosti]. *Ukrainskii istorik*, no. 1–3 (1974), vol. 11, part 1–3.

"Autobiography of Mykhailo Hrushevsky 1914–1919" [Avtobiografiya Mikhaila Grushevskogo 1914–1919]. *Ukrainskii istorik*, nos. 1–2 (1966), pp. 98–101.

Constitutional Acts of Ukraine, 1917–1920. Unknown Constitutions of Ukraine [Konstitutsiini akti Ukraini. 1917–1920. Nevidomi konstitutsii Ukraïni]. Kyiv, 1992.

Danilevskii, I. N., Tairova (Yakovleva), T. G., Shubin, A. V., and Mironenko, V. I. *A History of Ukraine [Istoriya Ukrainy]*. Saint Petersburg, 2018.

Front Ukrainian Congress [Frontovyi ukrainskyi s'iezd]. *Kievlianin*, no. 113 (1917), May 7, p. 2.

Hrushevsky, Mykhailo. Autobiography [Avtobiografiia]. Lviv, 1906.

Hrushevsky, Mykhailo. "Autobiography (1926)" [Avtobiografiia (1926)]. *Ukrainskii istorik*, no. 1–4 (1979), pp. 79–87.

Hrushevsky, Mykhailo. Autobiography [Avtobiografiia]. Kyiv, 1926.

Hrushevsky, Mykhailo. Autobiography [Avtobiografiia]. Toronto, 1965.

Hrushevsky, Mykhailo. "Autobiography" [Avtobiografiia]. *Ukrainskii istorik*, nos. 1–4 (1980), pp. 89–94.

Hrushevsky, Mykhailo. "How I Was Escorted to Lviv" [Yak mene sprovadzheno do Lvova]. *Ukrainskiiistorik*, nos. 1–4 (1984), pp. 230–237.

Karnishin, V. Yu. "'The Ukrainian Question' in the Political Journalism of M. S. Hrushevsky" ["Ukrainskii vopros" v politicheskoi publitsistike M. S. Grushevskogo]. *Izvestiya VUZov. Povolzhskii region. Gumanitarnye nauki*, 2014.

Lenin, V. I. *Collected Works [Polnoe sobranie sochinenii]*. Vol. 35. Moscow, 1974.

Petliura, Symon. "War and Ukrainians" [Voina i ukraintsy]. *Ukrainskaia zhizn,'* no. 7 (1914), pp. 3–7.

Plokhy, S. *Unmaking Imperial Russia: Mykhailo Hrushevsky and the Writing of Ukrainian History*. Toronto: University of Toronto Press, 2005.

Prymak, T. *Mychailo Hrushevsky: The Politics of National Culture*. Toronto, Buffalo, and London, 1987.

Revolution and the National Question: Documents and Materials on the History of the National Question of Russia and the USSR in the 20th Century [Revolyutsiya i natsionalnyi vopros: dokumenty i materialy po istorii natsionalnogo voprosa Rossii i SSSR v XX veke]. Vol. 3. Moscow, 1930.

Savchenko, V. A. *Adventurers of the Civil War: Historical Investigation [Avantyuristy grazhdanskoi voiny: Istoricheskoe rassledovanie]*. Kharkiv and Moscow, 2000.

Savchenko, V. A. *Symon Petliura [Simon Petlyura]*. Kharkiv, 2004.

Savchenko, V. A. *Twelve Wars for Ukraine [Dvenadtsat voin za Ukrainu]*. Kharkiv, 2006.

Vynar, L. "Autobiography of M. Hrushevsky from 1926" [Avtobiografiy M. Grushevskogo z 1926 roku]. *Ukrainskii istorik*, nos. 1–4 (1980), pp. 71–88.

Vynar, L. Autobiography of Mykhailo Hrushevsky from 1926 [Avtobiografiia Mykhaila Hrushevskoho z 1926 roku]. New York, Munich, and Toronto, 1981.

Zygar, Mikhail. *Interview with Rinat Akhmetov*, 2023.

CHAPTER 6

Dekulakization, Collectivization, Holodomor in Dnipropetrovsk Oblast (1929–1933): Collection of Documents [Rozkurkulennya, kolektivizatsiya, Golodomor na Dnipropetrovshchini (1929–1933 roki): Zbirnik dokumentiv]. Dnipropetrovsk, 2008.

The Famine-Genocide of 1933 in Ukraine: Historical and Political Analysis of Socio-demographic, Moral and Psychological Consequences [Golod-genotsid 1933 roku v Ukraini: istoriko-politologichnyi analiz sotsialno-demografichnikh ta moralno-psikhologichnikh naslidkiv]. Kyiv and New York, 2000.

Famine in the USSR [Golod v SSSR]. 1929–1934. In 3 vols. Vol. 1: 1929–July 1932, book 2. Moscow, 2011.

Gorskaya, N. A. *Boris Dmitrievich Grekov [Boris Dmitrievich Grekov].* Moscow, 1999.

Grekov, B. D. *Feudal Relations in the Kievan State [Feodalnye otnosheniya v Kievskom gosudarstve].* Moscow, 1936.

Grekov, B. D. *Feudal Relations in the Kievan State [Feodalnye otnosheniya v Kievskom gosudarstve].* Moscow, 1937.

Grekov, B. D. Formidable Kievan Rus' [Groznaya Kievskaya Rus]. Moscow, 2012.

Grekov, B. D. *Kievan Rus' [Kievskaya Rus].* Moscow, 1939.

Grekov, B. D. *Kievan Rus' [Kievskaya Rus].* Moscow, 1944.

Grekov, B. D. *Kievan Rus' [Kievskaya Rus].* Moscow, 1949.

Grekov, B. D. *Kievan Rus' [Kievskaya Rus].* Moscow, 1953.

Grekov, B. D. *Kievan Rus' [Kievskaya Rus].* Moscow, 2004.

Grekov, B. D. *Kievan Rus' [Kievskaya Rus].* Moscow, 2006.

Hrushevsky, M. S. *History of Ukraine-Rus' [Istoriia Ukrainy-Rusy]:* in 10 vols. Lviv, Kyiv, and Moscow, Viden', 1898–1936.

Hrushevsky, M. S. *Illustrated History of Ukraine [Illyustrirovannaya istoriya Ukrainy].* Saint Petersburg, 1913.

Hrushevsky, M. S. *Illustrated History of Ukraine [Ilustrovana Istoriia Ukrainy].* Kyiv and Lviv, 1911.

Hrushevsky, M. S. *Illustrated History of Ukraine with Appendices and Additions [Illyustrovana istoriya Ukrainy z prylozhenniamy i dopovnenniamy].* Donetsk, 2004.

Hrushevskyi, Mykhailo. "The Ordinary Scheme of 'Russian' History and the Question of Rational Ordering of the History of Eastern Slavdom" [Obychnaya skhema "russkoi" istorii i vopros ratsional'nogo uporyadocheniya istorii vostochnogo slavyanstva]. *Forum: Obshchestvenno-politicheskii zhurnal.* Munich, 1987, issue 17, pp. 162–171.

Ivnitsky, N. A. *The Famine of 1932–1933 in the USSR: Ukraine, Kazakhstan, the North Caucasus, the Volga Region, the Central Black Earth Region, Western Siberia, the Urals [Golod 1932–1933 godov v SSSR: Ukraina, Kazakhstan, Severnyi Kavkaz, Povolzhye, Tsentralno-Chernozemnaya oblast, Zapadnaya Sibir, Ural].* Moscow, 2009.

Ivnitsky, N. A. *Repressive Policies of Soviet Power in the Village (1928–1933) [Repressivnaya politika sovetskoi vlasti v derevne (1928–1933 gg.)].* Moscow, 2000.

Kondrashin, V. V. *The Famine of 1932–1933: The Tragedy of the Russian Village [Golod 1932–1933 godov: tragediya rossiiskoi derevni].* Moscow, 2008.

Kotenko, A. L., Martynyuk, O. V., and Miller, A. I. "'Maloross': The Evolution of the Concept Before World War I" ['Maloross': evolyutsiya ponyatiya do Pervoi mirovoi voiny]. *Novoe literaturnoe obozrenie,* no. 2 (2011).

Kulchytsky, S. *Why Did He Destroy Us? Stalin and the Ukrainian Holodomor [Pochemu on nas unichtozhal? Stalin i ukrainskii Golodomor].* Kyiv, 2007.

Malinov, A. V. *Philosophy of History in Russia: Outline of a University Course [Filosofiya istorii v Rossii. Konspekt universitetskogo spetskursa].* Saint Petersburg, 2001.

Plokhy, S. *The Gates of Europe: A History of Ukraine*. New York: Basic Books, 2015.

Plokhy, S. *The Origins of the Slavic Nations: Premodern Identities in Russia, Ukraine and Belarus*. Cambridge University Press, 2006.

Plokhy, S. *Ukraine and Russia: Representations of the Past*. Toronto: University of Toronto Press, 2008.

Plokhy, S. *Unmaking Imperial Russia: Mykhailo Hrushevsky and the Writing of Ukrainian History*. Toronto: University of Toronto Press, 2005.

Prymak, T. *Mychailo Hrushevsky: The Politics of National Culture*. Toronto, Buffalo, and London, 1987.

Russian State Archive of Socio-Political History (RGASPI), coll. 17, desc. 42, no. 80, p. 17.

Russian State Archive of Socio-Political History (RGASPI), coll. 82, desc. 2, no. 139, pp. 162–165.

Shchapov, Y. N. "Academician B. D. Grekov as a Historian of Kievan Rus" [Akademik B. D. Grekov kak istorik Kievskoi Rusi]. *Vestnik AN SSSR*, no. 9 (1982).

Tolochko, A. P. "The Chimera of 'Kievan Rus' [Khimera 'Kievskoi Rusi']. *Rodina*, no. 8 (1999), pp. 29–33.

The Tragedy of the Soviet Village. Collectivization and Dekulakization [Tragediya sovetskoi derevni. Kollektivizatsiya i raskulachivanie]. 1927–1939. Documents and Materials. In 5 vols. Vol. 2. November 1929–December 1930. Moscow, 2000.

Zygar, Mikhail. *Interview with Rinat Akhmetov*, 2023.

CHAPTER 7

"The Act of Proclamation of the Ukrainian State" [Akt provozglasheniya Ukrainskogo Gosudarstva]. *Samostiina Ukraina*, Stanislavov, July 10, 1941.

Antoniuk, P. "Hero of the Volyn Forests" [Heroy volynskikh lesov]. *Pravyi vybor*, March 7, 2013. [URL: https://web.archive.org/web/20180218142228/http://volnodum.live journal.com/714873.html]

Armstrong, D. *Ukrainian Nationalism: Facts and Investigations [Ukrainsky natsionalizm: fakty i rassledovaniya]*. Moscow, 2008.

Bandera, S. " My Life's Story" ["Moyi zhyttyepysni dani"]. *Volya i Batkivshchyna*. Lviv, 1999.

"The Battle of Hrabyne: How the Largest UPA Battle Against NKVD Took Place" [Bi—ñi pid Hurbamy. Yak prokhodyv naybil'shyy biy UPA proty NKVS]. *Tsentr dosl—ñdzhen vizvolnogo rukhu*, April 28, 2021. [URL: https://cdvr.org.ua/28939/2021/04/28/]

Bedriy, A. *OUN and UPA [OUN i UPA]*. New York, London, Munich, and Toronto, 1983.

"The Belgian in UPA: The Story of Radio Announcer Hazenbroek" [Belhiyets v UPA: istoriya radiodyktora Hazenbruksa]. *5 Kanal*, December 10, 2020. [URL: https://www.5.ua/suspilstvo/belhiiets-v-upa-istoriia-radiodyktora-hazenbruksa-231494.html]

Borovets, Taras Dmytrovych. Oleg Olzhych Zhytomyr Regional Universal Scientific Library. [URL: http://www.lib.zt.ua/ua/outstanding/node/6500]

Bulba-Borovets, T. *Army Without a State: Glory and Tragedy of the Ukrainian Insurgent Movement. Memoirs [Armiya bez derzhavi: Slava i tragediya ukrainskogo povstanskogo rukhu. Spogadi]*. Kyiv, 2008.

Chastyi, R. V. *Stepan Bandera: Myths, Legends, Reality [Stepan Bandera: mify, legendy, dialnist]*. Kharkiv, 2007.

Chernikov, S. "The Battle on Mount Lopata" [Boĭ na hore Lopata]. *Lviv X*, February 10, 2023. [URL: https://lvivyes.com.ua/ru/eternal-ru/bij-na-gori-lopata]

Danilevskii, I. N., Tairova (Yakovleva), T. G., Shubin, A. V., and Mironenko, V. I. *A History of Ukraine [Istoriya Ukrainy]*. Saint Petersburg, 2018.

"Death of the Polish General at the Hands of the Bandits from UPA Became a Signal for Operation Vistula" [Smert' pol'skogo generala vid ruk "banditiv z UPA" stala syhnaolom dlia aktsii "Vistula"]. *Gazeta.ua*, March 28, 2012. [URL: https://gazeta.ua /articles/history/_smert-polskogo-generala-vid-ruk-banditiv-z-upa-stala-signalom -dlya-akciyi-visla/428866]

Dziobak, V. V. *Taras Bulba-Borovets and His Military Units in the Ukrainian Resistance Movement (1941–1944) [Taras Bulba-Borovets i iogo viiskovi pidrozdili v ukraïnskomu rusi Oporu (1941–1944 rr.)]* Kyiv, 2002.

Encyclopedia of the History of Ukraine: Ukraine–Ukrainians. Book 2. Edited by V. A. Smolii and others. National Academy of Sciences of Ukraine. Institute of the History of Ukraine. Kyiv, 2019.

Encyclopedia of the History of Ukraine: Vol. 10: T–Ya. Edited by V. A. Smolii and others. National Academy of Sciences of Ukraine. Institute of the History of Ukraine. Kyiv, 2013.

Firov, P. *History of the OUN-UPA: Events, Facts, Documents, Comments [Istoriya OUN-UPA: Sobitiya, Fakty, Dokumenty, Kommentarii]*. Sevastopol, 2002.

"First Battle of the UPA Against the 'German Barbarians' and Further Struggle Against the Nazis" [Pershii bii UPA proti "nimetskikh varvariv" i podalsha borotba z natsistami]. *Veterano.ua*. [URL: http://veterano.com.ua/index.php?option=com_content&v iew=article&id=4755:pershij-bij-upa-proti-nimetskikh-varvariv-i-podalsha-borotba -z-natsistami&catid=36&Itemid=191]

"Full Alarm: How UPA Fighters Scared the Chekists in Stanislaviv and Didn't Lose a Single Fighter" [Povnyi alarm. Yak biitsi UPA nazhahaly chekistiv u Stanislavi y ne vtratyly zhodnoho biitsia]. *Reporter*, February 26, 2020. [URL: https://report .if.ua/istoriya/povnyj-alyarm-yak-bijci-upa-nazhahaly-chekistiv-u-stanislavi-j-ne -vtratyly-zhodnogo-bijcya-foto/]

Gorobets, S. "On This Day, the Organizer of the First Units of the UPA, Serhiy Kachynskyi, Died" [Ts'oho dnya zahynuv orhanizator pershykh viddiliv UPA Serhiy Kachynskyi]. Region Spekhor. [URL: https://speckor.net/tsogo-dnya-zagynuv-organizator-pershyh -viddiliv-upa-sergij-kachynskyj/]

Harkotová, S. "What the Banderites Were After in Slovakia (interview)" [O čo išlo banderovcom na Slovensku (rozhovor)]. *Aktuality*, January 28, 2019. [URL: https://www .aktuality.sk/clanok/656757/o-co-islo-banderovcom-na-slovensku-rozhovor/]

Heroes of Ukraine. [URL: http://heroes.profi-forex.org/]

Hohun, A. *Between Hitler and Stalin: Ukrainian Insurgents [Mezhdu Gitlerom i Stalinym. Ukrainskie povstantsy]*. Kharkiv, 2018.

Hrabovskyi, S. "Taras Bulba-Borovets: At the Origins of UPA" [Taras Bulba-Borovets: u ystokov UPA]. *Den'*, October 13, 2016. [URL: https://day.kyiv.ua/ru/blog/istoriya /taras-bulba-borovec-u-istokov-upa]

Isayuk, O. "The Great Blockade: How to Hold Elections in a Rebellious Region" [Bolshaya blokada: kak provesti vybory v nepokornom regione]. *Dzerkalo tyzhnia*, March 18, 2016. [URL: https://zn.ua/HISTORY/bolshaya-blokada-kak-provesti-vybory-v-nep okornom-regione-_.html]

Ishchuk, O. "Stepan Stebelskyi—'Khrin': On the 100th Anniversary of His Birth" [Stepan Stebelskii—Khrin': do 100-richchya dnya narodzhennya]. *Tsentr doslidzhen vizvolnogo rukhu*, October 23, 2014. [URL: https://cdvr.org.ua/22894/2014/10/23/]

"January 27." Gromadska organizatsiya "Vseukrainske ob'ednannya gromadyan "Kraïna." [URL: https://vgo-kraina.org/catalog/layer/27-sichnya]

Kovalchuk V. "Was UPA Created on October 14, 1942?" [Byla li sozdana UPA 14 okty-abrya 1942 goda?]. *Ukrainska Pravda*, October 22, 2007. [URL: https://www.pravda.com.ua/rus/articles/2007/10/22/4426156/]

Krychylskyi, S. "The Heroic Death of the First Commander of the UPA, Klym Savur" [Heroichna smert pershoho komandyra UPA Klyma Savura]. *Horyn.info*, February 12, 2022. [URL: https://horyn.info/posts/geroyichna-smert-pershogo-komandyra-upa-klyma-savura/]

"Letter of the Participants of the Interregional Meeting of Teachers from the Western Regions of Ukraine to Comrade Stalin I. V." [Pismo uchastnikov mezhoblastnogo soveshchaniya uchitelei zapadnykh oblastei Ukrainy tovarishchu Stalinu I. V.] *Izvestiya*, February 9, 1945, no. 33, p. 2.

Life and Activity of Stepan Bandera: Documents and Materials [Zhyttya i diyalnist Stepana Banderi: dokumenty i materialy]. Ternopil, 2008.

Matskevich, I. M. "A Criminological Portrait of Stepana Bandera" [Kriminologicheskii portret Stepany Bandery]. *Soyuz kriminalistov i kriminologov*, no. 2 (2014), pp. 7–41.

Mikoyan A. I. *So It Was [Tak Bylo].* Moscow, 1999.

Moskal, R. "The Last Battle of the Underground OUN: Ternopil Region, 1960" [Ostannii biy pidpillia OUN. Ternopilshchyna, 1960 rik]. *Istorichna Pravda*, March 28, 2011. [URL: https://www.istpravda.com.ua/articles/2011/03/28/33736/]

Motyka, G. From the Volyn Massacre to Operation "Vistula": Polish–Ukrainian Conflict 1943–1947 [Vid Volinskoï rizanini do operatsiï "Visla"]. Kyiv, 2013.

Myrchuk, P. *Ukrainian Insurgent Army 1942–1952 [Ukraïnska Povstanska Armiya 1942–1952].* Munich, 1953.

Olkhovskii, I. "On the Tragic Fate of Taras Bulba-Borovets' Wife" [Pro tragichnu dolyu druzhini Tarasa Bulbi-Borovtsya]. *Istorichna Pravda*, November 15, 2013. [URL: https://www.istpravda.com.ua/articles/2013/11/15/139565/]

"100 Years Since Colonel of the UPA Vasyl Halasa: Documents Published" [100 rokiv polkovniku UPA Vasylu Halasi: opublikovano dokumenty]. *Istorichna pravda*, November 12, 2020. [URL: https://www.istpravda.com.ua/short/2020/11/12/158449/]

Patrylyak, I., and Pahirya, O. "Military Conference of OUN (b) in 1942 and the Elaboration of Creation Plan of Ukrainian Armed Forces" [Viiskova konferentsiya OUN(B) 1942 r. i rozrobka planiv zi stvorennya ukraïnskikh zbroinikh sil], in *Z arkhiviv VUChK-GPU-NKVD-KGB*, no. 30 (2008), pp. 484–511.

Pisartsov, D. "The Battle of Stryhany" [Biï pid Stryhanamy]. *Shepetivka.com.ua*, May 13, 2014. [URL: https://shepetivka.com.ua/statti/inshe/1430-bii-pid-stryhanamy.html]

Plokhy, S. *The Gates of Europe: A History of Ukraine.* New York: Basic Books, 2015.

Posivnych, M. *Stepan Bandera—Life Dedicated to Freedom [Stepan Bandera—zhyttia, prysviachene svobodi].* Toronto, Lviv, 2008.

"Post-War Wars" [Poslevoennye voyny]. *Kommersant*, October 13, 2015. [URL: https://www.kommersant.ru/doc/2831262]

Posivnich, M. "Stepan Bandera in German Prisons and Concentration Camps" [Stepan Bandera u nimetskikh tyurmakh i kontstaborakh]. *Istorichna Pravda*, January 1, 2015. [URL: https://www.istpravda.com.ua/articles/2014/01/1/140665/]

Posivnich, M. "Stepan Bandera in Polish Prisons" [Stepan Bandera v polskikh tyurmakh]. *Istorichna Pravda*, March 9, 2011. [URL: https://www.istpravda.com.ua/articles/2011/03/9/29017/]

Program Resolutions of the Third Great Assembly of the OUN (S. Bandera) [Programni postanovi Tretogo Velikogo Zboru OUN (S. Banderi)], August 25, 1943. [URL: http://www.hai-nyzhnyk.in.ua/doc2/1943(08)25.oun.php]

Prymachenko, Ya. "Creation of the Ukrainian Insurgent Army" [Stvorennya Ukraïnskoï Povstanskoï Armïi]. *Tsei den v istorii*. [URL: https://www.jnsm.com.ua/h/1014T/]

Romanuyk, N. "Kolkhivska Republic: Territory of Ukrainian Freedom in the Whirlwind of War" [Kolkovskaia respublika–territoriia ukrainskoi svobody v vodovorote voiny]. *Ukrinform*, June 29, 2018. [URL: https://www.ukrinform.net/rubric-society/2488720 -kolkovskaa-respublika-territoria-ukrainskoj-svobody-v-vodovorote-vojny.html]

Rusnachenko, A. "Roman Shukhevych: The Leader of Fighting Ukraine" [Roman Shukhevych: kerivnyk voyuyuchoyi Ukrayiny], in Ukrainian Liberation Movement: Scientific Collection [Ukrayins'kyy vyzvol'nyy rukh: nauk. zb.]. Lviv, 2007, issue 10, pp. 223–243.

"Secret History" [Istoriya z hryfom "Sekretno"]: Christmas Battle of the UPA. Birch, January 7, 1946 [Rizdvyanyi biy UPA. Bircha, 7 sichnya 1946]. *TSN*, January 16, 2011. [URL: https://tsn.ua/analitika/rizdvyaniy-biy-upa-bircha-7-cichnya-1946.html]

"Secret History" [Istoriya z hryfom "Sekretno"]: Former Enemies. Hrubeshiv Operation of 1946 [Kolishni vorohy. Hrubeshivska operatsiya 1946 roku]. *TSN*, June 16, 2011. [URL: https://tsn.ua/analitika/istoriya-z-grifom-sekretno-kolishni-vorogi-gru beshivska-operaciya-1946-roku.html]

Skibchik, S. "The First Battle of the UPA, Which Took Place in Volodymyrets, Was Led by Friend and Associate of Bandera, Hryhoriy Peregyniak" [Pershyi bij UPA, yakyj vidbuvsya u Volodymyrci, ocholyv drug i soratnyk Banderi Hryhoriy Pereginiak]. *Volodymyrets City*, February 7, 2020. [URL: https://volodymyrets.city/articles/63910 /pershij-bij-upa-yakij-vidbuvsya-u-volodimirci-ocholiv-drug-i-soratnik-banderi -grigorij-pereginyak]

Smyslov O. Stepan Bandera and the Struggle of the OUN [Stepan Bandera i bor'ba OUN]. Moscow, 2011.

Snegirev, D. "Mykhailo Stepanyak. Communist and Member of the OUN Leadership" [Mykhailo Stepanyak. Komunist i chlen Provodu OUN]. *Istorichna Pravda*, July 4, 2011. [URL: https://www.istpravda.com.ua/articles/2016/02/10/148919/]

Snyder, Timothy. *Bloodlands: Europe Between Hitler and Stalin*. New York: Basic Books, 2010.

Snyder, Timothy. "A Fascist Hero in Democratic Kiev." *New York Review of Books*. February 24, 2010. [URL: https://www.nybooks.com/online/2010/02/24/a-fascist-hero-in -democratic-kiev/]

Snyder, Timothy. *The Reconstruction of Nations: Poland, Ukraine, Lithuania, Belarus, 1569– 1999*. New Haven and London: Yale University Press, 2003.

Soviet Occupation of 1944–1991, National Museum-Memorial to the Victims of Occupation Regimes "Lontskoho Prison." [URL: http://www.lonckoho.lviv.ua/istoriya /istoriya-vyaznytsi/radyanska-okupatsiya-1944-1991-rr]

Stepan Bandera in the Documents of Soviet State Security Agencies (1939–1959) [Stepan Bandera u dokumentakh radianskykh orhaniv derzhavnoi bezpeky (1939–1959)], vol. 3. Kyiv, 2009.

Tkachenko, S. *Povstancheskaya armiya: taktika bor'by [The Rebel Army: Tactics of Struggle]*. Minsk, 2000.

Tomchyshyn, Yu. "Third Assembly of OUN: 75 Years Ago" [Tretii Zbir OUN: 75 rokiv po tomu]. *Zbruch*, August 27, 2018. [URL: http://ukrpohliad.org/life/tretij-zbir-oun -75-rokiv-po-tomu.html]

Ukrainian Institute of National Memory. [URL: https://uinp.gov.ua/]

"Ukrainian Main Liberation Council—A Forgotten Page of History or . . ." [Ukrainskii Glavnyi Osvoboditelnyi Sovet—zabytaya stranitsa istorii ili . . .]. *Den'*, July 20, 1996. [URL: https://day.kyiv.ua/ru/article/podrobnosti/ukrainskiy-glavnyy-osvoboditelnyy -sovet-zabytaya-stranica-istorii-ili]

Ukrainian Nationalist Organizations During World War II [Ukrainskie natsionalisticheskie organizatsii v gody Vtoroi mirovoi voiny]. Documents in 2 volumes. 1939–1945. Moscow, 2012.

"Ukrainians Won Three-Day Battle" [Ukrayintsi vyhraly trehnevnyy boy]. *Gazeta.ua*, September 7, 2022. [URL: https://gazeta.ua/ru/articles/history/_ukraincy-vyigrali -trehdnevnyj-boj/1050617]

UPA—Attack on the Town of Kamień Koszyski, Raid on Transnistria. Copies [UPA—atak na miasto Kamień Koszyrski, rajd na Naddnieprowszczyznę Odpisy]. *Ukrainians in Poland in 1944–1956: Archives of the Branch of the Institute of National Remembrance in Warsaw*. [URL: https://web.archive.org/web/20190813092425/https:// ipn.gov.pl/pl/form/r826351637,UPA-atak-na-miasto-Kamien-Koszyrski-rajd-na -Naddnieprowszczyzne-Odpisy.html]

Vedeneev, D. "How Did Mykola Vatutin Die? Documentary Truth About His Injuries, Treatment, and Death" [Yak zahynuv Mykola Vatutin? Dokumentalna pravda pro poranennia, likuvannia ta smert]. *Istorichna Pravda*, January 10, 2011. [URL: https:// www.istpravda.com.ua/research/2011/01/10/8433/]

Vedeneyev, D. "How Shukhevych Died and What Could Have Happened to His Body" [Yak zahynuv Shukhevych i scho mohlo statysya z yoho tilom]. *Istorichna Pravda*, August 8, 2011. [URL: https://www.istpravda.com.ua/research/2011/08/8/50048/]

Vytvytska, O. "Vasyl Sidor—'Shelest' (24.02.10–14.04.49)—Colonel of UPA, Commander of UPA-West" [Vasyl Sidor—"Shelest" (24.02.10–14.04.49)—polkovnyk UPA, komandyr UPA-Zakhid]. *Istoriya UPA v Perehinsku*, October 6, 2016. [URL: http://www.upa-pereginsk.if.ua/?p=445]

Yankel R. "The Immortality of the Commander 'Chorny'" [Bessmertie komandira "Chornogo"]. *Dzerkalo Tyzhnya*, April 8, 2016. [URL: https://zn.ua/HISTORY/bessmertie -komandira-chornogo-_.html]

Yushchenko, K. "UPA Radio Station 'Aphrodite': 'You hear the voice of a free Ukraine . . .'" [Radiostantsiya UPA "Afrodita": "Vi chuete golos vilnoi Ukraini . . ."]. *Istorichna Pravda*, June 11, 2011. [URL: https://www.istpravda.com.ua/articles/2011/06/11/41933/]

Zygar, Mikhail. *Interview with Rinat Akhmetov*, 2023.

Zygar, Mikhail. *Interview with Andriy Yermak*, 2023.

PART II

CHAPTER 8

Address by Andrei Sakharov, "In Defense of the Poet Vasily Stus" [V zashchitu poeta Vasiliya Stusa], October 19, 1980.

Address by Vasil Stus to the Presidium of the Supreme Soviet of the USSR, July 1, 1976.

"Former Deputy Director of Chernobyl NPP: We started making such NPPs because of Arkady Raikin"[Byvshii zamdirektora ChAES: my stali delat takie AES iz-za Arkadiya Raikina]. *Interfax*, April 23, 2016. [URL: https://www.interfax.ru/world/505124]

Letter from Vasil Stus to Andrei Sakharov, February 15, 1978. [URL: https://khpg .org/1071389831]

Memories of Valentin Zgurski.

"My fate was bigger than my personality" ["Sudba moya okazalas krupnee, chem moya lichnost"]. *Istorichna Pravda*, September 10, 2015. [URL: https://www.istpravda.com .ua/digest/2015/09/10/148536/]

Solzhenitsyn, Aleksandr. "How Do We Build Up Russia?" [Kak nam obustroit Rossiyu?]. *Literaturnaya gazeta*, September 18, 1990, no. 38 (5312), pp. 3–6.

Statement of Vasil Stus, September 3, 1980. The Case of Vasil Stus, vol. 6, p. 168.

"Ukrainian Poet Vasil Stus: Destiny and Freedom" [Ukrainskii poet Vasil Stus. Sudba i svoboda]. *Sakharov Center*, May 4, 2014. [URL: https://www.sakharov-center.ru /blogs/main/all/ukrainskiy-poet-vasil-stus-sudba-i-svoboda/]

Zygar, Mikhail. *Interview with Archimandrite Cyril Hovorun*, 2023.

Zygar, Mikhail. *Interview with a source close to Metropolitan Volodymyr Sabodan.*

Zygar, Mikhail. *Interview with Ihor Yukhnovsky*, 2021.

Zygar, Mikhail. *Interview with Leonid Kravchuk*, 2021.

Zygar, Mikhail. *Interview with Oles Doniy*, 2021.

Zygar, Mikhail. *Interview with Serhii Plokhy*, 2022.

Zygar, Mikhail. *Interview with Stepan Khmara*, 2021.

Zygar, Mikhail. *Series of interviews with Mikhail Gorbachev*, 2008–2018.

CHAPTER 9

Correspondence, memorandums of telephone conversations and meetings between President William J. Clinton and President Leonid Kravchuk, 1993–1994, White House.

Dubnov, A. *Why the USSR Collapsed [Pochemu raspalsya SSSR].* Moscow, 2019.

Khomenko, S. "How Leonid Kravchuk Argued with Gorbachev, Collapsed the USSR, and Cried at the End" [Kak Leonid Kravchuk sporil s Gorbachevym, razvalil SSSR, a v kontse proslezilsya]. BBC News Russian, December 8, 2021. [URL: https://www .bbc.com/russian/features-59492080]

Khrushchev, N. S. *Time. People. Power. Memories: in 4 vols. [Vremya. Lyudi. Vlast. Vospominaniya: V 4 t.]* Moscow, 1997.

Memorandum of conversation between President George H. W. Bush and President Leonid Kravchuk of Ukraine, May 6, 1992, White House.

Memorandums of telephone conversations and meetings between President George H. W. Bush and President Leonid Kravchuk, 1991–1992, White House.

Memorandums of telephone conversations and meetings between President William J. Clinton and President Leonid Kuchma, 1994–1999, White House.

Stankevich, Z. A. "Minutes of the 'Novo-Ogaryovo Sages'" [Protokoly "novoogarevskikh mudretsov"]. *Natsionalnye interesy*, nos. 2–3 (2001).

Yashchenko, Anna. "Vasily Lopata Not Only Draws Hryvnias, but Also Writes About Them" [Vasilii Lopata ne tolko risuet grivni, no i pishet o nikh]. *UNIAN*, September 29, 2007. [URL: https://www.unian.net/society/67569-vasiliy-lopata-ne-tolko-risuet -grivni-no-i-pishet-o-nih.html]

Zygar, Mikhail. *Interview with Alexander Korzhakov.*

Zygar, Mikhail. *Interview with Andrei Chivurin.*

Zygar, Mikhail. *Interview with Anna Narinskaya.*

Zygar, Mikhail. *Interview with Archimandrite Cyril Hovorun*, 2023.

Zygar, Mikhail. *Interview with a source close to Metropolitan Volodymyr Sabodan.*

Zygar, Mikhail. *Interview with a source in the Kremlin close to Vladimir Putin.*

Zygar, Mikhail. *Interview with Dmitry Gordon*, 2023.

Zygar, Mikhail. *Interview with Ihor Yukhnovsky*, 2021.

Zygar, Mikhail. *Interview with Leonid Kravchuk*, 2021.

Zygar, Mikhail. *Interview with Serhii Plokhy*, 2022.

Zygar, Mikhail. *Interview with Stanislav Shushkevich*, 2021.

Zygar, Mikhail. *Interview with Tatyana Lazareva*, 2022.
Zygar, Mikhail. *Series of interviews with Gennady Burbulis*, 2020–2021.
Zygar, Mikhail. *Series of interviews with Mikhail Gorbachev*, 2008–2018.

CHAPTER 10

Basha, V. "Why Saburov Took the Crimea" [Zachem Saburov bral Krym]. *Novaya gazeta*, no. 48, December 1–7, 1997.
"Bragin's Murder: 'A Crime with Many Unknowns': 20 Years Later" [Vbivstvo Bragina: "Zlochin iz bagatma nevidomimi": 20 rokiv po tomu]. *FK Shakhtar Info*, June 6, 2019. [URL: https://shakhtar.info/zlochin-iz-bagatma-nevidomimi-20-rokiv-po-tomu.html]
"Corruption in Crimea Through the Eyes of the President" [Korruptsiya v Krymu glazami prezidenta]. *PASMI*, December 25, 2015. [URL: https://pasmi.ru/archive/131790/]
Fedorinova, Yu. "Interview: Victor Pinchuk, Founder of Interpipe Group" [Intervyu: Viktor Pinchuk, osnovatel gruppy "Interpaip"]. *Vedomosti*, September 15, 2005. [URL: https://www.vedomosti.ru/newspaper/articles/2005/09/15/intervyu-viktor-pinchuk-osnovatel-gruppy-interpajp]
Gordon, Dmitry. *Volodymyr Zelensky Interview*, 2018. [URL: https://www.youtube.com/watch?v=P8OBR9yjgFA]
Korzh, G. *Leonid Kuchma: The Real Biography of the Second President of Ukraine [Leonid Kuchma. Nastoyashchaya biografiya vtorogo Prezidenta Ukrainy]*. Kharkiv, 2005.
"KVN Artist and TV Host Volodymyr Zelensky: 'There are no friends in KVN and can not be'" [Kaveenshchik i televedushchii Vladimir Zelenskii: "V KVNe druzei net i byt ne mozhet"]. *Bulvar Gordona*, May 16, 2006. [URL: http://bulvar.com.ua/gazeta/archive/s20_3722/2225.html]
KVN Official YouTube Channel. [URL: https://www.youtube.com/channel/UCSZ69a-0I1RRdNssyttBFcA]
"'Most often in life I am guided by my sense of smell, hearing and sight . . .'" ["Chashche vsego v zhizni ya rukovodstvuyus nyukhom, slukhom i zreniem . . ."] A. Michnik's conversation with J. Brodsky. *Staroe literaturnoe obozrenie*, no. 2 (2001).
95th Quarter. Laughter Is the Meaning of Life [95 kvartal. Smekh—eto smysl zhizni], Interview, October 2002. [URL: http://lady-happy666.narod.ru/interview1.html]
"On Two Sides of the Ocean: Joseph Brodsky on Russia Interviewed in New York by Adam Michnik" [Pod dwu stronach oceanu. Z Josifem Brodskim o Rosji rozmawia w Nowym Jorku Adam Michnik]. *Magazin*, no. 3 (99), February 20, 1995, pp. 6–11.
Studio 95th Quarter YouTube Channel. [URL: https://www.youtube.com/@studiya95kvartal]
Troitskii, N. "The Inseparable Island of Crimea" [Neotdelimyi ostrov Krym]. *RIA Novosti*, January 20, 2011. [URL: https://ria.ru/20110120/323966474.html]
Zygar, Mikhail. *Interview with Adam Michnik*, 2022.
Zygar, Mikhail. *Interview with Alexander Voloshin*, 2015.
Zygar, Mikhail. *Interview with a source close to Leonid Kuchma*, 2022.
Zygar, Mikhail. *Interview with Borys Shefir*, 2022.
Zygar, Mikhail. *Interview with Dmitry Gordon*, 2023.
Zygar, Mikhail. *Interview with Leonid Kuchma*, 2006.
Zygar, Mikhail. *Interview with Oleksandr Rodnyanskyi*, 2022.
Zygar, Mikhail. *Interview with Petr Shchedrovitsky*, 2022.
Zygar, Mikhail. *Interview with Sergey Shefir*, 2022.
Zygar, Mikhail. *Interview with Sevgil Musaieva*, 2022.

Zygar, Mikhail. *Interview with Vladimir Voinovich*, 2018.

Zygar, Mikhail. *Interview with Vladyslav Rashkovan*, 2022.

Zygar, Mikhail. *Interview with Yuriy Lutsenko*, 2009.

Zygar, Mikhail. *Series of Interviews with Yury Luzhkov*, 2015–2019.

Zygar, Mikhail. *Series of Interviews with Valentin Yumashev and Tatyana Dyachenko*, 2015–2020.

CHAPTER 11

Apostrophe.ua archives [URL: https://apostrophe.ua/]

"A Resident of Novokakhovka Told How He Was a Guard for Yushchenko During the Maidan in 2004" [Novokakhovchanin rasskazal, kak byl okhrannikom Yushchenko vo vremya Maidana v 2004]. *Nova Kakhovka City*, January 14, 2018. [URL: https://novakahovka.city/articles/1864/novokahovchanin-rasskazal-kak-byl-ohrannikom-yuschenko-vo-vremya-majdana-v-2004]

Brodsky, M. "Kolomoisky bet me two million dollars that I would lose 27 kilograms and he would lose 14. I won. He paid up" [Kolomoiskii so mnoi na dva milliona dollarov posporil, chto na 27 kilogrammov ya pokhudeyu, a on—na 14. Ya vyigral. On rasschitalsya]. *Bulvar Gordona*, June 13, 2017. [URL: https://bulvar.com.ua/gazeta/archive/s632/eks-narodnyj-deputat-ukrainy-biznesmen-mihail%C2%A0brodskij-kolomojskij-so%C2%A0mnoj-na-dva-milliona-dollarov-posporil-chto%C2%A0na%C2%A027-kilogrammov-ja-pohudeju-a-on%C2%A0-na%C2%A014-ja-vyigral-on-rasschitalsja.html]

Bulvar Gordona archives. [URL: https://bulvar.com.ua/gazeta/archive/]

Censor.net archives. [URL: https://censor.net/ru/n45756]

Chervonenko, E. "I advised Firtash to return to Ukraine. He went through a lot, all gray-haired. He is angry with his mistake that he chose not Klitschko, but Poroshenko" [Firtashu ya sovetoval vernutsya v Ukrainu. On mnogo perezhil, ves sedoy. Obizhen na svoyu oshibku, chto vibral ne Klichko, a Poroshenko]. *Bulvar Gordona*, March 22, 2018. [URL: https://gordonua.com/publications/chervonenko-firtashu-ya-sovetoval-vernutsja-v-ukrainu-on-mnogo-perezhil-ves-sedoy-obizhen-na-svoyu-oshibku-chto-vibral-ne-klichko-a-poroshenko-]

Doroshenko, Y. "Yanukovych—President 2004. Destroyed issue of the 'Uryadovyi Kuryer'" [Yanukovych—Prezydent-2004. Znishchenyy nomer "Uryadovoho Kuryera"]. *Istorichna Pravda*, November 9, 2010. [URL: https://www.istpravda.com.ua/articles/2010/11/9/3469/]

Dzerkalo Tizhnya archives. [URL: https://zn.ua/]

Ivzhenko, T. "The resignation of the government of Viktor Yushchenko has taken place" [Otsatvka kabineta Viktora Yushchenko sostoyalas]. *Nezavisimaya Gazeta*, April 27, 2001. [URL: https://www.ng.ru/cis/2001-04-27/1_yushchenko.html]

Korrespondent.net archives. [URL: https://korrespondent.net/]

KP v Ukraïni archives. [URL: https://kp.ua]

Kuchma, L. *After the Maidan 2005–2006: President's notes [Posle maidana 2005–2006. Zapiski prezidenta]*. Kyiv, Moscow, 2007.

Lenta.ru archives. [URL: https://lenta.ru]

"L. Kuchma Accuses Both Candidates of Violating the Law" [L. Kuchma obvinyaet v narushenii zakona oboikh kandidatov]. *RBC*, November 28, 2004. [URL: https://www.rbc.ru/politics/28/11/2004/5703b68b9a7947783a5a5e07]

Lutsenko, Y. "Yanukovych told me: 'What do you, bitch, know about kvas? Those like you on my camp sucked snot from the dead!'" [Yanukovich mne skazal: "Sho ty, suka, znaesh pro chifir? Takie, kak ty, u menya na lagere sopli mertvyakov sosali!"]. *Bulvar Gordona*, January 22, 2019. [URL: https://gordonua.com/publications/lucenko-yanu kovich-mne-skazal-sho-ty-suka-znaesh-pro-chifir-takie-kak-ty-u-menya-na-lagere -sopli-mertvyakov-sosali-678296.html]

"Nemtsov: 'The brown revolution threatens us much more than the orange revolution'" [Nemtsov: "Nam korichnevaya revolyutsiya ugrozhaet gorazdo bol'she, chem oranzhe- vaya"]. *Personal website of Nemtsov*, November 20, 2005. [URL: https://nemtsov-most .org/2018/06/01/nemtsov-the-brown-revolution-threatens-us-much-more-than-the -orange-revolution/]

NEWSru.com archives. [URL: https://www.newsru.com/arch/]

RBC archives. [URL: https://www.rbc.ru/]

Roxburgh, Angus. *The Strongman: Vladimir Putin and the Struggle for Russia*. London: I. B. Tauris, 2011.

Smeshko, I. "I would not be completely frank if I said I did not have knowledge of all political players since 1991 and the origin of their financial influence" [Byl by ne do kontsa otkrovennym, esli by skazal, chto ne vladeyu znaniiami obo vsekh politicheskikh igrokakh s 1991 goda i proiskhozhdenii ikh finanso- vogo vliyaniya]. *Bulvar Gordona*, January 15, 2019. [URL: https://gordonua.com /publications/smeshko-byl-by-ne-do-kontsa-otkrovennym-esli-by-skazal-chto-ne -vladeju-znanijami-obo-vseh-politicheskih-igrokah-s-1991-goda-i-proishozhde nii-ih-finansovogo-vlijanija-660392.html]

Speech by Yuri Luzhkov on November 28, 2004, at the All-Ukrainian Congress of Depu- ties of all levels in Severodonetsk.

Stanko, A. "I sympathize with Zelensky in his confidence to achieve peace with the Kremlin, but this naivety will pass—political prisoner Mykola Karpyuk" [Ya spivchu- vayu Zelenskomu v iogo vpevnenost—ñ dosyagti z Kremlem miru, ale tsya naïvnist proide—politv'yazen Mikola Karpyuk]. *Hromadske*, March 17, 2020. [URL: https:// hromadske.ua/posts/ya-spivchuvayu-zelenskomu-v-jogo-vpevnenosti-dosyagti-z -kremlem-miru-ale-cya-nayivnist-projde-politvyazen-mikola-karpyuk]

Ukrainska Pravda archives. [URL: https://www.pravda.com.ua/]

"Unknown interview with Kushnarev: 'I am not an angel . . .'" [Neizvestnoe interv'yu Kushnareva: Ya ne angel . . .]. *Zhytomyr.info*, January 17, 2008. [URL: https://www .zhitomir.info/news_12064.htm]

Vakarchuk, S. "Marseillaises write before the revolution. After it—moon sonatas" [Marse- lyezy pishut do revolyutsii. Posle nee—lunnye sonaty]. *Ogonyok*, January 16, 2015. [URL: https://www.kommersant.ru/doc/2294659]

Vedomosti archives. [URL: https://www.vedomosti.ru/]

Yushchenko, V. *Private Secrets: Notes on the Shores of Memory [Nederzhavni taemnitsi: no- tatki na beregakh pam'yati]*. Kharkiv, 2014.

Zygar, Mikhail. *Interview with Alexander Kwaśniewski*.

Zygar, Mikhail. *Interview with a major Ukrainian oligarch*.

Zygar, Mikhail. *Interview with a Russian oligarch who had business in Ukraine*.

Zygar, Mikhail. *Interview with a source at the Viktor Yushchenko campaign headquarters*.

Zygar, Mikhail. *Interview with a source in the Kremlin close to Vladimir Putin*.

Zygar, Mikhail. *Interview with Borys Shefir*, 2022.

Zygar, Mikhail. *Interview with Daniel Fried*, 2022.

Zygar, Mikhail. *Interview with Davyd Zhvania*, 2015.

Zygar, Mikhail. *Interview with Demyan Kudryavtsev*, 2022.

Zygar, Mikhail. *Interview with Dmitry Gordon*, 2023.

Zygar, Mikhail. *Interview with Gleb Pavlovsky*, 2014.

Zygar, Mikhail. *Interview with Leonid Kuchma*, 2006.

Zygar, Mikhail. *Interview with Marat Gelman*, 2014.

Zygar, Mikhail. *Interview with Mikheil Saakashvili*, 2014.

Zygar, Mikhail. *Interview with Naum Borulya*, 2022.

Zygar, Mikhail. *Interview with Oleksandr Moroz*, 2006.

Zygar, Mikhail. *Interview with Petro Symonenko*, 2006.

Zygar, Mikhail. *Interview with Sergey Shefir*, 2022.

Zygar, Mikhail. *Interview with Stanislav Belkovsky*, 2015.

Zygar, Mikhail. *Interview with Viktor Yushchenko*, 2006–2015.

Zygar, Mikhail. *Interview with Vitali Klitschko*, 2006.

Zygar, Mikhail. *Interview with Vladimir Litvin*, 2006.

Zygar, Mikhail. *Interview with Yulia Tymoshenko*, 2006.

Zygar, Mikhail. *Interview with Yuriy Lutsenko*, 2009.

Zygar, Mikhail. *Series of interviews with Yury Luzhkov*, 2015–2019.

CHAPTER 12

Baker, Stephanie, and Voreacos, David. "Mueller Reveals Memos on Manafort Lobbying for Ukraine." *Bloomberg*, June 13, 2018. [URL: https://www.bloomberg.com/news/articles/2018-06-13/mueller-reveals-memos-on-manafort-s-u-s-lobbying-for-ukraine]

BBC News Russian archives. [URL: https://www.bbc.com/russian/]

"Conversation with Vladimir Putin" [Razgovor s Vladimirom Putinym], TV show, December 4, 2008. [URL: http://archive.government.ru/special/docs/2638/]

Documents published by court, *United States of America v. Paul J. Manafort, Jr.* [URL: https://www.justice.gov/archives/sco/file/1094146/download]

Gorchinskaya, Katya. "A Brief History of Corruption in Ukraine: The Yanukovych Era." *Eurasianet*, June 3, 2020. [URL: https://eurasianet.org/a-brief-history-of-corruption-in-ukraine-the-yanukovych-era]

Government's exhibit list, July 25, 2018, *United States of America v. Paul J. Manafort, Jr.* [URL: https://www.politico.com/f/?id=00000164-b049-d929-a5e4-b2f9d8e80000]

Government's reply in support of motion to revoke or revise defendant Paul J. Manafort, Jr.'s current order of pretrial release, June 12, 2018, United States of America v. Paul J. Manafort, Jr. [URL: https://assets.bwbx.io/documents/users/iqjWHBFdfxIU/rhjawP.n2.E0/v0]

Holovnia, A. Interview with Volodymyr Zelensky. *Film.ru*, February 1, 2012. [URL: https://www.film.ru/articles/kostyumery-ne-uspevali-menya-utolshchat]

Interfax archives. [URL: https://www.interfax.ru/]

Inter TV Channel archives. [URL: https://inter.ua/]

Kinopoisk archives. [URL: https://www.kinopoisk.ru/]

Komsomolskaya Pravda archives. [URL: https://www.kp.ru]

Korrespondent.net archives. [URL: https://korrespondent.net/]

KP v Ukraini archives. [URL: https://kp.ua]

"The Laughing Warrior: Volodymyr Zelensky, the CEO of 95th Quarter Is Not Afraid of the Crisis" [Voin smekha. Gendirektor Studii Kvartal-95 Vladimir Zelensky ne boitsya krizisa]. *Ekomik.ru*, December 14, 2008. [URL: http://www.ekomik.ru/byloe/1322-voin-smexa-gendirektor-studii-kvartal-95-vladimir-zelenskij-ne-boitsya-krizisa]

Lenta.ru archives. [URL: https://lenta.ru]

Lutsenko, Y. "Yanukovych told me: 'What do you, bitch, know about kvas? Those like you on my camp sucked snot from the dead!'" [Yanukovich mne skazal: "Sho ty, suka, znaesh pro chifir? Takie, kak ty, u menya na lagere sopli mertvyakov sosali!"]. Bulvar Gordona, January 22, 2019. [URL: https://gordonua.com/publications/lucenko-yanu kovich-mne-skazal-sho-ty-suka-znaesh-pro-chifir-takie-kak-ty-u-menya-na-lagere -sopli-mertvyakov-sosali-678296.html]

Memorandum from Paul Manafort to President Viktor Yanukovych, April 22, 2013, United States of America v. Paul J. Manafort, Jr. [URL: https://assets.bwbx.io/docu ments/users/iqjWHBFdfxIU/r3yELxhJbo30/v0]

Meyer, Theodoric. "New Manafort Docs Appear to Contradict Own Lobbying Claims." Politico, July 27, 2018. [URL: https://www.politico.com/story/2018/07/27/manafort -lobbying-documents-ukraine-evidence-745127]

Miller, Christopher, and Eckel, Mike. "On the Eve of His Trial, a Deeper Look into How Paul Manafort Elected Ukraine's President." Radio Free Europe/Radio Liberty, July 27, 2018. [URL: https://www.rferl.org/a/on-eve-of-trial-a-deeper-glimpse-into-how -paul-manafort-elected-ukraine-s-president/29394601.html]

"Money for Laughter" [Den'hy na khokhot]. Focus, March 30, 2007. [URL: https://focus .ua/news/1090]

95th Quarter Studio archives. [URL: http://kvartal95.com/]

"President Yushchenko Sold Weapons to Georgia, Taking It Off Combat Duty" [Prezident Yushchenko prodaval oruzhiye Gruzii, snimaya ego s boevogo dezhurstva]. Izvestiya, October 1, 2008. [URL: https://iz.ru/news/341307]

RBC Ukraine archives. [URL: https://www.rbc.ua]

RIA Novosti archives. [URL: https://ria.ru/]

Ruger, Todd. "Manafort Memos Reveal Influence Campaign." Roll Call, September 14, 2018. [URL: https://rollcall.com/2018/09/14/manafort-memos-reveal-influence-campaign/]

"Russia Has Found a Strategic Partner" [Rossiya nashla strategicheskuyu partnershu]. Kommersant, no. 179, October 3, 2008, p. 4. [URL: https://www.kommersant.ru /doc/1034951]

Segodnya archives [URL: https://www.segodnya.ua/]

Shestak, A. "Volodymyr Zelensky: 'On the cover of Forbes, I saw myself, and what was written beneath the cover was probably about me, someone else whom I don't know very well'" [Vladimir Zelenskii: "Na oblozhke Forbes ya sebya videl, i to, chto pod ob-lozhkoi, chital–eto, navernoe, pro menya, drugogo, kotorogo ya ochen plokho znayu"]. Bulvar Gordona, January 31, 2012. [URL: https://bulvar.com.ua/gazeta/archive /s5_65182/7292.html]

Sheth, Sonam. "Newly Unsealed Court Filing Shows Paul Manafort Was More Indebted to Putin Ally Oleg Deripaska Than Previously Known." Insider, June 28, 2018. [URL: https://www.businessinsider.com/court-document-shows-oleg-deripaska-loaned -paul-manafort-10-million-2018-6]

Sheth, Sonam. "We Read All 67 Pages of Mueller's Latest Court Filings on Paul Manafort: Here Are the Main Takeaways." Insider, April 25, 2018. [URL: https://www.business insider.com/mueller-manafort-court-documents-takeaways-2018-4]

TSN archives. [URL: https://tsn.ua/]

Ukrainska Pravda archives. [URL: https://www.pravda.com.ua/]

United States of America v. Paul J. Manafort, Jr., Exhibit 1. [URL: https://assets.bwbx.io /documents/users/iqjWHBFdfxIU/rQYA9OE6xvEw/v0]

Vesti.ua archives. [URL: https://vesti.ua]

"Volodymyr Zelensky: 'I hire my friends' wives at work.'" *Segodnya*, December 4, 2012. [URL: https://lifestyle.segodnya.ua/lifestyle/showbiz/Vladimir-Zelenskiy-YA-pristra ivayu-na-rabotu-zhen-druzey-401924.html]

"Zelensky: 'I can't become the President. Who will make the country laugh then?'" [Zel- enskyi: Ne mozhy staty presidentom. Khto zh todi bude smishyty kraïnu?]. *Tabloid*, August 7, 2007. [URL: https://tabloid.pravda.com.ua/person/471dff9d2718a/]

Zygar, Mikhail. *All the Kremlin's Men: Inside the Court of Vladimir Putin*. New York: Pub- licAffairs, 2016.

Zygar, Mikhail. *Interview with a former member of the Ukrainian government close to Viktor Yanukovich*, 2022.

Zygar, Mikhail. *Interview with Alexander Kwaśniewski*, 2022.

Zygar, Mikhail. *Interview with Alexey Chesnakov*, 2015.

Zygar, Mikhail. *Interview with Archimandrite Cyril Hovorun*, 2023.

Zygar, Mikhail. *Interview with a source close to Metropolitan Volodymyr Sabodan*, 2022.

Zygar, Mikhail. *Interview with Bogdan Sokolovsky*, 2014.

Zygar, Mikhail. *Interview with Borys Shefir*, 2022.

Zygar, Mikhail. *Interview with Burckhard Bergmann*, 2006.

Zygar, Mikhail. *Interview with Daniel Fried*, 2022.

Zygar, Mikhail. *Interview with Gleb Pavlovsky*, 2014.

Zygar, Mikhail. *Interview with Hanna German*, 2015.

Zygar, Mikhail. *Interview with Mikheil Saakashvili*, 2014.

Zygar, Mikhail. *Interview with Mustafa Nayyem*, 2014.

Zygar, Mikhail. *Interview with Petro Poroshenko*, 2013.

Zygar, Mikhail. *Interview with Sergei Livnev*, 2022.

Zygar, Mikhail. *Interview with Sergey Shefir*, 2022.

Zygar, Mikhail. *Interview with Serhiy Leshchenko*, 2022.

Zygar, Mikhail. *Interview with Sonya Koshkina*, 2023.

Zygar, Mikhail. *Interview with Vladyslav Rashkovan*, 2023.

Zygar, Mikhail. *Interview with Yulia Tymoshenko*, 2006.

Zygar, Mikhail. *Interview with Yuriy Lutsenko*, 2009.

Zygar, Mikhail. *Interviews with Viktor Yushchenko*, 2006–2015.

CHAPTER 13

"A Military Unit Is Stormed in Mariupol, Demanding the Surrender of Weapons" [V Marieupole shturmuiut voinskuu chast, trebuut sdat' oruzhie]. *0629.com. Mariupol City Website*, April 16, 2014. [URL: https://www.0629.com.ua/news/517713/v-mariupole -sturmuut-voinskuu-cast-trebuut-sdat-oruzie-videofotoreportaz-obnovlaetsa]

"Among the Moscow Law Enforcement Officers Who Dispersed the Students, a Former Head of the Kiev 'Berkut' Was Noticed" [Sredi moskovskikh silovikov, razgoniavshikh studentov, zametili eks-glavu kievskogo 'Berkuta']. *Moskovsky Komsomolets*, June 13, 2017. [URL: https://www.mk.ru/politics/2017/06/13/sredi-moskovskikh-silovikov -razgonyavshikh-studentov-zametili-eksglavu-kievskogo-berkuta.html]

"Andrey Chivurin: 'If Russia had not interfered in the affairs of Ukraine, there would be no "Liga Smekha"'" [Andrei Chivurin: "Esli by Rossiya ne vmeshalas v dela Ukrainy, 'Ligi Smekha'" ne bylo by]. *Mediannya*, October 26, 2015. [URL: https://mediananny .com/intervju/2312803/]

Annitova, I. "'Smart people tell who and when lost Crimea'—Former Commander of the Ukrainian Navy" ['Umniky rasskazyvayut, kto i kogda proigral Krym"—

eks-komanduyushchii VMF Ukrainy]. *Krym. Realii*, November 22, 2016. [URL: https://ru.krymr.com/a/28133358.html]

Antonenko, A. "'Sasha, you're at the finish line.' Big interview with former President of Poland Alexander Kwasniewski about Lukashenko, Putin, and Belarus" ["Sasha, ty—u finishnoy cherty." Bol'shoye interv'yu eks-prezidenta Pol'shi Aleksandra Kvasnevskogo o Lukashenko, Putine i Belarusi]. BBC News Russian, September 2, 2020. [URL: https://www.bbc.com/russian/features-53991945]

Apostrophe.ua archives [URL: https://apostrophe.ua/]

Artishchenko, A. "'Downed Pilots' Back in Action" ["Sbitie lyotchiki" snova v stroyu]. *Versiya*, June 2, 2022. [URL: https://versia.ru/na-osvobozhdyonnyx-territoriyax-v-xod-poshli-kadry-iz-kolody-viktora-yanukovicha]

"Azarov Explained Refusal from Association: 400 Thousand Ukrainians Could Lose Their Jobs" [Azarov obyasnil otkaz ot Assotsiatsii: 400 tysyach ukraintsev mogli poteryat rabotu]. *Glavred*, November 27, 2013. [URL: https://glavred.info/economics/264530-azarov-obyasnil-otkaz-ot-associacii-400-tysyach-ukraincev-mogli-poteryat-rabotu.html]

Balita V. "Lviv Universities Declare Their Support for Students" [Lvivski vishi zadeklaruvaly svoyu pidtrymku studentstvu]. *Zaxid.net*, November 23, 2013. [URL: https://zaxid.net/lvivski_vishi_zadeklaruvalo_svoyu_pidtrimku_studentstvu_n1297828]

BBC News Russian archives. [URL: https://www.bbc.com/russian/]

"Born on the Maidan: Memories of the People Who Started the Revolution of Dignity" [Rozhdennye na Maidane: vospominaniya lyudei, s kotorykh nachalas Revolyutsiya Dostoinstva]. *24 Channel*, November 21, 2021. [URL: https://24tv.ua/ru/rozhdennye-majdane-vospominanija-ljudej-kotoryh-gorjachie-novosti_n1799676]

Bubenshchykova, O. "Mysterious Death on Maidan" [Zahadkova smert na Maydani]. *Volynska Hazeta*. [URL: https://volga.lutsk.ua/view/2669/1/]

Bulvar Gordona archives. [URL: https://bulvar.com.ua/gazeta/archive/]

"Buses with Students from Donetsk Region Went to Kyiv in Support of Yanukovych" [Iz Donetskoi oblasti v Kiev otpravilis avtobusy so studentami v podderzhku Yanukovicha]. *Novosti Donbassa*, November 23, 2013. [URL: https://novosti.dn.ua/news/196991-yz-donckoy-oblasty-v-kyev-otpravylys-avtobusy-so-studentamy-v-podderzhku-yanukovycha-vydeo]

Butusov, Y. "Dmytro Yarosh: 'The first offensive battle of the war took place on April 20, 2014—volunteers attacked a checkpoint near Sloviansk'" [Dmytro Yarosh: "Pershyi nastupnyi biy viyny vidbuvsya 20 kvitnya 2014-ho—dobrovoltsi atakuvav blokpost pid Slov'yans'kom"]. *Censor.net*, April 22, 2016. [URL: https://censor.net/ru/r385673]

Chalenko, A. "Strelkov in the Light of Gubarev's Torch" [Strelkov v svete fakela Gubareva]. *Izvestiya*, October 27, 2015. [URL: https://iz.ru/news/594031]

Chervonenko, V. "Will Ukrainians Go to the EuroMaidan?" [Vyydut li ukraincy na Evromajdan?]. BBC News Ukraine, November 22, 2013. [URL: https://www.bbc.com/ukrainian/ukraine_in_russian/2013/11/131122_ru_s_protests_kyiv]

Chesnakov, A. "Surkov: I'm interested in acting against reality" [Surkov: mne interesno deystvovat' protiv realnosti]. *Aktualnye kommentarii*, February 26, 2020. [URL: https://actualcomment.ru/surkov-mne-interesno-deystvovat-protiv-realnosti-2002260855.html]

ChistoNews, May 14, 2014. [URL: https://www.youtube.com/watch?v=yFlvDb51VGA]

"The Chronology of Events on May 2, 2014 in Odessa." [Khronologiya sobytii 2 maya 2014 g. v Odesse]. *2 May Group*, December 8, 2015. [URL: https://2maygroup.blogspot.com/2015/12/2-2014-2.html]

"Chubarov: For the first time in 23 years, Crimean Tatars are forced to explain to the authorities how important it is to preserve historical memory" [Chubarov: Vpervye za 23 goda krymskie tatary vynuzhdeny obyasnyat vlasti, kak vazhno sokhranit istoricheskuyu pamyat]. *Bulvar Gordona*, May 17, 2014. [URL: https://gordonua.com/news/crimea/CHubarov-Vpervye-za-23-goda-krymskie-tatary-vynuzhdeny-obyasnyat-vlasti-kak-vazhno-sohranit-istoricheskuyu-pamyat-23072.html]

"City Council Deputy Sergey Smolyaninov Asked Putin to Send Troops into Ukraine" [Deputat horodskoho Soveta Sergey Smolyaninov poprosil Putina vvesti voyska v Ukrayinu]. *Sevastopolskaya Gazeta*, December 2, 2013. [URL: http://gazeta.sebastopol.ua/2013/12/02/deputat-gorodskogo-soveta-sergej-smoljaninov-poprosil-putina-vvesti-vojska-v-ukrainu/]

"Comment from Minister Vladimir Medinsky Regarding the Screening of the Film '8 New Dates'" [Kommentarii Ministra Vladimira Medinskogo po povodu prokata fil'ma "8 novykh svidanii"]. *Official website of the Ministry of Culture of the Russian Federation*, October 6, 2017. [URL: https://culture.gov.ru/press/news/kommentariy-ministra-vladimira-medinskogo-po-povodu-prokata-filma-8-novykh-svida20171006173921/]

Derenyuga, O. "Residents of Mykolaiv Resisted the Assault of Law Enforcement Officers at EuroMaidan" [Mykolayivtsi na Evromaidani daly otpor shturmu silovikiv]. *NikVesti*, November 22, 2013. [URL: https://nikvesti.com/news/politics/47315]

Deynichenko R. "US Warns Ukrainian Authorities Against Using Force Against Protesters in Kyiv" [SShA zasterigayut ukrainsku vladiu vid zastosuvannia syly proty mitynhuvalnykiv u Kyievi]. *VOA News*, November 29, 2013. [URL: https://ukrainian.voanews.com/a/1800282.html]

Documents of the President of Russia. [URL: http://kremlin.ru/acts/]

Dzerkalo Tizhnya archives. [URL: https://zn.ua/]

"Electoral Preferences of Ukrainian Voters, November 2013" [Elektoralni preferentsii vyborivtsiv Ukrayiny, lystopad 2013]. *Kyiv International Institute of Sociology*, November 28, 2013. [URL: https://kiis.com.ua/?lang=ukr&cat=reports&id=210&page=1]

Evening Quarter, April 12, 2014. [URL: https://www.youtube.com/watch?v=HJ_1kPGtYrw]

Evening Quarter, May 17, 2014. [URL: https://www.youtube.com/watch?v=2SWapAXBBic]

Fanaylova, E. "Kharkiv Maidan: Lessons of Confrontation" [Kharkovskii maidan: uroki protivostoyaniya]. *Radio Svoboda*, April 12, 2014. [URL: https://www.svoboda.org/a/25330078.html]

Fiasko misji Kwaśniewskiego na Ukrainie. "Porozumienie w Wilnie nie będzie podpisane," TVN24, November 21, 2013. [URL: https://tvn24.pl/swiat/fiasko-misji-kwasniewskiego-na-ukrainie-porozumienie-w-wilnie-nie-bedzie-podpisane-ra373473-3450798]

"15 Main Advisors of Poroshenko" [15 holovnykh radnykiv Poroshenka]. *Espresso*, June 10, 2014. [URL: https://espreso.tv/article/2014/06/10/15_holovnykh_radnykiv_poroshenka]

"The Fifth President: An Unknown Strategy for Victory" [Pyatyi prezident. Neizvestnaya strategiya pobedy]. *The Insider*, June 6, 2015. [URL: http://www.theinsider.ua/politics/557591a765d8e/]

Gordon, D. "Arseniy Yatsenyuk: 'I told Poroshenko: "Petro, you're next! Don't do it"'" [Arseniy Yatsenyuk: "Ya skazal Poroshenko: 'Petr, ty budesh sleduyushchiy! Ne delay etogo'"]. *Bulvar Gordona*, October 22, 2019. [URL: https://bulvar.com.ua/gazeta/archive/s755/arsenij-jatsenjuk-ja-skazal-poroshenko-petr-ty-budesh-sledujushchij-ne-delaj-etogo.html]

Government portal, documents archive. [URL: https://www.kmu.gov.ua/]

"Head of Crimean Self-Defense: 'The sniper disappeared into thin air'" [Glava samoo-borony Kryma: "Snaiper slovno rastvorilsya v vozdukhe"]. *Moskovsky Komsomolets*, March 19, 2014. [URL: https://www.mk.ru/incident/article/2014/03/19/1000914 -glava-samooboronyi-kryima-snayper-slovno-rastvorilsya-v-vozduhe.html]

"In Mariupol, Separatists Seize Prosecutor's Office. Searching for 'People's Mayor'" [V Mariupole separatisty zakhvatyly prokuraturu. Iskaly "narodnogo mera"]. *Ostrov*, April 5, 2014. [URL: https://www.ostro.org/general/politics/news/441786/]

"Interagency Coordination Headquarters on Social Protection of Citizens of Ukraine Who Move from Areas of Anti-terrorist Operation and Temporarily Occupied Territory" [Mizhvidomchii koordinatsiinii shtab z pitan sotsialnogo zabezpechennya gromadyan Ukraïni, yaki peremishchuyutsya z r100iniv provedennya antiteroristichnoï operatsiï ta timchasovo okupovanoi teritorii]. *State Emergency Service of Ukraine*, October 26, 2016. [URL: https://archive.ph/20161026185516/http://www.dsns.gov.ua/ua /Mizhvidomchiy-koordinaciyniy-shtab.html]

Interfax archives. [URL: https://www.interfax.ru/]

"In the Project of the Vilnius Summit Declaration, the Mention of Association with Ukraine Was Left in Parentheses" [U proekti deklaratsiï Vilnyuskoho samitu lishyly zhadku pro asotsiatsiyu z Ukrayinoyu v dudzkakh]. *Radio Free Europe/Radio Liberty*, November 26, 2013. [URL: https://www.radiosvoboda.org/a/25180987.html]

Kanygin, P. "I work in this country for Petro Poroshenko" [Ya v etoy strane rabotayu Petrom Alekseevichem Poroshenko]. *Novaya Gazeta*, December 23, 2013. [URL: https://novayagazeta.ru/articles/2013/12/23/57760-171-ya-v-etoy-strane-rabotayu -petrom-alekseevichem-poroshenko-187]

Karpinska V. "A Column of Hundreds of Cars and Buses Leaves Lviv for Kyiv" [Kolona z soten avtomobiliv ta avtobusiv virushyla zi Lvova na Kyiv]. *Zaxid.net*, December 1, 2013. [URL: https://zaxid.net/kolona_z_soten_avtomobiliv_ta_avtobusiv_virushila _zi_lvova_na_kiyiv_n1298329]

"Kernes: Who Ordered the Assassination Attempt on Me? Avakov" [Kernes: Khto za-kazav pokushennia na menia? Avakov]. *Bulvar Gordona*, March 3, 2017. [URL: https://gordonua.com/publications/kernes-kto-zakazal-pokushenie-na-menya-ava kov-176532.html]

Kondratova, V. "Debtors of the Maidan: How Poroshenko, Tymoshenko and Tyagnibok Were Nominated" [Dolzhniki Maydana: kak vydvigalis Poroshenko, Tymoshenko i Tyagnibok]. *Liga.Novini*, March 29, 2014. [URL: https://news.liga.net/politics/ar ticles/dolzhniki_maydana_kak_vydvigalis_poroshenko_timoshenko_i_tyagnibok]

Korrespondent.net archives. [URL: https://korrespondent.net/]

Koshkina, S. *Maidan: The Untold Story [Maidan: Nerasskazannaya Istoriya]*. Kyiv, 2015.

Koshkina, S. "Turchynov: 'I will destroy all of you! I will bury everyone!' Yanukovych Shouted, Running Around the Office" [Turchinov: "Ya vas vsekh unichtozhu! Vsekh— zakopayu!"—krichal Yanukovich, begaya po kabinetu]. *Levyi Bereg*, November 20, 2014. [URL: https://rus.lb.ua/news/2014/11/20/286541_turchinov_ya_unichtozhu-.html]

Kovalenko, E. "Video Appeared Where Poroshenko Helps the Wounded on Maidan" [Poyavilos' video, gde Poroshenko pomogaet ranenym na Maydane]. *Komsomolskaya Pravda v Ukraine*, February 20, 2019. [URL: https://kp.ua/politics/631253-poiavylos -vydeo-hde-poroshenko-pomohaet-ranenym-na-maidane]

Kozak, T. "Attack on Tetyana Chernovol: The Organizer Died in SIZO, the Suspect Fled to Russia, Only One Convicted Is in Detention" [Napadenie na Tatyanu Chernovol. Organizator umer v SIZO, podozrevaemyy sbezhal v Rossiyu, iz osuzhdennykh—tolko

odin v zaklyuchenii]. *Grati*, December 26, 2019. [URL: https://graty.me/napadenie
-na-tatyanu-chernovol-organizator-umer-v-sizo-podozrevaemyj-sbezhal-v-rossiyu
-iz-osuzhdennyh-tolko-odin-v-zaklyuchenii/]

Krivoshcheev, K. "Denis Pushilin: How to Build Novorossiya" [Denis Pushilin: Kak nam
obustroit Novorossiyu]. *Snob*, September 9, 2014. [URL: https://snob.ru/selected
/entry/80803/]

Kuzhel A. "The EuroMaidan Was Demolished in Chernihiv" [U Chernihovi znesly Yev-
romaidan]. Chernihivshchyna. *Podii i komentari*, November 25, 2013. [URL: http://
pik.cn.ua/6614/]

Lazorenko, R. "Armed People Seize City Council Building in Donetsk" [V Donetske
lyudi s oruzhiyem zakhvatili zdanie gorodskogo soveta]. *62.ua*, April 16, 2014. [URL:
https://www.62.ua/news/517014/v-donecke-ludi-s-oruziem-zahvatili-zdanie-goro
dskogo-soveta-obnovlaetsa-dobavleny-foto]

Lenta.ru archives. [URL: https://lenta.ru]

Levyi bereg archives. [URL: https://lb.ua]

Liga Smeha YouTube Channel. [URL: https://www.youtube.com/@LigaSmeha]

"New Ukrainian Ambassador to the UN: We were late with the decision to sever diplomatic relations with Moscow" [Novyi posol Ukrainy v OON: My oplazhdaly z resh-
eniyem o razryve dipotnoshenyi s Moskvoy]. *Evropeiskaya pravda*, December 23, 2015.
[URL: https://www.eurointegration.com.ua/rus/interview/2015/12/23/7042656/]

Nudyk, Y. "The National Historical Code Is Contained in 'Plyve Kacha'" [U "Plyve Kacha"
mistytsya istorychnyy kod natsiyi]. *Zbruch*, March 31, 2014. [URL: https://zbruc.eu
/node/20642]

"Owner of Former Airport Building: 'It was a sabotage act!'" [Sobstvennik zdaniya
byvshego aeroporta: "Eto byl diversiynyj akt!"]. *Novyny Kramatorska*, April 25, 2014.
[URL: https://hi.dn.ua/index.php?option=com_content&view=article&id=46269&ca
tid=55&Itemid=147]

"Pavel Gubarev: 'Their time has passed, and our time has begun'" [Pavel Gubarev: "Ikh
vremya proshlo, a nashe vremya nachalos"]. *Komsomolskaya Pravda*, May 4, 2015.
[URL: https://www.kp.ru/daily/26374.4/3255632/]

Pavlyk V. "Lviv Residents Seized the Building of the Regional Administration"
[Lviv'iani zakhopyly budivliu oblderzhadministratsii]. *Zaxid.net*, January 23, 2014.
[URL: https://zaxid.net/lvivyani_zahopili_budivlyu_oblderzhadministratsiyi_
n1301227]

Pivovarova, O. "DNR Fighters Seized the Krasnoarmiysk Police Department: Activists
Build Barricades" [DNRovtsy zakhvatili Krasnoarmeykiy gorotdel. Aktivisty vystroi-
vayut barrikady]. *06239. Site of Pokrovsk and Mirnograd cities*, May 1, 2014. [URL:
https://www.06239.com.ua/news/527094/dnrovcy-zahvatili-krasnoarmejskij-gorot
del-aktivisty-vystraivaut-barrikady-video]

"The Poroshenko Game: Between Power and Opposition" [Igra Poroshenko: mezhdu
vlastyu i oppozitsiei]. *The Insider*, January 14, 2014. [URL: http://www.theinsider.ua
/politics/52d42c187d29d/]

Prokhanov, A. "Who are you, 'Shooter'?" [Kto ty, "Strelok"?]. *Zavtra*, no. 47 (1096), November 20, 2014. [URL: https://zavtra.ru/blogs/kto-tyi-strelok]

Pushkar, A. "Big Interview with Turchynov: Sharp Moments" [Bol'shoye interv'yu s
Turchinovym: ostrie momenty]. Dankor Online, February 28, 2017. [URL: http://
dancor.sumy.ua/news/mosaic/196253]

RBC archives. [URL: https://www.rbc.ru/]

"'Referendum' in Crimean Tatar settlements in Bakhchysarai Has Failed—Umerov"

["Referendum" u krymskotatarskykh masyvakh u Bakhchysarai zirvanyi—Umerov]. *Radio Free Europe/Radio Liberty*, March 16, 2014. [URL: https://www.radiosvoboda.org/a/25298474.html]

"Resolution of the State Council of the Republic of Crimea on the Independence of Crimea" [Postanovlenie HS RK o nezavisimosti Kryma]. March 11, 2014. [URL: http://crimea.gov.ru/act/11748]

RIA Novosti archives. [URL: https://ria.ru/]

Rosbalt archives. [URL: https://www.rosbalt.ru/]

Rossiiskaya gazeta archives. [URL: https://rg.ru/]

Rudenko, A. "'There was a chance to "smoke out" the invaders from Crimea': How Russia Took the Peninsula" ["'Byl shans "vykurit" zakhvatchikov iz Kryma'. Kak Rossiya zabirala poluostrov"]. *Krym. Realii*, March 21, 2021. [URL: https://ru.krymr.com/a/anneksiya-kryma-rossiya-ukraina-igor-voronchenko-intervyu/31159026.html]

Russian State Duma archives. [URL: http://duma.gov.ru/]

Samorukov, M. "Neonazis Without Separatists: Who in Europe Supported Putin in Crimea" [Neonatsisty bez separatistov: kto v Evrope podderzhal Putina v Krymu]. *Republic*, March 18, 2014. [URL: https://republic.ru/posts/39056]

"Sashko Bilyi: Leadership of the Prosecutor General's Office and Ministry of Internal Affairs of Ukraine made a decision on my physical destruction" ['Kerivnitstvo genprokuraturi i MVS Ukraïni priinyali rishennya pro moe fizichne znishchennya'—Sashko Bilii]. *Chetverta Vlada*, March 13, 2014. [URL: https://4vlada.com/rivne/34078]

Segodnya archives. [URL: https://www.segodnya.ua/]

"Seizure After Seizure: In the Courtyard of the Horlivka Prosecutor's Office, a Bonfire Was Made Out of Documentation and Criminal Cases" [Zakhvat za zakhvatom: v dvore prokuratury Horlivky ustroyili kostyor iz dokumentatsii i ugolovnykh del]. *Gorlovka.ua*, May 1, 2014. [URL: https://gorlovka.ua/News/Article/6420]

Shargunov, S. "'We marched seventeen kilometers across the border.' Igor Strelkov Answers Sergey Shargunov's Questions" [Semnadtsat' kilometrov my shli marshem cherez granitsu. Igor' Strelkov otvechaet na voprosy Sergeya Shargunova]. *Svobodnaya Pressa*, November 11, 2014. [URL: https://svpressa.ru/war21/article/103643/]

"Source: Donetsk and Luhansk Separatists Are Controlled by People of Akhmetov and Yefremov" [Dzherelo: donets'kymy i luhans'kymy separatystamy keruyut' liudy Akhmetova i Yefremova]. *Ukrayinskyi tyzhden*, May 7, 2014. [URL: https://tyzhden.ua/News/106965]

TASS archives. [URL: https://www.tass.ru/]

Tolmachev, S. "Farewell to Slavyansk: Southeast Ukraine Slips from Kiev's Control" [Proshchanie Slavyanska. Yugo-vostok Ukrainy vykhodit iz-pod kontrolya Kieva]. *Kommersant*, April 14, 2014. [URL: https://www.kommersant.ru/doc/2452028]

TSN archives. [URL: https://tsn.ua/]

"Turchynov: In March 2014, Russia planned to storm all the deployment locations of our military units in Crimea" [V marte 2014 goda Rossiya planirovala shturm vsekh mest dislokatsii nashikh v/ch v Krymu—Turchinov]. *Censor.net*, February 27, 2017. [URL: https://censor.net/ru/news/429849/v_marte_2014_goda_rossiya_planirovala_shturm_vseh_mest_dislokatsii_nashih_vch_v_krymu_turchinov]

Ukrainska Pravda archives. [URL: https://www.pravda.com.ua/]

UNIAN archives. [URL: https://www.unian.net/]

Varlamov, I. "House of the Emperor Pshonka" [Dom Imperatora Pshonki]. *Ilya Varlamov*, February 25, 2014. [URL: https://varlamov.ru/1010198.html]

Vesti.ua archives. [URL: https://vesti.ua/]

"Vice Admiral Hayduk: 'In 2008, a professor at the Academy of the General Staff said, "Ukraine needs a small war to understand who we are"'" [Vitse-admyral Hayduk: "Prepodavatel Akademii Genshtaba v 2008-m skazal: 'Ukraine nuzhna malen'kaya voyna, chtoby ponat',' kto my takie'"]. *Fakty*, March 16, 2021. [URL: https://fakty.ua /ru/370923-vice-admiral-gajduk-prepodavatel-akademii-genshtaba-v-2008-m-ska zal-ukraine-nuzhna-malenkaya-vojna-chtoby-ponyat-kto-my-takie]

"Volodymyr Zelenskyy Calls on Yanukovych to Understand" [Volodimir Zelenskii zaklikav Yanukovicha vrozumitis]. *TSN TV Channel*, March 1, 2014. [URL: https://www .youtube.com/watch?v=OCvGLF4ePdI]

Yudin A. "Victims of the Clashes on May 2nd in Greece—Who Are They? The Facts of the Odessa Tragedy That the Press Is Silent About" [Zhertvy stolknovenii na Grecheskoi 2 mai—kto oni? Fakty odesskoi tragedii, o kotorykh molchit pressa]. *Rabochaya partiya*, August 10, 2014. [URL: http://workersparty-ioc.net/publ/sobytiya/zhertvy _stolknovenij_na_grecheskoj_2_maja_kto_oni_fakty_odesskoj_tragedii_o_kotorykh _molchit_pressa/13-1-0-89]

Zygar, Mikhail. *All the Kremlin's Men: Inside the Court of Vladimir Putin*. New York: PublicAffairs, 2016.

Zygar, Mikhail. *Interview with a source close to the Privat Group*, 2022.

Zygar, Mikhail. *Interview with a source in the Kremlin close to Vladimir Putin*, 2022.

Zygar, Mikhail. *Interview with Dmitry Peskov*, 2014.

Zygar, Mikhail. *Interview with Konstantin Malofeev*, 2017.

Zygar, Mikhail. *Interview with Mustafa Nayyem*, 2014.

Zygar, Mikhail. *Interview with Natalya Yemchenko*, 2022.

Zygar, Mikhail. *Interview with Radek Sikorski*, 2022.

Zygar, Mikhail. *Interview with Sevgil Musaieva*, 2022.

Zygar, Mikhail. *Interview with Svitlana Zalishchuk*, 2023.

CHAPTER 14

"Behind Zelensky Travels an Escort—a Minibus of the Company from the Privat Group of Kolomoisky" [Za Zelenskim yizdyt suprovid—mikroavtobus kompanii z hrupy "Privat" Kolomoiskoho]. *Bihus.info*, January 18, 2019. [URL: https://bihus.info/za -zelenskim-izdit-suprovid-mikroavtobus-kompanii-z-grupi-privat-kolomoyskogo/]

Brovinska, M. "Zelensky Expands His List of Intellectual Property: He Will Be Engaged in Clothing and Catering Under the TM 'Servant of the People'" [Zelensky rozshyryv spysok svoieyi intelektualnoyi vlasnosti: zaymetsya odezhdoi i keyteringom pod TM "Sluga narodu"]. *Dev.ua*, February 4, 2022. [URL: https://dev.ua/ru/news/zelenskii-™]

Brovinskaya, M. "Head of 1+1: TV Has No Other Interest Besides Politics" [Glava 1+1: TV ne predstavlyaet drugogo interesa, krome politiki]. *Liga.biz*, January 9, 2019. [URL: https://biz.liga.net/pervye-litsa/reklama-marketing/interview/glava-11-tv-ne -predstavlyaet-drugogo-interesa-krome-politiki]

Correspondence with European ministers published by the Russian Foreign Ministry on November 17, 2021. [URL: https://archive.mid.ru/documents/10180/4944950/%D 0%B4%D0%B8%D0%BF%D0%BB%D0%BE%D0%BC%D0%B0%D1%82%D0 %B8%D1%87%D0%B5%D1%81%D0%BA%D0%B0%D1%8F+%D0%BF%D0%B5 %D1%80%D0%B5%D0%BF%D0%B8%D1%81%D0%BA%D0%B0.pdf/795480b9 -c3da-4498-88c8-f0a723c62c6f]

Evening Quarter, May 23, 2015. [URL: https://www.youtube.com/watch?v=Et-mM92H PxQ]

Evening Quarter, September 10, 2016. [URL: https://www.youtube.com/watch?v=IAyl BO5NkiQ]

Facebook post by Margarita Simonyan on January 25, 2020. [URL: https://www.face book.com/margarita.simonyan.5/posts/10157839312052305]

"Giuliani Cancels Ukraine Trip, Says He'd Be 'walking into a group of people that are enemies of the US.'" Fox News, May 11, 2019. [URL: https://www.foxnews.com/politics /giuliani-i-am-not-going-to-ukraine-because-id-be-walking-into-a-group-of-peo ple-that-are-enemies-of-the-us]

"Giuliani Plans to Prod Ukraine in Cases That Might Aid Trump." *New York Times*, May 10, 2019, Section A, Page 1. [URL: https://www.nytimes.com/2019/05/09/us /politics/giuliani-ukraine-trump.html]

Hill.TV, March 20, 2016. [URL: https://www.youtube.com/watch?v=bRVVwa2aXEs]

"How the Business of One of the Most Popular Presidential Candidates Is Organized. Special Project" [Kak ustroen biznes odnogo iz samykh reytingovykh uchastnikov prezidentskoy gonki? Spetsproekt]. *Liga.net*, 2019. [URL: https://project.liga.net/proj ects/zelenskiy_business/]

"Igor Kolomoysky About the Seizure of Ukrtransneft and Deputy Leshchenko" [Igor Kolomoiskii pro zakhvat Ukrtransnefti i deputate Leshchenko]. *17 kanal*, YouTube channel. [URL: https://www.youtube.com/watch?v=k00iQ1GxERM]

"It Happened That Way: How the 'Servant of the People' Series Made a Showman and Businessman the President of Ukraine" [Tak poluchilos. Kak serial "Sluga naroda" sdelal shoumena i biznesmena prezidentom Ukrainy]. *Hromadske*, June 18, 2019. [URL: https://hromadske.ua/ru/posts/tak-poluchilos-kak-serial-sluga-naroda-sdelal -shoumena-i-biznesmena-prezidentom-ukrainy]

"Korban: In Kiev, there are thieves, and it's time for them to leave" [Korban: V Kieve sidyat vory, i im pora uiti]. *Ukrainska Pravda*, March 23, 2015. [URL: https://www.pravda .com.ua/rus/news/2015/03/23/7062435/]

Koshkina, S. "Igor Kolomoisky: 'God forbid to be in Turchynov's place!'" [Ihor Kolomoisky: "Upasi bog okazat'sya na meste Turchinova"]. *LB.ua*, May 16, 2014. [URL: https://lb.ua /news/2014/05/16/266620_igor_kolomoyskiy_ne_day_bog.html]

Kritskaya, I., and Gnennyi, K. "Problems Worth $880 Million: Which of Akhmetov's Businesses Suffered Due to the Conflict with Zelensky and Which Ones Could Suffer More" [Problemy na $880 mln. Kakie biznesy Akhmetova postradali iz-za konflikta s Zelenskim. I kakie eshche mogut silno postradat]. *Forbes Ukraine*, December 8, 2021. [URL: https://forbes.ua/ru/news/problemy-na-880-mln-kakie-biznesy-akhmetova-pod -ugrozoy-iz-za-konflikta-s-zelenskim-08122021-2932]

"Lavrov Explains Publication of Correspondence with Colleagues from France and Germany with the Word 'fed up'" [Lavrov ob"yasnil publikatsiyu perepiski s kollegami iz Frantsii i FRG slovom "dostali"]. *TASS*, November 18, 2021. [URL: https://tass.com /politics/12964879]

Medvedev, D. "Why Contacts with the Current Ukrainian Leadership Are Pointless" [Pochemu bessmyslenny kontakty s nyneShnim ukrainskim rukovodstvom]. *Kommersant*, no. 184, October 11, 2021, p. 3. [URL: https://www.kommersant.ru/doc/5028300]

Memorandum of telephone conversation between President Trump and President Zelenskyy, July 25, 2019. [URL: https://apps.npr.org/documents/document .html?id=6429015-Trump-Ukraine-Transcript]

"Offshores of Zelensky, Kolomoisky, PrivatBank, Ahmetov's Plane and the Crimean

Business of Hereg—the Key Takeaways from the Ukrainian Part of the Pandora Papers" [Ofshory Zelenskogo, Kolomoyskiy, Privatbank, samolet Akhmetova i geregi v Krymu—glavnoe iz ukrainskoy chasti Pandora Papers]. *NV Business*, October 3, 2021. [URL: https://biz.nv.ua/economics/pandora-papers-ofshory-zelenskogo-kolomoyskiy -privatbank-samolet-ahmetova-i-geregi-v-krymu-50187142.html]

"Over Thirty 95th Quarter Employees and Their Acquaintances Ended Up in State Positions in a Year" [Za rik na derzhavnykh posadakh opynylysia ponad 30 'kvartalivtsiv' i ikh znaiomykh]. *Committee of Voters of Ukraine*, May 15, 2020. [URL: http://www .cvu.org.ua/nodes/view/type:news/slug:za-rik-na-derzhavnykh-posadakh-opynylysia -ponad-30-kvartalivtsiv-i-ikh-znaiomykh]

Panina, N. V. *Ukrainian Society 1994–2005: Sociological Monitoring [Ukraïnske suspilstvo 1994–2005: sotsiologichnii monitoring].* Kyiv, 2005.

Piatin, A. "Zelensky Declared Income over $1 Million a Year" [Zelenskii zadeklariroval dokhod bolshe $1 mln za god]. *Forbes Russia*, May 31, 2020. [URL: https://www .forbes.ru/newsroom/obshchestvo/401867-zelenskiy-zadeklariroval-dohod-bolshe -1-mln-za-god]

"Putin Says Kiev Has Taken Course for Dismantling Minsk Agreements" [Putin zayavil, chto Kiev vzyal kurs na demontazh mins'kykh dohovorennostei]. *TASS*, February 8, 2022. [URL: https://tass.com/politics/13641525]

Putin, V. *On the Historical Unity of Russians and Ukrainians [Ob istoricheskom edinstve russkikh i ukraintsev].* July 12, 2021. [URL: http://kremlin.ru/events/president /news/66181]

Putin, V. *75 Years of the Great Victory: Shared Responsibility to History and the Future [75 let Velikoi Pobedy: obshchaya otvetstvennost pered istoriei i budushchim].* June 19, 2020. [URL: http://kremlin.ru/events/president/news/63527]

"Senior Ukrainian Official Says He's Opened Probe into US Election Interference." *The Hill*, March 20, 2019. [URL: https://thehill.com/hilltv/rising/434892-senior-ukrai nian-justice-official-says-hes-opened-probe-into-us-election/]

Smirnov, S. "'Kolomoisky's Puppet': The Story of the Ukrainian Oligarch Who Supported Zelensky" ["Marionetka Kolomoiskogo": istoriya ukrainskogo oligarkha, kotoryi podderzhal Zelenskogo]. *The Bell*, April 1, 2019. [URL: https://thebell.io/marionetka -kolomojskogo-istoriya-ukrainskogo-oligarha-kotoryj-podderzhal-zelenskogo]

Sociological Group "Rating": The Sixth National Poll: The Language Issue in Ukraine (March 19, 2022). [URL: https://ratinggroup.ua/ru/research/ukraine/language_issue _in_ukraine_march_19th_2022.html]

Sociopolitical Attitudes of Ukrainians: April 2018 [Suspilno-politychni nastroyi zhiteliv Ukrainy: Kviten 2018 roku]. *Kyiv International Institute of Sociology*, May 7, 2018. [URL: http://www.kiis.com.ua/?lang=ukr&cat=reports&id=764]

Solovyev, V. "Zelensky Talked About an Impending Coup, in Which He Himself Does Not Believe" [Zelenskii rasskazal o gotovyashchemsya gosperervorote, v kotoryi sam on ne verit]. *Kommersant*, November 26, 2021. [URL: https://www.kommersant.ru /doc/5098048]

"'Sudden actions': Enterprises of Akhmetov and Novinsky Are Being Searched by the SBU, BEB, Prosecutor's Office—Suspected of Not Paying Taxes in the Amount of UAH 18 Billion" ["Vnezapnye deystviya." Predpriyatiya Akhmetova i Novinskogo obyskivayut SBU, BEB, prokuratura—podozrevayut v neuplate nalogov na 18 mlrd grn]. *NV Biznes*, February 1, 2022. [URL: https://biz.nv.ua/markets/obyski-v-kom paniyah-ahmetova-siloviki-provodyat-sledstvennye-deystviya-na-kombinatah-metin vesta-50213162.html]

Tkach, M. "Kolomoisky After 8 Months in Geneva: 'It would be extremely foolish to go to Ukraine today'" [Kolomoiskii pislya 8 misyatsiv u Zhenevi: Poikhati sogodni v Ukraïnu bulo b ukrai neobdumano]. *Radio Svoboda*, May 17, 2018. [URL: https://www.radiosvoboda.org/a/schemes/29171015.html]

"Top Ukrainian Justice Official Says US Ambassador Gave Him a Do Not Prosecute List," *The Hill*, March 20, 2019. [URL: https://thehill.com/hilltv/rising/434875-top-ukrainian-justice-official-says-us-ambassador-gave-him-a-do-not-prosecute/]

"Tuka Revealed Sensational Facts About the 95th Quarter Studio: Footage Published" [Tuka raskryl sensatsionnye fakty o studii "95 kvartal": opublikovany kadry]. *Antikor*, September 1, 2016. [URL: https://antikor.com.ua/articles/124054-tuka_raskryl_sen satsionnye_fakty_o_studii_95_kvartal_opublikovany_kadry]

Vladimir Putin's speech at the 70th session of the UN General Assembly on September 28, 2015. [URL: http://kremlin.ru/events/president/news/50385]

"Vladimir Putin: The Real Lessons of the 75th Anniversary of World War II," *National Interest*, June 18, 2020. [URL: https://nationalinterest.org/feature/vladimir-putin-real-lessons-75th-anniversary-world-war-ii-162982]

Volodymyr Zelensky interview for *The New York Times. Official website of the President of Ukraine*, December 19, 2020. [URL: https://www.president.gov.ua/en/news/intervyu-volodimira-zelenskogo-new-york-times-65705]

"Volodymyr Zelensky's Anti-Rating Exceeded His Rating for the First Time: Why Did It Happen, and Can He Regain Popularity? Answered by Konstantin Skorkin: Carnegie.ru" [Antireyting Vladimira Zelenskogo vpervye prevysil ego reyting. Pochemu eto proizoshlo i smozhet li on vernut populyarnost? Otvechaet Konstantin Skorkin: Carnegie.ru]. *Meduza.io*, July 15, 2020. [URL: https://meduza.io/feature/2020/07/15/antireyting-vladimira-zelenskogo-vpervye-prevysil-ego-reyting-pochemu-eto-proizoshlo-i-smozhet-li-on-vernut-populyarnost]

"Zelensky Flew to Geneva and Tel Aviv, Where Kolomoisky Lives, 13 Times in Two Years" [Za dva roky Zelenskyi 13 raziv zlitav do Zhenevy ta Tel-Aviva, de meshkaie Kolomoiskyi—"Skhemy"]. *Radio Svoboda*, May 11, 2019. [URL: https://www.radios voboda.org/a/news-schemes-zelenskyy-perelyoty/29875430.html]

Zygar, Mikhail. *Interview with Alexander Kwaśniewski*, 2022.

Zygar, Mikhail. *Interview with a major Ukrainian oligarch*, 2022.

Zygar, Mikhail. *Interview with Andriy Yermak*, 2023.

Zygar, Mikhail. *Interview with a source close to the Privat Group*, 2022.

Zygar, Mikhail. *Interview with Borys Shefir*, 2022.

Zygar, Mikhail. *Interview with Dmitry Gordon*, 2023.

Zygar, Mikhail. *Interview with Ilya Khrzhanovsky*, 2022.

Zygar, Mikhail. *Interview with Maxim Galkin*, 2022.

Zygar, Mikhail. *Interview with Natalya Yemchenko*, 2022.

Zygar, Mikhail. *Interview with Natan Sharansky*, 2022.

Zygar, Mikhail. *Interview with Sergey Shefir*, 2022.

Zygar, Mikhail. *Interview with Serhiy Leshchenko*, 2022.

Zygar, Mikhail. *Interview with Sonya Koshkina*, 2023.

Zygar, Mikhail. *Interview with Svitlana Zalishchuk*, 2023.

Zygar, Mikhail. *Interview with Volodymyr Zelensky*, 2022.

Zygar, Mikhail. *Interview with Rinat Akhmetov*, 2023.

Zygar, Mikhail. *Interview with Viktor Pinchuk*, 2023.

INDEX

Page numbers in *italics* refer to maps.

ABOUT THE AUTHOR

Mikhail Zygar worked for *Newsweek Russia* and the business daily *Kommersant*, covering the conflicts in Palestine, Lebanon, Iraq, Serbia, and Kosovo before becoming founding editor in chief of Russia's only independent news TV channel, Dozhd, which provided an alternative to Kremlin-controlled federal TV channels and gave a platform to opposition voices. He won the International Press Freedom Award in 2014. He is the author of *All the Kremlin's Men*, a #1 bestseller in Russia that has been translated into over twenty languages and was called one of "9 books that can help you understand Russia right now" by *Time* magazine, and *The Empire Must Die*, a Kirkus Reviews Best Nonfiction Book of the Year.